JOHN SELDEN:
MEASURES OF THE HOLY COMMONWEALTH
IN SEVENTEENTH-CENTURY ENGLAND

D1598950

John Selden

MEASURES OF THE
HOLY COMMONWEALTH
IN SEVENTEENTH-CENTURY
ENGLAND

Reid Barbour

UNIVERSITY OF TORONTO PRESS
Toronto Buffalo London

National Library of Canada Cataloguing in Publication

Barbour, Reid
John Selden : measures of the Holy Commonwealth in
seventeenth-century England / Reid Barbour.

Includes bibliographical references and index.
ISBN 0-8020-8776-0

1. Selden, John, 1584–1654.   2. Great Britain – Politics and
government – 1603–1649.   3. Constitutional history – England.   4. Great
Britain – History – Stuarts, 1603–1714.   I. Title.

DA390.1.S4B37 2003   942.06'092   C2003-900215-2

University of Toronto Press acknowledges the financial assistance to its
publishing program of the Canada Council for the Arts and the
Ontario Arts Council.

University of Toronto Press acknowledges the financial support for its
publishing activities of the Government of Canada through the
Book Publishing Industry Development Program (BPIDP).

For Jessica Lynn Wolfe

Contents

Contents

Acknowledgments

This book was conceived in the parking lot of an airport. In those days before 11 September 2001, when you could wait at the curb of the terminal, my wife and I took the opportunity of a late arrival to discuss John Selden. I had always been a little nervous about the selective use of his works in my previous books, and Jessica challenged me to focus my attention on his complete career. I started the very next day, and since then, I have tormented my students, colleagues, and friends with Selden this, Selden that, John Selden for all occasions.

Selden's writings are so wide ranging, learned, and difficult that any attempt to explain what he thought or believed is bound to prove a perilous enterprise. I owe a great debt to those scholars (the few) who have written about Selden in the past, especially Paul Christianson, Jason Rosenblatt, Richard Tuck, J.P. Sommerville, D.R. Woolf, and David Berkowitz. The two anonymous readers for the University of Toronto Press were downright heroic; thank goodness they came to my rescue regarding a number of argumentative excesses and gaps. It would have been a better book had I possessed their expertise. At the Press, Kristen Pederson-Chew was an outstanding advocate for the book, and Catherine Frost made so many improvements to my style that I wish she would edit *all* my work.

Closer to home, I owe thanks to my colleagues Gerald Postema and Allen Anderson, Gerald for his expertise in matters of common law, and Allen for knowing how with his questions to get to the heart of a matter. John Headley has encouraged my work on Selden with his insight and enthusiasm. One of the exceptional benefits of my scholarly life has been the opportunity to work with and to learn from David Norbrook, whose writings on politics and literature of the early modern period rank among the best ever published.

I am grateful to successive chairs in the English Department – William Andrews and James Thompson – for their support in time and funding. The Institute for the Arts and Humanities at UNC also gave me time off and a congenial context for working out my ideas.

My graduate students have helped me in so many ways with thinking about the seventeenth century, especially the participants in the seminar on literature and culture in the English Civil War. I thank Brian Butler for a key reference, Melissa Caldwell for her incisive questions, and Amy Sweitzer for her vigorous encouragement. During the summer of 2000 Nigel Smith and Kate Flint allowed me to stay in their Oxford home when I was working in the Selden archive at the Bodleian. Jessica and I shared that wonderful house with the delightful Genelle Geertz-Robinson and Lynn Robinson, and with Nigel and Kate's three cats in what was an idyllic period for work on this book. In Chapel Hill, I have been fortunate in friends: Michael and Belinda McFee, Darryl Gless, Al and Janet Rabil, Lance and Marieke Lazar, Phil Gura, Erin Carlston, Megan Matchinske, and Mary Floyd-Wilson. My families in North Carolina and New York have given me love and support aplenty. I must thank my two dachshunds, Matilda and Ginger, for bringing me joy and laughter every day.

Jessica Wolfe not only provoked me to write the book, she also read earlier versions of the manuscript, helped me to improve countless sections, assisted me in translating and interpreting passages, set a standard of scholarly excellence for which I can only strive, and made me laugh with her New York sass. Without her, no book.

JOHN SELDEN:
MEASURES OF THE HOLY COMMONWEALTH
IN SEVENTEENTH-CENTURY ENGLAND

Introduction: John Selden and the Measures of a Holy Commonwealth

The twentieth century passed without publication of a single book on the complete corpus of the seventeenth-century polymath, intellectual, and lawyer John Selden (1584–1654). Good work was written on the remarkable Selden, especially by David Berkowitz and Paul Christianson on the 'formative years' and, more piecemeal, by Richard Tuck and Jason Rosenblatt on the later, Judaic phase.[1] Yet no book offered a reading of the lifelong cruxes of Selden's thought, in part because the wide scope and intricate detail of his scholarship have rendered the patterns of his convictions elusive even to those seventeenth-century contemporaries who considered him a walking encyclopedia of the law and a beacon of reason for troubled times. No wonder that some of Selden's readers, even those unafraid of his famously knotty Latin, have been apt then and now to take consolation in isolated phases of his life or in single categories or influences for his intellectual tendencies, above all, in the label 'Erastian.'

Towards the end of his life, Selden considered and embraced the genuinely held views of Thomas Erastus, even as he resisted the popular conception of the label that often replaces a careful study of those views. But Erastus affords us not merely something of an end-point to Selden's intellectual trajectory; the sixteenth-century controversialist on the question of excommunication also prompts us with one of the very best questions about Selden's literary and scholarly work in general. For throughout Selden's prodigious monuments to learning, and in so many different cultural arenas and modes of discourse, he explored the ways in which a comprehensively religious society might best be regulated, rectified, and normalized, only without an undue stifling of all the ineffable, elusive, and abnormal constituents that make up, and make thrive, that same society.

Despite his famous quips in the *Table Talk*, that civil magistrates determine the shape and practices of the religion of their people, the societies that Selden studies are – every one of them – comprehensively
religious. By the phrase 'religious society' I mean that the social unit in
question subsumes all of its practices, habits of thought, customs, institutions, and history under a predominantly shared sense of divine dispensations and warrants, and that, even if the social unit in question is a
colonized people, the religion of the colony provides this people with
the overwhelming share of their sense of purpose, identity, past, and
expectation. Thus, Selden's very Erastianism took it for granted (as did
Erastus himself) that a society whose civil magistracy would handle all
forms of coercion would nonetheless, even accordingly, be operating
under the aegis of a single, unified religion. Also, despite the fact that,
in his final Erastian phase, Selden was moving towards a notion that
spiritual labour might best be exerted and encouraged in social subsets,
coteries, or cantons, he never abandoned, never came close to abandon-
ing, the idea of a comprehensive, if imperfect and conflictive, religious
society. Far from it: the societies that he studied towards the end of his
life became more emphatically comprehensive in their religious orientation; the farther he moved from investigating early British pagan, early
British Christian, Greco-Roman, and 'Syrian' cultures towards his final
Judaic studies, the more the absolute integrity of religion in the society
under scrutiny became crucial. These societies might occupy the position of a conquered, colonized people or of an imperial people comprising many of the religions of the world; but Selden was fixated on the
ways in which either the colony or the colonizer managed its own coordination of the normative and adventurous constituents of their religious core.

By and large, Selden's experiments in the regulation of religious societies agreed with Calvin's commonplace assertion that 'civil government
is designed, as long as we live in this world, to cherish and support the
external worship of God, to preserve the pure doctrine of religion, to
defend the constitution of the Church, to regulate our lives in a manner
requisite for the society of men, to form our manners to civil justice, to
promote our concord with each other, and to establish general peace
and tranquility.'[2] In Selden's lifetime, however, English society came
apart over the question of whether a religious commonwealth can be
cohesive or a cohesive commonwealth can be religious. When it was put
back together in the 1660s, the English commonwealth was a delicate
civil artifice, and religious society was relegated more than ever before

to separate cantons situated in the interstices of that artifice. Selden himself would eventually become associated with the editorialized *Table Talk*, in which he was sometimes depicted as standing for the overwhelming hegemony of the civil domain over the religious. Yet in the early eighteenth century, his first major editor, David Wilkins, dismissed the *Table Talk* as a suspect production. More important, by the end of his life, Selden was still, more than ever, trying to construct a normative model of the comprehensively religious society, with Judaism representing both that comprehensive whole and the cantonizing tendency towards which religious community was moving.

On the one hand, then, William Davenant remarked to Thomas Hobbes in 1650 that the contemporary Jewish 'cantonizing in Tribes, and shyness of allyance with neighbours, deserves not the terme of mutual love, but rather seems a bestial melancholy of herding in their own Walks.'[3] On the other hand, albeit with some doubt and trepidation, Richard Baxter looked to the final Judaic work of Selden for the preservation of what Baxter called the 'holy commonwealth.' Baxter hoped that Selden might lead contemporary English Christendom in ensuring the future prosperity of the holy commonwealth in a time, the 1650s, that found its very survival under unprecedented threat from the radicals in religion and the Hobbists in politics. But Baxter also feared the truth of the widespread rumour that Selden himself was a crypto-Hobbist.

Both the hope and the fear emerge from Baxter's 'Additional Notes on the Life and Death of Sir Matthew Hale, Knight': 'I know you are acquainted how greatly he [Hale] valued Mr. Selden, being one of his executors; his books and picture being still near him. I think it meet therefore to remember, that because many Hobbists do report, that Mr. Selden was at the heart an infidel, and inclined to the opinions of Hobbs, I desired him to tell me the truth herein: and he oft professed to me, that he was a great adversary to Hobbs's errors; and that he had seen him openly oppose him so earnestly as either to depart from him, or drive him out of the room.' Baxter explains the significance of the anecdote with reference to Selden's late work on the Sanhedrin and the other (unnamed) writings in which the great scholar has proved himself 'Erastian' in its proper sense. As observed in Baxter's note, Selden 'owned the office properly ministerial; so most lawyers that ever I was acquainted with, taking the word jurisdiction to signify something more than the mere doctoral, priestly power, and power over their own sacramental communion in the church which they guide, do use to say, that it is primarily in the magistrate (as no doubt all power of corporal coercion, by mulcts and penalties, is).'[4] Selden and the Erastian lawyers understand, that is, that the holy commonwealth must be neither Hobbesian (in awarding all authority – even that over purely spiritual concerns – to the state) nor theocratic in assigning coercive jurisdiction to the saints or the clergy but a decorously apportioned yet mutually supportive coordination between the two.

As William Lamont has written, 'Baxter believed that it was men like Hale and Selden who understood best what a "commonwealth" meant.' In *A Holy Commonwealth* (1659), Baxter joined Milton and many others on the eve of the Restoration in a feverish (if still confident) attempt to reformulate the English government and its relationship with religion. Indeed, the title page of Baxter's aphoristic treatise advertises its inception in an invitation by James Harrington himself, one of the leading political theorists of the Interregnum. What would certainly please the political theorists and the lawyers is Baxter's overriding emphasis on the divine command that subjects remain obedient to their magistrate. This stress on obedience does not mean, however, that civil authority can proceed without regard to God or conscience for 'though Godlinesse give men no Authority, yet as Freemen, we have a certain Liberty; and Wickednesse may forfeit this Liberty; and therefore I shall thus far close with you, that the Church and Commonwealth should be very near commensurate, and that proved ungodly persons should neither Choose nor be Chosen' in political elections. Conversely, the history of Moses and the Jews makes it clear that God intends the magistrate to concern himself with certain 'matters of Religion.' In a 'holy commonwealth,' then, magistrates and ministers concern themselves with separate dimensions of human experience; yet those concerns and dimensions are laced tightly together no matter how different the nature of their threads. As a 'society of Gods Subjects ordered into the Relations of Soveraign and Subjects for the common good, and the pleasing of God their Absolute Soveraign,' the very concept of a holy commonwealth runs counter to, Baxter contends, 'some of the proud Pretenders to Politicks' in the 1650s, those who, 'opposing the Politician to the Divine, acquaint us that their Politicks are not Divine, and consequently none, or worse than none.' Like Selden, Baxter worked hard at expressing these relations accurately, for instance, in his aphorism that 'the Matter of the Church and Common-wealth should be altogether or almost the same, though the form of them and administrations are different.'[5]

As Baxter's aphorisms unfold, it becomes clear that he considers the political theorizing of his day to amount to so many utopian fancies, 'new Fantastical devices' concocted at the expense of 'the great Divine neglected Principles' available in the biblical history of Moses and the Jews. He opines, moreover, that such devices can only ever 'beautifie the Common-wealth in their own ways' rather than preserve the life of a truly holy society (126–7).[6] Whatever reassurance Baxter received from Hale about Selden's beliefs and commitments, some commentators in the years immediately after Selden's death imagined that the great scholar must have faced a choice between two masters, between the atheistic Hobbes and the godly Ussher. For all the inventiveness and learning of Selden's scholarship in the Interregnum period, some of Selden's contemporaries wanted him to be partisan, to have a 'side' in the wars of truth – but they were not always happy with the side on which they imagined him to be. Some maintained that his disregard for the early Stuart clergy had propelled Selden into atheism, in keeping with that ancient truism about the recoil from superstition into godlessness. These readers of Selden could speak with considerable hostility about his work. Others, responding especially to his edition of Eutychius, held the view that the same disregard for the clergy had rocketed Selden into the Congregationalist faction of the 1640s. Some of Selden's earliest readers expressed a vague disenchantment with him – vague because their admiration for his learning was so great and widespread – and they allowed that his densely packed and unfinished scholarly tomes on the Sanhedrin might simply offer their readers beauty rather than resolution and truth: even the publisher of the work ventured this mitigated praise. Writing in the early eighteenth century, David Wilkins concluded his life of Selden with an attempt to articulate precisely what Selden's religion had involved, essentially deciding that Selden was a proto-latitudinarian. Wilkins also found the essence of Selden's Protestantism in a remark that the scholar made in a dedicatory preface to Laud, hardly evidence that Selden hated the early Stuart clergy. What is more, Wilkins quoted a French manuscript in which that same remark to Laud is used as an argument that Selden should have kept his focus on the Protestantism of his native England rather than looking for answers to England's problems in the religious norms and histories outside that isle.[7]

Selden's legacy to the Restoration was, on the one hand, heroic, for he had devoted his career to assiduous scholarship on behalf of the foundering ancient marriage between holiness and civility. On the other hand, writers in the next generation were haunted, at times even infuriated, by the suspicion that Selden had either fallen short in his heroic enterprise or secretly joined forces with Hobbes in dividing theology from magistracy for evermore. Over the course of his evolving scholarship, contemporaries knew, Selden had explored the widely various forms of mediation between the holy and civil warrants of a commonwealth. In the 1640s and 1650s he had worked hard to imagine ancient ways in which a new commonwealth might be created when the old one had fallen apart. As the last book on the Jewish Sanhedrin trailed off into incompletion, Selden's editor allowed for the possibility that Selden's heroism was by its very nature a matter of delightful digressions to and through a utopia of arcane detritus, an odyssey without a return home into practice. In other words, Hobbes might well be right: the holy commonwealth was simply no longer viable in seventeenth-century Britain.

Selden's assessment of the offices, dimensions, and guarantors of such a society evolved richly and dramatically, even into speculation on the various ways in which 'moral action finds its natural home in small societies.'[8] By the end of his life, he was apt to relish the divine dispensations of zeal and love as they were shared among an intimate fraternity or community, whether among the ancient Jews or early Christians, whom he considered reformed Jews. But Selden's cantonizing of spirituality never overruled his prevailing emphasis on the problem of how to organize and normalize holistic societies with deep commitments to, and the encompassing framework of, a basically unified theology, ecclesiastical polity, and moral vision. The strain placed on this emphasis by the Civil War and its aftermath produced cantonizing tendencies, to be sure, and in his work on the Sanhedrin, he began to elaborate on the benefits of a basic distinction between the realms of civil magistracy and of spiritual labour; but the eruption of civil war, republicanism, and religious sectarianism also helped to renew Selden's resolve to uncover and devise a model, a Judaic one, for a comprehensively religious society that might cohere and prosper in the face of a cultural shift towards religious centrifuge.

Selden maintained that the challenge for contemporary as well as ancient and medieval peoples was how best to integrate norms or laws with a wide variety of often uncontrollable phenomena, from inspiration and prophecy to zeal and charity, but also including sexual desire and bloody violence, aristocratic privilege and royal prerogative, extemporaneous fancy and intellectual idiosyncrasy, historical change as well as the mysteries of divine dispensations and spiritual conversion. Too often, the arbiters of normative measures in the religious societies of the world had erred on behalf of legal restrictions on the unconventional and adventurous elements in their culture – witness the religious policies of Charles I and Archbishop Laud – while just as often religious societies had lapsed into the opposite problem of permitting their discontented, maniacal, and amorphous constituents to loose the ligaments that secured a society against adversity and gave the smallest private action a rich communal meaning. Whether he was studying the marbles of antiquity, the records of British history, or the clerical and legal institutions of the Jews, Selden unfolded the intricate ways in which human culture had devised both the rules and the releases implicit in what they understood to be their social order, their liberty under God, their proprieties, and their aspirations.

To make matters more difficult for his doubting intellect, Selden faced the challenges of unearthing and reconstructing norms for religious society in an early modern world in which religious schism, bloodshed, scepticism, mania, and persecution seemed the inescapable condition of post-Reformation Christendom. At least by the 1640s, during which time his own country had unleashed a civil war, the difficulty of regulating – while protecting the cutting edge and copious energy of – a religious society was eroding an optimism in Selden that was implicit mainly in his singular commitment to an astonishingly impressive scholarship on a wide range of societies and histories. In the *Table Talk* (first published decades after his death, its organizational focus his views of church and state) Selden is reported to have remarked that 'Disputes in Religion will never bee ended because there wants a Measure by wch the business should bee decided, the puritan would be judg'd by the word of God (if hee would speake cleerly hee meanes himselfe, but that hee is asham'd to say soe) ... One sayes one thing & another another, & there is, I say, no measure to end the controversie' (119). Elsewhere he is sceptical about the epistemology of measure as much as he is cynical about its political self-interest: 'We measure for our selves & as things are for our use & purpose so wee approve them ... Wee measure the Excellencie of other men by some Excellency we conceive to be in our selfes' (76). As a prime example of the absurdity of human measures, Selden relays an anecdote about Thomas Nashe, 'a poett,' whose tendency it is audaciously but ridiculously to measure the worth of all men, no matter how socially prominent, according to whether a person in question can compose a strong blank verse. When it comes to showing up the vanity of disputes in religion, however, it is also a poet, Ben Jonson, to whom Selden looks. In the *Table Talk*, poets epitomize the *reductio ad absurdum* of vain measure, but they also lead the way in exposing, perhaps in correcting, this vanity (76, 119).

It is typical of Selden both to engage and to criticize the competing, sometimes overlapping, norms available to English Protestant society and, in some cases, made more readily available to that society by Selden himself. For with utmost sobriety as well as a folksy humour, he prompted his contemporaries to rethink the diverse and often inwardly conflictual standards by means of which they sought to regulate the ineffable, the metamorphic, and extremist dimensions of their religious communities. For Selden, the problem of finding the right norms or measures for a religious society was as old as the creation itself; it had been most frustratingly fumbled by the early Christians; it was most damaging to societies when reduced to a logic of mutual exclusivity or to an overly neat dialectic; and it demanded that an accounting be made of essentially all human invention and experience, from poetry and music to sexuality and warfare, from natural order to social hierarchy, from interior autonomy and inspiration to obligation and community. The changing historical circumstances through which Selden lived, moreover, made a significant impact on the orientation and specificity of his thinking about the divine and human invention of normative standards, from his early fame as a wit, poet, critic, and historian in early Jacobean England, through his embattled, sometimes persecuted, interaction with James I then Charles I in the 1620s, to his involvement with the Long Parliament, Westminster Assembly, and English Republic in the 1640s and 1650s. Throughout this long and storied career, Selden bestowed on contemporary normative thinking his own subtle brand of humour and irony, his articulation of moral, religious, and political values within the domain of a dense and meticulous scholarly discourse, his idiosyncratic and at times innovative penchant for figures such as the Druids and for institutions such as the Sanhedrin; and his exploration of an extraordinary spectrum of normative genres, traditions, and instruments, in distinction from and in cooperation with one another, and each with its fair share of benefits and liabilities for ensuring the harmony and welfare of a religious society.

Over the course of his life, Selden creatively and doggedly developed the hypothesis that the problems haunting any religious society – how to calibrate church polity and civil government; how to establish the boundaries of liberty; how to determine the extent of toleration afforded irrational or supra-rational dimensions of religious authority and experience – were corollaries to the essential problem that he articulated so memorably at table: how rightly to isolate, codify, legitimize, and administer the best norms, standards, or laws against which rulers and their subjects in a religious society should be measured and rectified and from which to some degree they should be allowed to deviate. In Selden's own England, there were vivid examples of such legal authorities, who had pushed too hard for conformity with the canons of belief and behaviour: Selden's own patron, William Laud, or the Presbyterians in the Westminster Assembly; and equally dramatic cases of lawless frenzy in the name of the Holy Spirit: the Ranters and Quakers, who were just coming onto the scene in the decade of Selden's death. Yet Selden knew that it was easy enough for satirists to point the finger of shame at extremes; satirists themselves, however, for all their efficacy as normative authorities, would have to account for their own imperfections – their tendency towards parasitism, for instance. Taking the right and proper measure of a religious society was as difficult, Selden knew, as it was necessary for social welfare, even survival.

Given the various cultural or intellectual purviews into which Selden entered over the course of his life, measures differed considerably in their identities, as did those various deviations from measure on which any society must count. His penchant for scepticism entailed that he was never fully satisfied with or dogmatic about any one vision of religious society; but that same penchant drove him from one discursive mode to another in search of the criteria for satisfaction, and it also prompted him to retain, reinvent, and make use of each and every permutation of the holy commonwealth as he moved towards his Judaic studies. Selden was never fully satisfied with any one measure for holding the holy commonwealth together, but his career was ultimately more cumulative than disjunctive. Measure itself might serve as the very touchstone or criterion of truth; or it might oversee the normative coherence of the larger social order in such a way – it is hoped – that capacious zeal, moral fervour, and boundless love of individuals and smaller communities are encouraged to thrive, and violent and sexual urges, the wilfulness of the elite, and the rebelliousness of the many are directed into socially beneficial goals and acts.

In calling Selden an 'Erastian,' twentieth-century scholarship has largely denuded his thought of any real or sincere involvement with those aspects of religious culture, belief, and experience that fall outside the purview of civil regulation. In this reduction of Selden's understanding of religious societies, such scholarship was following in the footsteps of his contemporary critics in the Westminster Assembly, primarily di-

vines who deployed the term as abuse for the men they considered the
most secular minded of the participants in the synod. For these divines,
an 'Erastian' was the alias for a 'statist,' someone who was zealous to subordinate the church to the state, even to the point of complete spiritual
bankruptcy. Under the guidance of an 'Erastian,' these divines believed,
the state would cynically and selfishly manipulate the church in its every
detail, doctrine, and practice. The clergy would be made hapless servants to the carnal criteria of their masters and robbed of their ordination in the separate sanctity of church rituals, prayer, preaching, and the
other offices of spiritual ministry. The currency owed to God would be
diverted to the coffers of Caesar. From early on, Selden himself could
easily imagine such a state of affairs; for it was the situation that the
medieval historian Eadmer had captured and lambasted in a text to
which seventeenth-century readers gained admission in Selden's own
edition of the manuscripts.

Throughout the famous *Table Talk*, a record of his conversation selected and organized by an amanuensis, Selden appears to corroborate this
emphasis on his secularity, especially when he quips more than once
that church governance is carried out exactly as the state or the magistrate so desires (60, 101, 117). By the 1640s and into the 1650s Selden
has read and embraced the theses of Thomas Erastus to be sure, and he
is only too happy to take aim at the overreaching clergy. But the full
scope of Selden's understanding of the Erastian legacy is far more complex – and the legacy itself much less secular – than the Westminster
divines and Selden's modern secularizers have allowed. Having been
called an Erastian in so many hotly contested debates, Selden decided to
find out what the label really meant, and in his final great project on the
Jewish senate, the Sanhedrin, he rehabilitated the genuine arguments
of the sixteenth-century thinker. Like Selden, Erastus was a layman, a
doctor, attempting to advance theses about how the civil and spiritual
realms should be coordinated in the volatile years after the Reformation. As Selden emphasizes in *De Synedriis*, Erastus was grossly misunderstood, perhaps wilfully so, by those hostile divines who vilified his name
and caricatured his positions. For reasons that will become clear, Selden
was fascinated by the cultural and polemical processes by which Erastianism was invented and distorted, indeed almost as intrigued as he was
with the actual theses of Erastus.

If late in his life Selden came to align himself with Erastus's views on
excommunication, this alignment required his own recovery of what
Erastus had, in fact, argued. It represented, moreover, Selden's grandest

attempt to unite all the discursive and institutional permutations on which he had spent his entire scholarly career. Especially in the first two decades of the seventeenth century, he had been engaged with the reconstitution of normative poetry and didactic history, a project that would persist in his studies of classical culture, musicology, medieval history, and Judaic institutions. Most notably in the 1610s and 1620s he had concentrated his attentions on the common law and the Parliament as the arbiters and human guarantors of moral honesty and reformed religion in English society. This focus had involved Selden in political and legal practice and in the persecutory afflictions of living under monarchical prerogative, a brazen state of affairs that had in no small measure prompted his turn to natural law and to the distant, biblical past. During the 1630s he was addressing natural law but also the sacred identity and offices of the priesthood. If the former work (on nature) was his most utopian, it was nonetheless beleaguered by changing views of natural law, by conflicts in the largely Stoic tradition behind natural law, and by the sceptical demands on proof for transcendence that led Selden to the Talmud. The latter interest (in priesthood) was his most surprising. For Selden's preoccupation with the distinctive authority, status, and offices of the priesthood ran largely counter to his eventual reputation as a statist; decidedly began with his edition of Eadmer in the 1620s and almost ran aground in the face of disillusionment with the Westminster Assembly; was complicated by the patronage of two rival clerics, John Williams and William Laud, whose visions of church polity were at odds and were controversial in their own right; and dovetailed with his growing efforts in the 1640s to map out a domain in which prophecy, extemporaneous prayer, and otherwise counter-normative aspects of religious society might prosper, in coordination with the requirements of social regulation. In the 1640s and to this end, Selden followed through on his long-standing hunch that ancient Jewish society had managed both a thoroughgoing social cohesion and an intimacy with the divine will. He worked, moreover, from the presupposition that the divinely commanded legal institution, the Sanhedrin, had been largely responsible for ensuring this optimum state of affairs for a religious society committed at once to lawful behaviour and spiritual zeal. In turning to the Sanhedrin, he made strange bedfellows with some relatively radical figures of the Civil War and Interregnum periods, as surely as he worked to modify and normalize their excesses. After all, Fifth Monarchists were calling for an English Sanhedrin in the 1650s, the very decade in which the Cromwell government was considering readmission of Jews into

England as part of its apocalyptic vision; but Selden's Sanhedrin would be authorized to prosecute the sectarian acts of zeal, even as it was prepared to concede the extraordinary value of rapturous and violent zeal in the welfare of religious society.

Because Selden knew that the Sanhedrin could never be a panacea for all the ills encountered and produced by the subjects of such a society, he enfolded into his reconstruction of the Sanhedrin the purviews with which he had experimented: normative poetics; natural law; the separate and sacred offices of ministry; and the contractual relations into which local communities as well as whole societies enter. These discourses and institutions – poetry, natural law, consecrated church canons, and human positive law – had been the vehicles of Selden's Herculean labours to ensure the sanctity of law and the measure of sanctity. It was a career that rang through many changes, both in English society at large and in Selden's own scholarly focus and imagination, which ranged from the most artificial instances of the legal imagination to the cosmic and divine guarantors putatively behind human codes and arts. With the onset of civil war, regicide, and republicanism in the 1640s and 1650s, English society encouraged the vital intellectual experimentalism that had been Selden's stock in trade; but it also alarmed the sceptic in Selden himself that his religious society would never find its proper measure and indeed had never been further from the welfare that such measure might bring. In the wake of the great scholar's death, even his eulogists fretted that his life might come to represent not the unification of civil law and spiritual ineffability but rather their necessary separation, whether into mutual coexistence or into mutual exclusion.

In conceiving of Selden as a monist in the great scholar's 1640s Judaic phase, Jason Rosenblatt has perhaps come closest to articulating the polymath's overriding enterprise of coordinating legal norms and capacious spirituality in English religious society from the Elizabethan heyday of Richard Hooker to the war-torn Interregnum of Thomas Hobbes.[9] Ideals of a continuum between the dispensations of law and grace were impossible to abandon for the normative imagination of Selden, but also were hard for his scepticism to sustain. As much as he worked to envision a natural or divine fusion of regulatory norms and spiritual abundance, he kept returning to, and ended his life working on, an artificial coordination of legal coercion and spiritual labour that tended to reserve each in its own proper sphere. For Selden, it was above all the ancient Jews who had accomplished history's greatest accommodation of the legalists and the zealots.

As part of one entire society, unless the agents of law and the ministers in the spirit respected one another, cultivated the welfare of one another, and stayed away from one another, the artifice of religious society would crumble every time. If this was 'Erastianism,' then it was a long time in appearing in Selden's scholarship, and it owed almost as much to the liberty and largesse of spiritual labour as it did to the coercive powers of a judge-cum-senator. Almost – for in the 1640s and into the 1650s Selden had no doubts that the Holy Spirit had its advocates. With the Civil War, the destruction of the Church of England, and the beheading of the king, the question had become, increasingly, what to do about its measure. Whatever Selden thought about the regicide in January 1649, his Sanhedrin was, in essence, a special kind of parliament, the great judicial court and legal body of the ancient Jews, required of them by their God.

Thus, whatever his disenchantment over the search for measure in the 1640s, Selden went to his grave still fully engaged in a massive project to recover what might prove to be the optimum institution for curing the woes of seventeenth-century religious society, the Judaic Sanhedrin. All along, however, his multidisciplinary scholarship was bold and inventive in tracing the mental and cultural habits of a wide variety of times and peoples. In each case he studied the means of crafting a social instrument that might approximate the famous 'Lesbian rule' discussed by Aristotle. Metaphorically, this measure was a carpenter's rule or '*norma*' that combined the strengths of accommodating flexibility and judicial precision.[10] However arcane his scholarship might seem to modern readers, his most sympathetic contemporaries, from Lancelot Andrewes and Ben Jonson to Meric Casaubon and Ralph Cudworth, appreciated the fact that Selden was devoting enormous energy to discovering and fashioning appropriate norms for his religious society and to criticizing the improprieties of his own and others' norms.

As was true of John Milton, one of his greatest admirers, Selden devoted his maturity to strengthening the British understanding and possession of true liberty. For the sake of liberty, the leaders of a society must discern and facilitate those aspects of human experience that God would bind and those that God would unloose; and they would have to distinguish such a state of affairs from licence in two opposite but often complicit senses – the hyper-control of persecution and the debauchery of passions run amok. It is not surprising that Selden admired Ben Jonson's *Bartholomew Fair*, in which the extremes of control and enormity encountered one another, showed one another up, and in some measure found reconciliation in the end (*Table Talk*, 119–20). Later, in *Areopagitica*, Milton would warn the Long Parliament and the people of England that their greatest challenge was to avoid restricting what God would permit and permitting what God would restrict.

For the sceptical and scholarly Selden even more than for the rationalist heretic Milton, true liberty – the righteous and rational proportion between control and release – was exceedingly hard for a religious society to find and stabilize. Over the course of the *Table Talk*, Selden illustrates the difficulty of reviving liberty in so many ways – for instance, how he characterizes the bogeys of heresy and Congregationalism. 'Tis a vaine thing to talke of an Heretick,' he tells his auditors, 'for a man for his heart cann thinke no otherwise then hee does thinke' (88). Orthodoxy, then, was a state invention and imposition, but Selden does not make it clear in the context (as reported) just how good or bad that invention has been. One might be inclined to think that Selden has edged towards Milton's position that heresy, from its Greek root, simply means 'choice,' except for three problems in this linkage: (1) Selden's heretic does not choose his opinion but falls into it; (2) whereas Milton is utterly clear that the state has no business coercing the heretical conscience, Selden suggests simply that the state can gain no access to the heretic's thoughts, and so censorship is 'vaine'; and (3) Milton himself is prepared to put limits on what can be legitimately chosen in a godly society, even if 'opinion in good men is but knowledge in the making.'[11]

When he turns to discuss Congregationalism or 'Independency,' Selden's views on the relationship between control and release are intricate once again. He emphatically supports a coherence in the religion of English Protestants, a unity that at the highest level only a civil power can ensure. In Amsterdam, he jokes, they are overrun with distinctive churches that 'have nothing to doe with another' (57). Even so, Selden stops short of ridiculing the benefits deriving from the dispersion of authority in religious affairs. In primitive Christianity, he acknowledges, the local organization and neighbourly governance of the faithful were necessities; and in *De Synedriis*, Selden persists in declaring local communities of great value in the welfare of a religious society, even in limited forms of punishment. Yet he is also unhappy with the Independents and Presbyterians for wholly excluding the civil power (though not at all the laity) from their understanding of religious polity. In these remarks, Selden concedes that finding exactly the right levels of regulation and adventure requires all of the wisdom that God will opt to bestow and that learned men can muster.

No doubt Selden agreed with Hobbes that, among the peaks and val-
leys of history, the extraordinary seventeenth century in Britain was
among the highest of the hills. This is not to say that they imagined that
they were struggling with problems unimagined before: both Selden
and Hobbes understood that civil governments and the religious institutions and creeds interactive with those governments had experienced a
long history of tense mediation. Whereas Hobbes was convinced that
hope resided in leaving that history behind, however, Selden believed
that hope for the future was to be found (if anywhere) in the forms and
peoples of the past. In the *Table Talk*, Selden feared, in the vein of sceptics such as Montaigne, that human affairs would never be granted a
measure of appropriate rigour and flexibility. Yet in his study, the great
scholar never stopped looking. Within the perimeter of his Sanhedrin
he tried to find a place for normative vehicles with which he had
engaged in a serious fashion – with poetry and history, with natural law
and positive law, with a zealous spirituality allotted a protected domain,
and with the legal sages whose office it was skilfully to dispense and oversee that allotment. Over time Selden had come to understand that the
holy commonwealth needed all these guarantors in place; but as his
choice of the Sanhedrin also made clear, the holy commonwealth
needed both a singular devotion to law and an extraordinary intimacy
with God. The questions that he bequeathed his admirers and critics
alike were two: Was such an exceptional state of affairs possible in post-
civil war England? Had Selden's scholarship established 'Erastian' conditions for the holy commonwealth in which no commonwealth could
possibly remain holy?

Selden's life and work pose in a complex and dramatic way a further
question that obsessed his learned contemporaries: What in the world
can scholarship accomplish? Richard Tuck points out that, unlike many
of the leading intellectuals of his day, 'John Selden seems to have
printed most of what he wrote very quickly, but he did so sometimes
through cheap and unreliable printers and had to disown what had
been done to his text.'[12] Like his friend Ben Jonson, Selden believed
that writers seeking to reform the abnormalities of their society had the
responsibility to put their sage advice into print, in Selden's case most
often in the Latin language, which gave the international community
access to his ideas. Like Jonson, too, however, Selden had a very keen
sense of the value of the 'tribe' or 'coterie' – in Selden's case an international cast of scholars with whom he was in touch by means of letters;
aristocratic patrons who admired and made use of his brilliance; fellow

lawyers and leaders who consulted his expertise in the history of law;
and (apparently) the diners who enjoyed his witty company at table.
Such an investment in the semi-private domain of camaraderie is even
theorized in Selden's later Judaic phase, as he works out the possibility
that the most fruitful social reform takes place in smaller groups with
shared interests. Moreover, both the publishing Selden and the socializ-
ing Selden could speak in more than one register. While each could
speak of profoundest subjects with a learning uncommon for even a
learned age, each was equally brilliant in a more saucy, low-brow, and
folksy manner, from the satiric voice of a University Wit to the domestic
(yet incisive) analogies for contemporary conundrums. Jonson could
also write in a number of different voices spanning the social spectrum,
but Selden had a way of translating one register into another, at least in
the conversation attributed to him in the *Table Talk.*

Nonetheless, even Selden's contemporary supporters tended to
admit that he was not a great communicator in writing, or at least that
his 'understanders' might well be few. This, too, was a Jonsonian dilemma; for Jonson's emblem, the broken compass, took it for granted
that the normative writer would undoubtedly fail in communicating
reform to the world. So many things could go wrong. The audience
would in all likelihood be obtuse, Jonson believed, but there was also
the possibility that the genres in which one wrote lent themselves to corruption (in Jonson's case, the poetry of praise or the masque), or that
one's style would vacillate between the too elitist and the too vulgar, or
that one's person would be unable to sustain the authoritative ethos
necessary for normative writing. As Tuck reminds us, John Aubrey
brought out something deeply disjointed in the personae of Selden, the
one homely, the other profoundly learned: 'Selden's father was a poor
farmer in the uplands of Sussex, earning (according to Aubrey) no
more than £40 per year. Aubrey records the remarkably Hardy-esque
story of Selden as an undergraduate spending Christmas in the manor
house of an Oxford friend and finding his father at the bottom end of
the hall playing the fiddle for the farmers of the estate – a graphic illustration of how education could take a boy out of his former social
class.'[13] Jonson's social status similarly fluctuated: a gentleman's grand-
son, a parson's son, a bricklayer's stepson. Both Selden and Jonson
wanted to reform the habits of their contemporaries; both came in
touch with and spoke the languages of a broad range of their contemporaries; and both faced the very real possibility that their best points
might be lost on their contemporaries. No wonder smaller groups were

so appealing to both men. Yet Selden faced a dilemma in which Jonson only partly shared: the sceptical scholar's desire to get the distant past exactly right, and, in so doing, to give seventeenth-century readers authentic ways of thinking through the seemingly insoluble problem of measuring the holy commonwealth after the post-Reformation had generated so much fragmentation and violence.

The strange truth of Selden's life, works, and legacy was that he came to be associated with the destruction of the very holy commonwealth that he had laboured so monumentally and inventively to save. He was not, of course, the first to dedicate his energies to the rescue of the holy commonwealth in the face of growing secularism. Giovanni Botero was just one of those many sixteenth-century political writers who was faced with resisting – while absorbing – the subordination of religion to civil magistracy promulgated by Machiavelli.[14] Selden was certainly also not the first to offer bold new calibrations between the church and the state. Alan Gewerth writes of Marsilius of Padua that he 'shift[ed] the whole cast of the traditional medieval church-state debate. Where that debate had been between two different groups or authorities in society, each representing a different set of values – *regnum* and *sacerdotium*, temporal power and spiritual power – Marsilius subsumed both of these under a *universitas* which was at once *civilis* and *fidelis*, secular and religious, state and church, and equally infallible in both spheres, so that it was a single, all-inclusive locus and determiner of both spiritual and temporal values.'[15] Nor was Selden the first to admire the wisdom of the Jews and to imagine that it might contribute substantially to the harmony of contemporary religious society. Jean Bodin had made steps in that direction in his unpublished *Colloquium Heptaplomeres de Rerum Sublimium Arcanis Abditis.*[16] In the second half of the seventeenth century, however, Selden came to be seen as the end of the line for the holy commonwealth, either because that entity was found to have crumbled beyond repair – if the great Selden could not save the holy commonwealth, then who could? – or because Selden himself was charged with spearheading the 'Erastian' campaign for its demise. The slow, laboured birth of civil society did not bring with it the end of English concerns with religion. From John Locke to Sir George Savile, the Marquis of Halifax, writers proclaimed the supremacy of religion in the qualifications of English subjects and in the cohesion of the commonwealth so that 'Only the god-fearing could therefore be accepted as members of society.'[17] As David Wootton writes, Locke believed that 'the principles of Christianity were essential preconditions for any adequate political order, and [that]

Hobbes had been profoundly mistaken to think he could find an alternative to the fear of God in worldly self-interest.' At the outset of *Sacro-
Sancta*, John Maxwell declared that 'Piety and policy, Church and State,
prince and priest are so nearly and naturally conjoined in a mutual
interest that, like to Hippocrates his twins, they rejoice and mourn,
flourish and perish, live and die together.'[18] In the political entangle-
ments, persecution, and indignation over dissent, comprehension, popery, and toleration that followed hard upon the Restoration, however,
religion proved so contentious that it was eventually, if haphazardly,
excluded as the integrator or 'cement' of human society.[19]

Fears for the demise of the holy commonwealth ran rampant around
the time of Selden's death. As J.G.A. Pocock argues, Thomas May's
account of the English Civil War divulges the concern that 'the failure to
conduct an effective support of the Calvinist princes and churches is
being presented as the tip of the iceberg, both symptom and cause of a
deeper failure to maintain the Protestant structure of the English
state.'[20] Kevin Sharpe and Steven N. Zwicker pinpoint the consequences
of this 'failure' together with the persecutory subversion of religious
accommodation for Restoration society when they write that 'After the
civil war stability and order required the acknowledgment of diversity,
the acceptance – indeed legitimization – of differences, and, finally, a
political system fashioned and ordered by them.'[21] From the vantage
point of establishmentarians, 'The battle for a comprehensive (though
reformed) national church was lost' once 'the vision of an ordered, unified, godly community was challenged by sectarian and radical groups
who generated fears of moral chaos and confusion.'[22] However, the persecutory Anglicanism enforced by the so-called Clarendon Code of the
1660s turned the Church of England's closest allies into intolerable enemies, ending forever a dream of comprehension with the difficult but
also liberating realities of toleration. Whereas Hooker had concluded
the Elizabethan age with the 'classic expression' of 'the unity of church
and nation,' a hundred years later it was deemed insupportable that
'The consequence of the conviction that it was necessary to establish a
godly society was, inevitably, intolerance and persecution.' In the last
quarter of the seventeenth century, there appeared in political writings
'the suggestion that the only secure foundation for national greatness
was not virtue but a duly restrained vice,' a position that 'stood in opposition to the lengthy tradition that had aspired to establish a godly society.' 'It was necessary,' one author wrote, 'that some art should be found
out for the regulating cupidity; and this art is the politic order, or state-

government, which restrains cupidity by the fear of punishments, and applies it to the uses of civil society.'[23]

The progress of seventeenth-century history involves the widely ranging invention of the alternative ways in which the holy commonwealth might be perfected and, if not perfected, then at least rescued. For divines like Baxter and for lawyers like Hale, Selden was in the vanguard of both the invention and the resuscitation. As William Lamont explains, the English advocates of a genuinely Erastian thought in the 1640s were so committed to 'moral reformation' that, for them, 'Religion was too important to be left to clergymen, not a matter of indifference to be consigned to the magistrates.'[24] This belief underlies all of Selden's normative vehicles, from poetry to English law, from natural law to Judaism. His critics and enemies, however, preferred to paint the great scholar as a primary source of a spreading secularization. In this book an attempt is made to describe, to analyse, and to understand this strange truth.

chapter one

A Scholar's Life:
Duty, Scepticism, and Invention

During the 1580s, the decade into which John Selden was born, advocates for the Elizabethan establishment of a holy commonwealth found the clearest signs that providence was on their side, yet also ample opportunities for fretting that their settlement might come apart. In the 1530s Henry VIII had entitled himself the head of the English church, while on the Continent Calvin was instituting his theocracy in Geneva. The boy king, and Protestant, Edward VI had taken over the English throne in 1547, only to be succeeded after his premature death in 1553 by the staunchly Catholic Mary, who died in 1558. In 1584, the year of Selden's birth, the Protestant Elizabeth had survived on the throne for a quarter of a century, had managed to oversee the amalgamation of religious ceremony and Calvinist theology with a heavy stress on obedience, and in 1588 would be the putative focal point for God's gracious rescue of the English nation from the invasion of the Spanish Armada. That she remained unmarried was no doubt a mixed blessing for her subjects, for marriage would in all likelihood conjoin her with a partner from the Continent, where, especially in nearby France, the integrity and welfare of the holy commonwealth had never been so imperiled.

A dozen years before Selden's birth, the politics of the Reformation had been drastically altered. Before 1572 those Protestants theorizing a justification for resistance to idolatrous and ungodly princes had operated in the region of equivocation, caution, and contradiction; for the predominant injunction of both the Lutheran and the Calvinist branches of the Reformation was obedience to the magistrate. To be sure, writers entertained a handful of exceptions to this injunction and teased out justifications for some mild form of resistance that varied from the conscientious to the constitutional. The bogey of all these theorists was anarchy, however, and they worked hard at distancing their sense of the exceptions from anything smacking of violent revolt of the kind that had shocked Luther himself in 1524.[1]

In 1572 the St Bartholomew's Day Massacre changed this cautious, equivocal politics of the Reformation forever. Leading Huguenot thinkers were no longer content with crediting the Catholic leadership in France with good intentions. The crime of the massacre emboldened and radicalized their once fitful and bemused sense of whether papist tyrants ought to be resisted by force, and this change provoked once-moderate Catholics to abandon their own moderation, most famously Bodin. For, as Julian H. Franklin has argued, the absolutism of Jean Bodin's *Six livres de la république* (Paris, 1583) moved decisively away from the constitutional modesties of the earlier *Methodus ad facilem historiarum cognitionem*.[2] Especially with the accession of Henry of Navarre in 1589, the English were absorbed by and involved in the religious wars of France, from the newspapers and plays that were written about those contemporary events to the hordes of young men who went off to fight in France. His return to the Roman Catholic fold in 1593 dismayed Henry's English Protestant supporters with a wretched sense of betrayal, even as (in the words of the young John Donne) those English roustabouts continued to fight alongside the 'mutinous Dutch' and to court death in the 'fires of Spain.'[3]

Among the leading Huguenot theorists of resistance was François Hotman, whose *Francogallia* (published 1573) unfolded a constitutional history touting the elective basis of the French monarchy, indeed 'the greatest and most radical Huguenot treatise on the fundamental constitution of France.'[4] For Selden, Hotman's legal scholarship and historical methodology ranked him with the Jesuits, such 'Low Country men' as Grotius, and other sixteenth-century 'Lawyers of ffrance' as the most capaciously learned men, for 'the rest of the world make nothing but Homilies' (*Table Talk*, 71). But Hotman presented the Huguenots with a problem as much as a model. On the positive side, Skinner explains, Hotman's constitutional appeal to positive law pioneered Huguenot attempts to redress 'their two most pressing ideological needs ... On the one hand, it was essential for them to construct an ideology capable of defending the lawfulness of resisting on the grounds of conscience, since they needed to be able to reassure their followers about the legitimacy of engaging in direct revolutionary confrontation with the established government. On the other hand, it was no less essential to produce a more constitutionalist and less purely sectarian ideology of opposition, since they obviously needed to broaden the basis of their support if they were to stand any chance of winning what amounted to a pitched battle with the Valois monarchy' (2.310). In the 1620s and 1640s the less radical Selden would be faced with his own occasions for justifying resistance against the Stuart monarchy, but just as important, he would be struggling with a methodological and ontological problem that the Huguenots faced in the wake of Hotman's constitutional history. For that history, Skinner shows, proved undeniably vulnerable to Catholic critique and attack, provoking the Huguenots to seek out a conscientious and transhistorical justification for resistance in the realm of natural law. This move from positive to natural law was more deeply moral, yet also less exclusively religious, than previous Huguenot cases, and Skinner views it as essentially a foundation of political thought. Selden's own recourse to natural law would be subsumed, in turn, in his return to positive law as it was established by the ancient Jews and their God, his way of warding off the secularization of the commonwealth that was the mid-seventeenth-century purview of Thomas Hobbes. In the England of the 1590s, however, the appeal to natural law was being used to legitimize the general decency of the specific rituals practised in the established Church of England, newly and virulently under attack by respectful Presbyterians and saucy 'Marprelates' alike.

—— 1 ——

In the late 1580s and early 1590s the English were once again confronting the fissures in their own so recently resettled holy commonwealth. A secret press was releasing scurrilous satire on the offices, foundations, and practices of the episcopal chuch, while higher-brow theologians, such as Thomas Cartwright, were mounting learned scriptural assaults on the carnality of that polity. For Selden's Elizabethan generation, of course, Richard Hooker's *Of the Laws of Ecclesiastical Polity* was the grand monument to the putatively divinely appointed yet naturally and artificially decorous measure that Hooker took for granted in the Elizabethan settlement of English Protestantism. Selden's lifelong project of stabilizing and redefining the norms of religious society was the sceptical, non-partisan alternative to an Elizabethan polemical dogmatism that took its rightness for granted. Indeed, although Selden was born into Hooker's world, and even if he pursued the Hookerian project of devising and promulgating laws for English religious society, he was not one to take the official norms of English Protestant society simply as givens. Selden attempted to complete a search that Hooker never really started; one can see the difference even in their styles: the older man's reflective of a beautifully dispensed certainty, the younger man's difficult, digressive, and many toned.

It is likely that from Selden's vantage point, Hooker's version of the laws of ecclesiastical polity was as deeply flawed as it was grandiloquent. Hooker set the direction and agenda for the next (Selden's) generation in their efforts to stabilize and secure English religious society in the face of the polemical discord, scepticism, persecution, and civil war that wracked late sixteenth- and early seventeenth-century Christendom. But even if Selden sometimes took over terms like natural law that one finds in Hooker, the younger man's intellectual experiments in the laws of ecclesiastical polity were neither so polemical nor so systematic as Hooker's apologia. For even if in the 1640s and 1650s he ended where Hooker began, with a fervent disregard for Presbyterianism, Selden was attached to no one church and extensively considered the virtues of the presbyter; he could afford a scepticism and criticism that Hooker could ill afford; he was simply bolder and more widely ranging in his recasting of conventional norms; and he was not so averse to or perplexed by his more godly contemporaries as to resist their spiritualism altogether. At times Selden's scepticism might imply that it is far better to heed the laws and customs of the Sanhedrin, say, than to generate fanciful dogmatism of one's own. He had a regard for the sanctity of institutions and customs that Milton would have considered prone to tyranny. The most pervasive characteristic of Selden's sceptical historicism is that it tends to postulate, without ever finally promoting, templates and visions of lawful religion from the children of Noah surviving a deluge in 'inmost' history to the children of Selden's own generation surviving a civil war.

Selden was eight or nine years old when Hooker published the preface and first four books of his *Lawes of Ecclesiastical Politie* in 1593. Although Hooker was an ordained priest and Selden would become an ordained common lawyer, the trajectories of their careers were not dissimilar: both were extraordinary grammar scholars, Selden in Sussex, Hooker in Devonshire; both matriculated at Oxford; and each in his own capacity had connections with the Temple in London. Indeed, in the years immediately after Selden's birth, Hooker was embroiled in controversies with the Presbyterians in residence at the Temple; it was this very battle that provoked *Lawes of Ecclesiastical Politie*.

In his magisterial preface and over the course of the first five books, Hooker is intent on firmly grounding the hierarchical polity of the

Church of England in what he characterizes as the naturally unimpeachable warrant of law. Accordingly, his taxonomy and celebration of the presence of law in religion entail that laws and little else constitute the fabric of the cosmos, the orders of the angels, and the religious society of men. In responding to the spiritually zealous and wholly scripturalist Presbyterians emerging within his church, Hooker tends to supplant, ignore, or take for granted the ineffable warrant of spirituality and to dismiss as abnormal those parties that accentuate the supra-legal and especially Pauline penchant of Reformation spirituality.

In the eighth chapter of Book III, for example, Hooker is arguing for the value of rationality against those zealots who exclude all sources of wisdom save scripture and all instruments of religion save the gracious 'workings of the spirit.' Protesting that 'grave and learned' appeals to the 'testimony of the spirit' are not at all meant to short-change reason, Hooker finds himself in the middle of an uncharacteristic and a knotty exposition of how the spiritual and rational conveyances of wisdom relate to one another. He allows that the testimony of the spirit is exceedingly high matter, but such allowance entails that this testimony is very often mistaken and that there is little point in discussing it. 'Wherefore,' he concludes, 'albeit the spirit lead us into all truth and direct us in all goodnes, yet bicause these workings of the spirit in us are so privy and secret, we therfore stand on a plainer ground, when we gather by reason from the qualitie of things beleeved or done, that the spirit of God hath directed us in both; then if we settle our selves to beleeve or to do any certaine particular thing, as being moved thereto by the spirit.' With this return from a relationship between elusive if higher spirit and normative if lower reason, Hooker has grown impatient with the discussion of spirit: 'But of this enough,' he declares.[5]

The preface and first four books of Hooker's great work tend to proceed in similar fashion: the testimony of the spirit is not so much denied as taken for granted, elevated out of the discussion, and associated with misguided and fractious zealots. What matters is that the practices of the Church of England be granted a legitimate or normative authority, even if the warrant of that authority moves between nature, artifice, political will, and divine will. Sometimes the normative principle is not so much law – though it usually is – as it is simply everyday custom and expedience. Indeed, Hooker allows, no one would ever accuse the Presbyterians of having no canon; the problem is that their canon is, contradictorily, far too rigid in its polity (which can never change, whatever the time or the circumstances) and far too amorphous (since it is based in the testimony of the spirit and in fanciful readings of scripture); far too exclusive (scripture alone) and far too inclusive (too much lay intervention in the proper domain of the clergy).

Hooker's prefatory heading – 'No end of contention without submission of both parts unto some definitive sentence' – anticipates Selden's emphasis in the *Table Talk* on post-Reformation Christendom's urgent need for a guarantor of its claims on truth in the face of the disintegration of the church's integrity. But whereas in the 1640s Selden can sound as if the long hard search for such a measure is liable to come to nothing, Hooker argues as if no one but a foolish and incorrigible rebel would either abandon the laws of nature or feel the need to search beyond the unmistakable decorum of everyday life. Elaborating on how obvious it is that human beings require a rule, he does not, however, pursue the corollary that mortal corruption makes any human invention of such a rule automatically suspect: 'So full of wilfulnes and selfe-liking is our nature, that without some definitive sentence, which being given may stand, and a necessitie of silence on both sides afterward imposed, small hope there is that strifes thus far prosecuted, will in short time quietlie ende.' Adding an analogy between the Jewish Sanhedrin and the Elizabethan High Commission, he defines his goal as the normalizing and defence of the Elizabethan settlement 'which is in being,' and this resolution from the putatively stable status quo demands that he attack spiritual zeal as anathema to the 'observers of civility and decent order.' Frenzied, fanciful spirit destroys the normalcy of religion, whether that normalcy might find its embodiment in the music of the spheres or in 'the ordinary custome in every thing.'[6] Even when he characterizes scripture itself, Hooker is apt to emphasize its compendium of law. Hooker would enlarge the domain and reach of law, stress the lawfulness of God, exalt the linear rectitude rather than the spiritual abundance of virtue, and accentuate the social rather than the solitary experience of holiness. In short, decency and law are so in control of the limitlessly gracious spirit of Protestant faith that this spirit is allowed in Hooker's church only if it is properly groomed and normally behaved.

—— 2 ——

Insofar as Hooker's sixth and eighth books would not be published until 1648, the publication of his *Ecclesiastical Polity* essentially framed the lifespan of John Selden (the seventh book was first published twelve years after his death, which occurred in 1654). In those books, Hooker's concerns with bishops, presbyters, and monarchs and the authority of all three groups in religious society were singularly in keeping with Selden's own concerns in the 1640s and 1650s. But Hooker's defence of the status quo and his minimization of spiritual mystery or zeal are alien to the boldly inventive, sceptically searching, and religiously comprehensive polities conceived in the scholarship of John Selden. Selden did not need the turbulence of the 1640s to know that Hooker had not proved the superiority and stability of the bishops and their church, that he had only deferred the search for answers to the dilemma of how predominantly zealous and normative religions might marry for the good of societies and consciences alike. But the Civil War and its aftermath were not likely to convince Selden that, as Izaak Walton implies in *The Compleat Angler,* the Elizabethan church held the key to the ills of Protestantism. True, the Tudor Protestant church was rightly founded on parliamentary dispensations; but in contrast to Selden's approach to Judaic studies, Hooker had not taken the challenge offered by Jesus himself in the Gospels, namely, that even if God's law must not be altered, nonetheless it requires a gracious transformation and spiritual fulfilment.

In the 1640s Selden conversed about how the leaders in Protestant and Catholic Christendom had not solved the great but problematic double injunctions of the New Testament: of obeying the higher magistrates but also of fulfilling the law with the gracious afflatus of abundant spirituality. One could look with confidence neither to the Protestants, with their zeal for the Holy Spirit, their democratic tendencies, and their rampant preaching of God's word; nor to the Catholics, with their intolerance and military aggression. If the Tudor institution of the bishops had offered the best theoretical solution to mediating normalcy and zeal, the practice of that institution had proved rather less efficacious in the Caroline period. Yet Selden's published works on natural and Judaic law appealed to a wide variety of intellectuals and writers in search of sustenance for a wavering optimism that England might become the new Jerusalem, the best possible model of a holy commonwealth. Among Selden's advocates, John Milton looked to that body of scholarship both for hope that true religion might be found and for comfort in the likelihood that its discovery would be an arduous and complicated process. The more controlling or coercive his former allies, the Presbyterians and Independents, became, the more Milton moved away from a national polity. In the late 1650s he responded to the imminent failure of the republican experiment in English governance and of Congregationalism in English religion with treatises in which he italicized what he thought were the basic constituents of Protestantism: the Holy Spirit interpreting the scriptures to the individual conscience, a state of affairs protected by a carefully selected senate. God's law offered an invaluable warrant in Milton's vision of how England might recover its liberties, both the positive law laid down in the Bible and also the natural reason divinely dispensed to each individual. Milton's support of Old Testament law was highly fitful, however, and at times he would strike out at that law with an antinomian virulence worthy of Paul. Sometimes Milton did unto law and custom what Hooker tended to do unto spirit, a contrast made all the more ironic by their mutual dependence on concepts of natural law so radically different that they would have epitomized Selden's critique, in the *Table Talk*, that appeals to natural law are obscure at best and self-interested at worst. Selden continued to find a place for natural law in his vision of religious society, much as he continued to reserve a place for poetry; but by the end of his life, he had come to believe that natural law can prove far too malleable to private interests unless its dictates are directly linked to the will of God. Natural law represented Selden's most dogmatic and optimistic model for how spirituality might be normalized yet its zealous and adventurous edge retained – for how the Scylla of extreme scepticism might be avoided together with the Charybdis of the various dogmatic theologies on display. In working out that natural model over hundreds of pages in the 1630s, however, Selden was constantly moving back in the direction of positive law, understood both as a human artifice and as a divine appointment.

Even with the will of God on board, however, a religious society must come to terms with its need to invent some sufficient human authority to mediate that divine will. As Milton ran hot and cold with the religion of the Jews, Selden became more deeply committed to Judaism's religious society as a whole, including its pre-Pauline reformation in the communities of earliest Christianity. Selden would see in Milton's triangle of authorities – Holy Spirit, conscience, the Bible – a dearth of enforceable, contractual laws, as well as a cultural and intellectual blindness to the richly spiritual dimensions of the ancient Jews.

In his later Judaic work, Selden came to see that in the Gospel of Matthew, reformed Judaism – alias Christianity – offered a fleeting, hardpressed, but ripe opportunity for godly norms and a zealous spirituality to be married in one religious society. For so many reasons, however, it was an opportunity tragically missed, as he came to say in his treatise on

the Great Sanhedrin: with everyone under the pressure of Roman imperialism, the Jews refused to embrace the Christian reforms, and the
Christians eventually shook Judaism like so much worthless dust from
their feet. The tragedy was all the greater, Selden understood, given
Jesus' rabbinical status, defence of the law, and zealous reform of its
abuses. If Selden can be called an English Protestant, his is a Protestantism that pays little attention to Paul. More accurately, Selden invented
his own party of reformed Judaism in the 1640s, even if doing so meant
that in discussions of the Gospels he either avoided extensive analysis of
Jesus' trial or chalked up Jesus' persecution by the Jewish authorities to
the tendency of legal institutions to wane as well as wax within the circumstances of history.

As it was selected from the gospels, Selden's reformed Judaism would
be deeply and extensively lawful. After all, there was Jesus' own famous
warning: 'Do not suppose that I have come to abolish the Law and the
prophets; I did not come to abolish, but to complete. I tell you this: so
long as heaven and earth endure, not a letter, not a stroke, will disappear from the Law until all that must happen has happened' (Matt. 5:
17–18, NEB, 7). For Selden, Jesus' indictment of hypocritical rabbis and
Pharisees was part and parcel of a zealous commitment to Old Testament law; within the context of imperial persecution, the law's imperfect mediators, not the law itself, were to blame for the decline of Judaic
spirituality.

Jesus equally warns that true spirituality is not reducible to law, even
to God's laws for the Jews. A religion so immeasurably indebted to the
stewardship of the Holy Spirit would show itself by issuing in an unlim-
ited righteousness, even 'as your heavenly Father's goodness knows no
bounds' (Matt. 5:48, NEB, 9). At times Selden chooses to defer his discussions of apparent contradictions in the Gospels between a zealously
lawful Jesus and the Jesus on trial for violations of Judaic law. Over the
course of his final work on the Sanhedrin, however, he comes up against
the tragic possibility that the reformed Jews, or Christians, reeling under
pressure from Roman persecution, had also failed to coordinate the
warrants of law and spirituality. In *De Jure Naturali et Gentium*, Selden had
anchored the prospects for a sacred law on those basic principles of religion, moral honesty, and justice bestowed on human beings at their very
inception. In *De Synedriis*, he included vestiges of that foundation; but in
dwelling on the subsequent history of the Jews and of their human institutions, Selden raises the question of whether there was ever a just,
godly, and normative religion other than that directly handed on a plat-

ter first to Adam and Eve, and again (though not so politely) to Noah and his children.

Far too often in history, Selden knew, the arbiters of law had aborted spiritual fruits, and spiritual hotheads had abolished law. Unlike Milton, who was inclined to envision England's leadership in the Reformation, Selden tended to accentuate the centuries of religious conflict and laboured ecclesiastical negotiation in English history. On the civil wars of the 1640s, these features were writ large. In the early 1640s John Denham wrote, in 'Cooper's Hill,' that English subjects, clergy, and their monarch were about to become separated by a gulf between the extremes of fervid zeal and cold persecution that had severed the English commonwealth at the very commencement of the Reformation. Time and again, Selden's *Table Talk* testifies to the farcical tragedy resulting from the fact that in the 1640s English Protestants panicked over their own fractious dogmatism, profane scepticism, and bloodlust for the apocalypse. With the demise of the bishops and the treachery of their would-be successors, the Presbyterians, England was clearly failing to correct the extremes to which many of its church's best brokers had rushed, whether in the direction of law and prescription (Hooker, Charles I, and Archbishop Laud), or in obedience to the privatized fancies of the Holy Spirit (the antinomian radicals). More daunting, however, so many earnest and learned moderates had faltered across the spectrum between the extremes of law and spirit in their attempts to devise an English Reformation polity. Was there a humanly feasible model that they might follow? Or was coordination of law and spirit a utopian fiction, a *locus amoenus* as unreal as the Arcadia of those lyrical shepherds in a Renaissance pastoral? Were Selden's own attempts to fashion models for religious society read by his contemporaries in the same way that they might enjoy a diverting and exquisite romance, as a dazzling show of wit and the precious sublimation of a society's collective desires? Or was Selden understood to be devising a religious polity that would triumph where so many others – mere wits at long last – had spoken pompously, then had been deflated?

So many factors make such questions hard to answer. Selden's own dense allusiveness and elusive tone – sometimes late Elizabethan wit, sometimes sombre devotee of providential history, often cautious sceptic, often enough some strange mixture of all three – render his own scholarship as far removed from a straightforward speech act as discourse can move. Each of the normative personae in which Selden wrote implies its own tendencies towards inefficacy. Regarding the didactic poet and historian, Selden was closely affiliated with those authors (Drayton, Jonson, and Camden, for instance) whose high investment in a morally effective discourse was so often deflated by the obtuseness of audiences or by the parasitism and vanity of poets and historians themselves. Sages in the common law were struggling with the vagaries and obscurities of their own tradition and with the corruption in their own profession. The proponent of natural law was faced with sceptical demands for a new epistemological and demonstrative sophistication, under peril of rejecting Christian factionalism so thoroughly as to earn the moniker of 'atheist'; he also had to deal with the simple fact that natural law was as remote and unbinding as it was morally appealing. Selden's Judaic persona, for his contemporaries the boldest that he ever adopted, was liable to be criticized as irrelevant to Christian polities at best and as spiritually damaging at worst.

Selden's patron John Williams recognized early that the prodigious scholar faced his own battles against the force pulling young wits towards irreverence, inefficacy, and waste. When Selden had incurred the displeasure of James I and of some of the English clergy for his *History of Tithes*, the bishop wrote to the king with assurances that the author 'hath excellent parts, which may be diverted from an affectation of pleasing idle people, to do some good and useful service to his Majesty. He is but young, and it is the first offence he ever committed against the king.'[7] It would not be Selden's last offence against a king or the clergy. But Williams's view of the young Selden epitomizes a problem that emerges so strikingly from the great scholar's entire career in the study of law and religion: the question of whether learning's normative presence in the world is efficacious. Williams depicts Selden in the familiar guise of the prodigal son or 'Euphues,' a jokester on the order of a Thomas Nashe or Jack Donne or the 'university wits,' a wit who was wasting his considerable talent on smart-alecky satires or paradoxes, a roustabout style of living in taverns and with wenches – all for the sake of clever young men often found in Selden's own Inns of Court. In his early writings Selden sometimes adopts the style of such writers, and even in the *Table Talk* he recollects Nashe's saucy appropriation of cultural authority.

Williams protests that Selden's considerable talent can be redirected to good use, in particular, to the uses of the court. Like Ben Jonson, however, Selden was obsessed with the figure of the wit-turned-parasite, with an intellectual or literary talent that was sold away for the hire of an often corrupt patron's whims and desires. This danger was especially pronounced at a time when one of the major avenues for the normative influence of wits was through the poetics of praise. Still, Williams raises an important point: Selden's scholarship ought to serve some good public service, ought to intervene for the better in public affairs, and ought to operate as what David Norbrook has recently characterized as the speech acts cultivated in the training of young humanist intellectuals. Scholarship might apply itself as public action.[8] Selden would proceed to dedicate his edition of Eadmer to Williams, the contents of that edition boldly setting forth a vision of the church in which its liberty and labour in the world are protected from the contamination of politics and civil power. A decade later, Selden would dedicate work on the history and authority of priests to William Laud, no friend of Williams but in some measure a protector of Selden from the further wrath of a king. But in these works in support of the clergy, their autonomy, traditions, and resources, Selden made himself vulnerable to the charge levelled by some of his most hostile critics that the great scholar himself was a parasitic toady.

Together with the spectre of the parasite, there was for Selden a further problem with diverting oneself from the idle pleasures of what Nashe called 'lenten stuff' to the serious business of public intervention. In order to avoid parasitic careerism, the interventions of scholarship had to be premised on some conviction – the conviction of a prophet, of a principled senator, or of an honest adviser to the prince. Yet for Selden the integrity of scholarship depended in large measure on the suspension of convictions, on the ever critical acumen of the sceptical philosopher. In defending his historical work in the *History of Tithes*, Selden hedged his bets by remarking that he was leaving all theological debates about divine right to the theologians – this, despite the clear thesis in the work that at least the contractual basis of tithing was a human affair. In a preface to the same work, however, Selden argued ingenuously and strenuously that all great scholars must be sceptics at heart. The search for whatever truth one might find in history – whether that truth prove moral, religious, or factual – requires that writers not 'torture [their] brains or venture [their] credit to make or creat Premisses for a chosen Conclusion, that [they] rather would then could proue' (xii). Far from it, writers must apply a razor-sharp doubt to all vulgar opinions and suppositions, those 'which patient Idleness too easily takes for cleer & granted' (xiii). Selden's ideal scholar opposes the idleness of which he is accused by Bishop Williams, yet neither is he in the service of some ideology.

Nor is Selden's scholar a sceptic for the sake of idle doubting. Whether or not they wanted to do so, 'the old Sceptiques that neuer would professe that they had found a Truth, shewd yet the best way to search for any, when they doubted aswell of what those of the Dogmaticall sects too credulously receiud for infallible Principles, as they did of the newst Conclusions' (xiii). They were far too obsessively scrupulous, Selden concedes, and they were addicted to their witty games or 'Sophismes that permitted no kind of established Truth.' Like Bacon's vision of a doubting Pilate who would not wait for an answer to his questions about the nature of truth, or like the Elizabethan gallants and adventurers in Donne's 'Satire 3' – indeed, like Williams's own assessment of the young Selden – such fashionable sceptics are besotted, Selden adds, with 'their disputing Leuitie,' unmindful of the fact that 'their Libertie of Inquirie, is in the only way that in all kinds of studies leads and lies open euen to the Sanctuarie of Truth, while others, that are seruile to common Opinion and vulgar suppositions, can rarely hope to be admitted neerer then into the base court of her Temple which too speciously often counterfaits her inmost Sanctuarie' (xiii).

So the liberated scholar is neither idle nor servile. But is he a prophet or an adviser or a senator? Are his works tantamount to actions? Are they useful for the welfare of a religious society? What does the right application of that useful work require, first from the author, then from the readership? Selden's sceptical historian makes his way, cautiously yet boldly, into a sanctuary, indeed into the 'inmost' and most sacred area of a Solomonic temple complex. Is he a priest or an oracle? After all, Selden and his contemporary readers often made note of his oracular obscurity, and they struggled to place a value on it for better or for worse. It was possible that the obscurity was somehow appropriate for the preservation of truth, but the dispensation of that truth to a religious society at large would need some accommodating clarity. Selden's associates liked to point out that in person, in conversation, the great scholar was as crystal clear as he was confounding in his writings. Much is made among Selden's associates, and eventually in Selden's own writings, of the benefits that can accrue to religious societies from the rigour, honesty, and conversation of relatively small groups of citizens advising and rectifying one another. Along these lines, scholars are useful not as prophets, senators, barristers, or courtiers, but as friends and advisers. Again, anecdotes support documentary evidence that Selden was more inclined to give advice in matters of law than to work in his official capacity as a lawyer. However, this informal state of affairs leaves

wide open the question of whether the adviser's scholarship itself is
worth the considerable labour bestowed on it. If so, whence this worth?
Does value attach to the exquisite but nugatory grandeur of the
scholar's inventions, or to his remote encasement of a difficult truth or
pattern, its distance from a hapless society at once self-protective yet
ineffectual? In the first instance, the appreciative reader can rest from
the world turned upside down by all the contemporary problems that
the scholar ignores; in the second, the leading members of the society
are simply glad to know that a standard still exists, even if they would
never dare reach for it. In the first instance, the scholar devises mas-
querades for the library; in the second, he hovers around a rare and
illegible code preserved in his priestly, monkish sanctum. It is no wonder that Selden and Jonson found in one another such a kindred spirit;
for both were plagued by the fear that the most qualified arbiters of
norms in a religious society were also those arbiters likeliest to fail to
make any difference at all in that society.

In Selden's works and in contemporary responses to those works,
there is no ready, clear, or final answer to the problem of precisely what
gives the massive scholarship its value, efficacy, or authority. As Selden
sojourns in the domains of poets and historians, lawyers and priests, philosophers and governors, he tries on many guises for the persona and
stance of his scholarship, this in the course of experimenting with the
collective artifices in which religious societies might most becomingly
clothe themselves.

The dilemma of what makes scholarship worth the time and sweat it
requires reticulates throughout Selden's works and life with his ongoing
and evolving experiments regarding the invention of appropriate and
beneficial norms for religious society. Throughout his life, Selden displays both highly social or activist tendencies and a penchant for a law-
sage's version of monasticism: celibate, silent, and obsessed with Paradise. So too, the permutations of his normative discourse oscillate between highly practical and decidedly utopian inventions. On the one
hand, he works with the notion that a parliament, senate, or judicial
court must take the responsibility for ensuring the prosperity of a religious society, and in general that only carefully wrought human institutions can prevent the debacle of an overly licentious – censorial and
debauched – society in the wake of the Reformation. But, on the other
hand, in seventeenth-century Europe there were a great many extraordinary attempts to link canon and Canaan, law and Paradise, politically, discursively, and militarily, as well as etymologically.[9] As Selden pro-

duced three massive volumes in pursuit and invention of the Great
Sanhedrin, it remained unclear to the unfinished ending whether he
was in pursuit of a useful and workable institution, a utopian dream, or
a thing of beauty.

Sometimes Selden's normative arbitration clearly moves to one side
or the other, towards idealism or praxis. But as he engages the lessons of
poetry and history, the intricacies of the common law and the canon
law, the universal dictates of nature and the always changing artifice of
government, more often than not he lets the contents of his volumes
simply speak for themselves, without narrative guidance, with one seeming digression after another and largely stopping short of making a normative claim. Frequently, Selden accumulates documents from the past,
and even though he has selected and juxtaposed them, his scholarly persona makes no consistent thesis about what the reader should conclude.
He makes claims on historical accuracy, to be sure – about exactly when
Roman law most influenced English affairs, or about the proper translation of a Hebrew word – and all the while his labours towards accuracy
are promulgated in the service of those readers who would understand
anew how the leaders of religious societies – in England, Europe, Africa,
Jerusalem, in earliest antiquity, the Middle Ages, or in the years since
the Reformation – have struggled to mediate between civil and spiritual
dispensations. That is, he offers the fullest imaginable material for those
readers committed to the orderly, just, and righteous management of all
the different ways in which religious societies must permit (without
overly indulging) their neighbours' zeal, desire, inspiration, violence,
charisma, honour, love, and singularity. Yet Selden never finally says,
'this norm is the one we must follow so that our beleaguered England
will find measure, harmony, and true religion at long last.'

—— 3 ——

As will be shown in the chapters that follow, Selden's normative thinking developed in a loosely chronological fashion through periods of
emphasis on a variety of foci: (1) didactic poetry and history; (2) the
human institutions of positive law, whether common-law courts or parliament; (3) natural law; (4) churches and their spiritual labourers left
to their own peculiar devices; (5) the Sanhedrin. The permutations in
Selden's scholarship were shaped by the circumstances in which he
engages these norms, criticizes them, subordinates and reworks them.
Even as one focus supplanted another, Selden tended to revisit and

coordinate anew all of them, so that his last focus, the Sanhedrin, is decidedly hybrid or comprehensive in its conception of a holy commonwealth. Selden's views of poetry and history, of common law and natural law, of Erastian magistracy and spiritual labour developed in fits and starts, with shifting emphases and in dialogue with themselves and with the salient issues and events of different periods in his life.

Selden was born in Sussex on 16 December 1584, the only surviving son of a musician and a gentlewoman. Educated as a boy in Chichester, he spent his university days at Hart Hall in Oxford from 1600 until he enrolled at Clifford's Inn in London (1602). Having entered the Inner Temple in 1603, he began to publish his studies of English history, law, and customs and, though we have very little direct data on this important matter, pursued the study of the wide range of languages in which he developed expertise. In the second decade of the seventeenth century, he was already well known for his scholarship – at this time, Michael Drayton requisitioned his commentary on the poet's *Poly-Olbion* (1st ed. 1612) – and he added substantially to that reputation with the *Titles of Honor* (1st ed. 1614); an edition of the medieval legal authorities John Fortescue and Ralph de Hengham (1616); contributions to *Purchas's Pilgrimage*, including an anti-Semitic squib concerning 'the Jews some time living in England' (1617); his first major instalment in a subsequently lifelong study of Near Eastern cultures with a focus on the Old Testament idols, *De Dis Syris* (1st ed. 1617); and the *History of Tithes* (1618).

As England moved into the 1620s, years in which the aftermath of the Synod of Dort and the continuation of the Thirty Years War were dramatising religious division on the Continent, his study of tithes reaped Selden a fair share of controversy, polemical abuse, and royal censorship. Having twice met with Selden for a discussion of his work, and in addition to commanding him never to publish another word about tithes, James I sought to make use of Selden's religious scholarship in requesting that the author redeem himself with studies of the number 666, of a passage in Calvin, and of Christmas. Privately, Selden continued to defend and explain his views on church economy. Not all the English divines attacked him; one of his biggest supporters was Lancelot Andrewes, who, according to Selden himself, understood that the thesis of the *History of Tithes* – that is, when Selden was prepared to admit that there was one – would benefit rather than impoverish the church.

Selden's troubles with the king worsened, however, when in 1621 the lawyer assisted Parliament in recovering the full scope of its rights and privileges, an enterprise for which he earned a spell in prison, not for the last time. During his time in prison, Selden was studying the manuscripts of the historical writings left by Eadmer, monk and secretary to Anselm; in 1623, after his release from prison, Selden published an edition of and commentary on that work, dedicating it to Bishop Williams. In 1624 and throughout the remainder of the decade, Selden took a seat in the House of Commons and was a leader in the group of MPs who resisted the over-extension of the king's prerogative, especially in matters of royal finance, of due process in the law, of favouritism at court, and of the determination of orthodoxy in the Church of England. During this dramatic period, Selden also found time to heed the call of a patron, Thomas Howard, Earl of Arundel, and a fellow scholar, Sir Robert Cotton, in piecing together, editing, and glossing the famous marbles recently removed from the near east to the earl's garden next to the Thames. Selden's *Marmora Arundelliana* appeared in 1629.

In the first decades of his scholarly career, Selden had cultivated many leading lights as friends and patrons, including Drayton, Jonson, and Cotton among the former and featuring Henry Grey, Earl of Kent, and the Earl of Arundel, among the latter. When Charles put an end to parliaments in 1629 for what would prove to be over a decade, however, Selden was royally rewarded for his leadership in the Commons with extensive prison time. Finally released in May 1631, and then only on the pretext of helping certain patrons with a legal matter, Selden published a second, substantially revised and newly prefaced, edition of the *Titles of Honor,* one that corroborated his supreme authority in matters of positive law. Also, he began to produce his series of Judaic works, beginning with *De Successionibus in Bona Defuncti, Ad Leges Ebraeorum* (1631; written during his prison term). This study, concerning the inheritance laws of the Jews, was republished with *De Successione in Pontificatum Ebraeorum* in 1636, a volume dedicated to Archbishop Laud. In the first half of the 1630s he also participated in the committees selected in 1633 for the organization of a masque that might redress the damage done the reputation of the Inns of Court by William Prynne's *Histriomastix* (1632); for Prynne was a lawyer who had taken it upon himself to launch a massive attack on the theatre, on the effeminate manners of the age, and (it was perceived) on the queen herself. Selden was no friend of court culture and for the most part was suspicious of Charles's extralegal devices. In addition to the masque, he also prepared for publication his *Mare Clausum*, written for James I but for political reasons not published, at the behest of Charles. It was this publication that would prompt Selden's critics to accuse him of being a toady to the monarch who had persecuted him, a charge that he carefully refuted.

In 1640, in addition to publishing his *De Jure Naturali et Gentium*, Selden took his seat in the Long Parliament as a member for Oxford. Over the course of the 1640s he remained a participant in the Commons, involved in a wide range of committees concerning matters such as the trial of Strafford, ship money, the Court of Honor, the 1640 Convocation, bishops and the impediments to their spiritual offices, religious grievances, control over the military, and the privileges of the parliament. Committed as he was to helping Parliament to articulate the rule of law, he was also critical when it ignored that rule. In religion, Selden was caught between a client's loyalty to Archbishop Laud, who wrote to Selden for help with Parliament, and a lawyer's commitment to the Commons that would put the prelate on trial for his life. Clearly, however, he remained firmly supportive of the work of Parliament and was awarded a large sum of money in 1646 for having been persecuted by Charles in 1629–31. His former parliamentary patron, the Earl of Hertford, invited him to join King Charles at York in 1642; instead, Selden worked on the case against the royalist commissions of array.

In the early 1640s Selden participated in the Westminster Assembly of Divines as one of the laymen appointed by Parliament. He was quite active in this body, keen to keep it on course in its charge of reinventing the Church of England and eager to check the divines when they overreached themselves. His edition of a passage from the Arabic historical work of the Patriarch Eutychius (*Eutychii Aegytii*, 1642) dovetailed with contemporary religious debates; for it testified to the leadership of presbyters (as against bishops) in the early church of Alexandria, and in Selden's notes there are interventions in controversies such as the dispute between the respective supporters of extemporaneous and liturgical prayers. Selden's Judaic scholarship continued in 1644 with his *De Anno Civili et Calendario Veteris Ecclesiae*, a study of the calendar year in Judaism, with important work on the Karaites, a scripturalist group in rivalry with the normative Judaism of the rabbis. In 1646 he brought out the *Uxor Hebraica*, a study of Judaic laws and rituals regarding marriage and sexuality. His magnum opus, *De Synedriis et Praefecturis Juridicis*, a study of the Judaic court and senate known by its Greek name, the Sanhedrin, appeared in three parts, in 1650, 1653, and 1655. The third part was posthumous, since Selden died on 30 November 1654.

By the end of his life, Selden was predominantly devoted to Judaic studies, but not entirely so. In his *Ad Fletam Dissertatio* (1647), he posed an argument about the relationship between common and civil (Roman) law in English history, which he had begun to elaborate in his 'Review' to the *History of Tithes*. In his introduction to a collection of ten medieval historical writings in 1652 he continued to contribute to the welfare of his nation's historical documents, a goal dear to him also in his role as the keeper of the records for the Tower of London. There is no indication that Selden ever married, though some have speculated that he married his patroness, Elizabeth, Countess of Kent, after her husband's death; he certainly lived and died in her residence at White Friars and was buried in the Temple church. Although he accrued many admirers and friends over the years, he also continued to be attacked by enemies, a state of affairs that led to publication of his *Vindiciae de Scriptione Maris Clausi* in 1653 (see *Opera Omnia*).

The phases of Selden's normative thinking – pronounced yet never neatly partitioned, none ever quite abandoned, and indeed each recuperated in his work on the Sanhedrin – were intricately entangled with the events of his life. Especially in the first two decades of the seventeenth century, Selden investigated the claims made by poets and historians for the didactic value of their distinctive but overlapping discourses. In this enterprise he joined the leading cultural brokers of late Elizabethan and early Jacobean England, the noble Sidney, the robust Jonson, the saucy Nashe, the antiquarian Camden, and the nostalgic Drayton. He worked among old records, stuffed his prose with often obscure allusions, combined sobriety and humour, and took stock of the vehicles of narrative, praise, and blame by means of which poets and historians attempt to instruct and fashion their societies. Rather than take for granted that English didactic writers had found their best medium, Selden joined these diverse cultural brokers in their efforts to concoct the best possible historical poem or poetic history, a labour motivated by clear convictions yet complicated by divided loyalties.

Selden's complex involvement in the reconstitution of normative poetry and history often leaves its shifting rhetorical mark. Thus, in his commentary on Drayton's *Poly-Olbion*, one series of notes can interlace the toothy satire so popular among the wits of the time – 'Observe here the difference twixt the more ancient times and our corrupted neighbour ages, which have been so branded, and not unjustly, with dissembled bestiall sensualities of Monastique profession ... [and the] shamefull discoverie of Sodomites and Incontinent Friars' – with a sympathy for Drayton's mythological and romantic dreams of Britain, together with a feckless dismissal of readers and historians alike, even amid a show of uncommon historical learning: 'How my Reader tastes this, I know not; therefore I willingly quit him; and add only, that *William* of *Malmesbury* grossely erres in affirming that this *Bangor* is turn'd into a Bishoprique; but pardon him, for he lived in his Cloister & perhaps was deceived by Equivocation of Name, ther being in *Carenarvan* a Bishoprique of the same title to this day, which some bodie later hath on the other side ill taken for this.'[10] For all this *sprezzatura* in the vein of Sidney, however, for all this Nashean carelessness, Selden shared Jonson's and Drayton's commitment to preserving and concocting a normative literary discourse that would rectify the moral honesty and transmit the valuable traditions of their newly powerful Britannia.

Selden appended to the songs of Drayton's poem his own feckless dismissals, dense allusions, and ironic dodges as something of a critical historian's distancing from the poetic history itself, even as his rhetoric also mounted what Sidney, Nashe, and Jonson in their very different ways considered shields against the almost inevitable failure of normative poetics. As he constructed his own version of the community of cultural brokers in which didactic history and poetry might best thrive, a gathering of bards and critics with complementary talents, Selden also evinced his suspicion that this discursive community was unlikely ever to assemble. Despite England's being at peace in the first decades of Jacobean rule, and despite the fact that a political and religious comprehension overrode any internal discord, his work on and in history and poetry were rife with a scepticism that resisted any old-fashioned reconciliation between the heroic-cum-didactic and evidentiary orientations in representations of the past.

During the 1620s peace and comprehension deserted Selden's England, and with that change, his role as a guarantor of norms for his religious society altered markedly. It is true that Selden's studies of poetry continued throughout his life, to his exploration of the value of metaphor in the Talmudic tradition. But when in the late 1620s he provided his patron with a commentary on the history of music and poetry as part of his reconstruction of the Arundel Marbles, Selden was taking a break from his leadership in the legal and parliamentary activism at the forefront of an exploding combat over the religious and political values of early Stuart England. Indeed, when Selden turned his attention in the 1630s to natural law and to Judaic institutions of law and priesthood, this shift responded in part to the failures and afflictions of an activism that had once promised a more immediate and binding reform than dreamy poets could ever deliver. Yet Selden would shift back to a focus on the legal ties that bind a holy commonwealth; for he always believed that without binding ligatures no such commonwealth could prosper for long.

In the first two decades of the century, times of peace and prevailing consensus in England, Selden had commenced his legal career and published some of his pioneering research into the records of English legal institutions. In the second decade of the new century, he had published an edition of the work of one of the proudest advocates of English law, Sir John Fortescue, whose treatise begins with praise for the sanctity of that law and for the Mosaic legacy of its judges. At the end of the second decade, then throughout the 1620s, however, the security, peace, and consensus of Selden's religious society evaporated (where illusory) and collapsed (where sturdy in fact) – and this at so many levels of the young scholar's experience. In Europe, a massive religious war broke out between the Hapsburg emperor and the supporters of his German Protestant rival for the rule of Bohemia, Frederick, the Elector Palatinate, whose soon-to-be-exiled wife was James I's daughter. European Protestants were hardly unified among themselves, as exemplified by the divide between Calvinists and Arminians in the Synod of Dort. At home, among Protestants in England, tensions rose and protest erupted over a series of affairs, beginning with the controversy over just how England should intervene in the continental war, with the more aggressively Protestant voices calling for a military engagement with the papist Antichrist, while James sought a bargaining leverage with Catholic Spain to which peace might entitle him. The actual play for leverage was even more upsetting in England than the simple fact of neutrality in the war; for not even James was happy with Prince Charles's dangerous journey to Spain in hapless search for a papist bride, and the godly sort of Protestants among his subjects were appalled at both the danger and the goal of the journey. During the 1620s the perception that the source of courtly misrule and corruption derived from the Duke of Buckingham, Charles's fellow on that journey and James's favourite, would divert the anger of critics from the Stuart monarchs. But in the 1620s James (increasingly) and Charles (uniformly) were impatient with any show of opposition to any person or policy falling in what they considered the purview of their prerogative. In the early 1620s James attempted severely to restrict the political and religious content of sermons, while in the second half of the decade Charles lost patience with one Parliament after another for an unwillingness to fund adequately the wars for which they had clamoured, at least not without redress to their complaints in the threatened demise of true religion and lawful propriety in their homeland.

In the 1620s, whatever the differences from one parish to the next, no one with a sense of the national religious community would have claimed that English Protestantism was at peace with itself. Indeed, common lawyers and members of Parliament led the charge against the prominent and energetic articulation of what the godly tended to dub 'Arminian' positions, by which they meant a number of related but unequal tendencies: the support by certain royally patronized clergy for détente with Roman Catholicism; the visible relaxation of Calvinist hegemony in the rhetoric of English orthodoxy, with a corollary tendency to posit a greater role for free will in the *ordo salutis*; a higher profile in the services of worship for physical beauty, ecclesiastical formality, and clerical ritual, with pronounced official advocacy of these accoutrements of worship; and a monopoly on preaching, lecturing, and general authority in the church for clergy ordained in and subservient to the dictates of a royally delineated ecclesiastical polity. Far more than James, Charles considered any resistance to or non-conformity with this polity clear evidence of rabid insubordination and anarchy.

As is clear from parliamentary leadership in the critique of Arminianism in the 1620s, the contentions over 'true religion' implicated the institutions and energies of the whole of English society, not only the clergy, the church, and any exclusively sacred domain. This fusion of civil and religious concerns was sealed once the peacetime of Jacobean England – whatever the discontent it raised among the 'godly' sort about non-involvement in the international Protestant cause – gave way to Charles's fumbling war efforts against both Spain and France. These ambitious military enterprises obviously created a great financial burden, which meant that Caroline parliaments would be summoned on account of their long-standing responsibility for the award of subsidies, that they would therefore have a forum in which to air the serious grievances about the state of religion, and that the king's attempts to circumvent his dependence on Parliament would lead him to financial expedients with such controversial legal grounding that the most basic values and presuppositions of the national community would suddenly be on the agenda for parliamentary sessions, with Selden in the middle of the stocktaking of the norms most integral to his world.

Impatient with parliamentary stinginess, whining, and ingratitude (as he saw it), Charles believed that the necessity of the times authorized his use of prerogative in raising money by whatever means he saw fit, including forced loans. His paranoia over and prosecution of what he considered the chief rebels against his divinely bestowed authority and contaminants of his sacred honour led only to further battles over the precedents for and legality of his rule. Critics of his exercises of prerogative were apt to direct their barbs against those counsellors and rhetoricians who (they believed) had seduced the king into the extremes of popery and autocracy, from the queen herself to Buckingham, but also including preachers such as Robert Sibthorpe and Roger Maynwaring, whose pulpit rhetoric elevated the king's will dizzily far above any warrant in law, propriety, or ancient liberty for the subjects.

Selden found himself in the role of intellectual and rhetorical leader of the lawyers and parliamentarians defending the religion and proprieties of English society in the late 1620s. His work on the second edition of *Titles of Honor,* together with his publication of the *Mare Clausum* in the 1630s followed by the edition of the *Ad Fletam* in the 1640s, testified to his ongoing commitment to the normative value of a humanly devised law for the needs and welfare of a commonwealth. Also, legal sages or magistrates would play an invaluable part in his vision of a holy state centred on the Sanhedrin. Even so, Selden was not entirely convinced by some of the loftier claims made for the immemorial and natural merits of the common law, as surely as he was never wholly or even predominantly content with the apologies for instructive poetry. Selden was always sceptical about the most grandiose theories behind the notion of an immemorial and inviolable common law, those promulgated by Edward Coke, and he participated in a widespread critique of the common-law artifice, whose every aspect, from style and method to scope and content, was under attack during the very time of its ascendancy. When he shifted his focus from the common law per se to its parliamentary modifiers and advocates, no doubt Selden deemed the king's ability simply to dispense with Parliament at will as evidence that English legal institutions could prove too unreliable, their often aristocratic leaders too imperfect, for the welfare of English religious society to depend on its control and authority. The conflicts and dramas of the 1620s confronted Selden with the displeasure and manipulativeness of monarchs who could gravely afflict his person or severely restrict his intellect if they disliked his views on tithes or felt stung by his legal opinions in parliament.

In the 1620s, then, Selden embodied the assumption that the human institutions of positive law are largely responsible for whatever sanctity and honesty perseveres in the fallen world. Indeed, his contemporaries looked to him as the embodiment of the legal norms of their world. At some level, too, his scepticism itself was supportive of this move towards engagement with the remedies of positive law in human institutions, since, according to one trend in that philosophy as articulated most recently by Montaigne, our own artificial constructs are all that we human beings ever finally have. Selden's criticism of the naturalizing myth currently situated at the source of English common law recognized with irony that those myth-makers, fallen human beings each and every one, are wholly responsible for the corruption from which sanctity, propriety, justice, and honesty nonetheless need their protection.

Selden's involvement in the intensely contentious Caroline parliaments as a member and as a legal orator held out the promise of normative results more socially definitive and contractual than any effect a Jonsonian poet might have on the solitary reader. Yet the penal consequences also were decidedly tangible and binding. In the late 1620s and early 1630s Selden was imprisoned for leading Parliament in its aggressive critique of the illegal and impious ways in which the king and his ministers had been governing England's Protestant society. In the 1630s, with England again at peace, Parliament dissolved, and conflicts over religion at first more submerged than in the 1620s, Selden diverted his attention to three overlapping but quite different concerns: the warrant of natural law, with its claims on universality and transcendence over the stage-play human world; the separate canons or, alternatively, the spiritual labours defining the ministry; and the legacy of Judaism, especially rabbinical Judaism, with its promise to return human beings to the period and conventions of their greatest intimacy with God.

Each concern emerged somewhat piecemeal at first, then intensified in the 1640s. With natural law, as he had done with the golden world of Sidneyean poetry, Selden attempted to project the norms of a religious society beyond the gross imperfections of merely human justice. This higher law factored into Selden's elaborate taxonomy of law in the *Mare Clausum*, but it could not be said to dominate his works until he published *De Jure Naturali* in 1640. The second concern – with church canons, the priesthood, and spiritual labour – is harder to trace and at times sits uneasily with Selden's disputes with the established clergy. During his earlier imprisonment by James, Selden had turned his attention briefly to a writer who supported the autonomy and proprieties of the church against the civil government: the historian Eadmer. He had also sought patronage and protection from a clergyman, John Williams, a moderate who would eventually come into conflict with William Laud yet survive his own prison sentence to emerge victorious over Laud. In dedicating work on the Judaic priesthood to Archbishop Laud, Selden flirted with that controversial advocate of the theory that religion is best protected by those priests ordained into its inmost circle. Selden admired Laud for the prelate's vigorous support of scholarship, and Laud was utterly sympathetic with research that resurrected the meticulous laws according to which the ancient Jews measured the qualifications for priesthood on the basis of everything from facial moles to moral blemishes. In his preface to the prelate, Selden offered some watered-down Laudian sentiments that in Wilkins's eighteenth-century biography would even be used to epitomize Selden's religious positions: the idea that there are two kinds of Protestants, the healthy ones who embrace tradition and the peevish ones who destroy the peace of the church in advancing their own innovative explications of scripture.[11] But Selden clearly did not support Laudian notions of the power of the clergy. He offered his services to Laud as a pioneer seeking out learned materials for the intellectual refurbishing of the Church of England. He simply never forthrightly claimed to support Laud's vision of the church in which the prerequisites, rites, and status of proper ordination were central to clerical authority; in which the clergy were responsible for exacting canonical conformity in religious practices whenever and wherever the children of the *ecclesia anglicana* worship; and in which those practices were supposed to be reverential to the extent to which they were ornate, beautiful, and formal.

In the 1640s and 1650s his understanding of ministerial autonomy would reject the clergy's claims on worldly jurisdiction for a purified sense of their labours with the spiritual instruments of salvation. Of all Selden's notions of how law and spirituality might be coordinated, then, the presupposition behind the history of canon law was no doubt the one that most often repelled him. Selden was immeasurably more supportive of lay intervention in religion than he was of clerics left to their own devices, and he could be and often was fervently critical of overreaching clerics who appropriated the offices of the laity. His very presence at the Westminster Assembly was symbolic of the Long Parliament's control over that body, and in the *Table Talk*, he quips that laymen must attend the convention of divines to ensure that they did not make a mess of English society and law. Even so, he ended up believing that spiritual labour required its own ontological and cultural space, a space in which the lack of magistracy or worldly authority was read by the various parties of the mid- to late seventeenth century as a fatal weakness and a diacritical strength. Above all, he insisted that Erastianism required the protection of the spiritual realm of experience as surely as it paradoxically demanded the civil status of all jurisdiction, including that involving religious issues.

Concerning Judaism, whose history he mined for both natural and priestly codes, Selden began to strive for something far more, for a holistic vision of a normative religious society comprising poetry and nature, priests and secular lawyers, epistemological protection derived from the Talmud, and the most transcendent warrant of all, the first and continuing expression of God's will in history. Selden's burden in setting forth this vision would be, first and foremost, the coordination of all these normative strains.

Selden had shown great interest in Old Testament studies before – in his *De Dis Syris* (1617) – but in that text he was interested in idolatrous deviations from the standards of Judaic worship. In the 1630s and 1640s normative Judaism took centre stage in his thoughts and writings. In 1640, with a major impetus from the work of Hugo Grotius, the two legacies of nature and Judaism came together in Selden's *De Jure Naturali et Gentium*. But they also pulled against one another in the author's attempt to study the small slate of universal religious laws dictated from God to Adam, Eve, and Noah in the form of 'nature' and the positive laws designated by God for the Jewish people alone. By the 1640s Selden was showing discomfort with staking so much on natural law, not least because natural law is always vulnerable to subjective and political manipulation. One might even say, and Selden does say, that it is virtually meaningless to base a religious society on natural law; that, at best, natural law offers guidance to the individual conscience attempting to protect itself from the vicissitudes of the world. If natural law exists – and Selden at times questions whether it does – it is often impractical beyond the internal economy of the constant Stoic sage, unless it can be enlisted in defence of a specific cause or transmuted into the clearly expressed will of God. Selden's own treatment of natural law in the *Mare Clausum* was criticized virulently for being a political tool of a royal court as well as political security for its periodically imprisoned author. In the 1640s Selden was turning back to (if he ever fully left) his belief that the human institutions of positive law must be integral to the welfare and arrangement of any religious society. Indeed, he never really abandoned that conviction, for he was at work on the Sanhedrin from the late 1630s through to the end of his life.

Yet the context in which Selden posed his cases for the role of the civil magistracy together with the partial autonomy of the church drastically changed between the 1620s and the 1640s. The Eadmer edition let its monkish historian speak largely for himself, and it served in some measure as a qualification, no doubt a politic one, of the impression left by Selden in the *History of Tithes* that the church should surrender its resources to the civil jurisdiction. John Williams, the patron of the Eadmer, exemplified the infiltration of civil office by the clergy rather than the invasion of sacred office by the laity. So, too, did Laud when in the 1630s Selden's research on the Jewish priesthood was recast under the prelate's auspices.

In the 1640s Laud was in prison, on trial, and under the executioner's axe. Moderate Episcopalians, Presbyterians, and Congregationalists were in agreement that substantial reform was needed for the bishoprics of the Church of England, and the Westminster Assembly and Long Parliament were engaged in the work of that reform. Civil war was breaking out in England, in no small part over the question of church polity, with fissures subsequently opening between the parties, who agreed only that some reform was needed but radically disagreed on whether that reform entailed a strictly delineated national Presbyterian church, a loosely defined national gathering of Congregationalist churches, or an apocalyptic radicalism in which inner lights, antinomian grace, and the monarchy of Jesus were the dominant markers. In this extraordinary and rapidly changing context, Selden was considered a stalwart scholar on behalf of the church, an unbiased critic of the errors and excesses discoverable on all sides of the debate over the future of the church, and an Erastian heretic on his way to damnation. Some contemporaries looked to him for rigorous, fruitful, and conciliatory interventions in the debates over the future of the church, while others dismissed or vilified what they considered to be his spiritually sterile secularism.

In the 1640s – years of uncommon promise, urgency, and frustration for the leading arbiters of religious polity in England – one finds Selden trying to carve out a middle ground between supporters of liturgical and extemporaneous prayer (in his edition of Eutychius); thinking through the benefits and liabilities of each ecclesiastical proposal in turn, from bishops to presbyters to congregations to inspired zealots and prophets; and coming up against the painful recognition that normative thinking about religious society might well need to shift towards models for keeping spiritual labours and civil enforcements conveniently apart.

The problem for Selden with leaving the church to its own devices was always that no one was hungrier for power than the majority of leading clerics. Given all the different pitfalls that open when civil magistrates invade the realm of spiritual labour or spiritual labourers usurp civilian offices, it is no wonder that Selden devoted much of the 1630s to a newly sophisticated defence of natural law, with its positing of common notions that transcend differences among and within religious cultures. By the end of his life, the scope that he allotted to natural law had shrunk from a set of common notions overarching all of history and filling the artifices of all cultures to a supporting role within an overarching artifice of religious society, a role most vividly instanced in the very private moral strength of afflicted individuals. Selden could remain in the paradise of nature only so long, much as he always suspected that poetic Bards needed outside critics to keep them honest. And much as the intensely conflictual 1620s provoked him out of an orientation towards didactic history and poetry and into a direct involvement with the practical workings of human law, so, too, the even more militant and divisive 1640s spurred him out of nature back into the contractual institutions of church and civil government. But Selden did not repeat his mistake of the 1620s, during which time much of his intellectual devising had given way to workaday politics. For in the 1640s, even as he debated questions of church polity and instruments of worship in the Westminster Assembly, Selden kept a certain distance from the war and the assemblies. He was very much an inhabitant of the scholar's cell in the last years of his life, hard at work on his reconstruction and reinvention of the religious society that might prove a remedy for an England in total disorder.

In his final works Selden argued that the protection of spiritual labour from civil coercion can work only if the domain of spiritual labour is properly laid; but this delineation was difficult for him, especially as he grew increasingly committed to the holistic, Judaic notion that there can be no distinction between the sacred and profane. In God's chosen society of the Jews, the Sanhedrin considers all kinds of cases, and all of law is religious, whereas all religion is lawful. Most obviously, rabbis are theologians as surely as they are legal-cum-judicial sages. Yet, Selden maintains, the redemptive dispensations of God's spirit are a fundamental and pervasive constituent of Judaic society, and the early Christians are simply zealous Jews in search of that dispensation again. In one of the most poignant passages in his works, he interjects into his study of the Sanhedrin a lament for the circumstances

under which the ancient Jews squandered much of their spiritual treasure, even if their motives for doing so – cultural, political, and legal survival in the world of Roman tyranny – were understandable. Selden also
laments the early Christian failure to persevere in its original commitment to Judaic law, even if its motives for breaking away from Judaism –
the influence of Pauline dualism and eventually the prospect of imperial power – are equally clear.

As Selden invented his model of the Sanhedrin, his attempt to coordinate law and ineffable spiritual largesse in one comprehensive vision of
a holy commonwealth made use of both the poetic and natural legacies
with which he had been involved. Poetry and nature, like human institutions of justice and the separate and sacred labours of the priests and
ministers, claimed their proper place in what amounts to Selden's own
conceptual temple complex. In the three tomes he rarely addresses the
fissures that open up between the compartments of his never-finished
volume, in which much more is promised about the law of nature, and
leaves off with a tortuous yet powerful digression in which the value of
flawed but tangible human inventions is posed against the universality
and purity, yet elusiveness, of natural law. He makes a case for civil
authority to control excommunication, makes another case for the separate domain of labours in the spirit, yet his temple complex never gets
much further than the archway, a crucial metaphor with which he introduces the work.

Even though the tomes on the Sanhedrin touch on the issues of governance under unprecedented debate and contention in the England
of the late 1640s and early 1650s, Selden rarely, if ever, plants his attention firmly on relevant points of contact between ancient Judaism and
his contemporary situation. There is much ado in the work about how
the ancient Jews dealt with the relationship between kings and law sages,
about the subordination of ancient Judaic priests to those same
sages, about the level of autonomy that the Jews granted to spiritual
zealots and prophets, about the qualifications for the priesthood, and
about the extent to which legal judges should control religious culture.
In the 1650s, however, Selden kept his distance from the rival parties,
the sectaries and Independents, Presbyterians and royalists. Refusing to
accept Cromwell's offer that he help to design the new English government, Selden left unclear just how his Sanhedrin might relate to the
rival contemporary dreams of the Judaic institution and the temple that
housed it: the Fifth Monarchists' call for a Sanhedrin in their apocalyptic vision of the New Jerusalem in England, as distinct from the temple

that had once filled the sermons of Laud and comforted the imprisoned Charles I in 'the pages of the commentary on Ezekiel by the Jesuit Villa-lpandus,' which featured 'the learned Jesuit's conception of the Temple at Jerusalem, a majestic classical fantasy which had influenced Inigo Jones in his designs for Whitehall.'[12] It is not evident whether Selden would have been more pleased with the Nominated Parliament of 1653, itself a sort of contemporary Sanhedrin in its designs for the rule of the fittest godly men though few, or the Restoration Parliament of the 1660s and 1670s, in which persecution in the name of conformity replaced the inner light of radical reform.

Its massive scholarly reconstruction unfinished, it is not clear whether Selden's Sanhedrin was to be received as a golden, poetic construct or as a recommendation to the policy-makers of contemporary Britannia. His favourable contemporaries, however, tended to read the lessons of his later work as at once extraordinarily brilliant for the few readers equipped to read him and almost entirely lost on the brazen world of civil war Britain, their need for his valuable if difficult lessons notwith-standing. Other readers, those especially supportive of clerical author-ity, were simply not favourable. Indeed, contemporary accounts of his last days tend to interpret the scene of his death as the moment at which the great scholar had to make a final decision between service to the civil government and devotion to the church. In their divisiveness over which choice Selden had made, they reflected their own growing sense that the enterprise of integrating civil magistracy and religious experi-ence into one social order might be a wrong-headed and impossible undertaking after all.

In the realms of poetry and history, of positive law, natural law, and the separate offices of spiritual labour, Selden was both critical of and engaged with the potential of humanly mediated norms to help to secure and enrich a society's holiness, harmony, and honesty. His Sanhe-drin, or the cultural and ideational complex that surrounds it, attempted to comprise all of them. But Selden's last Judaic study is silent on whether its project of inventing a measure for religious society is a useful labour or a grandiose vanity. Many of Selden's associates would have agreed with Richard James that the great scholar generated 'heroic thought.'[13] Contemporaries celebrated the courage, honesty, labour, and brilliance with which he mediated between the civil and spiritual requirements of a prosperous society and brought such enormous learning and precise method to bear on the problems of their day. In the 1620s and 1630s, however, there was decreasing certainty about whether an internal and intellectual heroism might boldly assert itself in changing the shape or direction of English Protestant society.[14] Then, in the 1640s and 1650s difficult questions about the abstraction so integral to Selden's scholarly identity – liberty – were at the centre of the violent upheaval and extraordinary experimentation in that society, especially the execution of the king, the initiation of England's first and only republic, the surge of radicalism from the Army debates and eventual Leveller mutiny to the outgrowth of sects and the intention to nominate and select only saints for the 1653 Parliament, and the inauguration of the Protectorate under Oliver Cromwell. In England, never before had the struggle to coordinate zealous spirituality and lawful order been so exciting yet also so chaotic for the labourers in polity. Cromwell, who enlisted Selden's help in vain, wanted social order but also reformed justice, property as well as unprecedented godliness, political representation but also the triumph of the saints.

In these years just before his death in 1654, Selden struck his contemporaries as magnificently fulfilling the promise shown throughout his formative years in regard to the history and mastery of normative thinking, whether classical or biblical, Jewish or Christian, pan-European or simply British; but his was a heroic fulfilment whose harvest might well include public insignificance. In *De Synedriis*, Selden moved simultaneously towards his most coercive vision of a religious society – the Sanhedrin would oversee and prosecute all human affairs – and towards a separation of civil society from the spiritual labours of a godly faith that the proponents of liberty in his final years deemed essential. In the end, Selden left his contemporaries with monumental questions about the dynamics of liberty, without clearly instructing them on the direction they ought to take in the heady, traumatic years of the 1650s. Jonson, had he lived, would have sympathized with the broken compass of Selden's scholarship, the centred fixed foot unable to transmit its measure to the always imperfectly rendered circumference of the world.

—— 4 ——

For all the scholarly details and sceptical hesitations of Selden's persona, the overriding problem undertaken in his work emerges into the open: the challenge facing religious societies as they seek to cultivate laws that will not commit rapine on their spiritual bounty or zeal, on their adventurous edge in thought and belief, on the socio-political intangibles according to which the community has functioned well, and on the procreative desires and licences to kill that the God of the Old Testament most certainly authorized. In turn, religious society must be able firmly and ubiquitously to rely on normative measures for the social ligatures so vital in religion itself. In his studies of tithes and titles, or of ancient Britain, Greece, and Israel, Selden's intellectual experiments in the normative of a religious society reach for a perspective between the inner sanctum of history, in which priests simply believe and obscurely chant what they have been taught, and the profanity of the idle sceptic with no concern for a truth that will delight and instruct his beleaguered society. Those perspectives vary in purview: they can reside in the domain of poets or historians, natural philosophers or rabbis, monkish ascetics who promote a this-worldly agenda or judicial and parliamentarian activists who seek clearer answers in a book. They also differ in warrant: some ancient or medieval, others modern; some abstractly principled, others concretely contractual; some likened to the precision of optical geometry, others invested in the misty authority of Druids and Bards. In search of the best perspective, moreover, Selden alternates his role between the priest and the critic, in the hope that his sceptical scholarship will return from doubt's boundless sea with an intellectual discovery that might rectify the standards and correct the vision of a contentious religious society. Indeed, he tells Laud in 1636 that whereas some students of Judaism enlist that culture in behalf of their already formed and hotly polemical dogma, Selden himself pioneers a course to Judaic notions of a lawful religious society that might well help to move English society beyond the factionalism, incoherence, and spiritual decrepitude that afflict it.

Of all Selden's associates, perhaps the one who came closest to fretting this dilemma of stance and method was his good friend, the poet and playwright Ben Jonson, whose emblem of the broken compass captured the normative writer's frustration over a private integrity that never quite rectifies the circumference of the world outside the honest self. Far too many intellectuals between 1590 and 1650 were ready to thrust their normative visions on English society rather than to suffer the scholarly and argumentative pain that the invention of a fully moral and spiritual normalcy might be devised. Indeed, if Selden was born into the world of Richard Hooker, he died in the England of Thomas Hobbes. In the *Leviathan* (1651), Hobbes locates many of the problems plaguing English society in the wildly fanciful permissiveness bestowed on putatively spiritual claims. Like Hooker, though with different results, Hobbes is sick and tired of the spirit.

By contrast, Selden was unwilling to surrender his vision of religious society to those extremists who force a choice between normative regulation and all the ineffable experiences and authorities to which members of a society might lay claim, from poetic prowess to spiritual charisma, from scholarly talent to the immeasurable love celebrated by the early Christians. As the *Table Talk* makes clearest in its humorous, homespun fashion, there is much at stake in his normative experiments: exactly how tolerant or inflexible a religious society should be; exactly how the faith so dear to a tender conscience should be treated within the coercive jurisdiction of a magistrate whose responsibility it is to strengthen the social ligatures in a religious community; and whether it is possible for the church and the state to be separated without the marriage of law and spirituality simply fracturing in divorce.

For some of Selden's eulogizers, however, as for some of his lifelong critics in the clergy, his career was a testimony to the simple biblical admonition that a man cannot serve two masters. Yet the masters in question were not mammon and the word of God; they were the masters of civil law and holy spirit promoted side by side within God's own word. Far from believing that he was serving two disparate masters, Selden premised his Judaic work on the belief that the biblical God encouraged both spiritual zeal and legal wisdom, a holy zeal in the law and a lawful approach to a sometimes violent zeal. As his final work wore away in digressions and indirection, however, his posthumous publisher hedged on whether the Sanhedrin would be useful to English society or simply grand and beautiful. Selden's career might be construed, then, as the noblest of failures, as the failure of a historian to realize that the historical imagination itself has sufficient social benefits, or that a political activist cannot make any difference in the world if he is always distracted by paradise. During the controversy over his *History of Tithes*, Selden protested that he was not making theological claims, that he was merely a historian after the facts of the case. Like Sir Philip Sidney's ideal poet, Selden was not simply tied to the facts; he was committed to inventing models of a religious society that showed England what it might be, not only what it had been. Like Sidney's poet, too, Selden left the readers to decide whether those golden inventions might be better worlds or simply other, whether they might spur reform, provide delight, or only very subtly advise new directions.

That the problem of how to invent or discover the best norms for a religious society was Selden's primary obsession, one shared by his closest associates, emerges with obvious clarity from even a cursory reading

of the *Table Talk*. Obsession, however, does not translate into flatness or
sameness in his scholarship. Far from it, the permutations in Selden's
normative thinking that constitute the following chapters are highly distinctive and richly detailed, even if they are not mutually exclusive,
either in substance or chronology. The overlaps between the discursive
experiments are everywhere to be seen. For instance, the normative
thrust of Jonsonian poetry gathers much of its authority from appeals to
a Stoic notion of natural law, and both discourses – didactic poetry and
the philosophy of natural law – figure into Selden's scholarship. Yet
neither are his various notions of how best to regulate a religious society
interchangeable; for they represent markedly differentiated constructs
in his writing as well as locatable phases in his life. Differences arise not
only in the question of the status of law – whether it is natural, humanly
positive, or divinely willed – but also, even especially, in the nuances and
characteristics of the numinous, divine, or ineffable realm of experience as Selden imagines it.

At one end of the spectrum, the essence of spirituality for Selden is
moral honesty. In the *Table Talk*, Selden wishes that sermons were more
like Assizes, since 'The thinges between God & men are but a few, &
those forsooth wee must bee told often of, but the things betweene man
& man are many, those I heare not of above twice a year, att ye Assizes or
once a quarter att sessions, but few come then, nor does the Minister
ever exhort the people to goe att these times to learne their duty
towards their Neighbour' (106). It is unclear exactly what Selden imagines the vehicle of human responsibility to be here – the sermons
preached at the Assizes certainly often took on themes appropriate to
the judicial proceedings – but the joke about how ministers never
exhort their parishioners to attend the Assizes suggests that duty is to be
learnt from the judicial proceedings themselves. For as J.S. Cockburn
has written, the 'itinerant justices [were] compared in popular metaphor to visiting bishops, circling planets, or the streams of paradise.'[15]
What is clear, however, is that the judicial session replaces the church
proper in Selden's quip as the best context in which to learn the very
essence of religious obligation.

In his work on natural law, in his advocacy of Jonson's didactic poetry,
in his conviction that the human institutions of positive law are largely
responsible for the cultivation of sanctity and true religion in England,
and in his characterization of communal monitors in the study of the
Sanhedrin, Selden edges holiness towards an honesty premised always
on reverence for and worship of God. 'They that cry downe morall hon-

estye,' he says elsewhere in the *Table Talk*, 'cry downe that wch. is a great part of Religion, my duty towards man: for Religion consists in these two, my duty towards God & my duty towards man' (83).

Dutiful moral honesty, as sturdy and reliable as it seems, is not the whole story of Selden's notion of holiness. Just as often in his Judaic works, moral strength takes the form of holy violence, manic prophecy, and unnatural zeal. In the same breath that praises moral honesty, Selden acknowledges that moral duty, indeed morality itself, is not a sufficient warrant or definition of spirituality. He warns that 'Morallity must not bee without Religion, for if soe it may change as I see convenience, Religion must governe it' (83). Yet this admonition is not as clear as it might be. 'Religion' per se might be canonical prescription, restricting a zealous conscience that has a tendency to run amok just as claims on the Holy Spirit do. Or, as in the case of Grotius's work on natural law, it might be a more numinous, supernatural level of reality and experience, an incalculable abundance such as that supposed in divine grace, spiritual love, mystical transmigration, or inspired zeal. From his earliest work on British history and poetry through his latest scholarship on Jewish society and law, Selden confronts head-on the inevitable, attractive, but also dangerous media in which members of a society operate or think outside the confinement of convention, decorum, and law. With regard to poetry, his friend Jonson, committed as he is to decorum, also articulates justifications for deviation from the norm; with regard to revolutionary thought and spirituality, his admirer Milton looks to Selden for the case that liberty must factor in a 'venturous edge' of trial and error as much as the restrictions implicit in a moral vision of society. But whereas for Milton, restriction is best when it is generated from within the individual, Selden is committed to the notion that religious societies need an Areopagus, a Sanhedrin, to delimit, mediate, and prosecute the often wild, incalculable fancies of their violent zealots, inspired prophets, incomprehensible dreamers, charismatic leaders, and those softer souls banqueting in the largesse of a love they consider integral to brotherhood in God. One sign that Selden is invested in the dimensions of spiritual ineffability as well as the restrictions of norms and canons emerges from his intertwining attitudes towards nature. In keeping with the latter, he is devoted to the rigour or precision of the 'new philosophy'; in keeping with the former, he is fascinated by the legacies of theosophy from Pythagoras and the Neoplatonists to Renaissance cabbala and the 'Mosaic philosophy' of Selden's physician, Robert Fludd. So it is that Selden draws analogies between his critical, sceptical scholarship and the greater precision afforded by natural philosophers such as Copernicus, but returns on many occasions to conceptions of transmigration in which entities, once thought fixed and stable, enter then escape one framing boundary after another.

Even as the older Selden began to invoke his friend Ben Jonson's rhetoric of the centred Stoic sage in his last vindication of his controversial life and works, his legacy was no fixed persona and no constant poetics; rather, the great scholar bestowed on the world a legacy of stunning, seemingly infinite variety in cultural models, normative alternatives, and details of social practice. Fellow scholars looked for a light in the darkness of civil war and national trauma when they turned to Selden's work on the Patriarch Eutychius, on the Jewish rites of marriage, on the common notions of religion transmitted from Adam and Eve through the children of Noah to seventeenth-century England, on the Talmudic rabbis and their chief critics, the Karaites. There was much extraordinary historical detection on display in Selden's work on the Arundel marbles, in his genealogy of the titles of honour whose cheapening the subjects of King James were protesting, and in his bold foundation of tithing in human arbitration. Selden had offered his contemporaries a new and detailed familiarity with their own history, laws, and institutions; had given voice to the great lawyer Fortescue but also to the monk-historian Eadmer. He had delved not only into the Old Testament record of idolatry in all the countries in the vicinity of the 'promised land,' but also into the norms governing international conflict as they were tested in the crucible of one issue, the ownership of the seas. Selden had reviewed the various arbiters of the British past – the Druids and Bards, knights and kings, for instance – and also the legal sages held responsible by God for preserving justice among the ancient Jews. Selden's contemporaries and successors were confronted with rival ways of understanding this formidable variety: either Selden's career testified to the many ways in which a religious society might properly be normalized, or it heaved the last powerful gasp of the entrenched illusion that social polities should be anything other than simply civil.

chapter two

Ancient Bards and
Inmost Historians

In the first two decades of John Selden's life (1584–1603), the last two of Elizabeth I's reign, the normative and didactic value of poetry – its power to shape the morals, actions, and beliefs of Protestant England – was both vigorously defended and scathingly attacked. Having been composed a year or so before Selden's birth, then published twice in 1595 and once again in 1598, Sir Philip Sidney's *Apology for Poetry* was the most brilliant exemplar in a bumper crop of defences of poetic art. For a historian in the making like Selden, it was significant that even though Sidney elevated the moral value of poetry over and above that of history, he included among the ranks of excellent poetry such prose histories as Xenophon's *Cyropedia*; for it, as much as Spenser's *Faerie Queene*, could instruct, delight, and inspire its readers with images of ideal virtue. In verse and in prose, in obvious fantasy but also in accounts of history, poets were for Sidney the best possible legislators of righteousness and virtue for the gentlemen of Elizabethan England, who in experiencing the golden world invented in poetry would be charged to embrace and defend true religion, beleaguered virtue, and good governance in the brazen or fallen world. Good poetry might be guilty as charged of lying, Sidney quipped, but from those lies came the stuff of the military, political, and religious heroes on whose virtues the welfare of a society depended. As Blair Worden has argued. Sidney's elevation of poetry over history 'posits a false antithesis, for in Sidney's mind history is not the rival of poetry but its partner.'[1] In this convergence, Sidney shared much in common with Samuel Daniel.and Ben Jonson, for whom 'historical and dramatic writing could seem alternative and complementary means of recovering the lessons of the past. History, like drama, was conceived as an exercise of the imagination, in which historians, like

dramatists, asked themselves what a given character would have said or
done in a given situation.' Historians joined poets in the intent 'to ex-
cite their readers to imitate virtue and renounce vice.'[2]

Throughout the *Apology*, Sidney boldly defended the supposed lies
that poetry told for their ability to convey virtue as it ought to be in
golden images that would impress themselves on gentlemen striving to
be better than mortal frailty tends to allow. Supremely legitimized by the
inspired psalms of David but more solidly realized in the mimesis of the
'maker,' poetry educated and inspired readers in the moral virtues far
more effectively than the historian, who was stuck with telling stories as
they happened in fact, and the philosopher, whose truths were lofty but
not efficacious. Compared with the poet, the straight historian was especially worthless and petty, even if more accurate in a narrow sense: 'But
the Poet (as I sayd before) neuer affirmeth. The Poet neuer maketh any
circles about your imagination, to coniure you to beleeue for true what
he writes. Hee citeth not authorities of other Histories, but euen for hys
entry calleth the sweete Muses to inspire into him a good inuention; in
troth, not labouring to tell you what is, or is not, but what should or
should not be.' According to Sidney, whom Selden lauded as 'That wonder of humane excellence,' poetry would be normative in the best, fullest sense: it would supply its gentle readers with an ideal moral standard,
yet incite in them the zeal with which to invent that standard in their
control over the religious society of Elizabethan England in a time of
unprecedented combat with those forces of evil and vice soon to be allegorized in Spenser's *Faerie Queene*.[3]

Ten years after the first edition of the *Apology*, however, in *The Advancement of Learning* (1605), Francis Bacon would draw different conclusions
from the belief that the poetic imagination eludes the ties that bind the
plodding historian to the way things actually are. According to Bacon,
this attribute rendered poetry lawless, unable to transmit valuable norms
to human readers and societies: 'Poesie is a part of Learning in measure
of words for the most part restrained: but in all other points extreamely
licensed: and doth truly referre to the Imagination, which beeing not
tyed to the Lawes of Matter, may at pleasure ioyne that which Nature hath
seuered; and seuer that which Nature hath ioyned, and so make unlawfull
Matches & diuorces of things' (73). Already Bacon was moulding an
understanding of natural law that was more mundane and concrete than
the moral and rational standard inherited by his contemporaries from
the Stoics and Aquinas among others. Yet even if debates over natural law
could be set aside, Sidney himself had hedged somewhat on the question

of whether poesy's inventions were better than – or other than – the brazen world in which human beings live and act. Nor had the apologist for poetry ever denied that poetry lies; he had simply made the case that its lies were well worth telling and reading; for they could fashion the behaviour of sinners in the direction of a more holy and virtuous standard.

Sidney was not alone in defending poetry from its detractors. Chief among the other normative poets in Selden's lifetime were Michael Drayton and Ben Jonson, both of whom vilified those closeted poets who had reneged on their public duties to reform manners and mores. But Drayton's and Jonson's insistence on publication – rather than the manuscript circulation of gentle amateurs like Sidney – indicates that the tribe of normative poets in Selden's early years itself was highly various and even contentious within its own ranks. Although they might share some basic assumptions and ancient legacies for their poetics, Sidney, Drayton, and Jonson differed considerably from one another about the constituents of an ideal poet and poetry. Sidney's was an aristocrat gifted and instilled with courtly *sprezzatura*, the ironic and playful wit associated with the humanist praise of folly, an indifference to the wider public (he never published his *Apology*), an investment in romantic and Protestant heroism, and a classical eclecticism that embraced Plato, Aristotle, and Horace. He had no interest in recuperating the value of history as such. Although Drayton wrote in some genres that attracted Sidney – the sonnet, for instance – and in those genres could approximate Sidney in terminology (Drayton's 'idea' resembling Sidney's 'foreconceit'), the author of the *Poly-Olbion* was a public and nationalistic bard, whose norms were attributed to historical tradition rather than to the poet's own wits or even to mimesis. Indeed, Sidney showed disregard for those poetasters addicted to, and in no small measure constitutive of, the lifeless conventions of English verse. Like Drayton, Jonson was a proudly public poet, one whose deep involvement in court culture was indicative of a professional relationship rather than his own social nobility or *sprezzatura*. Jonson might aspire to write a national epic like Drayton's and praise the virtues of Sidney's family at their country estate; but aside from his late, uncharacteristic, and poorly received play, *The New Inn*, his normative values were unromantically Stoic. In their most efficacious capacity, natural law, right reason, and virtue – the moral foundations of good poetry – would connect the wise man to the greater cosmos by means of duty, but in the end the wise man could depend only on himself. And Jonson would never allow true poetry to lie.

In short, poetry was highly celebrated in Selden's early life as the greatest means of teaching moral, civic, and religious values to English Protestant society. Far more readily than straight history, it could aspire to a consecrated status and authority, and its mode of instruction promised greater efficacy in the transmission of virtue. Yet poetry was also highly controversial – its detractors were both loud and articulate; and inwardly conflictual – its supporters often disagreed about what its constituents should comprise. As confident as poetry's apologists might sound, they were assembling the theoretical framework for their art even in the process of defending it.

Early in his life, Selden had strong intellectual and biographical links to some of the most committed normative poets of his time, especially to Ben Jonson and Michael Drayton. He was Jonson's friend and unofficial adviser and Drayton's collaborator in print. Yet unlike those poets, who were angered by their own and their contemporaries' failures to sustain the vision of their poetics, Selden grappled to come to terms with the question of whether the enterprise of a normative poetry should be undertaken in the first place. His struggle, moreover, was heightened by the fact that unlike Sidney, Jonson, and even Drayton, he was first and foremost a historian, and one faced with deeply conflicting models of how historical writing might best gain access to truth. One model of history – idealized and didactic – coincided with Sidney's Xenophon, the historian who for Sidney is in reality a golden poet. The other – unflinchingly empirical, sceptical, and methodical – was mocked in the *Apology* as a pedantic antiquarian more interested in dry bones and dirty rags of the past than in any goodness or holiness that the past might transmit. If normative poetry was being assembled in Selden's day, a providential and normative history was being challenged by a rival, more critical brand of evidentiary history. Thus, in weighing the claims of normative poets, Selden faced two challenges: to reconceive the role of a critical sceptic in the making of poetry; and to reshape history itself so that it might subsume the benefits of poetry rather than (as Sidney has it) having its moral and heroic dimensions appropriated by the poets themselves. Selden's critical historian would have to find his proper place in the groves of the bards, but also to open a space for the bards within the discourse of a critical history.

—— 1 ——

To Ben Jonson, William Browne, Michael Drayton, and John Suckling, Selden was one of the most judicious readers of contemporary poetry.

For Jonson, who spent much of his poetic energy vilifying wits shallow, wits obscure, wits fantastical, and wits parasitical, the understanding reader was as rare a commodity as the right rational poet who shaped society by means of a poetry itself carefully shaped and reshaped. Yet Jonson was confident that Selden's censure was indispensable to his poetic mission, one committed to right and good norms in language and manners alike, and to the correction via learned praise and searing blame of the epidemic enormity in his world.

When Jonson was having doubts about a crucial stage convention in contemporary theatre, he turned to Selden for his learned and judicious guidance. The practice was cross-dressing, a convention that in the *Table Talk* Selden can be found defending from impiety and linking to the decorum of everyday society: 'I never converted but two, the one was M^r. Crashaw from writing ag[ains]t playes, by telling him a way how to understand that place (of putting on womans apparell) wch has nothing to doe with the business (as neither has it, that the fathers speake ag[ains]t playes in their time with reason enough, for they had reall Idolatry mix'd with their playes, haveing three Altars p[er]petually upon the Stage') (95–6). Selden is pleased with his conversion of the Puritan divine, which entails not only Crashaw's newly found appreciation of the morality of theatre but also his genuine comprehension of 'reall Idolatry,' the ancient and biblical features of which Selden explains to Jonson himself by request.

The letter to Jonson, dated 28 February 1615, corroborates Selden's enjoyment of Jonson's *Bartholomew Fair*, a play that satirizes the inflexible and ineffectual normative interventions of a Puritan divine (who despises theatre) and a justice of the peace (who scorns poetry). Just as the puppet-actor at the fair proclaims the innocence of theatre by pulling up its frock and exposing its lack of genitals, so Selden supports the religious and moral legitimacy of theatre by removing cant and revealing the Bible's lack of any bias against theatre. In Deuteronomy, he argues, the prohibition against male armour on women and of female garments on men pertains in its Judaic context to the interdict against worshipping pagan deities, especially Mars (for whom women would don armour) and Venus (for whom men would adorn themselves with a habit) (Deut. 22:5). Selden not only adduces rabbinical evidence for this claim but also operates as a surrogate or lay divine. With the help of cross-textual analysis and Talmudic commentary, he uncovers a common misconception – found in Philo and Josephus among others – that the practice of cross-dressing corrupts 'the publick preservation of hon-

esty in both sexes, lest in corrupt manners by such promiscuous use of
apparel the least forwardness of nature might take the easier advantage
of opportunity.'[4] No doubt already hard at work on *De Dis Syris*, Selden
assesses the authority of the impressive and exotic material that he col-
lects: he promotes the trustworthiness of Maimonides; traces the transmission of myth from Babylon to Africa, Greece, and Rome; clarifies the
double gender of ancient deities and the conflation of their names; and
generally brings to bear the 'relicks of antiquity' on the learned Jonson's rectification of dramatic and social custom. It is clear from the letter that Selden takes seriously his charge as a scholarly gauge of Jonson's
comic vehicle for moral norms in Jacobean England. It is less clear
exactly what kind of authenticity Selden is meant to bestow on Jonson's
theatre. Contrary to Sidney's disdain for historians, Jonson is convinced
that those poets responsible for shaping English mores have a special
need for an antiquarian to tell them 'what men haue done' (Sidney,
156). But why?

   After all, in his letter to Jonson, Selden delegates the correction of
moral norms to the playwright: 'as it tends to morality,' the scholar cautions, 'I abstain to meddle' (Rosenblatt and Schleiner, 74). Nonetheless,
the second conversion commemorated in the *Table Talk* once again
demonstrates that Selden directs the transmission of mores by means of
shaping the media of transmission, this time a message about cosmetics
as conveyed through the vehicle of a sermon. The second convert, he
says, 'was a Doctor of Divinity from preaching ag[ains]t painting, w^{ch},
simply in it selfe, is no more hurtfull then putting on my Clothes, or
doeing any other thing to make my selfe like other folkes that I may not
be odious or offensive to the Company' (96). Much as a puppet in *Bartholomew Fair* converts the zealous Puritan to an appreciation of theatre
by exposing the truly sexless status of the diminutive players, Selden
converts the divine to what might be called the normative poetics of Jonson and, in their own ways, of Michael Drayton and William Browne.
This poetics seeks to guarantee the moral, godly, and rational grounding of decorum, custom, and any other formalized expectations that
afford communities with what they perceive to be a natural and artificial
coherence. In their exchange over cross-dressing, it is clear that Selden
and Jonson understand themselves to control the formation of norms
that will reflect the consent of learned, rational, and virtuous men.
These norms must not languish in obscurity or singularity; they should
not confuse vulgarity with accommodation; they should not require the
damaging compromise of rationally and morally centred souls; and they

should not disguise, much less abet, the vicious designs of powerful men. Like Jonson, who is often suspicious of the cosmetic veneers in society, Selden immediately qualifies his commitment to the sociable arts with a moral proviso: 'Indeed if I doe it [put on my clothes or paint my face] with an ill Intenccion, it alters the Case. Soe, if I putt on my gloves with an intenccion to doe a mischeife, I am a villaine' (*Table Talk*, 96). But his mediation between theatrical conventions in particular and social customs in general is situated by the organizer of the *Table Talk* under the category of 'Poetry.' Selden's honest intention is offered in support of decorous poetic fictions, not as a wholesale disdain for artistic ornament.

The case of cross-dressing epitomizes a basic tenet for the defenders of poetry among Selden's contemporaries. Poetry is best able to convey moral and religious ideas, norms, or laws – it is best able to discipline human reason and the human soul – if it can manage its more indecorous and wonderful dimensions without violating its own mores. Sidney's golden poetry and Jonson's honest poetry require a moral law, to be sure, but they need a power, delight, and wonder that cannot be reduced to a law or an idea. Just as Sidney knows that the poet must neither 'build Castles in the ayre' (*Apology*, 157) nor sacrifice vitality, delight, and wonder for 'Mouse-eaten records' (162) or 'certaine abstract considerations' (163), so Jonson knows that the best poetry requires more than norms of reason, virtue, duty, and piety; more than decorum; and more than scholarship. It is Jonson's obsessive and ridiculous justice of the peace, Adam Overdo, who thinks that normative authority can dispense with poetic delight, compassion, and metaphor. To write poetry is to cross-dress the habits, languages, and beliefs of a religious society so that it might be transformed as well as entertained. And just as Jonson conceives his poetic endeavours as a collaboration with the ancients, so he looks to Selden as a contemporary collaborator in fashioning the best normative poetry according to the 'consent of the learned' and the 'consent of the good.'

In the years immediately before Jonson's death, Selden was actively involved in defending the value of poetry against its most heated detractors. As Selden's friend Bulstrode Whitlocke recalls the year 1633, the Inns of Court sought to express 'their love and duty to their majesties' (Charles I and Henrietta Maria) in the 'outward and splendid visible testimony of a royal mask.' The reason: 'the few societies joining together' wished to defend the solemn performance of masques against 'Mr. Prynne's new learning,' that prodigious attack on theatre contained in William Prynne's *Histriomastix*. To this end, the Inns chose representatives, including Selden, for a committee, whose charge it was to produce the masque and whose work was carried out in subcommittees: 'one for the Poeticall part, another for the properties of the Masquers & Antimasquers & other actors, another was for the dauncing, & to Wh[itelocke] in perticular was committed the whole care & charge of all the Musicke.' The members of the committee were assigned not only to this one masque but to the defence of a principle – that panegyric art can reconstitute and consecrate the Christian mores of English society. In his final assessment of the masque, however – 'Thus was this earthly pomp and glory, if not vanity, soon passed over and gone, as if it had never been' – Whitlocke suspects that panegyric always risks a parasitism regarding the same royal authority that had so recently imprisoned Selden for his parliamentary defences of the English subject's liberties against unlawful imprisonment.[5] The normative value of poetry might be deflated not only by its cosmetic vanities but also by its complicity in unlawful, indeed tyrannical practices. If poetic custom were to secure and dispense the expectations of good and rational men, then Selden, Jonson, and others like them would have to work hard to save poetry from a frivolous dishonesty associated with court culture.[6]

The commendatory poems traded between Selden and the public poets affiliated with him demonstrate the criteria informing their assiduous pursuit of a judicious and normative poetics. In a poem affixed to Selden's *Titles of Honor*, Jonson makes the point that the book's combination of two approaches to history – one monumental and didactic, the other critical and antiquarian – stands to make a mighty contribution to this pursuit. Histories (or stories) and poems attempt to realize the dream of an art that teaches what 'ought' to be, only now both forms carry the added burden of proposing norms amid those intricacies of scholarship indebted to French judicial humanism and to antiquarian historiography. At best, critical scholarship will make the idealized virtues more muscular to do combat in a sceptical and corrupt age; at worst, the 'ought' will get lost in or even undercut by the mass of details comprising what Sidney called the 'bare *Was*' (168). For Jonson and Selden, the poetic ideal is embodied in a robust sphere of virtues, replete with moral athleticism, substantial learning, a complex of duties owed by the individual to his society, and all those delightful and pro-

vocative qualities associated with wit. In the duress of everyday life, however, even the best of poets will sometimes encounter the various
demands on their talent as if those demands represented irreconcilable
masters.

Jonson understands that such a discourse – one artful but not uncriti-
cal, learned but not pedantic – is exceedingly hard to achieve, making
collaboration among judicious men all the more valuable. In his poem
to Selden, Jonson confirms the unadorned trust and freedom that he, a
poet, and Selden, a historian, have come to share in assessing one
another's work. Their minds are knitted by duty and judgment, not by
the vices of that patronage that exacts the 'penance' of dishonest praise
from a parasite. Jonson concedes to Selden, however, that one powerful
medium for normative poetry – praise – renders this dishonesty exceptionally hard for even the good poet to avoid:

> Though I confess (as every muse hath erred,
> And mine not least) I have too oft preferred
> Men past their terms, and praised some names too much,
> But 'twas with purpose to have made them such.[7]

Jonson protests that his apparent parasitism is owed to an understandable human error, and that he has learned from his mistakes – learned,
that is, to 'turn a sharper eye / Upon myself, and ask to whom, and
why, / And what I write? And vex it many days / Before men get a verse:
much less a praise' (148). Selden himself has 'vexed' the 'fables' and
'Opinions' that have passed for history, and so he serves as a model for
that painstaking acuteness to which Jonson aspires in refashioning his
poetry.

According to Jonson, however, the reverse is also true: Selden fashions
his historiography according to the morally and socially normative aims
of Jonson's poetry. After all, it is Jonson who takes as his mission the making of mores rather than the compiling or sifting of records. On the one
hand, then, Jonson's poet needs a scholarship: thus, at the poet's request,
Selden's *Titles of Honor* includes among its rites and formulae a history of
the poetic laureateship. On the other hand, however, Jonson praises
Selden's scholarship in such a manner as to credit its normative power. In
seeking out the rivulets of aristocratic and royal titles, in disabusing the
judicious reader of 'Impostures ... blots and errors,' Jonson's Selden has
accomplished far more than the amassment of minutiae. He has also 'rectified / Times, manners, customs,' and so established the provenance of

hierarchy that, 'besides the bare conduct / Of what it tells us,' the study of titles offers its readers a 'story ... weaved in to instruct' (148–9). And Selden has woven this story, Jonson declares, in a rich, 'manly,' and appropriate style, one that avoids the obscurity of a scholarship conducted for its own sake as well as the prettiness of those verses devoid of critical judgment and sinew. Selden's discourse, Jonson concludes, is at once sharp, wise, and artful.

In his poem to Selden, Jonson leaves no hint about whether he himself might be refashioning in the *Titles of Honor* those qualities that readers have found wanting in the young scholar's prose. Is Jonson praising Selden as the latter 'ought' to be? Where other readers might find the *Titles of Honor* obscure and digressive, Jonson dubs it well seasoned and coherent. According to Jonson, Selden's is a history that has the focus, breadth, and wit of a normative poetry: its geometrical compass is centred on what is true, yet its circle is naturally capacious in 'general knowledge.' Only 'the round / Large clasp of nature, such a wit can bound,' Jonson protests, then emphasizes how judicious Selden is 'In sharpness of all search, wisdom of choice.' In a characterization that resembles his own theoretical statements about poetry, Jonson praises Selden's language for embracing the best of the ancient and the modern. Like Jonson's ideal poet, his Selden is committed to rectifying the estates of great men in English society, yet maintains his own virtuous, rational, and pious 'state / In offering this thy work to no great name,' that is, to Edward Hayward, Selden's chief understander and 'chamberfellow' at the Inner Temple (149). In keeping with Jonson's own moral values, especially the standard of a rare friendship shared between two honest 'understanders,' Selden is said to integrate the Stoicism that preaches duty with the one that advises autonomy; to reconcile the demands of celebration and integrity; to write a history that morally fashions what society should be and do in the laborious process of recovering what society has been and done; and to convey these norms in a style at once accommodating and rigorous.

Albeit less elaborately than Jonson, other seventeenth-century poets praise Selden for his custodial authority in rectifying the weaknesses and legitimizing the strengths of their poetry. As if the choice were self-explanatory, Suckling seats Selden at the head of his imaginary 'Sessions of the Poets'; perhaps Suckling's rationale was simply that the laureateship should be decided by the great historian of that title, but he does not say.[8] Robert Herrick appeals to Selden as the premier arbiter of a public, corrective, and ceremonial poetics. In verses directed 'to the most learned, wise, and Arch-Antiquary, Master John Selden,' he looks for the just recompense owed to a would-be laureate who has offered his priestly services in officiating over those lyric rites that commemorate merit as they dispense favour:

> I Who have favour'd many, come to be
> Grac't (now at last) or glorifi'd by thee.
> Loe, I, the Lyrick Prophet, who have set
> On many a head the Delphick Coronet,
> Come unto thee for Laurell, having spent,
> My wreaths on those, who little gave or lent.
> Give me the *Daphne*, that the world may know it,
> Whom they neglected, thou hast crown'd a Poet.
> A City here of *Heroes* I have made,
> Upon the rock, whose firm foundation laid,
> Shall never shrink, where making thine abode,
> Live thou a *Selden*, that's a Demi-god.[9]

Herrick strikes a Jonsonian note here: Selden can be trusted to bestow the laureate wreath on those deserving poets neglected by the very patrons that such poets edify and exhort. Yet like court masques as Whitlocke assesses them or the kind of nugatory verse that Suckling and Herrick liked to write, the fault lines in the patronage system supporting normative verse are often on display in the lives and works of these very poets. Its constellation of heroes can glamorize a parasitic and unjust economy, and beatitudes that begin in virtuous duty commonly end in pleasure and escapism. In all, English Protestant society suffers from a dearth of reverence, justice, and goodness when those poets most equipped for public duty retreat into their own version, no matter how innocently pleasurable, of Elysium, another world if not better than the brazen world in which fallen humanity lives.

For all the normative and didactic claims of the poets, they are compelled to admit that actual poetry rarely achieves a public effect, either because of the poetry's own weaknesses or because of the readers' inadequacies and stubbornness. In part as a symptom of its fantastic status and in part in response to its failures, poetry tends to lure its proponents away from the world of men. The escapes of poetry are construed to be many: into the womb of Stoic autonomy; into the closet of the coterie; into the realm of Platonic ideals; into romantic fictions of the hero; and into the fortunate isles of a pastoral imagination that loses

the pleasing but strenuous *nomos* – at once law and music – in the delica-
cies of *numus*, the Elysian groves of fancy. In Canaan there is law and
pleasure; in Elysium the golden fancies of poetry are antinomian. Once
Camden's *Britannia* gives way to Browne's *Britannia's Pastorals,* Jonson's
New Inn, or Drayton's *Muse's Elysium,* then Selden's favourite group of
poets has edged away from law-giving through idealized images towards
a golden-world poetics in which, it is hoped, love and fellowship require
no law. So, too, over the course of decades Selden moves from a long
discussion of *nomos* (harmony and law) in the *Arundel Marbles* to an
extensive gloss on *numus* (grove) in his preface to the *Decem.* Yet Selden
never abandons the commitment of these normative poets to the witty
human artifice whose responsibility it is to strike a balance between
binding moral norms and the pleasurable wonder that inspires the
heroic leaders of a religious society.

In *Titles of Honor,* Selden establishes precedents for the notion that he,
a legal sage, can strengthen and support the dutiful poetry of Drayton
and Jonson. Amid the regal and aristocratic dignities traced in that tome,
Selden records how in 1616 at Strasbourg, '*Thomas Obrechtus* a professor
of Law and a *Count Palatin*' made use of an imperial patent in solemniz-
ing the poet laureateship in a ceremony for Joannes Crusius (3rd ed.,
333). At Jonson's prompting, Selden affixes to this account a brief history
of other such creations of the laureate as well as documentary evidence
of the ritual formulae. Thus, Jonson asks Selden to arbitrate the customs
of a public poetics as surely as Herrick and Suckling invite Selden to
bestow the laureate wreath itself, a collaboration made all the more valuable by virtue of the fact that the normative enterprise of poetry has been
challenged of late by a breed of manuscript, coterie poets.

Selden's collaborator, Michael Drayton, bitterly complains that coterie poets are too dainty and 'incloistered' for the reader's serious attention. Such poets conceal their verses 'In private chambers ... As though
the world unworthy were to know, / Their rich composures'; and they
abandon the poet's didactic office for fear of nothing worse than 'publique censure.'[10] In the *Table Talk,* Selden puts the same point the other
way around: coterie and aristocratic poets ought not to embrace the
role of the public poet lest they ludicrously botch those precious offices:
'Tis ridiculous for a Lord to print verses, 'tis well enough to make them
to please himself but to make them publick is foolish. If a man in a private Chamber twirles his Band string, or playes with a Rush to please
himselfe, 'tis well enough, but if hee should goe into Fleet streete & sett
upon a stall & twirle his bandstring or play with a Rush, then all the

boyes in the streete would laugh att him' (96). In contrast to the nugatory verse-making of the private chamber, Selden celebrates the ideal poet as a holy figure whose oracular and hortatory *carmina* should comprehend in its sacred circle the rectitude of law, the vision of the seer, the invention of the orator, the wisdom of moral philosophy, the instruction of monumental history, and the integrating force of ritual. All these qualities also should be tested against the prodigious learning and critical method of a French judicial and philological humanist.

Selden recognizes that the harnessing of moral and critical criteria in one poem is no easy endeavour. If, as Anne Lake Prescott has argued, 'Selden was fortunate in his liminality,' that is, free to vacillate between critical and fictive approaches to history, he also powerfully contributes to the contemporary clarion call to pry fables and histories apart. In envisioning the criteria of history and poetry, both together and apart from one another, Selden attempted to engineer a new historical poetics that avoids the useless empiricism of some antiquarians as well as the outright lies of some poets.[11] Selden takes seriously the responsibility the leading public poets of early seventeenth-century England handed him: nothing less than the modernization and legitimization of historical poetry and poetic history.

Even when poetic history is not his immediate concern – in the 1618 dedication of the *History of Tithes* to Sir Robert Cotton, for instance – Selden wards off two opposite monsters of such danger to the advancement of legitimate poetry, the Scylla of fable and the Charybdis of pedantry: 'For, as on the one side, it cannot be doubted but that the too studious Affectation of bare and sterile Antiquitie, which is nothing els but to be exceeding busie about nothing, may soon descend to a Dotage; so on the other, the Neglect or only vulgar regard of the fruitfull and precious part of it, which giues necessarie light to the Present in matter of State, Law, Historie, and the vnderstanding of good Autors, is but preferring that kind of Ignorant Infancie which our short life alone allows vs, before the many ages of former Experience and Obseruation, which may so accumulat yeers to vs, as if we had liued euen from the beginning of Time' (A2v). If antiquarianism without purpose is motivated by a humoral compulsion and yields an idle senility, a poetized history without the fruit, treasure, and light of inmost antiquity leaves a society in the state of perpetual childhood, from which (Selden says in the *Table Talk* [96]) serious authors must graduate. For Selden, the poets Jonson, Browne, and Drayton and the translator Thomas Farnaby occupy the desirable vantage point between dust and air.

In his *carmen protrepticon* (hortatory song) to Jonson, Selden lauds the poet for his powers of discrimination, for plays and poems comical yet dignified and learned, at once modern in their application yet ancient in their mores. Yet the normative poet has singularly failed to reach his audience, in keeping with Jonson's own emblem of a broken geometrical compass whose centre is fixed but whose circumference can never be fully or exactly drawn. In response to this failure, Selden is eager to bestow the laureate crown on Jonson's brow and so to consecrate the poetic labours that have been so misjudged. Indeed, such a ritual might provide the normative poet with precisely the legitimacy he needs among those countrymen who secretly want pleasing and exalted letters but fear the exceedingly powerful light of Jonson more than they fear shadows.

In thrice conferring the laurels on William Browne, the author of *Britannia's Pastorals*, Selden insists that his own serious Muse has not drifted into unmusical pedantry. For all her learning, she still deserves to participate in the pleasurable rites of poesy:

> So much a stranger my severer muse
> Is not to love-strains, or a shepherd's reed,
> But that she knows some rites of *Phoebus* due's,
> Of *Pan*, of *Pallas*, and her sisters meed.
> Read, and commend she durst these tun'd essaies
> Of him that loves her (she hath ever found
> Her studies as one circle.)[12]

In other poems to Browne, Selden is set on proving his familiarity with love as it is represented in the osculatory play of Anacreon and Catullus, but his circle image in the poem on behalf of the 'severer muse' redirects love away from mere eroticism or favour and towards the capacious yet precise and integrated sanctity of a new normative poetry. Love and music are praised for integrating a poetics from which they, more than any other element, might be jettisoned without substantial loss. For also in the circle are heroic virtue, social custom and law, religious wisdom, natural philosophy, and indeed Selden's own learning in the margins of the verses. Yet pleasing harmony in the 'tun'd essaies' is responsible for holding the elements together and for conveying the mysterious centre of the circle outwards into the world of readers who, Selden prays, will 'be with rose and myrtle crown'd' just after the experience of Browne's poetry if not before (*Opera Omnia*, vol. 3, col. 1720). Browne's poetry

either transmits a harmony audible to those few initiates who can hear
it, or creates a wider social harmony where before there was none.

In his commendatory verses to Michael Drayton's 1619 volume of
poetry, Selden lends mythic stature to the systemic integrity, balance,
and harmony of what he considers an ideal poetics:

> I must admire thee (but to praise were vain
> What every tasting palate so approves)
> Thy martial *Pyrrhick*, and thy *Epick* strain,
> Digesting wars with heart-uniting loves,
> The two first authors of what is compos'd
> In this round system all; its ancient lore
> All arts in discords and concents are clos'd
> (And when unwinged souls the fates restore
> To th'earth for reparation of their flights,
> The first musicians, scholars, lovers make
> The next rank destinate to *Mar's* knights
> The following rabble meaner titles take)
> I see thy temples crown'd with *Phoebus* rites,
> Thy bay's to th'eye with lilly mix'd and rose,
> As to the ear a *diapason* close.[13]

Selden claims that all readers of the 1619 collection admire Drayton's
odes, satires, and pastorals, but this imaginary unanimity is the social
companion to Selden's attribution of a cosmic holism to the poet's artistic world of love and strife. In the highly flawed and unpredictable world
of social interaction and of idiosyncratic readers, the cohesion of the
values holding human affairs together itself is a poetic construct, the liturgy for an imaginary ritual in which the figure of a priestly poet is
meant to officiate. This artifice is lent considerable weight if it is supposed to correspond with the actual cosmic order. In practice, however,
readers too often idolize the pleasurable strains and erotic stimulants
that have been invented in the service of an inaudible moral harmony.

A marginal note explains why Selden places scholars with lovers and
musicians; for each must cultivate harmony and beneficence within a
discursive context that might well produce satiric discord or destructive
violence, or the softer perturbations of sex and taste. He underscores
the cosmic harmony with which he associates Drayton's poesy by invoking the Platonic myth of the transmigration of souls, according to which
in the *Phaedrus* the souls 'eminent for true worth' are set apart from

lower souls as well as sorted from one another.[14] However, Selden's version of this process differs from that of Socrates. Having compared the soul to that charioteer whose one horse jerks him downwards to earth and whose other one carries him towards heaven, Socrates maintains that souls have wings whose potential for upward movement depends on whether each soul is divinely wise or freighted by earthly corruption. On the basis of this proportion, the cosmic powers distribute souls to their appropriate persons, the hierarchy of which descends from lovers of wisdom and beauty to lawful kings and martial rulers; then on to businessmen and politicians, gymnasts and physicians, priests and prophets, poets and other creative artists, craftsmen and farmers, sophists and demagogues, and tyrants. Each must wait a set duration before a new assessment is made of the justice of each soul: the law or *nomos* of this process is that those philosophers remembering truth arise, and the vile descend even into beasts.

In his poem to Drayton, Selden has elevated poets and soldiers to the level of those philosophers whose wisdom embodies cosmic law, while he lumps all the rest under the 'meaner titles' of the rabble. Elsewhere he explores the Pythagorean matrix of harmony, law, and transmigration; and clearly that interest is tied to his search for compelling ways of gaining access to natural-cum-universal norms of belief and behaviour. What becomes visible in the poem to Drayton but remains unclear is the question of just how this musical naturalness interacts with the artifice of those norms made by pastoral, heroic, and satirical poets; made and imposed by warriors and governors alike; and made rigorously by those scholars with whom Selden replaces philosophers at the top of Plato's transmigratory scale. Selden celebrates an ideal poetry that conjoins sanctity and moral law in one pleasing music. Less clear, however, is exactly what the source and character of that sanctity, the status of that law, and the force of that harmony are.

—— 3 ——

Selden's admiration for historical poetry is evident in a variety of contexts. In his research on English history he often quotes with respect the archaic verses of Robert of Gloucester. In one of his own poems, Selden praises Thomas Farnaby's edition of Lucan, whose invented speeches were high in the list of strategies associated with poetic history and who offers via Farnaby some access to the 'ancient and recondite rites ... from the inmost part of the temple' – a claim that might well encompass the secrets of poetry, history, philosophy, and religion.[15] For Selden, the public poets of his own day update Lucan's own powerful commitment to the preservation of noble mores in critical times and to the gauge of human enormity.

Selden's response to Jonson's *Bartholomew Fair* demonstrates his belief that normative poetry can offer religion itself a measure for its seemingly endless disputes. In the *Table Talk*, Selden has been lamenting the tendency of Puritanism to supplant the authority of churches and even the scriptures by force of the arrogant self. At this point, he applauds the puppet scene in Jonson's play for satirizing the vanity of the divinity that eschews an accessible standard or rule. Elsewhere in his conversations, Selden recommends frequent trips to the local Assizes for a strong dose of law and justice in the religious life of English Protestants; but in Jonson's play, Adam Overdo, an overzealous justice of the peace, is just as flawed as Zeal-of-the-Land-Busy in uncharitably and inequitably prosecuting enormity at the fair. Over the course of the play, however, Adam reforms his own office and remembers his own enormities, inviting the company to supper and declaring his new aim to correct and edify rather than to destroy. By play's end, Adam has learned the value of hospitality and a better way of applying his measure, all thanks to the authority of comedy.

In many of his plays and throughout his poetry, Jonson envisions his literary enterprise as a normative one, according to which the 'consent of the learned' and the 'consent of the good' arbitrate the manners, arts, and values of English society. In *Cynthia's Revels*, Jonson calls his arbiter Crites, a name that in Selden's efforts to integrate poetic and scholarly histories can prove divisive. Jonson's character is only, and judiciously, divided from the vanities and humours of the world around him, a world in which custom has abandoned any pretence to goodness or learning and is playing the bawd. By contrast, Crites possesses a humoral balance; a discourse at once uncommon and effective; a vigilance over his own judgment and learning; and a virtue sufficient against the vicissitudes of fortune. In short, he illustrates the Jonsonian hero as a moral and rational norm that is fundamentally natural yet constantly remade.

The critic was not always welcome in contemporary debates over the endeavours of poetry and history, and even when welcome, he often played an inglorious role. One can see his shaky status in Elizabethan and Stuart debates about whether historians should offer ornate monuments to virtue or naked authenticity and accuracy by way of philology,

numismatics, and an acutely sceptical analysis of texts and their chronologies. In this controversy: at best, the 'critic' cleaned the Augean stables
of legend and anachronism; at worst, he traded the moral value of history for a show of pedantry. There is no question that Selden admired
and emulated the Herculean critic and no doubt that he resisted the
showy pedant. Even with the undignified, if nonetheless heroic, labours
of the purging critic, however, Selden wanted more from history than
simply sanitation. He wanted a clearer perspective on those 'inmost'
norms of history that might yield the most abundant fruit in redressing
the ailments of contemporary society. Selden's ideal history was at once
more profound, more accurate, and more useful.

Selden shows his admiration for the critic in his choice of cultural
heroes, in his writings on historiography, and in his own historical practice. To Joseph Scaliger and the French legal humanists, he looks for a
critique of, and new standards for, the ways in which historians handle
evidence. As Anthony Grafton has shown, Scaliger focused on philology
and chronology for the rebuilding of evidentiary standards, using his
commentaries as 'a highly flexible instrument of instruction.'[16] Resisting the fascination woven by fabulous, heroic, or otherwise shrouded
eras of the past, the critic cherishes non-textual, physical vestiges of the
knowable times.

As it was practised on the Continent, however, criticism was not mono-
lithic. If in one instance it was meant to move history and law beyond
the realm of the poetic, it was also intended to generate an improved
poetry. On the one hand, then, one finds in Selden's writings a love of
philology, antiquarianism, synchronism, and interpretive suspicion. On
the other, one sees clear evidence of his attempts to help historical
poetry attain new standards of greatness. Selden's heroes – Scaliger,
Hotman, and Camden, for instance – had certainly not decided that
poetry must be forsaken for philology, law, or chronology. After all,
Scaliger's father had written a treatise on poetics that Selden admired.
Among the French humanists, as Donald Kelley argues, Budé believed
that 'historians and poets as well as lawyers should be granted authority,
since they were cited in the Digest and were obviously necessary for its
understanding.'[17] Selden admired many of the poets whom Camden
quotes frequently, from Ausonius and Claudian onward.

In fact, the critical scholars to whom Selden looked for historical
exactitude disagreed on the purpose of their work as much as they
agreed on the basics of its method. They differed over the value of
moral and philosophical content; over the value of poetry against law,

and of the Roman code against their own nation's medieval laws and customs. If these critical scholars were prepared to remove the layers of fable, error, and distortion so that the truth of history might emerge at last, they did not always agree on what the nature or scope of that truth might be. Nor could they guarantee its normative value outside the domain of what Edmund Bolton called 'Grammatical Criticks (from whose Pens let no man greatly hope for any thing in History noble).' Like Selden, Bolton treasured the 'steel Rule' of the critics' honest and demystified history, but not at the expense of those godly and moral fictions found in 'every Historical Monument or Historical Tradition.'[18]

That Selden was a 'critic' in his methods is obvious. That his criticism set him against the poets is another, much more complicated matter. In a chapter called 'Poets and Critics,' Edwin Johnson captures the divide in Selden's thinking about the value of normative poetry: 'Great as were the critical powers of Selden, he was not able to efface from his imagination that ideal retrospect which he had learned at school, and which his friend Camden was teaching the children at Westminster.'[19] Conversely, one of these students, Ben Jonson, could not erase from his conscience the demands of scholarship that his master had instilled in him, great as were his poetic abilities. So it was with Michael Drayton's request that Selden provide a scholarly commentary on the *Poly-Olbion*: normative poets operating in Selden's purview grasped the value of enlisting the modern critical historicism at the risk of their own demise.

Selden's commitment to the ways of sceptical criticism is as clear as any other factor in his work. In a 1622 letter to Augustine Vincent, for instance, he attributes Vincent's prowess at uncovering error to his careful attention to manuscripts, a key ingredient in antiquarian history. True, the pilgrim in the vast 'records of this kingdom' will find the 'right way to truth' a rough one, but the ancients have set good precedent, Selden urges, and a grand vista of 'the world of historical matter both of church and state' awaits those historians who persevere through the difficulty. For the most part, he laments, English historians have devoted too much effort to stylizing their narratives, which 'is but to spend that time and cost in plaistering only, or painting, of a weak or poor building, which should be imployed in provision of timber and stone for the strengthening and enlarging it' (*Opera Omnia*, vol. 3, 1692–4).

Elsewhere Selden elaborates on the tools and materials needed for fortifying and expanding the architecture of history. Commending philology as a 'fit Wife' for learning in general, he places her together with 'her two Hand-maids, *Curious Diligence* and *Watchfull Industrie*' in a

'raised Towre of Iudgment' from which she 'discouers to vs often ...
many hidden Truths, that, on the leuell of any one restraind Profession,
can neuer be discerned' (*History of Tithes*, xix). It is not surprising that
his investment in the 'restraind Profession' of antiquarianism is at once
deeper and more discontented than his marriage of philology with
learning. As D.R. Woolf has shown, Selden's debts to his antiquarian
associates, with their virtually exclusive focus on English materials, did
not hinder him from expanding their scope, methods, and purpose.
Indeed, he followed the course of this expansion into the Talmud and
partly out of history, critically defined, into what Woolf calls the 'supra-
historical disciplines.'[20] Poetic history already testifies to that impulse,
which accounts for the ways in which Selden alternately respects and
equivocates the border 'between antiquities and true history' (213).
According to Woolf, Selden attempts to integrate an English antiquarianism (with its love of coins, inscriptions, and manuscripts); the philology and textual criticism of Scaliger and the French legal humanists;
and didactic narrative. That is, he would ground historical narrative
in antiquarian research; methodize and internationalize antiquarian research with philology and humanist criticism; and instil in philology,
criticism, and research 'a larger concept of history' with the 'answering
of broad questions' that lend history its value (220).

As the historian recommended by Degory Whear to his students, the
one heralded by Henry Peacham as 'the rising star of good letters and
antiquity,' Selden undertook the challenge of preserving – by redefining and strengthening – the poetic, sacred, and normative values of history.[21] Camden was the beacon lighting the way of this endeavour, not
only for Selden but also for Jonson, who claimed 'an intention to perfect an epic poem entitled *Herologia*, of the worthies of his country,' and
who liked the plan if not the execution of Drayton's *Poly-Olbion*[22]; and
for Drayton himself as well as Browne, both of whom attempted to
secure British legends by converting them either into chorographic sub-
deities or into a pastoral *locus amoenus*. For Camden wrote large not simply the labours of preservation but the conflict over historical values: as
Kevin Sharpe explains, he epitomized the Tudor antiquarian 'mixture
of medieval didacticism and credulous repetition with a new, more
refined critical treatment of the evidence.'[23]

In the enterprise of rebuilding poetic history and historical poetry,
Selden's Inner Temple became the Temple of the Muses, with which he
often associated that London site. There, as in Jonson's 1629 Pindaric
ode for Lucius Cary and Henry Morison, the poet doubles as priest in

order to invent and preserve the sanctified and rectified expectations for behaviour in early Stuart England. In the ode, Jonson touts the duties, virtues, and the faith in 'that bright eternal day: / Of which we priests, and poets say / Such truths, as we expect for happy men.'[24] But even in celebrating and officiating over the rites and customs of the normative yet also spirited society, Jonson understands that such customs and values cannot be entrusted to the devices and desires of the public at large, and that even those supposedly great and good men to whom he directs his praises must be made and sustained in their heroic virtues by the poet himself. As natural as moral norms ought to be in the consent of the learned and the good, Jonson is committed to the notion that, like good poetry, the offices and virtues of a social order must be made and remade, repaired, dressed, and exalted.

For Jonson, Stoic models support the normative endeavours of good poets more than most templates, not least in the Stoic emphasis on the convergence between duty ('offices') and personal integrity. Yet Jonson's moral society is also very much a religious one; for together with social duties, performative rites, and private virtues celebrated in his ode, he imagines that the prematurely dead Morison has leapt into heaven, 'Possessed with holy rage' (214). This leap of the faithful dovetails, however, with other images of retreat in the poem: the opening image of an infant's retreat from worldly chaos into his mother's womb, for instance. As a 'fair example' of virtue and honesty, the two aristocratic friends celebrated in the poem offer 'a law' to society at large, but they also daunt the members of that society with their mysterious love and with the suspicion that such ideals are fictions to be read and admired rather than instructions to be accomplished (215).

Selden's friend Jonson advanced normative poetry as far as it could go: in an analogy sustained throughout the ode to Cary and Morison, the good life and the good poem are said to share the same qualities of proportion, fullness, and beauty. At the heart of this poetics was a more widely applicable belief that, as one contemporary remarked of dutiful advisers, 'that rule had need to be verie straight in itself that will squarr others.'[25] The classical qualities and virtues best captured in poetry, Jonson argued, were also relevant to history, philosophy, oratory, and sermons, in short, to any discourse whose responsibility it was to square the imperfections of a society. In the requirement that the carpenter's rule itself be straight and level, Jonson understood that, more often than not, actual wits fell far short of the ideal. Jonson's theorization of decorum, however, like Selden's conception of the law, entailed that the arbiters of human rectitude faced an even greater challenge, as Sharpe explains, of flexing the 'verie straight' rule of behaviour so that it might accommodate and measure the changeable circumstances of experience (229).

Jonson believed that the good poet was the best adviser and rule for others, but among Selden's associates, the arbiters of discursive straightness varied from the critic to the moral philosopher, and from the legal sage to the poet. Even at its best, the style and content of poetic history was increasingly thought to require some outside measurement from the sharp edge of a philological and evidentiary scholarship – as surely as moral philosophy and true religion were needed for an inspection of the justice, goodness, and holiness of its values. More than any other text of its time, the collaboration between Drayton and Selden on the *Poly-Olbion* testifies to the difficulty posed for authors and audiences in coordinating a set of clearly conflicting criteria.

Even though Camden alternated between a critical and tolerant approach towards dubious evidence, he wished mainly to praise and memorialize worthy places, things, stories, and persons in his own land, a cue taken by Drayton, who took the next step and converted memory into myth. If Camden does not cherish the title of 'historian,' he does not prefer the moniker of 'critic' either. He would demystify the past but not desiccate it; recast traditions rather than repudiate them; and make use of poetry rather than dismiss it.[26]

In devising the 'intermixtures' of the *Poly-Olbion*, Drayton held Camden and Selden to be advocates of and collaborators in his labours. Their mutual aim, he believed, was to rescue a sacred and didactic historical poetry from the 'Idle Humerous world' of coterie verses and from 'the thicke fogges and mists of ignorance' about antiquity.[27] Even before William Browne declared a 'Crisis' in poetic history upon the bad reception of Drayton's great poem and despite George Wither's claim that Drayton would save this Muse from oblivion, the poet himself was dismayed but certain that his verses required annotation as well as apology (393–6). For English readers willing to be guided and abetted in their travail by Selden, Drayton promises that the religious and moral recompense will be immense: industry will lead them back to the groves of the Bards and Druids, to a *locus amoenus* that surrounds the monuments of British virtue, piety, and law. In this sacred grove or *numus*, there thrives what Selden will later identify as *nomos*: custom, law, and music.

Given his own sometimes sportive and ambivalent attitude towards the 'Arcadian deduction' of historical poetry, Selden offers Drayton an assistance with the poem that can be devoted, suspicious, equivocal, or haphazard (ix). Whenever his glosses begin to resonate with the classical principles of Jonson's poetics, it is easy to see that Selden would find less trouble – but also less historical matter – in Jonson's poems. The antiquarian's first commitment to Drayton's readers lies in clarifying the poem's fictional layers or folds: 'What the Verse oft, with allusion, as supposing a full knowing Reader, lets slip; or in winding steps of Personating Fictions (as some times) so infolds, that suddaine conceipt cannot abstract a Forme of the clothed Truth, I have, as I might, *Illustrated*' (viii). In abstracting the form of a dressed or folded fiction, he often justifies its appropriateness. Selden's role, however, is not that ancillary: he must also censure and, in judging, rectify and refashion the fiction according to his own critical square, reminding the readers that the ancient Bards themselves were also rectified by public censure. What is more, he must accomplish his critical purpose without doing violence to the sanctity of the poetic fiction.

Thus, when Selden tells us that 'Being not very Prodigall of [his] Historicall Faith, after *Explanation*, [he] oft adventure[s] on *Examination*, and *Censure*' of Drayton's traditions, the illustrator is staking out his own normative role as Jonson understood it: the critic-poet is vexed into suspicion of hyperbole or inaccuracy, and commits himself to vexing the fabulous by means of what Selden characterizes as 'weighing the Reporters credit, Comparison with more perswading authority, and *Synchronisme* (the best Touch-stone in this kind of Triall)' (viii). Indeed, Selden applies terms to his illustrations and himself – 'rectified' and 'vext' – that Jonson features in his praise of Selden, all in announcing his opposition to 'intollerable Antichronismes, incredible reports, and *Bardish* impostures, as well from Ignorance as assum'd liberty of Invention in some of our Ancients' (viii). Whether attributable to bad scholarship or to poetic invention, 'such palpable Fauxeties, of our Nation ... are even equally warrantable, as *Ariosto's* Narrations ... *Spensers* Elfin Story, or *Rablais* his strange discoveries,' that is, not at all (ix). Yet the illustrations often convey just how difficult it is to pry poetic norms out of romantic groves without squandering the sanctity of the poetry.

A dialogue develops between Drayton's Muse and Selden's critic in their efforts to preserve and to strengthen the normative force of historical poetry on the reader, to whom the glossator's notes often appeal with advice and exhortation. Regarding the 'credit' owed to 'Hyperbolies ... of *Bevis*,' the romantic hero, Selden entrusts the readers' 'owne judgement, and the Authors censure in the admonition of the other rivers here personated' (46). In the same breath, he complains that neither readers nor poets can always be trusted with history and that they require an impartial judge: 'And it is wished that the poeticall Monkes in celebration of [Bevis], *Arthur,* and other such Worthies had containd themselves within bounds of likelyhood; or else that some judges, proportionat to those of the *Graecian* Games, (who alwayes by publique authority pull'd downe the statues erected, if they exceeded the true symmetry of the victors) had given such exorbitant fictions their desert' (46). This ancient model of public censure for artistic representation is part and parcel of the Jonsonian investment in ancient forms such as the Pindaric ode; in fact, in Selden's note it is the power of Pindaric poetry over human belief – 'The sweet grace of an inchanting Poem (as unimitable *Pindar* affirmes) often compels beliefe' – that necessitates an equally forceful and rectifying censure (46). All the more reason to fault those 'indigested reports of barren and Monkish invention,' their expansions 'out of the lists of Truth,' and 'their intermixed and absurd fauxeties' (46).

Yet Drayton's poem itself depends for its value on intermixture; he leaves it to Selden to decide where his inventions are legitimate and to censure the absurd. Regarding one passage, Selden attributes the illegitimacy of its fiction to the author's own passions – the '*Affection*' of panegyric and the '*Hate*' of satire – then urges readers 'not to credit' the very material that he introduces as a gloss (x). He emphasizes that his explanations, disclaimers, insertions, and censures are designed to guide or at least to 'please an Understanding Reader.' Selden's aids to such a reader come in a variety of strategies: sorting ancient, medieval, and contemporary authorities; differentiating the best methods for attaining a reliable if still distant vantage on 'inmost' history, from that 'rash collecting (as it were) from visuall beam's refracted through anothers eye' (xii); marshalling observations and records that might corroborate or even fashion the propriety of Drayton's conceits; tracing the progress of Drayton's assiduous Muse; providing Continental, Syrian, and Judaic analogues for British legends and myths, even when Selden severs 'Prose and Religion' from the invocations of 'Poetry and Fiction'; and categorizing poetic fictions as variously ludicrous, amorous, allegorical, satisfactory, or sufficient (15, 62).

Drayton's passionate impersonation of landscape and his heroic monuments to ancient virtue are not simply at the mercy of Selden's collaborative censure. Rather, the poet mounts an impressive theory and defence of those age-old stories and verses that are expressly filled with lies. Selden is prepared to allow 'Poeticall' as against 'Historicall liberty' and to correct Drayton's liberties with chronology and records (155), but Drayton in part convinces Selden that such critical distinctions and revisions are irrelevant, even harmful to the availability and value of history. When Selden (like Camden) frets over the temptation that he 'should untimely put on the person of an Historian,' it is evident that Drayton's project seeks to convert him to, and into, the impersonations of historical poetry as surely as the antiquarian seeks to square or measure the fictions (246). As Selden unfolds narratives and anthologizes poems, he moves closer to the sacred Muse with whose power to compel belief he 'would therin joyne with the Author' if 'Prose and Religion' allowed (15). Poet and critic belong in the holistic sphere of learning – or so Selden likes to believe – but it remains uncertain whether one figure must become the other if they manage to move into the same discursive space. Of the two taskmasters distancing Selden's Muse from Drayton's, the former (prose) enlists a conventional modesty for the critic, while the latter (religion) is harder to pinpoint: either Selden is attempting to laugh off the differences between Drayton's antique magic and his modernist rigour, or the scholar is wary of his implication in superstition and idolatry if he allows Drayton's poesy to compel his own belief.

At the simplest level, Drayton lauds poetic history as the fortress built against the ruins of time. Where there is no Homer for history, there is no survival of history. Even more, however, Drayton turns a celebration of the ancient British Bards into a theory of how tradition connects the practices and suppositions of the present to the worthy, if sometimes inaccurate, norms of the past. For Selden, the music of the Bards was clearly collaborative with the laws of the Druids in the groves that Caesar must have witnessed. But Drayton concurs with Sidney that poetry might reach its highest status when it fabricates an idea not available to the vision of the most critical history.

— 4 —

In *The Church History of Britain* (1656), Thomas Fuller congregates the group of offices with which early Stuart writers tended to associate the ancient Bards. Unlike the Druids, who were 'philosophers, divines, lawyers,' Bards served the Britons as 'prophets, poets, historians.'[28] The latter, thrice-blessed figures exerted a morally civilizing influence over

their people, commemorated the heroes and values of the past, yet also
bestowed on all human experience a providential trajectory and spiritual warrant. All three of their offices converged, and cast the mythic
persona of the Bards as a Janus; for their 'rhyming verses ... looked both
backward in their relations, and forward in their predictions.' Fuller
condemns the 'wild conjectures,' vulgar 'credulity,' and false doctrine
(transmigration) that contributed to the honorable reputation of the
Bards, and stresses that it was mainly their musicality that was responsible for their impact on the British people (vol. 1, 5). There is no denying, however, that the Bard's historical-cum-poetic-cum-prophetic music
assumed a comprehensive and integral role in the public memory,
morality, aspirations, and beliefs of ancient British pagans.

Throughout the *Poly-Olbion*, Drayton invokes the 'sacred Bards' or
'old British Poets' who sang to their harps of the heroes, genealogies,
and oracles integral to the identity and mores of their people. He wishes
that he might reincarnate the spirit of those Bards, presumably with
Selden doubling as a Druid priest and sage regulating all 'British rites ...
in darksome Groves, there counsailing with sprites.'[29] At times, Selden
rebuffs the 'truth-passing reports of Poeticall Bards,' or insists that any
defence of legend needs a 'more then Poeticall forme'; but like Camden, Selden opposes the 'critique age' that automatically rejects its
myths of origin 'because of their unlikely and fictitious mixtures' from
the fabulous age (21). He also digs deeply for authentic scraps from that
age, including obscure and fragmentary writers such as Nennius and
'*Taliessin* a great Bard' (21). Selden conveys some hope that new evidence might be found for the fabulous and deems reasonable Geoffrey
of Monmouth's claim that he is translating his history from a now-lost
Welsh book. Unlike Sidney, who allows no room for fables in history –
the historian must rely on the naked facts of the past – Selden shares
with Drayton the hope that the putatively fabulous traditions of the past
might be granted their place in history. Even if the myth of origins is
illusory, Selden suggests, its enchantment has helped to instil discipline,
hope, and moral values in all European peoples. An argument for the
alternative transmission of Trojan blood by way of Roman colonists or
even Gallic ancestors – an option also pursued by Camden – represents
the scholar's attempt to save a normative poetic history from the critics.

Selden understands the major point that Drayton would make, that
tradition has been treated by all peoples, not least the Jews, as a precious
'antique and successive report'; and the illustrator exhorts that readers
'shall enough please *Saturne* and *Mercury*, presidents of antiquity and

learning, if with the Author [they] foster this belief' (23). That is, the Trojan Brute is Britain's Talmudic Moses, suspected of egregious lies and mystifying fictions but still valuable and, as their 'highest learning,' true in his own way. Somehow that learning must be measured by a reliable standard, but Selden is unsettled by the divide between the Talmud's norm (God's holy word) and the gauge of British historical fictions (criticism). All the same, he persists in his analogies between Jews and the British: both peoples have been misunderstood and misrepresented by their Roman conquerors; and both mingle gigantic fictions with their laws and norms.

As Selden's commentary on the Bards accumulates details, it locates an institution of criticism within the communities of those Bards. Having identified Taliessin as a 'learned' poet and 'the chiefest of the Bards,' he explicates the '*Stethva*' as 'the meeting of the *British Poets* and *Minstrels*, for tryall of their Poems and Musique sufficiencies, where the best had his reward, *a Silver Harpe*' (83). One can still find evidence of this custom, he says, in the twelfth century 'under *Rees ap Griffith*, Prince of *South-wales*,' and it is praiseworthy: 'A custome so good, that, had it beene judiciously observed, truth of Storie had not beene so uncertain' (83). Not only were there prizes for the best songs, he continues, but also rectification of the flawed: 'for there was, by suppose, a correction of what was faulty in forme or matter, or at least a censure of the hearers upon what was recited. As (according to the *Roman* use) it is noted, that *Girald* of *Cambria*, when he had written his *Topography* of *Ireland*, made at three severall dayes severall recitals of his III. distinctions in *Oxford*; of which course some have wisht a recontinuance, that eyther amendment of opinion or change of purpose in publishing, might prevent blazoned errors' (83).

Having commended the British censure of erroneous historical poetry, Selden rehearses the ancient Roman treatments of the Bards as 'Poets and Minstrels' – especially those found in Athenaeus, Ammianus Marcellinus, and Lucan, authorities who in other contexts induce Selden to stress the parasitical tendencies of the Bards' heroic, panegyric, and oracular songs. In the commentary on Drayton, however, they resemble the Greek *rhapsodoi*, reciting epic poetry and converting wisdom, virtue, theology, and the social order into sweet and musical conventions that might compel belief in the ideals providing the ligatures that unite a religious society.

At times in the Drayton commentary, Selden's glosses on ancient music tend towards the scholarly analysis of poetic quantities, musical

instruments, the 'chiefest forme[s] of the ancientest musique among
the Gentiles,' and 'the elaborat institutions' of language (83–4).
Throughout this discussion, however, the illustrator keeps the poetry of
the Bards answerable to what in the *Arundel Marbles* he will call *nomos*,
understood as either law or harmonic mode, at times as both. In one
instance, a prince of North Wales 'reformed the abuses of those Minstrels by a particular statut, extant to this day' (84). In another, he notes
the division of British music into a variety of modes and measures, the
particulars of which Selden confesses not fully to understand. Allowing
the military, heroic use of sprightly Phrygian music among the Irish, he
nonetheless emphasizes the prominence of 'the mind-composing
Dorique' creative of harmony, holism, and gentleness within the 'assemblies' of the British and other 'Western people' (84). Thus, as censure
rectifies poetry, music facilitates censure. Those Bards still need correction 'by a great critique,' but criticism profits from their music (87).

When Selden applauds William of Malmesbury's argument that
Arthur and other inspiring heroes were 'right worthy to have been celebrated by true storie, not false tales,' he desires a 'perswading authority'
that 'rectifies the uncertainty' in such celebrations (88–9); but for
Drayton, there can be no inspiration without the 'false tales,' and moral
value is always preferable to precision. As 'Musician, Herault, Bard,' the
ancient British poets and their harps have a remedial effect on their
people as well as the power to save past customs from oblivion. In this
blindly critical age, Drayton laments, no one believes in the heroic past,
and fools defame those 'credulous Ages' that 'layd / Slight fictions with
the truth, whilst truth on rumor stayd' (118). Where Bards blended fiction with truth, the lies were small in the 'credulous Ages,' then pur-
poseful in the critical ages for preventing lazy neglect of the past. Slight
as they were, these toys provided the 'appetite' of the audiences with the
'varietie' that the human mind requires in its expense of moral labour.
In short, it is better for more critical ages to receive the past dressed in
'fictive ornament' than not to have that truth at all (118). The Bards
knew enough to accommodate the human condition, their harps proving nothing less than symbols of this beneficent compromise.

According to Drayton, the past itself is 'decrepit' and so must 'leane /
Upon Tradition.' The norms afforded by history might limp on their
poetic crutches, but at least they advance, and the critic who removes
that prop is comparable to that other precisionist, the Puritan, 'Who for
some Crosse or Saint they in the window see / Will pluck downe all the
Church' (118–19). Taken to iconoclastic extremes, then, Selden's own

severe Muse approaches the overdone justice and busy zeal that dispense with any human art that might preserve what is sacred, instructive, and valuable about the past. Such a false zeal might well remove the guarantor of continuity and immediacy that 'Time hath pind to Truth.' As 'Soule-blinded sots that creepe / In durt, and never saw the wonders of the Deepe,' critics nullify the normative sanctity gathered from human experience, and they ruin the beautiful temples that house the only truths worth having from the past (119). Such critics have no sense of what sanctity needs to survive in the world.

Drayton concludes that the critics get what they deserve: the story of their own people told only by the brutal and ignorant imperialists who retain little of the Bards' epic songs and bowdlerize what fragments they have. How ridiculous, he argues, for critics to baulk at the dearth of early bardic material when the critical demotion of such materials resembles the destructive rage of the Romans, Picts, Saxons, and Danes, whose invasions yielded 'sacrilegious wrack / Of many a noble Booke' (120). In Song 10, the last of the Welsh songs, Drayton personifies the River Dee as the last voice of expiring poetic history: she blames the British for allowing Brute to be dishonoured and the 'ancient *British* Rimes' forgotten. In their fixation on Caesar and other putatively legitimate sources, the critics have abandoned the ancient, oracular Taliessin and other 'immortall men.' In fact, Drayton protests, British genealogies are more reliable than the 'idle tales' of the Greeks insofar as the Bards had critical judges: they, 'from the first of Time, by Judges still were heard, / Discreetlie every yeere correcting where they err'd' (207). These discreet judges helped the Bards to execute their art more carefully and persuasively, even learning from the Druids that the transmission of custom was more secure and medicinal in the human heart than in the storage of writing. In the words of the River Dee, human breasts are better than books for ensuring historical memory, since a book is readily destroyed while memory almost inevitably develops into tradition. Lies develop as well, but without some standard such as the Bible, lie-prone tradition is a people's only way of receiving the sacred norms of inmost history. Just so, without the Holy Spirit's authorization of scripture, the only reason to believe in Mosaic law and history is found in witty rabbinical tradition, the '*Jewish* Fiction' (as Selden himself calls it) wrapped together with law (152).

In her last image of history, Dee imagines historians sailing past an impressive 'promontory steepe,' gazing awestruck at what they see so close by, then haplessly moving well out of sight of the monumental setting (209). The Bards were on this ship as it passed, Dee supposes, and the best that modern critics can accomplish is to find some vantage between now and then for their surveying instruments. Without the sacred Bards, the critics will not see the monumental cliffs at all; they will see instead the clouds cast over the sacred norms of antiquity by the ruins of time and by imperialism, too.

If Drayton positions Selden as the judge who will correct his bardic song, Selden identifies himself as a judge open to the music and liberties of the Bard. He concedes Drayton's point that Roman accounts of British customs are largely ignorant and hostile, meant to destroy a people rather than to integrate them. Quoting Horace's ninth epode to suggest that bardic music mixed the Doric and Phrygian modes, Selden privileges the former, calming mode over the envigorating latter. At their best, the Bards helped to keep law and order with a music that would 'charme ... & compose [British] troubled affections.' That is, music inseminated lawful harmony into human hearts, a 'conveniency of use' that Selden appreciates (121). The illustrator adds that the bardic power to pacify violent passions has 'authentique affirmance,' not least in Aristotle's *Politics*, in which music and mind are keyed to one another mimetically (122). Just as effectively, Selden explains, the Bards of Tacitean fame were skilled in inciting war as well as in ensuring peace; theirs was a music of two modes, of double *nomoi*, as Horace knew, in support of the sacred laws of war and peace.

In addition to maintaining the normative sanctity of the Bards, Selden makes the more obvious case that Roman sources are insufficient for a British history that has moral utility as well as authenticity. His point, however, is not that tradition sustains those truths that lost texts, if found, would corroborate; rather, he worries that lost texts – for instance, the Welsh model for Geoffrey of Monmouth – might have been our only access to tradition. Noting the unanimity on the claim that Roman and Greek history would be filled out by lost sources, Selden wonders why it is so hard for his critical readers to believe in the lost sources of the British, 'devoured up from posterity, which perhaps, had they bin left to us, would have ended this controversie' (214). Unlike Drayton, Selden situates the sacred customs of native Britain not in tradition but in Elysium, in that grove to which all lost works of monumental and 'instructing use' retire. Prescott has shrewdly argued that Selden's fascination with Elysian spaces testifies to his plaintive (if also sportive) tendency towards methodological impasse or thresholds.[30] In later works, both Drayton and Selden join William Browne in their commitment of imaginative and intellectual labour to a reconstruction of the fortunate isles in which the grove of the Bards and Druids encloses the sanctity of a lawful and hortatory poetry, only a few steps away from Selden's own turn to natural and Judaic versions of an elusive yet transcendental law. Already in his early works, he suspects that the rabbinical sages double as fanciful poets whose metaphors coexist with their laws in the Talmud.

In keeping with his censorial collaboration with Drayton's historical poetry, Selden uses his illustrations as an anthology for British poetry; as an opportunity to rectify that poetry; and as occasion to serve up miniature normative histories as well as, perhaps, his own oracular and priestly hymns. Early on, Selden promises his readers an abundance of archaic and native '*Rimes*,' including personal favourites such as the historical poet Robert of Gloucester; the pastoral satire in *Piers Plowman*; and the fairy poetry of Spenser. These rhymes have three warrants for the illustrator: they 'justifie my truth,' provide 'variety' in imitation of Drayton's 'pleasanter Muse,' and – more mysteriously – transmit the spirit of the past, 'even breathing antiquity.'[31] In addition to collecting these verses, Selden also identifies himself as one of the 'Judicious reformers of fabulous report,' like those ancient judges of the 'best of the *Bards*' (157–8). This role helps to explain apparent digressions such as the extended gloss on an Arabic term in Chaucer's *Troilus and Criseyde*, found in Selden's own preface to the *Poly-Olbion* (xi).

Often the glossator seeks to impress values on his readers, including Christian, legal, political, and moral norms. In a wide range of notes, Selden abstracts the normative legacy from a bulk of historical matter; resists the violence of the 'great Critique' with the power of 'an old Panegyrist' (163); rebukes harmful fables and vices by means of comic satire in Lucian, Rabelais, Plautus, Aristophanes, and Langland; holds historical error against 'the square of *English* law & policie' (164–5); expressly allegorizes and moralizes the 'worth' of historical evidence; theorizes the 'sufficient justification of making a Poem' (287) for the sake of expressing 'worth' (168); censures 'vulgar' tales (288); declares the problems faced by anyone attempting to rectify the 'uncertainties, if not contrarieties' of history (289); revises the history of clerical-lay relations; and separates obvious fictions from their 'couvert' and 'difficult' counterparts (299).

It is in this matter of fictive obscurity – whether in the bardic oracles or topical satire – that Selden's justification of poetic history comes closest to self-defence. In his preface, he asks for the 'Common Curtesie in

Censure' of his errors and infelicities, not least in that archaic obscurity of style that he attributes also to his '*Historicall deduction of Our Ancient Lawes*' – his own work, the *Janus* – 'wherein I scape not without Tax' (xii). Like his beloved Scaliger, who had a penchant for the strange dignity of archaism, Selden accepts the charge of obscurity levelled at him 'as if [he] had been the author of a Saliarian hymn' ('Saliaris *Carminis*') (xii). Even his earliest admirers, Clarendon among them, would attribute such an oracular obscurity to his writings, but Selden tries to justify his own obscurity.

In Elizabethan and early Stuart England, obscurity was a much discussed literary quality. Allegorical poets such as George Chapman maintained that the mystifying cover of darkness lent highest truths protection from the masses but also retention in the few readers who worked hard for the meaning. Juvenalian satirists such as John Marston claimed that obscurity was a symptom of their indignation as well as a shield from the authorities. Jonson generally preferred perspicuous poetry, but literary decorum entailed that obscurity was sometimes appropriate – in histories or speeches rendered in perilous times, for instance – such as those one finds in the works of Tacitus. Why might Selden cultivate obscurity?

Selden knew that the Saliarian hymn was a form assailed in the works of Cicero, Aulus Gellius, and Lucian, while Horace and Quintilian converted it into a watchword for obscurity. The Saliarians were those ancient priests thought to have been instituted by the great lawgiver Numa, with a strong connection to Mars, whose weapons and shield they bore. In the *Fasti*, Ovid connects them to Numa's law, which, together with their awesome religious rites, served to temper violent military zeal so that 'Men put off savagery, justice was more puissant than arms.'[32] In addition to having some connection with the horned deity Faunus, these priests were famous for their ritual dances performed throughout the city in formulaic steps and pauses. Selden himself provides those references to Horace, Ovid, and Apuleius that inform the reader of the Salierian hymns, solemn dances, clashing shields, and post-ritual feasts. Through the medium of their archaic obscurity, the Salierians were impressive poets whose offices were priestly, epic, law giving, and choral; they were mesmerizing dispensers of ancient laws, beliefs, virtues, and social concord. Classical rhetoricians attacked them in terms that Ben Jonson approved of in his search for a perspicuous and appropriate poetic language. But Jonson himself would write a Pindaric ode in which a priestly poet works through choral ritual, and Selden would defend them as cousins to Drayton's Bards. The Salierian priests epitomized, then, everything that was powerful and dangerous about the medium of oracular hymns for the dispensation or performance of *nomos*.

According to Quintilian, the Saliarian hymns are prominent examples of excessive and obscure archaism, their *reductio ad absurdum* reached when their language was 'scarcely understood by its own priests.' But Selden quotes Quintilian's concession to archaic language: 'Archaic words not only enjoy the patronage of distinguished authors, but also give style a majesty and charm,'[33] and the ancient orator adds that religion prohibits our tampering with old sacred hymns. Nonetheless, Quintilian, like Jonson long after him, insists that language should be clear enough to communicate its message without an interpreter, and that orators should cull the newest of the old and the oldest of the new. In response, Selden defends obscurity with the help of 'Latine Critiques' like Lipsius, who through philology have inured students of the past to the 'Saturnian' language found in 'the admired Ruins of olde Monuments.'[34] Scholars of Ovid's *Fasti* have pointed out that the leaping dance of the Saliarian priests was an ancient form of magic meant to ward off bad spirits and disastrous harvests, and that these priests might well have called on Saturn in their dances. Selden, however, defends the poetics of such ritual magic as much as he celebrates its fusion of law, epic, dance, and mystery. Like Jonson, he certainly does not always support 'Antique Termes,' agreeing that 'as Coine, so words, of a publique and knowne stamp, are to bee used' (xiii). Yet he is well versed in the Elizabethan and Jacobean poetic tenet that obscurity often attends the most ambitious normative discourse, whether it be affirmative (in the case of soaring Neoplatonic allegory) or condemnatory (in the case of roughshod topical satire).

Quintilian's directives notwithstanding, Selden defends 'that way I offend' – the way of priestly obscurity – as an imitation of a singular hymning language that entitles his authority to more than naked innocence. In Cicero's *De Oratore*, Crassus articulates what this surplus might be: in a paean for those rhythms and words to which human beings almost viscerally respond, he touts the 'extremely powerful influence' of poetry or song on the human affections, a power that King Numa understood in establishing the Salierian verses.[35] The effect that Selden admires in the Salierian hymns, the one that Jonson wishes to achieve in his Pindaric ode, the response that Sidney has – against his better judgment – to medieval ballads: in all, the point is that the ritual effects of

hymnody and of heroic poetry lend normative discourse a neurological
control over its auditors. Thus, the judge becomes the Bard, the lawyer
becomes the priestly poet. In the *Table Talk*, Selden lauds Ovid's *Fasti* for
its extraordinary fusion of religious law and poetry, only to lament the
erosion of this coupling by ravenous time.

Yet Selden suspected the power of this fusion for granting too much
credence to the zeal or honesty of its source; too much importance to
the manipulation of audience passions; and too much stock in the
impressive obscurity of its language. He was too much the critic fully to
give himself to the Bard. At best, modern poetry recreated the public
forum in which ancient Bards were corrected by Druid judges in the
groves of Britain. At worst, Selden's collaboration with the normative
poets of his day edged towards a divorce between the priests and their
critics, between the poet and the lawyer – with the Bards suspected of
the very parasitism that Jonson dreaded in panegyric poetry. With common law itself accused of wilful, self-interested, and sacerdotal obscurity
in their time, however, Selden and Jonson could not rely on any simple
dichotomies as they sought to fashion a normative discourse as rigorous,
rational, and learned as it was sacred, compelling, and uplifting.

—— 5 ——

In his collection of records from British and English history, the *Analecton Anglo-Britannicon* (dedicated to Sir Robert Cotton in 1607; published
in 1615), Selden confronts head-on the legacy of the sometimes
inspired, sometimes parasitical Bard. Regarding the poets of ancient
Gaul and Britain, he cites the praise of Ammianus Marcellinus – they
'sang to the sweet strains of the lyre of valorous deeds of famous men
composed in heroic verse' – and of Lucan:

> You too, ye bards, whom sacred raptures fire
> To chant your heroes to your country's lyre,
> Who consecrate in your immortal strain
> Brave patriot souls in righteous battle slain,
> Securely now the tuneful task renew,
> And noblest themes in deathless songs pursue.[36]

Selden also invokes Diodorus Siculus, who emphasizes the praise and
blame meted out by these lyric poets as well as the British obedience to
their civilizing sway over wild passions among armies. According to

Diodorus, the Bards possess the magical power to discipline passion with wisdom.[37]

In the *Analecton*, however, the civilizing Bards give way to Knights and Druids as the normative leaders of the British. In keeping with this displacement of the poets, Selden's prefatory division of the audience into candid understanders and inept calumniators relies on optical metaphors rather than on oracular warrant: the Druids, after all, conjoin expertise in natural philosophy with their wisdom in matters of law and religion. Worse still for the Bards, the collector stresses the complete omission of their hero Brutus in the ancient records, invoking those classical authorities who disapprove of bardic means of and intent in compelling belief. In Aelian, for instance, a painter has captured poets' swallowing the vomit spewed from Homer; and what these poets spew, in turn, as theogonies and epics, is simply incredible. As one source, quoted also by Camden, states, 'These Poets love to overreach, / Beleve them not, when so they teach.'[38] It is true, Selden concedes, that Bards teach ethics, natural philosophy, and religion by means of their myths. It is equally true, as the historian Tritemius explains, that many nations trace their customs back to Troy. But the complete omission of Brute from classical records leads Selden to conclude, with Possidonius in Athenaeus's *Deipnosophists*, that the British Bards were degenerate parasites who constructed and sweetened custom as their patrons saw fit (*Analecton*, preface, 865).

The passage from which Selden takes his notion of the parasitical Bard traces the corruption to royal and aristocratic patronage: '"The Celts [Possidonius argues], even when they go to war, carry round with them living-companions whom they call parasites. These persons recite their praises before men when they are gathered in large companies as well as before any individual who listens to them in private. And their entertainments are furnished by the so-called Bards; these are poets, as it happens, who recite praises in song."'[39] Nothing was more dreaded by the Jonsonian panegyrist than the trap of parasitism that an aristocratic patronage system opened for him. No wonder that Jonson prefaces so many of his praise poems with rules on how not to praise dishonestly; for there is a fine line between telling a patron what he ought to be and flattering a patron as what he wishes to be.

The history of the poetic parasite is not so simple. Crucially, Athenaeus's dialogue on parasites also recalls a time when their social and ritual functions were sacred and integral to the values of a community. Even if Selden's preface to the *Analecton* elides this claim, his own interest in its treatment of the parasite had a clear contemporary relevance. For the dialogue's celebration of a special dignitary at priestly sacrifices and sacred feasts – of a singer who came 'from men of mixed descent, and their children, according to ancestral custom' – these criteria suit the Jonsonian poet and the Saliarian priest quite well. By law and custom, parasites had been honoured officials in state religious ceremonies and in the feasts that concluded them; but over time, the laureate title of honour 'shifted its meaning to apply to a disreputable thing,' to a hanger-on ever willing to gratify his patron in service to his own belly rather than to the corroboration of 'ancestral custom.'[40] In the past, the honour of attendance at rituals and festivals had been thrust on the modest parasite; over time, it happened that parasites could not be thrust from the board.

The dialogue of Athenaeus served as Selden's *locus classicus* for the early Jacobean disgust over how a poetry once presumed to be reverential and normative had degenerated into fulfilling the basest human desires. Sometimes Selden follows Drayton in trying to recover the Bard's estimation. In the preface to the *Analecton*, however, Selden implies that even when they are earnest, the labours of such Bards are impressively ridiculous, but he formulates his critique of shameless poetry in such a way as to redeem a standard of *nomos* that has no restricted basis in merely positive law. Sometimes that standard is nature – as it is when Selden introduces the work of Galen as his gauge. In his argument that Geoffrey of Monmouth brazenly lies about the past, however, that standard is still historical poetry: indeed, the collector allows that historical fictions are not improper provided that they are poetic – for instance, Virgil's verses on the building of Carthage. In other words, one learns more from the history in poetry than one does from those dreamy fictions in history; but the nature and value of what one learns – whether it is narrowly evidentiary or more generally normative – is less clear as Selden turns from his preface to the historical collection itself.

The *Analecton* reveals a young Selden attempting to work out how his historical research understands the relationship between the factual 'was' and the didactic 'ought': he is indebted to the antiquarian conviction that a commitment to fact must supersede any longing for idealism; but he is also involved in the poetic endeavour of inventing golden worlds above the brazen. Selden's shift in emphasis from poetics to positive law, especially as that shift is played out in the 1620s, is motivated by his hope that somehow what 'ought' to be can be derived from what 'has been.' Thus in *Mare Clausum*, he posits that 'as the point of *Law* hath many things mingled with it, which manifestly arise from matter of *Fact*; so this of *Fact* comprehend's [*sic*] not a few which relate unto that of *Law*' (1–2). In turn, Selden's work on natural law (including his discussion of it in the *Mare*) and his final Judaic phase represent attempts to reinvest positive law with a superhuman authority to which the always humanly invented poem, no matter how excellent or virtuous, can scarcely lay claim.

For the most part, Selden accentuates the value of his collection in its marshalling of the providential and moral wisdom to be gained from the orbits of sacred and civil government in the history of his native isle. Early on, he argues that all the great changes in that history have been heralded by physical and celestial omens sent from God. Often addressing the reader with the lesson to be learned from such phenomena, Selden seeks also to silence the blasphemous assaults on God's power made by philosophers who subordinate divine agency to immediate, mundane, or secondary causes. Bringing his history of omens up through current times, he includes the comet presaging the death of Elizabeth I, as well as the 1605 fireball that forecast the divine rescue of England's leadership over true religion from the treachery of the Powder Plot. Adducing numerological and divinatory warrants, Selden praises the Homeric image of the golden chain and Manilius's fatalistic astrology for defending the strange ways in which natural omens establish the horizons of human expectation. In this providential history, Selden's bardic historian edges closer towards the prophecy, magic, and divination of the Druid (*Analecton*, col. 867), even as he labours to continue fulfilling the criteria of the empirical and sceptical critic.

Providential history and Stoic fatalism themselves epitomize a second key value in the *Analecton*, the assets of situating early Anglo-British history within the framework of biblical, 'Syrian,' and Greco-Roman chronology. Selden's interest in the writings of the Chaldaic priest Berosus, in Berosus's fabricated alter ego, and in the Egyptian historian Manethius generates two hard-to-reconcile conclusions. For one, England's revolutions unfold as epicycles in the larger circuits of providential history, which include the divine creation, Noah's flood, and the dispersion of Noah's children. As the macrocosm extends outward from a Noachian centre, Selden argues for cross-fertilization between the large and little (human) worlds, maintaining that Josephus and other Judaic sources might help with conjectures about Britain's first inhabitants. After all, Camden himself has conjectured that the Gomerians settled in Gaul and Britain. Selden's second conclusion is that the critical historian

must debunk fraudulent attempts to fill the gap of 2000 years leading up
to recorded history, such as those one finds in the lineage devised by
Pseudo-Berosius. One needs a mediator between Britain, Rome, and the
Syrian-biblical world, but Pseudo-Berosius's mediations are as false as his
religion is idolatrous. Selden's search for the best normative and sacred
discourse proves nothing less than the pursuit of a measurable paradise
– a world in which illumination and law come together in support, not
at the expense, of one another (cols 868–71).

Selden's efforts to gauge what bardic Britain has gained and lost in its
cross-fertilization with other cultures or peoples redouble when he
turns in the *Analecton* to the Roman invasion of Britain. Prior to this
point in his narrative, he has rehearsed the stories of Brutus, Locrine,
Lear, Gorboduc, and all the other early British royalty who teach vital
lessons about obedience, unified rule, the evils of civil war, the remedial
power of law, and the emergence of true religion. Clearly Selden picks
and chooses from his sources so as to accentuate the intertwining and
equally potent legacies of law and true religion in the history of Britain.

Once he moves from the early Britain so beloved by Drayton to the
more reliably evidential Roman invasion, however, Selden's commitment to rigorous method joins forces with his complex understanding
of the cultural mixture in British history, with the result that his fashioning of the values that benefit religious society is less clear-cut. On the
one hand, Roman self-aggrandizement and parasitism are liable to his
attack, for instance, as they appear in the courtly historian Velleius,
whose lies include the claim that Caesar twice penetrated Britain. On
the other, the civility of Rome is in no small measure responsible for the
normative poetics and historiography taught by Camden, practised by
men like Jonson, and held by such learned men to enshrine and transmit the most essential virtues of a pious British society. Accordingly, the
record of British resistance to Roman invasion is treated with an uneven
hand in the *Analecton*. Selden includes but greatly condenses and neu-
tralizes Geoffrey of Monmouth's highly patriotic account of King Cas-
sivellanus's resistance to Rome, then the collector introduces a more
recent Roman invasion, the Gunpowder Plot of 1605. The Plot, with its
scheme of a combined assault on the institutions of British governance
and the survival of the Protestant religion under the watch of that government, provokes Selden out of his more indifferent historian's persona into an immediate address to and applause for his readers, who
have manifested the faith of their pious ancestors. In 1605 the mores of
ancient British government and religion are thriving under the gracious

providence of God: 'Quibus & tuum, lector, numen habeamus placa-
tum, dum paululum a serie temporum digressi (cum Romanorum iam
& quasi publica fide editorum testimonia proxime suppeditentur)
administrationis Britannicae reipublicae speciem circa Caesaris adven-
tum, dynastarum item philosophorumque in eadem mores exinde sub-
nectamus [with which (sacrifices), reader, we have found favour with
your God when, a very short time ago, when so recently public testimonies were offered up in abundance, indeed testimonies of faith for our
command over the Romans, we secured our mores under the same sort
affiliated with the British government, dynasty, and philosophy at the
time of Caesar's invasion]' (col. 877). If Selden at times conveys the
impression that his accumulative method is shorn of values, at other
times he aggressively solicits the reader to be mindful that history is a
value-laden rite over which a priestly poet officiates in a formulaic
medium for expected truths.

In the *Analecton*, Selden's two main normative purviews – law and religion – resoundingly converge in the records of how early English Christians attempted to standardize the doctrine and practices of their
church. Their first Christian king, Lucius, cared about nothing more,
we are told, than nurturing his Christian commonwealth, and he
wanted to institute suitable laws so that its piety might flourish. In a letter to the Pope, Lucius seeks the guidance and mandate of Roman law –
indeed he lives in the age of Marcus Aurelius and Ulpian – but the Pope
(according to John Foxe) reminds the king that Roman law should matter far less to the English Christians than God's law. Selden emphasizes
that as Christ's vicar, the godly ruler has, as his greatest burden, the
fusion of holiness and civility in the administration of law, and Lucius
supplements his legal lessons with accomplishments in God's honour,
working for British freedom, resisting idolatry, and propagating the true
religion (cols 895–8). Before too many chapters have passed, Selden is
looking to Gildas and Bede, and to Constantine as well, for evidence
that the early history of Britain features inventive and earnest attempts
to integrate the demands of civil justice with the warrants of God's holy
spirit. The fashioning of this integrity persists throughout the Anglo-
Saxon and Norman sections of the collection as well as the British and
Roman.

From the debilitating vices of Vortigern to the Norman preservation
of English laws, Selden authenticates the sanctity and civility of norms
by means of a nitty-gritty study of documentary rolls and records. Those
norms also give purpose and direction to the records. Turning to Ger-

ald of Wales rather than to Bede and Geoffrey of Monmouth for his
account of the Pelagian heresy in Wales, Selden opts to underscore the
orthodox habits of worship rather than the prominence of miracles,
focusing on customs of tithes, confirmation, charity, penance, church
building, worship, and sanctuary (cols 907–8). In keeping with his
emphasis on their lawful piety, Selden does not quote Gerald's conclusion that the Welsh perform all things, whether pious or evil, in
extremes. With Bede and Gildas, Selden disapproves of the British failure to instruct the pagan Angles in the true faith – that is, the British
willingness to leave the Germans to their own idolatrous myths performed in ancient *carminae*. But he lays greater stress on that apostle to
the English, Augustine; on the providential marriage between the pagan
Ethelbert and the Christian Bertha; on the auxiliary monks who accompanied Augustine; and most of all on Augustine's assiduous efforts to
secure the orthodoxy of English religion as measured by the square of
canon law. Consulting Pope Gregory on matters of church discipline,
Selden's Augustine receives instructions on tithing, monasticism, and
incest laws (cols 909–13).

Skipping other documentary matters such as the variations in masses
or the punishment of thieves, Selden above all wants his readers to
appreciate the industry and piety with which Augustine, Ethelbert, and
other leaders of the English Christian world undertook the inculcation
and invention of orthodoxy without ignoring or violating the immediate
experience and powerful spirit of Christian devotion. Readers are
induced to understand, moreover, that seekers after the best fusion of
law and spirit must vex many versions, records, and caricatures of the
truth before that fusion is found.

Concurrently with his treatment of the history of English Christianity,
Selden traces the development of the laws securing English liberties
through the records of the Anglo-Saxon heptarchy. Thus, Bede's complaints against idolatry appear cheek by jowl with the institutions assuring the dispersion of political authority – another way in which Selden
strikes his keynote of the fusion between zealous religion and civil justice. In learning about the laws of Ina or the exemption of the church
from Danegelt, readers are also advised to trust in prayers more than in
arms. The ratification of agreements proves to have sacred formulae
and gestures; kings are faced with organizing law, duty, and religion in
rapacious times; modes of punishment are estimated for their understanding of sin; kings dilate the greatness of church discipline and secular law alike; miracles confirm the legal views of English clerics, while

the English law sages invent juries and other legal institutions. King Canute takes a pilgrimage to Rome during which he beseeches pope and emperor for help with safeguarding church discipline and with regulating the English people more equitably.

Throughout his collections, Selden foregrounds the evidence epitomized in the Danish Canute's resolve to preserve and enforce English customs and laws, especially those formulae regarding tithes, festivals, priests, and calendars that adhere 'ad certam aliquam religionis normam [to some certain norm of religion]' (col. 938). As Selden likes to remind the reader, the decrees of Canute were attributed later to King Edward, not because the latter established them, but because he observed them. As it intertwines the sacred and civil realms of experience, Selden's history depends less and less on what the Bards have made and more on the artifices owed to lawyers.

Normative poetry does not vanish altogether from the *Analecton*. Among his records about the laws concerning rape and adultery, Selden invokes Juvenal's second satire condemning hypocritical and debauched censors, rulers, and lawmakers who so often violate the virtuous rules that they tout, and such a Roman satirical vein is very much part of Selden's own roughshod style (col. 940). Indeed, satire is the discursive version of that public shame that Selden takes note of in Plutarch's question about those women made to 'ride the donkey' (col. 940). As Selden will continue to argue to the end of his life, the making of law cannot replace shame and its poetic trumpets, not least because the lawmakers themselves commit some of the worst transgressions. Poets help to decide when a set of behaviours – cross-dressing for instance – abets the moral influence of the theatre or the decadence of the audience. Whereas Selden's critical historian is keen on collecting what he would consider documents, the materials of his collection persist in the promulgation of praise and blame: the Roman poet Claudian is summoned to laud the preservation and adaptation of sacred law amid the vicissitudes of history; and satirists are invoked to denounce the uglier side of conquest, with fields destroyed, temples razed, and morals lost along with the language of poets and lawyers alike.

For Selden, the lawyer-poet might have the best possible normative discourse for the welfare of contemporary religious society. It is also possible, however, that such a figure struck the satirists of Selden's day as ridiculous (if woefully common). The marriage between legal historian and poets was no simple matter for Selden, not merely because the former is supposed to tell the story of the past truthfully, while the latter

is licensed to make that story up. Far from it, Selden increasingly understood in the first quarter of the century that if some legal arbiters
tended towards hypocrisy and corruption, others, the legal sages of the
society, had an impressive ability to preserve the virtues and values of
the past when the works of the Bards have perished or found discredit.
In the *Analecton*, law already rivals poetry in leading the rescue of essential native values from the vicissitudes and violence of time. For instance,
the English-Danish alliance bolstered law just prior to the Norman conquest; and even as the English became 'gallicized,' the Normans
retained English laws about the church, tithes, Danegeld, captives, and
ordeals by fire and water. With civil and church officials cooperating,
the Normans found it unnecessary to strip away most English customs
and laws; in mixing the old with the new, they made it possible that, as
Selden wittily remarks, 'omniaque ... Normanniam tamen & Normam
redolerent [all matters smelled of Norman and norm]' (col. 949).
When next Selden uses the term 'redoluerunt,' the Normans stand
alone in power, having internalized the indigenous norms on which
Selden's own religious society depends (col. 954).

   In the closing pages of the *Analecton*, Selden summarizes the purpose
of his collection: to build columns in commemoration and explication
of the sacred norms of the past (col. 954). In this arbitrator and maker of fame, Drayton found a kindred spirit, yet in no small measure he
ended up in discourse with a stranger. When in his final chapter Selden
assembles the beliefs of Saxon religion alongside with the formulae of
judicial ordeals and duels, he anticipates what in the second and third
decades of the century he will consider poetry's main rival as the normative guarantor of English religious society, namely, the institutions of
positive law in the common-law courts and in parliament. In both Jonsonian poetry and English positive law, aristocrats are problematic elements, potentially providing moral and spiritual leadership for their
lesser contemporaries yet often encouraging the parasitic, wilful, and
violent elements in their world. Nonetheless, the legalist formulation of
procedures for ordeals and duels, an enterprise to which Selden devotes
a separate tract, serves finally to spotlight the folly of basing judicial process on theogonic poets such as Hesiod, Homer, Orpheus, Musaeus, or
Pindar, whose first line in Olympic ode 1 – 'Best is water' – might be
blamed for the madness of aquatic ordeals (cols 957–60). The Bards
might rhapsodize over the values of religious society so as to provoke a
visceral response and collective memory in their audience, but legal
sages have a better chance of restraining those responses and rectifying

those memories – of binding religious society more firmly together – if the nerves get out of hand and memory gives way to self-interested invention.

Even as he collaborates with the poets, Selden deems rash and illusory a full and extra-legal commitment to the power of compelling belief that he finds claimed for Hebraic allegorists and British Bards as well as Pythagoreans and Druids. In this merger between prophetic poets and hierophantic magicians, Selden recognizes that in natural law as in poetry, the benefits of a numinous warrant and of an awesome medium produce equally obvious liabilities in the provocation of violent passions, in the foisting of superstition and lies on the unsuspecting, and in the greedy or arrogant motives into which so many Bards and magi have lapsed. The *Analecton* suggests, then, that the critical historian and legal sage must be prepared to reconstitute the normative ruins of the past without the afflatus of divinity, the sweetness and power of music, the superhuman prowess of magic or prophecy, or even the protection of patronage. It is less clear whether the contractual bindings and evidentiary concretion of common law and parliaments can make up for what is lost when religious society can no longer rely on rhapsody and divination. Thus, he continues to enlist the poets.

—— 6 ——

Even as he collaborated with the poets in the first decades of the century, Selden delved deeply, inventively, and boldly into the classical and biblical history of normative artistry. With a scholarly scope larger than the legacies of contemporary verse, that is, he pursued major research projects that explored the diverse media – poetic, musical, visual, and narrative – in which human fictions reflect, shape, and deform the values of the religious societies in which they operate. In two works especially, one on the Arundel marbles (*Marmora Arundelliana*, 1628), the other on the Syrian gods (*De Dis Syris*, written 1605; 1st ed. 1617; 2nd rev. ed., 1629), Selden explores the ancient ways in which norms were transformed into beautiful, enticing, and mythical monuments, for better or worse.

In the late 1620s, when Jonson was reconstructing the Pindaric ode as a surrogate ritual that might consolidate the expected truths for good, happy, and pious aristocrats at the helm of British society, Selden was attempting to piece together the carvings on those ancient marble fragments in the earl of Arundel's garden – indeed, with no small help from

Pindar and his scholiasts. Selden's work on the marbles does offer respite from his entanglement in the fervidly controversial and politically dangerous parliamentary debates over the principles of English religion, liberty, and property. Within his intricate scholarship on the marmoreal inscriptions, Selden comes upon and focuses on a concept according to which human law might recover some dignity, beauty, constancy, and truth: the complex notion of *nomos*. At its most capacious, *nomos* comprises the naturalness of harmony; the changing yet progressive history of human music in which actual instruments, strings, chords, and sounds are developed; and the human laws ensuring the justice, piety, and moral living of a society. In 1629 Selden turns his archeological focus to the exploration of an ideal in which the human laws (his trade in the 1620s), a transcendent natural law (to which he is about to turn in the 1630s), and the music and poetry of human artistry might be wonderfully fused.

So, too, in his Pindaric ode, Jonson imagines that normative poetry, natural law, musical proportion, and the specific social arrangement of the English aristocracy fuse (if only rarely) in one heroic embodiment. In some measure, the marmoreal and poetic acts of classical recovery are similar: Jonson conceives his poetic imitation as the careful placement of verbal stones in a wall celebrating a rational and dutiful piety, while Selden's scholarship on the marbles prompts his scholarly labours to resurrect the meanings of a principle at the very crux of normative art in the classical period, the *nomos* of law, literature, history, religion, and music. Like Jonson, Selden seeks in the fragments of the past the formulae of beautiful artistry that might buttress the expected truths of a society against the ravages of time. Both men are especially eager to explore the intersections between natural law and poetic artifice, but more than Jonson, who was an eager student of Selden's scholarship on the Syrian gods as well as titles, Selden is attuned to the odds against the satisfactory recovery of ancient ways; holds in his very hands the physical reminders of those ravages; and is prepared to supplant imaginary fictions from the centre of authority in religious society if their enticements erode the apparatus of contracts, distort the godly warrant behind contracts, or seduce the most well-meaning subjects into moral and social transgression. For Jonson, normative poetry and music can and must be reformed; for Selden, they can be severely demoted among a society's leading arbiters of value, even if they can never be nullified.

According to the *Oxford Classical Dictionary* (*OCD*), there were, in fact, three senses of the word *nomos* in ancient Greece.[41] Setting aside its use as 'the Greek term for the administrative districts of ancient Egypt,' the word pointed to two areas of Greek culture in which Selden is interested (*OCD*, 1047). It could refer to 'law' as against '*physis*,' or nature, but its more complicated sense involved the 'seven canonical types [of song] used either with *kithara* (lyre) ... or with *aulos* (pipe),' some of which were performed with vocal accompaniment (*OCD*, 1047). From very early in Greek history, the musical *nomoi* were implicated in and supportive of religious ritual, their rhythms and harmonies of a simple nature. Thus, changes in Greek music reflected either the development of the connection between religion and song or the weakening of that connection. Choral music, for instance, that 'indissoluble blend of poetry, melody, accompaniment and, [*sic*] dance' came to embody for Pindar and Aristophanes 'the pinnacle of the ancient, simple, educative, and edifying style' (*OCD*, 1006), in keeping the conviction of ancient music theory 'that music affects moral character; that music of different styles and structures affects it differently; that appropriate musical training is essential to a citizen's education; and that music of the "wrong" sort is morally and socially pernicious' (*OCD*, 1006–7). But the moral theorists who supported the *nomoi* and choral music viewed the advent of experimentation, sophistication, and virtuosity as a collapse into precious insignificance at best and 'the individualistic, questioning modes of thought exemplified in the sophists and Socrates' (*OCD*, 1006). That individualism offered more than philosophical scepticism; it purveyed the spirit of change in society and politics and the break of music from ritual. For all its presumed role in the putative 'downfall of an integrated art closely allied to religion and civic tradition,' music accrued strong links to an even higher, cosmic order: 'since music is a paradigm of harmonious order,' theorists argued, it could be deployed 'to describe the ordering of the whole cosmos and of the soul in terms of similar numerical relations and principles,' not least in Pythagorean thought (*OCD*, 1006, 1007).

In his glosses on *nomos*, Selden conveys a fascination both with the traditions and with the changes in music history. At its best, music can unite natural law, human law, and poetic art; but changes in the *nomoi* suggest either the fleeting nature of any such unity, or the adaptability of societies – via criticism, scepticism, and innovation – to the very changing circumstances of human life. Indeed, the fragmentary status of the marbles is a constant reminder of how easily lost are culturally constructed vehicles of harmony and of how these constructs can be recovered only with the help of great learning, patience, and care. The

marbles are not unlike the sonnets and panegyrics of Selden's Elizabethan and early Stuart contemporaries: they tantalize with their offers
of a humanly constructed immortality, only to provoke sceptics into
remembering that any attempt to embody the values of a society in
heroic monuments is unlikely to survive the wars, conflicts, and vicissitudes of time. If early Stuart scholars have the fragmentary records of
ancient Greek musicology, they have even less – indeed nothing – of the
music itself. Selden's commentary on *nomos* and the marbles thus revisits the concerns of his commentary on Drayton's *Poly-Olbion*, which celebrated ancient monumental fictions alongside its valediction to the
Bards. Selden's study of the *nomoi* offers to remove the beautified norms
of a religious society from the realm of parasitism to which poetry is liable. Yet music is also quite elusive in its claims on normative efficacy: it is
not wholly natural, nor does it necessarily share the assets and liabilities
of legal or poetic language – not necessarily, since of course some
ancient music and its early modern imitations are poetic. The location
of music in the history of Greek society ensures that the *nomoi* cannot
boast a freedom from the political pressures and traps with which parasitic poetry is saddled. Nor can classical culture claim the intimacy with
the true God on which Selden's Judaic studies will soon insist, a problem that he has already begun to explore in *De Dis Syris*.

Of Asian provenance but Greek in language, the mutilated marbles
enticed the English scholars Robert Cotton, Patrick Young, Richard
James, and their friend Selden with the promises of inmost history. Just
as the ancients believed, these stones have preserved their records – a
treaty and a chronology among them – where codices would have perished. The Hellenistic chronology alone afforded historians an invaluable tool for synchronizing human affairs, without which the principle
formulae and patterns of history diminished in significance. Meanwhile, the treaty exemplified the value of formulae themselves, a notion
that was carried over to Selden's study of religious ritual and dramatic
genre. Both concerns – with chronology and with formulae – converged
in Selden's commentary on the ways in which ancient peoples calibrated or systematized their expectations (for instance, in calendars);
and on the ways in which they elevated, performed, and preserved the
laws, customs, and suppositions carried over from the past. The concern
with formulae led Selden to an extensive essay on the concept – part
musical, part legal – of *nomos*.

For the most part, Selden confines his study of *nomos* to musicology,
with a special focus on how early musicians changed the music itself by

developing new instruments or by adding strings to old ones. Yet Selden, whose own scholarship keeps coming back to those old music theorists the Pythagoreans, lived at a time when philosophers such as Kepler, Mersenne, and Selden's own doctor, Fludd, are dedicated to a new understanding and assertion of cosmic harmonies during a period of upheaval in natural philosophy. It is not surprising that his exploration of *nomos* moves beyond strings to a taxonomy of the concept that ranges from law and custom to musical modes. *Nomos* can signify all the laws pertaining to civil administration, but it also mediates between two levels of music: between the prescribed rules of sound, chord, voice, tautness, intervals, and tone; and specific songs performed in distinctive modes. Throughout his discussion, Selden persists in detailing how actual music was adapted to fixed standards as well as how it accommodated the various circumstances of the ancient auditors. That is, *nomos* is divisible into law, music theory, and performance mode; but it also names the Greek obsession with adapting art to law and with shaping human society and the human spirit by means of art (*Marmora*, 78). In the classical texts compiled by Selden, *nomos* is under investigation for the promise it might hold in abetting a society's harmonization of a rigorous law and an amenable, uplifting spirit.

This impulse to integrate law, theory, and performance is, as Selden suggests, at once epic and pastoral – the former whenever there is an emphasis on compelling action, the latter whenever there is an emphasis on preserving intact the expectations of happy men. That is, *nomos* touches at one end the muscular didacticism of Jonson's Pindaric ode, which risks an overdoing zeal; at the other end it edges towards Browne's and Drayton's Elysian Fields, in which the values making British society flourish are protected by fairy magic and myth so long as the reader never wakes from the dream. Law is left to find its proper place along the social version of the generic spectrum, exhorted to do battle on one side, sung into loving conciliation on the other. Indeed, Jonson himself has shifted his play writing in the direction of Shakespearean romance in these very years, as if he were trying to rediscover his normative register.

Citing Pindar on the heroic side of the spectrum, Selden quotes Athenaeus for an account of how, in Arcadia, boys from infancy 'are accustomed to sing according to laws, or *Nomos*, those singular hymns and paeans by which the custom of their country might be preserved; they celebrated the gods and heroes of their people' (quoted in *Marmora*, 78, along with the Latin version: 'Cantare solent iuxta leges, seu Nomos, hymnos & paeanas quibus singuli, vt mos patrius obtinet, Gentis suae heroas & Deos celebrant'). Athenaeus adds that rhythmical dancing accompanied the music, a link between pastoral songs and the choral odes of Pindar that for Jonson ritualized the consent of the learned and the good in a turn, counter-turn, and stand. Just so, Selden includes Plutarch's view that the ancient *nomos* was composed from heroic songs, a practice that Pindar himself adapted (*Marmora*, 78).

If the poetic and musical modes of law make strange bedfellows of the shepherd and the hero, it is equally the case that in Selden's commentary, *nomos* insists on a differentiation of music into modes capable of quite diversely shaping the putatively sacred ends of a society. In this regard, he purveys a more analytical or precise understanding of poetics, citing treatises from Aristotle to Julius Caesar Scaliger. For instance, when Selden draws the distinction between *nomoi* and other choral songs, he notes that in the *Problems*, Aristotle says that the *nomoi* are more diverse and flexible than the others, and so are better able to mold a moral character. Whereas Selden does not believe the notion that *nomoi* were limited to reverence for Apollo, he credits Aristotle's argument that before people could write, they sang their laws in order to remember them. They entrusted law to music as surely as Drayton's oral tradition entrusted law to Bards – or perhaps they did so more surely, if the cosmic embodiment of harmony were always naturally present as a guarantee. After all, the music of the spheres might be hard to hear, harder still to imitate, but it surely could not lie, wear out, or be seduced by patronage. Other Greeks, Selden adds, record the ancient custom of singing laws, and that notion would persist, for instance, in Martianus Capellus's willingness to take it for granted that many of the Greek cities recited laws and decrees accompanied by the lyre.

When Selden turns to gloss the use of the term *nomos* on the marble under study, he rules out the sense of legal singing that he has just recovered; and he doubts a usage indicating the laws of music. As is the modern custom, he notes, musicians proceed with little attention to the authority of music theory. Probably, he concludes, the marmoreal *nomos* refers to music defined as a specific style of performance, perhaps as a musical mode. That is, the term is descriptive, not prescriptive, and is more than likely directed towards those Phrygian songs dedicated to Cybele, the mother of the deities. The point of such a song, Athenaeus tells us, was to establish a 'specific character or feeling' appropriate to honouring the goddess 'amid the flutes beside the mixing-bowls of the Greeks.'[42] In this instance, then, *nomos* defines the coherence of a social order, not by preserving its laws, still less by theorizing its harmonies, but by evoking a collective frenzy within the decorum of religious ritual, the powerful and irrational performance of belief. In this context, Selden deems it apt to invoke the Bards as just such poet-singers who were skilled in the art of compelling belief and its regulated outpouring.

In another note on the Arundel marbles, Selden elaborates on the Phrygian *nomoi*, sung as they were to Bacchus and Pan as well as to Cybele and generally characterized as 'religious' by Apuleius. As Strabo explains, the Phrygian *nomoi* were performed in religious communities – among the Curetes, for example – especially those prone to inspired Bacchanalian frenzy, terrific in their dances, and feverish in their sacred rites. This *nomos* is a far cry from that understood as a philosophy of music or as a code of law in music. In these *nomoi* consecrated to deities, Selden argues, one finds an amazing and often puerile harvest of theogonies, portents, fables, frauds, amours, and exotica, but when it comes to societies giving vent to the power of custom, he concludes that the *nomos* could not be otherwise.[43] So it is (Selden advises) that we ought to revise our understanding of *nomos* as it is presented in a famously tricky passage in Aristotle's *Metaphysics*, the italicized part of which Selden quotes: 'The effect of a lecture depends upon the habits of the listener; because we expect the language to which we are accustomed, and anything beyond this seems not to be on the same level, but somewhat strange and unintelligible on account of its unfamiliarity; for it is the familiar that is intelligible. The *powerful effect of familiarity is clearly shown by the Laws* [*nomoi*], *in which the fanciful and puerile survivals prevail, through force of habit, against our recognition of them.*'[44] Thus understood, *nomos* embodies the sheer power of habit or custom over and above whatever else is critically accurate or strictly lawful. Might there be some way to retain the power of expectation and familiarity yet remain in tandem with reformative law, critical analysis, and the more dispassionate measures of a socially based religion? Might frenzy and philology marry? For Selden, *nomos* affords one last imperfect, exploratory collaboration with Drayton and the normative poets of his time.

Aristotle concludes that students must be trained in various argumentative modes and be alerted especially to the difference between precise and poetic methods. They must come to understand the dynamics of expectation, whether incited to a frenzy by musical poetry or restrained in its passions by law. Expectation can be rectified, though it remains unclear whether the modified habits of thought will retain something of their force. Selden applies the Aristotelian passage to those many histor-

ical records that have habitually encased English custom and law in
fables. At any time, he notes, there are inept reporters of law, though
ineptitude includes the craft of lawyers and the inaccuracy of scholars as
well as the puerile fables of the poets. One need not look to music for
distortions of law; and silly fables at least have the capacity to unify society even when they serve personal interests. If Jonson's Pindaric ode celebrates a strenuous virtue ultimately made manifest in 'holy rage,'
Selden's marbles integrate ancient athletic contests with the religious
mysteries that made up a key component of those displays of heroism.
At its best, *nomos* reconciles musical harmony, religious passion, duty,
and law in one work of art.

Again and again, Selden returns in his notes on the marbles to a history of music and to an analysis of *nomos*. Terpander is especially
famous, he tells us, for having added poetry to music and then for having rewritten Spartan laws in metrical verses. Selden insists that among
his many sources, the term *nomos* virtually never means simply 'civil law.'
Among the very early Hebrews and Greeks, civil laws were sung – and
the mention of the Jews indicates in two ways Selden's movement
towards natural law as a replacement for normative poetry. For one,
they help to establish that musical law was practised widely; for another,
they might well have a special access to natural law. Or even if Selden
insists on grounding *nomos* in some positive code of law, the Jews might
well have had a code that evades the problems plaguing the normative
efficacy of English law.

Already in the work on the marbles, Selden is veering in the direction
of Judaism: he studies the lunar calendar of the Hebrews and its demise
in Greece; his preface is devoted to Joseph Scaliger's exhortation that
the scholar who sojourns in Palestine will gain access to inmost history;
and the final section of his study concerns fragmentary stones found in
Aldersgate and inscribed with the Hebrew of medieval Jews living in
London, the stones no doubt transferred from a synagogue to the gate.
In his discussion of the these Jewish sepulchral stones, Selden offers
something of a survey of Jewish life and law in medieval London, including data on the laws regarding Jewish goods, loans, mortgages, usury,
and worship. Moreover, Selden writes plaintively of the exile of Jews
from England, a tragedy that he believes too many English citizens have
wholly forgotten. Unlike his earlier disparagement of rabbinical fictions
or of Jewish infanticide, Selden is redefining his classical world as princi-
pally the biblical world and refashioning his understanding of poetic
laws as divinely dispensed natural laws.[45] As Josephus reminds him, the

ancient Jews grasped the value of inscribing their legal wisdom on stone. Perhaps the Jews hold the key to a normative discourse at once natural, positive, godly, and artificial – one neither fabulous nor critical, neither puerile nor pedantic, neither rigid nor chaotic, at once supremely true, morally powerful, and physically resistant to the ravages of time, fire, and flood.

Selden's discussions of divination in his commentary on the marbles also suggest potential problems with basing the measure of social expectations on nature. Looking at the ways in which people have predicted the future from their understanding of natural patterns, he includes a long, sometimes ironic and jocular treatment of omens, magic, and astrology. He examines the supposed alliance between daimons and fortune, along with practices such as casting lots and reading horoscopes. Recognizing that one set of his readers will have a vain devotion to divination and astrology, Selden directs his efforts to another group, to those who soberly and respectfully investigate ancient philosophies and the ruined vestiges of the arts. Accommodating even these sharper readers with an astrological chart, he acknowledges how easily ancient formulae of measuring, stabilizing, and representing expectations can be distorted, especially in the act of earnest imitation. Natural law will need a critical measure. Yet the offer of a chart itself registers Selden's awareness that natural law will also need some impressive vehicle of transmission; and that human invention must manage to communicate the norms that critical judgment can rectify only by a severely limited, if learned, standard.

——— 7 ———

For Selden, the poesy of sacred norms can entice societies back towards paradise, to a golden age in which human beings had no fears that their mores might be lost or contaminated in transmission. Such an enticement itself can prove illusory, irresponsible, and vicious, though it might also afford the members of a community with an unparalleled coherence in, desire for, and access to their inmost beliefs. Yet a society's recourse to and development of a mythopoetics, with the graphic and literary arts that unfold its creeds and mores, can also start or register its hapless fall into the brazen world, even in the efforts of those societies to adapt an ancestral faith to contemporary sensibilities and local customs. *De Dis Syris* offers an intensive study of the distortions of religious truth into idolatrous myth, deformations that occur in the process of

earnestly imitating a divinely true normative poetics. For, as an anticipation of his later treatment of religious arts in the full-scale Judaic phase
of his scholarship, Selden is neither so harsh on the idols of history as a
fervent iconoclast would be, nor so forgiving of the common impulse to
make graven images as seventeenth-century students of comparative
religion – say, Selden's friend Edward Herbert – tend to become. For
Selden, the logics and vehicles according to which societies represent
their most cherished presuppositions and expectations are at once
understandable – indeed, they are shared – and so grotesque as to elicit
censorship on the part of their seventeenth-century surveyor.

As Selden's first work to capture the attention and respect of the European community of scholars, *De Dis Syris* is a history of those biblical idols
with which the Protestant poets of his day, not least Milton in *Paradise
Lost*, had to come to terms, for those idols encapsulated the error-prone
human impulse to engrave or to incarnate the divine. The work focuses
first on the idols in the Pentateuch, then on the idols of the prophets,
but always with its scope aimed at the spread of a myth or deity from a
loosely defined Syria to Africa, Greece, and Rome. There were, he
explains, two main types of ancient theology: the worship of created
things, especially planets; and the devotion to daemons. There is a clear
set of media for such worship, for instance, the columns, steles, hymns,
invocations, images, and pillars of antiquity. Even as Selden deems this
worship a symptom of hobbled reason and sinful human error, his attitude is often hard to pinpoint: he is neither the pagan sympathizer that
his friend Edward Herbert would prove, nor the brazen iconoclast; or
perhaps he is both at once. Whatever the attitude of his scholarly persona, the key dynamic that he traces is consistent if also complex: idolatry involves the imitation and distortion (*depravatio*) of true religion,
with the truth (a '*norma*') most clearly embodied in the religion of the
obedient Jews and early Christians.[46] Tertullian teaches that the devil is
at work in showing heretics how to divert, intercept, or embezzle sacred
worship, and Selden sends us to the church fathers for preparation
against such evil. But he also gives relatively sympathetic portraits of
those pagans whose idols derived from some sacred norm when they
sought to adapt, adorn, or console their own habits of imagination and
worship in relation to the beliefs and practices of God's chosen people.

Selden clarifies how the human circumstances of life, conflict, and
especially death inaugurate and strengthen daemonic worship in particular; for mythic daemons and heroes afforded the ancients with more
proximate surrogates for their deceased loved ones than did stars and

planets. It is endemic to the religious imagination that some transfer of honour be made from the dead to monuments (ceremonies, grave markers, and hymns), then onward to daemons, heroes, perhaps even stars. Selden need not mention that such transfers are part and parcel of contemporary poetics: for instance, when Jonson urges Lucius Cary to transfer his honour for Henry Morison to regard for the Pindaric ode, for Castor and Pollux, and for Gemini, a rededication officiated at by the priestly poet. For proponents and opponents have made this claim in their own ways, the former claiming that panegyric raises the living towards the level of a moral ideal, the latter responding that hero worship is always pagan, and often parasitical, idolatry. Selden himself indicts the greed, superstition, and vulgarity of priest craft, with its corrupt tendency to multiply effigies, fables, rites, and deities in order to manipulate passions and expectations for the sake of profit; but he expressly refuses to wallow in the most gruesome details of idolatry, remaining committed to tracing the commodious power of mythic imitation. Whether the deity is a thing or a force, Selden stresses that social needs generate mythic accommodations, or rather that mythic accommodation itself is a social need. In the last phase of later Judaic scholarship, after the debates over the value of artistry in worship had intensified during the Civil-War decade, the accommodating role of sacred art factored prominently into Selden's most comprehensive understanding of how a religious society might best be organized. In *De Dis Syris*, however, Selden's focus is more narrowly on the processes and permutations according to which the widespread impulse to create mythic stories and images deforms the very truths that those vehicles would and must serve, especially given the inevitable distance of cultures and times from the God of Adam and Eve. Like his letter to Jonson on the legitimacy of cross-dressing, Selden's work on the ancient idols is really an investigation of the cultural poetics implicit in theology. In the later Judaic phase, Selden's explorations of poetics are part of his investigation into the comprehensive means by which a religious society might regulate its practical obedience to God's commands.

Sometimes, according to *De Dis Syris*, the pagans come very close to a notion that Selden and his contemporaries consider religious truth, for instance, when their most learned ancients are shown to have constructed genderless deities. In this matter, the hierophants resisted the power of vulgar familiarity and secretly inserted a kernel of religious truth in their myths. These pagan priests neither divulged this truth in opposition to familiar custom nor completely dissolved their sacred mys-

teries in the power of that custom. Rather, they devised rites or hiero-
glyphs affording saner minds access to hidden truths, the most valuable
of which was the divine unity. Selden singles out the sphere as a symbol
for this unity, one used in his own efforts to articulate a holistic wisdom
and in Jonson's own Pindaric ode to an integrated virtue. Such symbolism must be neither elite nor vulgar; accordingly, the sphere is both a
simple and a mysterious symbol for monotheism. Even if its graphic displays are concealed in sacred chests and grottoes, the symbolism is most
unifying of a people if that people at least knows where the chest or
grotto is kept and that the priests are legitimate and holy (107–23).

Making use of a passage from the *Hermetica*, Selden accentuates the
point that at its best, mythology expresses the noble human endeavour
to be with and like God. So it is that human beings construct statues to
be animated by sense and spirit; and that learned men master divination, magic, spirits, astrology, music, and geometry. For such vatic and
pneumatological rites embody their greatest optimism that the mundane *nomos* can intersect with the sublime. Selden's fascination with
Roger Bacon, the Chaldeans, the Pythagoreans, and the Druids – all lawmakers, hierophants, and magi – writes in small his eagerness to take
the poetry of norms to a higher, more secure level than the monuments
of bardic tradition or of didactic history could ever achieve. For Selden,
however, this movement towards magic, theosophy, and cabbala has its
own potential fanaticism, ambiguity, corruption, and error. It can never
be as contractually concrete as positive law, and its basis in the will of the
true God is shaky at best. Natural law offers an alternative to monstrous
fable and an escape from the tyranny of mere custom, but it risks the
loss of representational power and vividness that derive from stories and
images. Like normative poetry, natural law can conceal a recklessly oti-
ose hankering for pleasure groves within its claim that its golden worlds
enshrine those foreconceits, Platonic ideas, or purified notions on
which the truth of human religious thought must always depend. In recognition of this potential for deception in the poetry and philosophy of
norms, Selden reverts to the third side of Sidney's triangle in the *Apology*, to a history in which the critical attention can be retrained on some
very familiar institutions, workaday procedures, and punishable obligations. In the 1620s Selden looks to the common legal and parliamentary
basis for English mores and religion. In the 1640s he has learned the liabilities of the workaday procedure as surely as he has worked through
the inadequacies of poetic and natural mythologies. Selden turns to the
Jews for a religious society with a capacity for poetry, nature, legal insti-

tutions, and (more emphatically than ever before in his normative work) concessions to the mysterious and even violent inner workings of God's will and spirit.

In *De Dis Syris*, however, Selden takes on a subject virtually assured of repelling his audience, and he rethinks those mythic idols for the ways in which they peculiarly frame and instil the sacred norms of a society confronting the complex circumstances of cultural practice, the elusive and various subjectivities of the worshippers, and a distance from the one true God of the Hebrew Bible that only grows with time. This review of the idols as they transmigrate from culture to culture is Selden's worst-case defence of a normative and sacred poetics; yet he shoulders the burden of reclaiming valid accommodation from superstitious debauchery when, for example, he makes a case for Baal as an allegory of the divine and ineffable Creator.

If his study of the idols confronts the potential monstrosity of myth-making, Selden is also keen to penetrate the veneer of normative poetry's best-case scenario, the impulse towards golden-age or paradisia-cal rhetoric in the imaginary literature of Elizabethan and early Stuart writers. On a number of occasions, he reassesses the legend that Britain was Elysium, the Fortunate Isles, the *locus amoenus,* or grove, in which shepherds, Druids, and Bards once joined forces in fashioning sacred laws and perfecting those chants in which the laws might be sweetly hymned. In his doubting mode, from the commentary on *Poly-Olbion* to his introduction to ten medieval histories anthologized in 1652, Selden is intent on getting at the motives of this thirst for a paradise for British devisers, pipers, and magi. He expends great energy parsing the rele-vant documents, whether papal dispensations, geographical accounts, alchemical allegories, etymological studies, emblem books, or 'Poeticall' and 'Mythique inventions' such as the 'fabulous relation' of Saturn's imprisonment in Britain.[47]

For the 1652 anthology Selden's approach to the myth of a British paradise is less complex, perhaps more nostalgic, but largely disengaged from the socially and morally formative potential of a specifically British pastoral fantasia. This farewell to a specifically British tradition of his-tory and poetics – for he has by no means bid farewell to poetry and fiction-making in Judaic culture – emerges when he investigates the basis for a panegyric in the *Imagines Historiarum* of the pious Randul-phus de Diceto, the upshot of which is that Britain is the most divinely blessed of all the islands (*Historiae Anglicanae,* xxx–xxxv). Greek and Roman explanations of why Britain might be Elysium take Selden into natural theosophy, especially theories of transmigration that have recurred throughout his work, sometimes in association with poetic fictions and sometimes on their own. As the blessed seat of the dead, Britain has been considered the cosmic recipient of souls travelling from other lands, especially (according to ancient and medieval Greek sources) of those heroic souls making their way as a strange cargo of fish on mercantile ships. Selden is not prepared to believe in the geographical or historical accuracy of this myth, of course, but even if he entertains the power of such fictions to incite the heroism that they decorate, he knows the dream of transmigrating fish to belong to the realm of fairies, maypoles, and 'merry old England,' with its myth of a rural life in which parish religion, natural cycles, social hierarchy, customary morals, communal fantasy, and licit pleasure amount to the simplicity and perpetuity of human happiness under the providence of a God at once classical, biblical, and English. Robert Herrick accumulates the shards of that fracturing monument in his *Hesperides* of 1648. In the early 1640s John Denham can write of a mythological landscape in the English countryside as still present though elusive to 'All but a quicke Poëticke sight'; but in his revision of 'Cooper's Hill' in the early 1650s, Denham reckons that 'This scene had some bold Greek, or Brittish Bard / Beheld of old, what stories had we heard, / Of Fairies, Satyrs, and the Nymphs their Dames, / Their feasts, their revels, & their amorous flames.' Protesting that such scenes are still, perhaps always 'the same,' Denham's praise for the lively vision of the Bard is rendered in the context of a valediction to a harmonious society that cohered in large part thanks to its communal narrative imagination.[48]

Inside Herrick's anthology of the 'littles' adding up to a mythic religious society, the reader finds Herrick's request that Selden award him the laureate crown; Selden's normative authority over English poesy is enshrined, therefore, among the golden apples in Herrick's collection. In 1652, however, Selden entertains a specifically British poetics of a mythic religious society only as part of his preface to medieval histories and so as part of the reader's apparatus for deciphering a world that has passed by in the mid-seventeenth century. Selden is not happy to jettison the poetic dreams of Elysium that might conjure powerful images of piety and virtue as part and parcel of one holistic cosmic and social vision. His melancholy for the loss of a British Elysium is captured in many places, for instance, in his quotation of Claudian's plaintive verses on the weeping spirits that flit on wings by furthermost Gaul (*Historiae Anglicanae*, xxxii). But as he explains to the readers of the anthology, his work on the volume's introduction is made possible by virtue of a break in his consuming Judaic studies. Clearly, Selden understands the latter studies as serious work on a religious society, while his preface to the anthology is more of a recreation and a palliative.

As Prescott argues, Selden's fascination with Elysium derives from his desire to rest from the labour of separating fact from fiction, to leave off worrying about 'anachronism and the ruins of time.' Such a paradise, she concludes, always verges for Selden on Rabelais's Macreon Island, which means that it 'is Selden's own paradise, ideal analogue of his own enterprise; it is where good antiquarianism goes when it dies, where history and Time might even be cured and story verified through decoding strange letters and interviewing the famous.' As Prescott says, Selden turns to the art of poetry as a way of hinting at 'longings and hesitations about his own project that are difficult to articulate directly.'[49] At the most public level, however, his 'project' runs contrary to poetry altogether: in his legal-cum-parliamentary career but also in many of his greatest writings, Selden looks to the documented and positive legacies of common law, parliamentary law, and social custom as the guarantors best securing the sacred norms of his society. When that public career lands him in (and cannot release him from) prison, Selden tends to ask for the works of Lucian and those of the largely unknown Byzantine historian Anna Comnena, both powerful representatives of the literature of blame and praise so valuable to Jonson, Drayton, Browne, and Camden.

Selden's release from prison in 1631 was made possible in large part by patrons in need of his services, an indication that lawyers, like poets, were involved in a social system of clients for hire. Like Jonson, Selden sometimes exerted his independence from such a system, for instance and ironically, in the prefatory matter to the *Titles of Honor.* As Selden's work on the histories of poetics, music, the marbles, and the idols tends to emphasize, normative poetics was often bound up in such a system, the benefits of which were the cultivation of heroic virtue, the liabilities of which were bloated aristocrats and degenerate parasites in their service. Selden himself was praised as an intellectual hero and demigod, for instance, in Herrick's panegyric. Jonson's 'Cary-Morison' ode epitomized the extent to which normative poetics sought the embodiment of its virtues and offices in heroic men and women. One of Selden's attractions to the English and Judaic codes of positive law was that, if approached rightly, they might subordinate the heroic individual to institutions, customs, covenants, and offices; less might be riding on the hero and on a discourse invested in inflating that hero's ego. Yet in jettisoning the hero, a moral leadership and mythic vitality might be squandered so that the legal contract proves less viscerally binding than the rhapsodic *nomos* of the Bard. Sidney reminds the readers of his *Apology* that a ballad can stir the sap of virtue with an immediacy that a barren document is unlikely ever to produce. Selden knows, however, that there must be ways of restricting that response to potent fictions if it threatens the social fabric that in its finest hour it might well save.

In directing his energies to the past, present, and future of English positive law, however, Selden confronts head-on the contemporary assignment of heroic leaders to human codes of law as well. Those heroes of the English law – perhaps the aristocrats in the House of Lords, whose titles he would trace through history, perhaps legal sages like Selden himself, men with little or no social distinction and in conflict with the nobler sort of law student at the Inns of Court – might well burden the law they represent with their imperfections and wilfulness, with their obnoxious penchant for violence and rivalry. Natural law also will yield from Selden its heroes: the Druids of antiquity or the astronomers of modern times, again with contentions between them and blemishes among them. In the everyday life of a religious society, heroes might offer an impressive and inspiring fiction, but what more? Might they lend wisdom and coherence to communities in peril of blindness and disintegration, or rather perpetuate an ethos of arrogance and sham honour at odds with both true religion and social unity? No small part of Selden's substantial scholarship in the history of honour involves his attempt to resituate the heroes of a religious society within its codes, laws, documents, and obligations, not outside in service only to will, desire, or impulse.

In this effort to restrain heroic charisma by means of lawful devices, Selden straddles the divide between the enterprises of law and poetry. Like the Jonson of the Pindaric ode celebrating the aristocratic Cary and Morison, Selden wrestles with the problem of how distantly the heroes of a religious society should reside from the restrictions on the rest of humanity, perhaps so far away as Castor and Pollux among the stars, perhaps so near as the judge at an assize, and perhaps somehow both at once. So, too, Jonson urges Cary to live on in embodiment of the dead Morison, who remains a distant ideal glimmer; so, too, Jonson idealizes the Sidney estate at Penshurst, yet satirizes the many members of the aristocracy whose degeneracy and competition are all too human. Selden's early involvement with the normative poets of his day shapes not only his understanding of how artificial beauty might lubricate the

reception of often morally severe laws, but also his disquisitions on especially perilous – because so powerful and unpredictable – social artifices,
those that have the greatest chance of invigorating or eviscerating the
coherence of a religious society. Sidney positions the poet in the service
to heroes; but Selden, like Jonson, opens up the possibility that the normative inventor himself is heroic in showing heroes what and how they
must serve.

In his commissioned introduction to the ten histories of 1652, Selden
summarizes and illustrates poetic principles from Geoffrey of Vinsauf's
Poetria Nova (*Historiae Anglicanae*, xxxix–xl). That is, to the end of his
life, though usually in the context of quite different models of normative discourse, Selden is committed to the basic assumption in Sidney's
Apology, that poetry possesses a superiority over straight philosophy and
accurate history as far as teaching human beings what they ought to do
in life. Yet Geoffrey of Vinsauf's very title reflects the ongoing need to
give poetry a measure, law, or rule. If poetry is to discipline, unite, and
uplift religious societies, its own most excessive fables must be excised
with the knife of criticism; be dispelled by the right reason of nature; be
exorcised with a Mosaic rod; or at least be framed by the context of
positive law. Once it is acknowledged that the arbitration of norms in a
society with deep commitments to spiritual zeal or divine inspiration
depends on human artifice rather than more immediately on divinity or
nature, then the work of the legal scholar as Selden understands it can
never be to dream of some cosmic fusion between our obligations to
and permissions from a transcendent authority. Instead, the legal sage
must struggle towards an imperfect, irregular coordination between the
devices that bind human action and all the powerful forces that move
the human spirit. Selden rarely moves far from the work of this coordination into dreams of a golden world without the traceable ligatures
and boundaries of documentary law.

chapter three

Legal Sages and Parliamentary Religion

In the 1620s Selden devoted a majority of his attention to the practice of that legal profession for which he was trained at the Inns of Court. At no time before had he, and at no time in the future would he, practise law to the extent that he did during that contentious decade in which James I grew impatient with his more zealous or 'puritan' critics, the Spanish Match blew up in the faces of King James and Prince Charles, polemical warfare exploded over the perceived rise of Arminian and crypto-papist sentiments in the Church of England, military failures against Spain and France dishonoured the English monarchy, a theorist in divine right (James) gave way to a relentless and tactless practitioner of its prerogative (Charles), and parliamentary sessions became the crucibles in which the ideals so integral to English society – proportionate government, property, legal procedure, and fervent Protestant faith – were enunciated, reassessed, and reasserted. In this decade, Selden practised law, not as a barrister in the courts of the land but as an unimpeachable standard to which other lawyers and members of Parliament could look for the right and historical understanding of their own responsibilities and privileges as guarantors of the mores and creeds of Protestant England.

In his scholarship as well as in his consultations with and membership in Parliament, Selden early on earned the reputation of an extraordinary legal sage. The problem with Selden's leadership of the common lawyers and parliamentarians in their vigorous and brave claims to be Protestant England's most reliable normative guardians was that he was acting bravely and perilously on behalf of a set of human inventions and institutions whose limits and imperfections he was the first and best fitted to criticize. At the most immediate level, Selden joined Coke in thinking through the relations between the three constituents of English law. As Glenn Burgess explains, these three were 'common law (which was also called common or general *custom*, or a law of reason); statute law; and (particular or local) custom.'[1] In a more far-reaching way, however, the premier legal thinkers of the 1620s embraced the office of reassessing and reasserting the value of human legal institutions to the holy commonwealth in its entirety. Christopher W. Brooks cautions that 'it is probably dangerous to ignore the possibilities for the interaction between religion and law at any point in the sixteenth and seventeenth centuries.' As Brooks goes on to show, there is ample evidence for the interaction – including William Lambarde's dalliance 'with the idea of casting the charge for the commissioners of the peace under the headings of the Ten Commandments' – and the possibilities range through a wide variety of levels, from 'campaigns for moral reformation' through squabbles over jurisdiction. In the sixteenth as in the seventeenth century, the Ciceronian 'notion that positive law was the prime defender of civilised life and a bulwark against its disintegration into a brutish state of nature was also a constantly reiterated theme'; and law was often heralded as the finest of God's gifts to humankind.[2] In the 1620s, however, Selden and Coke embodied best what Brooks has called 'a great defensiveness about the common law and its practitioners' (224), which means that they understood the charges against the law's vulnerabilities and responded with extraordinary commitment to the conviction that their holy commonwealth could not thrive without the law of the land.

Like poetry, so too the common law: Selden was committed to sifting the probable truths and usable fictions from the worthless lies among the records of the past. In the British society to which the imperial Romans came, the Bards had not been unique in guiding the people towards what they should believe, emulate, and expect. Rather, in a passage often cited and greatly prized by Selden, Julius Caesar explains that Gallic peoples tended to acclaim 'two privileged classes,' the Druids and the Equites. The Druids took responsibility for legal and religious affairs – they were priests-cum-lawyers – but they 'are exempt from military service and do not pay taxes like other citizens.' The Equites, or knights, took care of war. In Caesar's account, there is a mention of poetry – the students of the Druids 'memorize a great number of verses' – but his analysis of Gallic institutions differs conspicuously from the triad of Bards, Druids, and Euhages found in the pages of Ammianus Marcellinus and Strabo. Caesar omits Gallic poetry and natural philosophy; his attention rests entirely on the sacerdotal lawyer and the aristocratic warrior, complementary but segregated offices in the dispensations of justice, and also very different from the Tacitean image of that Druidic fury performed so stunningly at the vanguard of battle.[3]

Unlike Edward Coke, who clearly preferred Caesar's account of Gallic customs to any other, Selden was both more eclectic and more critical in his search for the heroic paradigms behind English legal and parliamentary institutions. He was especially cautious in exploring the ancient evidence supporting a premise in which his study of tithes put great stock, namely, that a humanly contrived law might afford Protestant England its best measure of resolution in the face of even theological and ecclesiastical controversy. In England, this legal invention comprised two separate but overlapping components. First, there was the common law, whose wise supremacy is the theme promulgated in Selden's 1616 edition of Sir John Fortescue's *De Laudibus Legum Angliae*. As Selden knew it, the shape and legacy of this law had developed most crucially through the workaday customs and precedents of the judicial courts in the land, but also through those texts in which attempts were made to record, explain, and organize that vast, unwieldy material. It was a law to which Selden in the *Table Talk* attributed more religious and moral value than he was ready to concede to most sermons. Second, there was the proposition that the English Reformation itself was what Selden called a 'parliamentary religion.' In the parliamentary debates of the 1620s as well as in the *Table Talk*, Selden lent support to the boldly civil argument that the creed and practices of the English Reformation depended on parliamentary statutes and acts.

For Selden, the recourse to judicial and parliamentary law had the advantage over normative poetry and natural law that, as an arbiter of conflict, its hold on the members of an existing society was more securely binding and enforceable, not left to the members' own visceral and epistemological responses. If tithes were based in a documented, humanly devised law, then they would have to be paid. If Parliament had sponsored the standard texts and practices of the Church of England, then conformity among and between the religious communities could be monitored and exacted. This greater contractual bind did not ensure, of course, that enforcement would perfectly succeed, worse still, that judges would always be equitable and just, and, worst of all, that the contents of the laws would be righteous and honest. Parliaments and judicial courts themselves would have to require legal sages capable of guiding those institutions away from the extremes of antinomian chaos and hyper-legal persecution. These sages, moreover, would need to be exceptionally learned in all the domains over which parliaments and judicial courts possess authority.

As much as Coke, Selden believed in the value of positive law for the prosperity of the holy commonwealth. But far more than Coke, Selden was eager to monitor and to correct the vulnerabilities in England's own institutions of law. As Alan Cromartie explains, Coke's emphasis on the artificial and unimpeachable rationality of the common law 'greatly discouraged any sense that its origins were messily contingent,' but for Selden common law was particular, local, and consensual rather than universal and perfect expressions of a natural law, 'less evolutions of reason than authoritative actions of the "state."'[4] J.W. Tubbs has shown in his study of the famous 'common law mind' that Coke, rather than Selden, was in the minority of medieval and early modern contributors to the theory and practice of English law; for both theory and practice were always less consistent and certainly less uniformly interested in or supportive of the law's 'immemorial' status than Coke would have liked to believe. Tubbs concludes that in the seventeenth century understandings of the common law were essentially divided between men such as Coke and Sir John Davies, who stressed the immemorial customs of their law, and others such as Selden and Finch, 'who brought either their educations in philosophy, logic, and other legal systems or their training in the methods of humanistic scholarship to bear on their consideration of the common law; hence, they are less prone to limit their discussions to traditional formulas.'[5] It is possible to argue that Selden was divided with himself over the ability of the common law to ensure the welfare of the holy commonwealth. His edition of Fortescue promulgated the image of the sage, even Mosaic common lawyer, yet its scholarly apparatus lent a critical refinement to that image, as surely as his collaboration with Drayton was meant to offer a tough critical support to the Bard. His work on the *Mare Clausum* showed his strong commitment to the autonomy of England, while his work on the *Fleta* in the 1640s proudly argued England's legal autonomy from the influx of the Roman civil law (*Ad Fletam Dissertatio*, 1647). As we will see, the second edition of *Titles of Honor* (1631) reveals a Selden downplaying his allegiances to the normative poets and intensifying his identity as a legal expert. There is evidence, however, that Selden could not fully sustain his 1620s involvement in the case made for the common law and Parliament as the best guardians of the holy commonwealth. For one, he became deeply invested in natural as well as Judaic law, perhaps models for the common law but laws decidedly closer to the divine in Selden's estimation. For another, even where Selden was fully prepared to grant the common law its peculiar power as a form of artificial reason, he conceded that it would have to reckon with the imperfections of its own artifice: hence (for example) the indignation he unleashed against judges in the *Table Talk*. Selden argued in the commentary on Fortescue that the common law, like all positive codes of law, had derived from natural law; but no amount of mystique shrouding the origins of common law in some timeless source could dispense with the contingency of that law's humanness. Like poetry, so too the common law and the parliament: Selden's Judaic studies involved the recasting, and by no means the repudiation, of native English means for reforming the sanctity and honesty of the commonwealth. Given his cumulative rather than disjunctive tendencies, it is helpful to remember that in the 1640s and 1650s Selden was still very much involved in the study of English law and history that had interested him from the beginning of his career.

In the early seventeenth century, the legal imagination was alive with the possibility that lawyers and MPs held the keys to the most cherished of moral, social, and religious values in England. But these years were also controversial for English institutions. The artificial reasoning of the common-law courts, the equity of chancery, the jurisdiction of Parliament, and the men responsible for advising the king on policy and principles: each apparatus for the accomplishment of lawful measure in English Protestant society faced its rivals and critics. Some of the king's men, even preachers like Sibthorpe and Maynwaring, showed utter disregard for the law, while – as Selden, better than anyone, knew – law itself was divided into rival codes and jurisdictions. The very civil law from which Selden claimed such autonomy for the common law was still taught in the universities and even practised in some of the special courts in the land. Given Selden's concern to recover a higher legal legacy with a closer intimacy with the divine, it seems reasonably clear that he fretted over the extent to which a simply human law might suffer as a standard for religious society; for all its ability to bind contractual partners, it lacked the harmonies of poetry, the universality of nature, and the more obvious sanctities of rabbinical and canon laws. Indeed, the ancient Druids and the rabbis represented the hope of a possible link between human legal elaborations and either the natural law or God's own positive law. Like Coke, Selden participated in the consecration of common law; with his fellow MPs in the 1620s he supported the parliamentary derivation of English Protestantism. Unlike those others,

Selden looked far beyond the institutions of English law to see if he
might discover law's surest access to the divine.

In Jacobean England, Selden and his fellow legal scholars and practitioners generated many ways in which to reconcile the warrants of poetry
and common law. The Inns of Court thrived as centres of literary activity
and patronage, at least until during the course of James I's reign when,
according to Wilfrid Prest, emphasis somewhat shifted in the Inns from
poetry to 'political and theological concerns.'[6] Masques celebrated law,
while lawyers wrote poetry commonly enough to be satirized as a type.
Selden himself wrote poetry and befriended poets; admired works such
as Ovid's *Fasti* for their fusion of law and verse; traced the history of the
poet laureate to an occasion on which a professor of law bestowed that
honour; and modelled his career on those French legal humanists
whose sophisticated criticism was applicable to poetry, civil law, and
native law alike (*Table Talk*, 95). At the very least, both English poetry
and the English common law were inventions with national pride written all over them. No doubt Coke's connections to poetry were less
intentional than Selden's. Nonetheless, as Richard Helgerson argues,
Coke's proud defence of English law bears many points of comparison
to Samuel Daniel's or Edmund Spenser's promotion of English verse[7];
and Coke's students saw fit to versify his legal work in keeping with Caesar's report that Gallic law was memorized in verse. Indeed there was a
long-standing tradition of encapsulating complex legal analyses in maxims. Even if Selden's fullest study of the possible conflation between
music and law in *nomos* would appear near the end of the 1620s in his
work on the Arundel marbles, he had begun to investigate that key concept in his history of English law, the *Jani Anglorum Species Altera* (1610).
In that survey, Selden traced the usage of *nomos* and the appeal to *Euno-
mia* in early Greek poetry, calling attention to the convergence between
law and song in that poetry (11–12).

   In the *Jani Anglorum*, Selden also makes the case that whatever their
points of convergence, poetry and positive law must eventually arrive at
a crossroads, at which point the welfare of a society requires them to
part. In his formative years, no doubt, he noticed some disenchantment
with poetry among the French humanists. Conversely, there were
famous ancient and Renaissance poets who resented their expense of
spirit in a waste of legal studies. Later, in the *Table Talk*, Selden confi-

dently recommends the putting away of poetry in the vein of the biblical requirement that spiritual adults set aside childish things. In the *Jani Anglorum*, however, Selden conveys the sense of historical drama and of normative loss in what is nonetheless the crucial maturation from poetry to law proper, the spiritual gains of returning to childhood notwithstanding. There are many ways in which the titular Janus may be understood in Selden's history of English law – pre- and post-Norman, custom and statute, abstraction and particularity, continuity and change – but he also accentuates the rivalry of those discursive media, verse and prose, in which legal oracles must choose or be moved to speak.

Yet in his collection of English laws, and its synopsis in *England's Epinomis* (1683), his break with poetry was not decisive, neat, or final. In the phases of his career or in the places in his work where he prefers positive law to poetic norms, Selden recognizes that a certain felicity will be lost with childhood, and that other imperfections will accompany maturity. Poetry has a place in his Sanhedrin, as does the natural law about which he also expresses criticism.

As the English translation promises, in *Jani Anglorum Species Altera* Selden assembles 'All that is met with in Story Concerning the Common and Statute-Law of English Britanny' (title page). Selden's collection stops short of the most active medieval period for the law, but its pages offer a ready access to the most significant legal matter up to the time just prior to that period. The text's seventeenth-century translator identifies in Selden's style a difficult mixture of opaque historical poetry and crabbed legalism: 'His ordinary Style, where he delivers himself plainest, is as to the Matter of it, so full of Historical and Poetical Allusions, and as to the Method ... so Intricate and Perplex, that he seems, even where he pretends to Teach and Instruct, to have intended only to Amuse and Confound the Reader. In very deed, it is such a style, as became a Learned *Antiquary*, which is to be *Antique* and Oracular; that one would think, the very Paper, he wrote upon, was made of the *Sibyll's* old-worn Sheets, and that his meaning could not be fisht out without the assistance of a *Delian Diver*' (translator's preface, n.p.). As Selden's own preface to the *Jani* opens, the author records his desire to clarify early legal procedure along with the substance of pre-Norman laws; but the preface itself offers a complex of quotations from classical writers such as Ovid (the *Fasti*), Athenaeus, Horace, and Claudian. Whatever his promise to improve the study of an amorphous, obscure, and undigested law by providing a more faithful and compendious measure, 'method and connexion,' Selden's own oracular style greets the reader with heavy archaism and allusion;

accordingly, it contributes to the notion that the law has its own special sages, its modern-day Druids not so far removed from the Bards. His edition of Fortescue expressly makes this boast.

Over the course of this preface, however, Selden wrenches opaque law and oracular poetry apart. At the start, he defends the barbarous style of the legal records by reminding the reader that in other disciplines – in philosophy and divinity, in particular – a flawed or unpolished surface often covers a precious core. In support of a forbidding legal style, he tends to feminize the products of poetic wit as dainty and 'golden Flower-amours,' 'the graces of words and beauties of expression' that befit the lyrical Muse. Law, he repeats, is closer to theology; for 'how the most abstruse Mysteries even of highest Urania, of Divinity it self, are laid open without [the care of exact speaking] ... Schoolemen ... know well enough' (a3r). Added to this honour roll of barbarous genius are certain natural philosophers, especially 'Aristotle's crabbed Lectures of natural Philosophy,' and all of these imitators of the Silenus – ugly outside but beautiful inside – are preferable to a poetry so 'spruce' or 'neat' as to gratify the most niggling grammarian (a3v).

'As to the neatness of Poetry,' Selden concludes in debt to Plutarch that 'Apollo himself hath been outdone by Sappho, Homer, Hesiod' (a3r). In Selden's source, Plutarch's essay on the 'Oracles at Delphi No Longer Given in Verse,' the interlocutors debate the potentially conflicting claims made for elegance and wisdom in oracular utterance. During this exchange, even the poet Sarapion defends the truth – though crabbed – of prophecy over the sweetness of ornamented language. But if Sarapion advocates philosophical verses, it remains for the interlocutors to explain why the oracles have abandoned verse entirely. The absence of verse in oracles manifests, they say, an epochal shift from a time that 'produced personal temperaments and natures which had an easy fluency and a bent towards composing poetry' – a promptitude and agility of imagination – to a more prosaic time, whose mindset works as providence sees fit to sift truth from the 'more impressive utterance' of decorative poetry and to couch that truth in an economical and putatively unambiguous plainness.[8]

Plutarch's argument for the new prosaic age is that in preferring philosophy to poetry, it 'welcomed clearness and teachability in preference to creating amazement, and pursued its investigations through the medium of everyday language' (329). A people tired of ambiguous circumlocution forced oracular discourse to disengage from its epic heritage or strategies of mystification in what amounted to 'a revolution in belief' (329). Were the people ever to want metaphor again – and the interlocutors acknowledge that they might well do so – in effect, they would relapse into a childhood in which imaginary rainbows replaced the sun.

Warning his readers that 'the whole Body of our Common-Law' is a far more valuable social resource than the pretty gloss of artistic 'workmanship' (*Jani*, a3r), Selden temporarily distances his work from the neat and spruce poetry, but neither does he claim the ready and plain quality of the new oracles. As his translator notes, the *Jani Anglorum* languishes in a difficult style whose obligations are torn between an allusive poetics and a notoriously crabbed common law. Throughout Selden's survey, poetry continues to play a major role in the transmission of English norms, sometimes at such crucial and difficult moments that it is hard to see exactly what he hopes poetry will add to the legal point at hand. More often than not, these troublesome places in the survey involve the vexed relations between common law and the church.

When in *Epinomis* Selden epitomizes his *Jani Anglorum*, this reduction is made in part to deliver law from poetry and in part to reclaim common law from its own lack of clarity, purpose, relevance, and authority. For it is a law assailed at home and abroad with obscurity, disrepute, remoteness, and uncertainty; and while obscurity might benefit the priestly mystique for which some common lawyers have striven, it scarcely qualifies the Assizes for accomplishing what Selden in the *Table Talk* claimed those congregations could do, namely, teach the moral tenets of English society to the laity far more effectively than the majority of sermons.

For human law to work as a measure for religious society, it must avoid the famous extremes of profanity – too human, too worldly – and superstition, too much hocus-pocus in the guise of profundity. On the one hand, the *Jani* includes the history of religious controversy in England; on the other, it suggests a distinction between divine law and secular law made more explicitly in the *History of Tithes* and the *Ad Fletam*. No doubt one reason why Selden turns to Judaic models of the holy commonwealth is that Judaic history makes it easier to integrate the competitive realms of social experience than Selden's sense of English legal history could ever do.

—— 2 ——

In the late Tudor and early Stuart decades, common law was even more controversial than poetry. Poetry might require Sir Philip Sidney to defend it from those enemies who found only lies and lechery in the golden verses of the day; and normative poetry might need Ben Jonson to protect it from the poetasters giving true poesy a bad name. Yet at the most basic level of existence, the common law affected the lives of everyone, directly and tangibly so; in more academic or intellectual terms, the common law was subjected to critique, iconoclasm, rivalry, and calls for reform.

Among the great common lawyers in these years, Selden understood that the sanctity and reliability of the common law should be neither rejected out of hand nor taken for granted. If English people were to put stock in the ability of common law to measure their mores in a just and righteous fashion, that law had to be studied, assessed, and reinvented as carefully as possible. In the *Jani* and his edition of Fortescue, he sought to transmit a reverence for the common law and for the sage figures who oversee it, but by means of the critic's exposure of fraudulent records as well as his modification of some of the more extravagant claims made on its behalf. The problem that Selden encountered with poetry – how to retain its sanctity while correcting its errors – carried over into his treatments of the common law. For there was every chance that the measure of law would simply be ruined by the fables found in poetic history, and every chance that the law's sacred aura would be dispelled without something like fable. In turn, the mediation between the aims of sanctification and criticism intersected with the *Jani*'s most persistent problem of all, namely, how the ecclesiastical and civil realms had been and ought to be coordinated in the Christian commonwealth of Britain.

Throughout the *Jani Anglorum*, Selden attempts to rectify and celebrate the history of English law, to operate as both critic and sage. As critic, he rebukes bogus sources such as Geoffrey of Monmouth and Berosus – who can, at best, claim an allegorical and 'Poetick' legitimacy – and he relegates naïve claims for the evidence of positive laws in earliest Britain to the region of Aristophanes's city of birds. But Selden allots a more serious attention to the utopian tendencies of the early part of his history when he delights in the natural sanctity of the legendary Trojans. 'The gravest Writers do acknowledge,' he adds after the allusion to Aristophanes, 'that those most ancient times were for the most part free from positive Laws' (10). If some authorities have surmised that the will of princes amounted to law, Selden asserts that early people lived according to 'Natural Equity,' a principle comparable to 'the Lesbian Rule in *Aristotle*, being adapted, applied, and fitted to the variety of emergent quarrels, as strifes, ordered, over-ruled, and decided all Controversies' (10–11). These societies were not coterminous with the golden age, but neither were they far removed from that lawless, innocent age. Their law was essentially natural conscience or moral honesty; their leaders were divinely appointed shepherds, driven by duty and a 'provident tenderness' (11). Speaking of the Trojans, Selden praises their commitment to virtue, 'the worship of their Gods and those things which belong to Religion' (11). The next step in ancient society was the invention of *nomos*, that principle 'to be met with in those old Poets' as the harmony of law and the '*Law of Song*' (11–12). In this account, then, natural law gave way to the artifice of poetry, after which positive law developed as the arbiter and guarantor of mores, harmony, justice, and religion in human societies. Poetry's standard was and had to be more rigorous and forceful than nature's – more concrete, more capable of producing shame and other visceral responses, more formulaic in its embodiment of conventional values – yet poetry was not so enforceable as positive law. Ideally, however, the later standards were so fashioned as to retain something of the earlier assets: the flexibility of natural conscience or the lyric harmonies of lawful song.

Yet once he has proceeded into the recorded history of law, Selden offers fewer vestiges of a common law invested with innocent nature or promulgated in harmonious song. Even straightforward testimonies to the basic sanctity of English common law are few. Aside from recurring praise for Coke, Selden invokes the concept of musical *nomos* (11–12), celebrates the consecration of the Inner Temple (7), and idealizes the musical harmony of the English estates in government (94). For most of the survey, however, the flexible Lesbian rule clearly gives way to 'the straightest and surest bond of safety in every Common-wealth, and such as can by no means be without Justice' (94). Once history proper is under way, it is clear that for Selden, the sanctity, truth, and goodness – the *nomos*, even the music or poetry – in law cannot be presupposed; rather, it must be reconstituted, cultivated, and rectified through scholarly intervention.

The most discordant feature of Selden's legal history proves to be the interactions between church and magistrate. Having advertised to his reader that he will concentrate solely on the 'profane' law, Selden takes a major step towards asserting the artificial order of English law when, in emphasizing the Norman retention of older English laws, he agrees with one of his heroes, William Lambarde, that the outline of an 'archaenomia' might be glimpsed in English legal customs. In anticipation of Coke, Lambarde represents for Selden the groundswell of arguments for stabilizing and completing the medieval standardization of the law's artificial reasoning. At one point, Selden even wistfully longs for a godlike vantage or a divine record book in which he might survey all 'humane affairs' and gather the truth from English legal history (12). Methodological dreams aside, he knows that if the fragments of the law are to arise into 'the frame and model' of a proper structure, he must find a way 'to give some closure and cement, such as it is, (i.e. some method and connexion) to the scattered and disjointed bulk' (a2v). From start to finish, the burden of devising the 'connexion' in the laws of the commonwealth is heightened by the question of whether, when, or how much the common lawyer is meant to intervene in specifically religious concerns. Accordingly, Selden engages the question that in the preface he offers to set aside, the matter of whether a specifically English civil code, together with the lay institutions that produce it, can serve as a measure for manners and even for the creeds and practices within the English church.

On the one hand, the *Jani Anglorum* promulgates the authority of the common lawyer in regulating controversies or cases of great concern to the church. After all, as a common lawyer himself, Selden corrects the record of the Clarendon constitutions over which Henry II and Thomas à Becket were at loggerheads, and he advocates the lay jurisdiction asserted by those constitutions over the clergy as well as their use by Coke in defence of James I's own 'Ecclesiastical Jurisdiction' (72). In selecting the material of his survey, Selden features those English kings from Lucius to Henry VIII who have engineered a partnership between English governance and spirituality at the expense of the bondage to the Romans engineered by means of the civil and canon laws. On the other hand, Selden either diminishes his own authority in religious matters when he retreats from a full account of lay-clerical conflict, or simply rejects the relevance of sacred matters to a survey of the common law. The *Jani* evinces a young Selden undertaking his first, uncertain steps towards a holistic vision of a religious commonwealth; and indeed, the endeavours of coordination can be so uneven and unsure that he interrupts his straightforward account of the legal history with any number of poetic and rhetorical diversions: the archaic 'Law rhythms' of Robert of Gloucester that he prefers over the poesy of 'dainty finical Verse-wrights' (51); breezy, poetically allusive digressions on kissing, adultery, drinking laws, and the nobility of women; and the idle if provocative banter made famous in the 1580s and 1590s by Thomas Nashe, one of Selden's minor cultural heroes, whose defences of the Church of England against the Marprelate satirists were so explosive and unkempt as to worry the very officials of that polity (*Table Talk*, 76–7). Yet the legal survey that opens with a clear distinction between profane and sacred concerns concludes with a virtually obsessive reportage of all the ways in which those two areas of concern have become entangled in English history.

Selden's distinction between what he calls the 'Jus Prophanum' and everything 'held by the Religion of the Church' is set forth clearly in the author's preface to the reader. As the translator's note on the distinction elaborates, Selden is severing *'common and statute law'* from the 'Sacred and Ecclesiastical' so as not to meddle 'with the Canons and Rules of the *Church*' (105). In keeping with this notion, also acknowledged by Selden himself, that it is not the business of the common lawyer to intervene in matters divine, the historian makes only the vaguest attempts to consecrate the profane dimension of law: pagan myths of justice connect law with divinity; the ancient Jews are invoked on a handful of occasions for analogues with early British customs (5, 19, 21); and trial-by-ordeal is connected to the fiery representation of God in the Bible. But Selden undercuts his inclusion of that last point by reminding the reader that the Bible is often misinterpreted, that it is none of his business how ordeals came to be commonplace among Christians, and that in any case the Bible seeks to accommodate the weakness of 'mortal conception' (85).

Unlike the soon-to-be published edition of Fortescue, then, Selden's *Jani Anglorum* is not interested in uplifting the common law out of the profane into the realm of the sacred. In the sixteenth chapter, however, with the introduction of Christianity to the island, Selden inaugurates what proves to be an ongoing record of the interactions between church and magistracy in regard to legal history. In the first instance, King Lucius is exhorted by Pope Eleutherius to prize the law of God far above the law of Caesar – no real problem for Selden, whose admiration of the English common law often entails his argument that this law has resisted the incursion of the Roman civil law. Even so, the Pope's advice is bold: Lucius is urged to put divine dispensations over human, this as a key element in his repudiation of 'the pitiful fopperies of the Pagans, and the Worship of their Idol-Devils' (28).

When Selden next focuses on the relations between magistrates and religion, he has moved into the Saxon phase of his survey – indeed the Lucius episode is the last of the British phase. With assistance from the

Venerable Bede, Selden relates the campaign of ordinances and decrees unleashed by King Ethelbert on all sacrilegious crimes against the church and its property. Like Lucius, so too Ethelbert: the legal actions in support of the Christian faith are carried out by kings, not by judges or parliaments, a distinction that will matter eventually in the survey. Nonetheless, there can be no question that in these instances, if no-where else, the profane and the sacred have collided, and in both instances the sacred has gained the upper hand.

Religion does not keep the upper hand over the profane for long. Under Alfred, the king and the prelacy work out a harmonious relationship in which, according to Ingulph, 'There was no choice of Prelates ... that was merely free and canonical' – not simply left to the church, that is – 'but the Court conferred all Dignities, as well of Bishops as of Abbots, by the Kings Ring and Staff, according to his good pleasure' (42). The king, however, is so good as to confer that dignity as his churchmen see fit: 'The Election or choice was in the Clergy and the Monks; but they desired him whom they had chosen, of the King' (42).

In the next chapter, focus shifts from the pleasure of kings to the 'publick debate of Parliament' (43), and at once the records assessing the relations between magistracy and the church become more complicated. Selden's juxtaposition of Ingulph and Matthew Paris telescopes the events leading to the church's deprivation of its full exemption from taxation, one according to which they had been given 'a concession of all things for the release of our Souls, and pardon of our sins to serve God alone ... to the intent that the Clergy might wholly attend Divine Service' (43). This exemption having been taken for granted in Saxon times, records show that during the time of Henry III, 'the ancient State, Freedom, and Government of the *English Church*' came to be compromised by the preponderance of '*Leeches*, Jugglers and Decoys of *Rome*,' whose aim it was to deprive the people of their wealth 'to the great prejudice of the Common-wealth' (43). Now relations between the two key constituents of the English commonwealth, one civil and the other religious, is far more contentious: some 'stand for the priviledge of the Church,' while others are 'not so much inclined to countenance that liberty of the Church' and set 'the publick advantage of the King-dom' over the liberty of the church in certain critical matters.

Indeed, after the Norman Conquest, the English commonwealth can fairly be said to have a perennial problem in just how civil and religious claims might best be coordinated. The records show two faces of William the Conqueror in relation to his church. First, he attacks the liberty of the church when he deprives bishoprics and abbacies of their exemption 'from all Secular service,' especially 'Military service' (48). But his final act – final as sequenced by Selden yet 'not to be accounted among the last or least of his' (57) – is more sensitive towards the clergy. The Conqueror takes advice from prelates and nobility alike about 'the amendment of the Episcopal Laws,' with an eye towards reforming deviations from 'the Precepts of the holy Canons' (58). The upshot of the royal decree is to protect ecclesiastical jurisdiction in its 'Government of Souls' from lay encroachment. So it is that the secular magistrate can take an active interest in protecting the church from secular aggression, hardly the image of the post-Conquest world that emerges from Selden's edition of Eadmer a few years later.

The image of the post-Conquest world that emerges from the remaining chapters of the *Jani* reveals a variety of fortunes in the legal relationship between secular magistracy and the holy church. In the sixth chapter of Book 2, Henry I ranks among the very best rulers of a holy commonwealth, which means that he 'took care' of injustices and enormities in the secular and ecclesiastical realms alike. Having worked to correct 'what had slipt far aside from the bounds of Justice,' Henry offers to free the church, in the sense 'that [he] will neither sell it, nor will [he] put it to farm, nor upon the death of Arch-Bishop, or Bishop, or Abbot, will [he] take any thing of the domain of the Church, or of the men thereof, till a Successor enter upon it' (60). As Henry cleans up the main 'evil customs' in his commonwealth, so he oversees the proper delegation of authority to the ecclesiastical realm, especially with regard to wills and inheritance, a component of canon authority according to the 'ancient Constitution, intrusted to the Church by the consent of the King and Peers' (62).

Two chapters later, however, such harmony between the secular and the sacred realms has dissolved. Anselm, the hero of Selden's Eadmer, is at odds with the king over the question of who should invest bishops and abbots with their authority. 'There was a sharp bickering about this business,' we are told (65), a squabble that comes in Eadmer's mind to epitomize the sacrilege of lay invasions in the sacred jurisdiction of the church. Much of the remainder of the *Jani* is a record of this 'bickering.' On the one hand, the Pope exerts pressure on Henry II in protesting 'that the secular Court of Justice did not at all suit with them [the clergy], upon pretence that they had a priviledge of Immunity' (69). In England, however, the Clarendon Constitutions emblematize and contribute to the surge of secular power over clerical affairs – 'the Advowson and Presentation of Churches' (69), for instance, or the prose-cution of clerical crimes, the travel abroad of prelates. Contrary to Selden's eventual Erastian position that excommunication is a civil mat-ter, the records show that both lesser excommunication ('an Interdict or prohibition' from participation in worship services) and greater excommunication (removal from the community of the faithful itself) is carried out by the church, but the king and his judicial representatives have a strong say in determining the appropriate circumstance for such a punishment.

Chapters 11, 12, 13, and 14 of the *Jani*'s second book are dominated by the secular laws governing church affairs, not least by a corrected list of the Clarendon Constitutions. But three key changes appear in Selden's treatment of the 'bickering.' The first is that Selden draws a brief analogy between the medieval past and his own times, informing his reader that 'the famous Sir Edward Coke' has recently deployed a medieval law con-cerning the order of appeals 'to assert and maintain the Kings Ecclesias-tical Jurisdiction' (72). A second twist in the discussion, one that quietly modifies the first, arises when, during the discussion of the Clarendon Laws, Selden returns to the tragic tale of Thomas à Becket. Having cred-ited Henry II with an appropriate indignation at the 'insolence' of the Pope, he illustrates the way in which this angry king lost control of his pas-sions when he levied a punishment on the innocent families ('both by Marriage and Blood' [79]) and posterity of criminals. Even though this royal excess is only briefly narrated and is made understandable by the excesses of the papacy, nonetheless Selden begins to emphasize what he has suggested all along in the *Jani*, that the English commonwealth has a far greater chance for harmony if its secular power is shared among the king, Parliament, and the judicial authorities.

The third change is that, in the record of the tragic controversy between Becket and Henry, Selden uses archaic poetry not as ornament but as the main vehicle of transmission. The verses of Robert of Glouces-ter bear the burden of explaining 'which of those [Clarendon] Laws were granted by Thomas a Becket, which withstood'; the prose commen-tary is disregarded as an interruption to the '*Glocester* Muse' (77). It is not entirely clear why Selden makes this change. Poetry has been in evi-dence throughout the *Jani*, but in shifting the burden of the records to verses, Selden might be accentuating the normative significance of the conflict, or obscuring his own account of an uncommonly complicated episode in secular-sacred relations with what he calls an 'ancient Dia-lect' (74). Evidence for this latter position comes at the end of the final chapter on the affair, when Selden admonishes the readers that they 'are not to expect here the murder of *Thomas a Becket*, and the story how King *Henry* was purged of the crime, having been absolved upon hard terms' (80). Is this because the *Jani* really means to deal only with secular matters? Is this because Selden deems such a sensational scene inappropriate for his more factual legal record? After all, Robert the poet has been described as returning 'upon the Stage' (74), a remark that offers one more reason why poetry might be used – as an appropriate medium for historical tragedy. In fact, Selden ends with the Latin tag, 'Conveniunt cymbae vela minora meae [Smaller sails are more appropriate for my boat]' (80). What Selden admits with this Latin tag is that the medieval contention between church and magistrate is too profound a driving force for his vessel of law. But he does not leave the matter altogether. In chapter 18 of the second book, he adds a handful of laws that favour the clergy (90). Even as he protests that the *Jani* is all about the common law in its purely secular instantiations, the text of the survey reveals a young scholar fascinated and vexed by the history of both the harmony and the bickering between the two major components of the holy commonwealth, the church and the magistracy.

With his 1616 edition of Sir John Fortescue's *De Laudibus Legum Angliae*, Selden offers his readers a very different way of understanding the common law from his emphasis on its secularity in the *Jani*. For, whatever modern scholars might think about its significance in legal history, *De Laudibus* makes a bold claim for the sanctity of the common law. What is far less clear is the extent to which the editor and commentator, Selden himself, supports the grandiose claims of his medieval authority. In the commentary, Selden demystifies some of the more extravagant claims made for the immemorial constancy of the common law; but he also reformulates some of those same claims in keeping with praise for the English legacy of justice.

By celebrating the sanctity of lawyers, Fortescue – who was lord chief justice and lord chancellor for Henry VI – is both mimicking and subordinating the sacerdotalism of Roman civil law on display in Justinian's *Digest*, in which lawyers occupy a priesthood in the dispensation of virtue and justice. In *De legibus et consuetudinibus Angliae*, Henry de Bracton also adopts this notion together with the argument that God is the fountain of justice.[9] In *De Laudibus*, however, Fortescue stages a dialogue between the lord chancellor and England's heir apparent on the biblically supported holiness of the common lawyer, a status that he attempts to elevate above that of the civilian claim. Selden forewarns would-be critics of

Fortescue that the dialogue aims at instructing and inspiring the future Edward IV during a time of civil war and exile. In other words, Sir John offers devotion to, not analysis of, the common law. According to Selden, the reader who resents this fact resembles those parasites who ignore 'an establisht and vniuersall proceeding or position' yet rely entirely on the gauges of their appetites (*De Laudibus*, 'To the Reader,' n.p.). With parasites, criticism is simply corrupt desire in disguise.

Fortescue's persona of the lord chancellor argues as follows. It is appropriate that the prince has mastered arms, but now he must devote himself to the study of law. He must indeed be rearmed with law. The chief source for this claim is Moses, who 'doth by the authoritie of God straitly charge the Kings of Israel to be readers of the law all the dayes of their life' (5r). Leadership entails two factors: the prince's own essential knowledge of the sacred law; and his reliance on those lawyers advanced in legal wisdom and scholarship. To know the law is to strive to know God's will and wisely thereafter to fear God's justice, 'For the principall point of all seruice is to knowe the will and pleasure of the lord or master to whom seruice is due' (6r).

The prince responds that surely the Mosaic Law differs from the human laws of England, but the lord chancellor assures him that all law is holy insofar as it measures the divide between good and evil, 'so that in this respect a man may well call vs *Sacerdotes*, that is to say, giuers or teachers of holy things ... Forsomuch then as the lawes are holy, it followeth that the ministers and setters forth of them may right well be called *Sacerdotes*, that is giuers & teachers of holy things' (8v). Compiling biblical citations in order to clinch the holiness and certainty of English law, the lord chancellor reiterates the prince's double obligation: to rule legally and to entrust the mysteries of the law to the consecrated lawyers and judges. Then, by insisting that the prince study common, not civil law, the lord chancellor clarifies what gives law its religious force: in addition to its source in the spirit and justice of God, and aside from its moral uprightness, common law is the ligament or sinew that binds the people together and ensures their mutual welfare. Thus, Fortescue drives home the etymological ties that bind law and religion together.

For Selden, however, Fortescue's next point moves the commentary beyond the acceptable limits of sanctified law into the realm of fable and mystification. The lord chancellor opines that English common law is, in fact, superior to civil law with regard to the greatness of its antiquity and the justice of its customs. By contrast to the customs, procedures, and rules generated in the common-law courts, statutory law is harder for the lord chancellor to idealize. He emphasizes the representative breadth of Parliament and the mechanisms for revision in the case of parliamentary error. But his greatest praise is reserved for those customs so old and so just as to have been embraced without fundamental changes by the British, Roman, Anglo-Saxon, Danish, and Norman inhabitants of the island. The artifice of common law borders on the innocent state of nature itself.

In rejecting Fortescue's myth of an unchanging and primordial common law, Selden takes a number of approaches, some more conciliatory than others. First, he offers readers the actual meaning of the claim that English law is a mixture concocted in turn by each of the reigning peoples. Then, in more dismissive fashion, he links the claim for a supremely ancient British law to the fables of Brutus, and undercuts both in their dependence on those parasitical Bards whose livelihood derived from flattery. The antiquity of English law is better argued, he continues, in the revisionary vein of William Camden, who maintains that the Gallic people derive from Japhet, and British law derives from the Gauls. The problem with this line of argument is that it sacrifices superiority for antiquity.

Wanting to corroborate the holy status of common law, yet resistant to fraudulent historical claims, Selden resorts to natural law as the immutable yet adaptable standard from which all legal codes flow. Natural law is limited as, or channelled into, positive law for two reasons: because weak human reason must interpret natural law and because 'the seueral conueniences of divers States' require different rules ('Notes on Fortescue,' separately paginated, 18). If the naturalization of the common law prohibits any bogus claims for the superiority of England, it also defends English law from the charge that it is new and unstable. Having downplayed the collaboration between poetry and positive law, Selden concedes in his recourse to nature that contractual obligations benefit from some higher religious warrant. English law is emphatically artificial; but in comparing English law to a ship whose materials have been replaced section by section until nothing original remains, Selden is able to transfer to that artifice something of the continuity that adheres much more securely to natural law than it ever could to Drayton's beloved traditions of the Bards. In the humanly devised identity, practice, and purpose of that ship, Selden reserves a precious cargo hold for its only 'immutable part of nature' ('Notes on Fortescue,' 19). Thus emboldened, he ventures to maintain that if measured according to the standard of continuous practice, civil law has much more to fear than does common law.

—— 3 ——

The idea of a consecrated legal sage stayed with Selden over the course of his career, but it always competed with Selden's insistence on a substantial distinction between lawyers and priests. In the *Table Talk*, Selden is fond of drawing analogies between priests and lawyers: 'Those words you now use in makeing a Minister (receive the holy Ghost) were used among the Jewes att the makeing of a Lawyer' (78); 'Onely he is made a preist ... by designacion, as a Lawyer is called to the barr' (78); 'Like a Doctor of Law in the Universitie,' or a civilian, a minister 'has a great deale of Law in him, but cannott use it, till hee bee made some bodyes Chanceller' (78); and the method of study in divinity should mimic that of an education in the common law (80). But as with all analogies – and some of Selden's are famously homely – the comparison maintains a distance between the two things whose isolated similarity is wittily remarked. Sometimes, however, Selden's sense of the wide distance between the courts and the church is manifested in his anti-clerical conviction that the courts should perform – would better execute – the duties fumbled in the pulpit and the parish church. Thus, protesting that the core doctrine of religion ought to focus on a 'morall honestye,' he finds that core better taught in the Assizes than in sermons, so much better, in fact, that Selden would have ministers 'exhort the people to goe att these times to learne their duty towards their Neighbour' (106). Clearly, the Assizes included sermons, but Selden does not specify them apart from the full context of the deliberations. Setting aside his disaffection for judges and the clergy alike, Selden draws the conclusion that it is better to hear the deliberation of legal and moral controversies, corroborated by suitable lessons taught in the Assizes sermons, than to absorb some minister's singular and fanciful interpretation of abstruse theological points extrapolated from scripture.

From the very beginning of his scholarly career, Selden had few if any illusions that the institutions of English positive law would rectify the manners of the English people without a fair share of crises in the instrumentation of the law. Even the hero of his Fortescue, a lord chancellor consecrating the whole of English law, was an ideal conceit in contrast with the actual lord chancellors in Selden's formative years, who figured centrally in the hotly contested debate over those laws and procedures spun out in the judicial courts. The lord Chancellors were involved particularly in the challenge delivered against the supreme value of the common law by its corrective counterpart, the arbiters of equity. Selden's own role in the development of equity was at times advisory – he addressed *A Brief Discourse Touching the Office of Lord Chancellor of England* to Bacon; and at times laudatory – he dedicated his edition of Eadmer to John Williams, who from 1621 to 1625 revitalized the medieval tradition of clergy at the helm of the equity court of chancery. At least by the 1640s Selden was fervently critical of chancery's erosion of standard measures in law, a critique that in his view was paralleled by the erosion of all measure in religion by the claims made on the singular dictates of conscience.

By Selden's time, the claims of conscience in the evaluation of circumstances in cases of law had long been considered a chief means of keeping a godly spirit in the common law. The classic treatment of conscientious equity was Christopher Saint German's *Doctor and Student,* first published in 1523 and comprising a dialogue between a theologian and a law student. As the prologue to that work tells us, the upshot of the dialogue reconciles the claims of conscience and the principles of law. The obvious problem arises, however, of whether equity monitors law or vice versa.

Saint German's Doctor of Divinity softens the conflict by accentuating the godly status of the common law: he traces its origin to rational and divine law, though it is difficult (he says) always to find one's way back with confidence. Like Fortescue, he stresses the etymological links between law and religion by means 'of Ligare: that is to say to bynde,' in keeping with the premise that law profits moral honesty, spiritual piety, and social cohesion alike (27). But the theologian is equally clear that positive law or its application can be irreligious, and it is the role of equity to restore its conscience by modifying its rigour.

As seventeenth-century supporters of equity were apt to point out, the responsibilities of equity and the chancery could not fairly be reduced to the blunting of legal teeth. In the *Table Talk*, however, Selden fuses equity with conscience in order to attack both. One can never be entirely sure when the bons mots of the *Table Talk* were uttered, whether they were accurately reported, or in precisely what tone or context Selden intended his squibs to be received. Yet the thrust of his declarations on law's relationship to conscience is clear: at some point, perhaps late, in his life, Selden believed that equitable appeals to conscience were destroying the normative authority of the law's holy warrant. The sibling of the problem with equity – claims on the spirit among antinomian Protestants – is included in Selden's comparison of a tender conscience to a skittish horse or a frightened child to which law should bring a confident maturity. He supposes that 'an Anabaptist comes and takes my horse; I sue him he tels me; he did according to his conscience; his conscience tells him all things are common amg^{ts} the Saints, what is myne is his what is his is mine therefore you doe ill to make such a Law – If a man take anothers horse he shall be hangd. What can I say to this man; he do's according to his Conscience; why is he not as honest a man as he y^t pretends; y^t A Ceremonie established by Law is against his conscience? Generally to pretend conscience against Law is dangerous, on some cases haply wee may' (35).

In the last clause, Selden acknowledges the occasional justice of an appeal to conscience, and the entire passage leaves open the likelihood that the Court of Chancery would purvey conscience more lawfully than the Anabaptist. In his work on the Sanhedrin in the 1640s and 1650s Selden is intent on establishing ample room for zeal, inspiration, and conscience within the holy dispensation of divine and human law in the model society. In the *Table Talk*, however, Selden returns often to the mutual need of justice and religion for a standard so strong that conscience cannot undermine it. One sees this emphasis in his exhortation that contract is at the heart of law and religion and that divines can moralize this fact but lawyers must apply it. It is especially clear in Selden's quip that 'Equity in Law is ye same y^t ye spirit is in Religion, what ever one pleases to make it' (43). Giving the concept an aristocratic alter ego to the Anabaptist, Selden complains that 'Equity is A Roguish thing, for Law wee have a measure know what to trust too' (43). Donning its habit of expensive guises, equity is, in fact, unreliable and waggish, utterly vague, irresponsible, and arrogant. Selden is even prepared to call names: he criticizes the chancery itself, arguing that each Chancellor's conscience, like his shoes, will differ in size from the others. Even the golden rule must be stabilized according to a consensual measure, he argues, rather than according to what private persons and judges desire. The problem with the common law, of course, is that consent and contract are themselves human inventions prone to the social diseases and mortal fancies attributed to equity and conscience.

During the 1630s and 1640s Selden attempted to locate a stable coordination between and higher standard for the otherwise disputatious rivals, contractual law and conscientious equity. In the 1620s, however, Selden himself is a central figure in the national test of the hypothesis that the sages of the common law can provide that arbitration. More often than not, Selden's links between law, conscience, and sacred warrant are neither so confident as Fortescue's panegyric nor so negative as the conclusion that a harmonious balance between kindly equity and rigorous law will always be elusive. In the *Table Talk*, Selden is still offering guidelines for working out this nexus: responding to the impasse that law can too tightly bind conscience, while conscience too wildly subverts law, he explains that we must scrutinize both the justice and the purpose of a law. He is most confident in these recorded conversations when he recaptures the rhetoric of his parliamentary years in the 1620s, according to which positive law and its lawyers serve to establish, authenticate, and regulate the values and creeds of English religion more effectively than priests. For Selden, however, Fortescue's English version of the Mosaic law is rarely so far away from the musical myths of the Bards as a contractually minded lawyer would prefer.

In the 1620s the common law was gaining ground as a body of customs, cases, and procedures in which England's most sacred principles and liberties were preserved and transmitted. But that law was also severely under attack. Sir Edward Coke's reverence for the common law reached sacerdotal proportions: for him, knowledge of that law was divine, honest, grave, and upright; and its certainty, however disputed by others, entailed 'that the just shall flourish like the palm-tree, and spread abroad as the cedars of Libanus.' Behind the infinite variety of common law, and whatever its human distortions, Coke posited a coherent unity comparable to those streams or flowers that derive from a source or root. In common law, as in flowers, he maintained, 'this admirable unity and consent in such diversity of things proceeds only from God, the Fountain and Founder of all good laws and constitutions.'[10] According to David Little, Coke's common law comprises a 'total self-consistence and inner harmony' reflective of 'the coherence and continuity of social life itself.' It possesses a 'circular unity,' offers 'the measure and source of virtue,' and amounts to a religion with sacerdotal lawyers.[11] Like Selden himself, Coke likes to invoke the Druids as arbiters of religion and law alike. Even where common law is said by Coke to be an artificial reasoning, it is an artifice that distils what natural reason struggled in vain to say.

In *The Ancient Constitution and the Feudal Law,* J.G.A. Pocock's notion of a 'common-law mentality,' with its penchant for mystical and insular myths of that law, loosely describes Coke's approach, but not, finally, Selden's. As Tubbs has written, 'if there was a common law mind in the period, it was divided.'[12] Coke embraces Fortescue and the *Mirror of Justice* – the latter a text that Selden eschews – and he leads the charge in laying claim to a 'fundamental law' in common law, a term as vague as it was useful for warding off the universalist indictments made by civil and natural lawyers against an English common law that they depict as woefully particular, transient, and unstable. Indeed, Coke is so pleased with the extensive preparation required of the common lawyer that, aside from excellent reporting and 'the advised and orderly reading over of the books at large,' he does not share in the contemporary concern that common law needs a method or at least an abridgment. Whereas Selden has many unpleasant things to say about judges, Coke likes to emphasize 'the way of righteousness' that judges – like Moses, that 'first reporter of law' – were summoned to follow. To those critics of barbarous style in the common law, Coke responds that one can find the richest substance in a 'homely receptacle.' Truth, he adds, is often lost in varnish; it belongs in residence between the judgment of the head and the simplicity of the heart, with 'the right rule and reason of the law' requiring the same particular mastery and simple piety that the Old Testament heroes displayed in the Pentateuch.[13] Coke has faith that utmost particularity manifested 'the reason of the common law,' that is, the abstract or fundamental principles comparable on the one hand to pillars of the commonwealth, and on the other, to a 'golden and straight mete-wand ... and not to the incertain and crooked cord of discretion' that equity tried to sanctify.[14]

For many 'godly' writers in the 1620s true English religion had always shared a warrant and an integrity with the English institutions of law. In *High-wayes of God and the King*, Thomas Scot italicized the intimacy between common law and true (non-Arminian) religion. Such polemicists against contemporary abuses in the church and royal court alike were not as careful as some of their common-law successors thought they might have been to differentiate the common law proper – worked out in judicial courts, cases, procedures, and a variety of legal writings – from the authority or doings of Parliament. So it happened that in the 1629 Parliament, Selden came to embody, as well as to espouse, the close kinship of religious and legal ideals within the halls of Westminster.

Men like Coke recognized the weighty opposition to the claim that English positive law might serve as the foundation for and touchstone of religious orthodoxy. After all, it was a matter of considerable conflict in his day simply whether statutory law as made by the monarch in Parliament readily superseded common or case law; constituted a portion of common or case law; or mended common law from outside and only very cautiously at that. Coke argued that the skilled common lawyer developed a perfected reason, but as Tubbs has shown, the medieval treatises (Bracton and Glanvill, for instance) and the Year Books often were inconsistent or ambiguous in their theories of the common law, or for that matter simply not interested in theory in their discussions of legal argumentation and practice. If some seventeenth-century lawyers came to speak of their code as 'fundamental,' they were innovating against a medieval legacy that never did so, that showed little consistency about whether the common law was a matter of immemorial custom, and that varied on the question of whether 'contrary actions or enactments are invalid.'[15]

In defence of common law as a key ingredient in godly religion, an anonymous writer declared that English laws 'are at this day more agreeable to ye Law of God than ye Civill or Cannon Lawes, or any other Lawes in ye World.'[16] Writing most likely in the 1620s, this writer cherished much of the pre-Norman history of the positive law that Selden had recovered, including the correspondence between King Lucius and Bishop Eleutherius in which the latter urges adherence to divine law rather than to civil or canon law. For the anonymous writer, this advice corroborated a harmony between common and divine law that persisted over time and warrants an analogy between the legal dispensations to Israel and to England.

If, in the 1620s, godly Puritans and common lawyers could at times agree on their role in reforming early Stuart society, this convergence of interests and ideals had more than its fair share of problems. Each measure alone, true Protestant religion and English common law, was liable to virulent attacks from staunch opponents. For the former: towards the end of his reign, James I had attempted to restrict what he considered the 'Puritan' encroachments from the pulpit on his prerogative and their equally contentious preaching on the *ordo salutis*, so controversial in the wake of the Synod at Dort. Despite a brief honeymoon with the godly sort of Protestant, Charles I was not long on the throne before making it perfectly clear that for him Puritanism was the polar opposite of orthodoxy. Meanwhile, the common lawyers were liable to a wide variety of criticisms and abuses from the equity court in Chancery. And Charles had little patience for the challenge that common lawyers posed to the application of his prerogative in securing funds to fight those wars for which the godly themselves had been hankering.

If, apart from one another, the godly and legal critics of Caroline orientations, policies, and practices were subject to polemical assault, their conjunction of forces was peculiarly disturbing to opponents and even at times to themselves. Sometimes the terms of abuse hurled at 'Puritans' and common lawyers were similar in aim (for instance, both groups were accused of being quarrelsome and of canting). It is also the case that some of the advocates of godly Protestant religion and of common law found their more intimate partnership objectionable. There was certainly no shortage of common lawyers resistant to the notion that the basis of their vocation was as amorphous, insubordinate, and fanciful as that of a zealot. Selden's favourite play, *Bartholomew Fair,* attacked both a busybody justice of the peace and a hypocritical Puritan, and there is a similarity between the two characters' views of the fair. Jonson, however, redeems only one of them, the J.P., in basic agreement with Selden's conviction that an everyday court session is more likely to convey more of religious substance than by far the majority of sermons. In the *Table Talk* as well as in his work in Parliament, Selden offered clear if not abundant evidence that he derived the English Reformation from the doings of the early Tudor Parliament. In 1628, however, he defended the proprieties of English subjects – liberty and property – as so widely embraced that he 'never heard it denied, but in the pulpit, which is of no weight' (*Opera Omnia,* vol. 3, col. 1994). This dismissal of the place of sermons in the promulgation of law is mitigated by the likelihood that Selden had in mind solely those two preachers widely believed to be courtly parasites, Maynwaring and Sibthorpe; but in the late 1620s especially, Selden inclined towards the notion that the institutions of positive law could accomplish more for the welfare of true religion than the self-proclaimed prophets of godly Protestantism could ever effect for positive law.

Conversely, some godly English Protestants objected in the 1620s that the common law, like Mammon, was a far too worldly standard to support an analogy with faith in God. Politically, they complained, the common law misdirected English energies and intellects towards exclusively domestic affairs, while (by contrast) godly Protestants were eager to join forces with their kindred spirits at war with the Antichrist on the Continent. Any such suspicion cast on the putative sanctity of the common law was abetted whenever attempts by early Stuart supporters of that law to consecrate its code in the vein of Fortescue met with serious criticism from within the legal community itself. In a series of treatises, Lord Chancellor Ellesmere offered one of the more incisive indictments of common law pieties, his aim the exposure of abuses and of instability in the procedures of that law. A careful reader of cases and statutes, Ellesmere believed that those statutes devised by the king in Parliament were legally superior to the common law. After all, he says, human law and

judiciary interpretation could claim only a temporary validity and therefore required, in the words of Louis A. Knafla, a 'continual evaluation,
analysis, and reframing to meet the needs of the present.'[17] Thus, if
equity could be charged with a wilful, unpredictable irrationality,
common law could be subordinated to statute and to chancery as a
makeshift construct of use for only a short time. It was a debate that culminated in the first quarter of the seventeenth century and amounted
to nothing short of a struggle over which English legal apparatus or
system approximated most closely the power and certainty of sacred
principle.

In sum, Selden undertook to collect and assess the records of the
common law at a momentous time in its history. If English law struck
young John Selden as potentially a more mature, concrete, and reliable
norm for moral honesty and godly duty than either the oracular poetry
of Drayton or the perspicuous praise of Jonson, this conclusion was
always highly imperfect and tentative for him, especially once other
alternatives to the common law – natural law, Judaic law – were added to
the range of resources by means of which a religious society might best
harness its passions, mysteries, abnormalities, and excesses. For the
common law could prove very inadequate in its obsolescence, confusion, contrariness, and infertility, never mind the irregularities and corruption of its lawyers and judges.

In the very years of Selden's maturation, then, common law was a
highly controversial vehicle for ensuring that English Protestant society
was guided by the most sanctified measure available to that society.
'What gave this period such a critical nature,' Knafla sums up, 'was the
coming together of several complex developments: the rise in prominence in new courts of law, the conflict of jurisdictions, the impact
of new social and economic demands, and the growth of litigation.'
He adds: 'The legal problems which emerged baffled even the most
learned of contemporary lawyers. At the heart of these complexities lay
a fundamental transformation in the law itself – the changing pattern of
litigation. The competition among lawyers for new legal remedies, their
enlargement of legal fictions, the advent of written pleadings, the shift
in personal actions to trial by jury, and the proceeding to trial by demur-
rer or special verdict had caused an opening up of legal procedure that
was giving rise to a renaissance in legal thought.' With rebirth, however,
came pain – conflict over tutelage, status, and mission in the law. Attitudes ranged from a pious devotion for the interpretation and application of law, to disgust that the law was so swollen, tangled, and opaque. If

'William Fulbecke and Sir John Davies believed that the common law had reached its greatest hour,' and that even 'increased litigation and uncertainty in the law reflected a society of individuals in search of true justice,' legal reformers were convinced that common law was hopelessly amorphous in its vestiges at any one time and in its evolution over time.[18]

Whereas the legal term 'enormity' referred specifically to a crime judged to be beyond the scope of the common law, the common law itself was widely accused of a comprehensive abnormality. Legal reformers differed, however, on the severity of and solutions for the common law's 'enormities.' Although his attack on the common law's uncertainty and impracticality encouraged the induction of legal maxims, Bacon also steadfastly resisted the scaffolding of a specific method. By contrast, Henry Finch appealed to natural law as the source of all common laws, but also worked hard on a method for this 'golden & sacred rule of reason.'[19] In something of an ironic reversal, given Selden's distinction between mature law and childish poetry, some common lawyers had recourse to verses as a means of clarifying, simplifying, and taming an unwieldy and barbarous body. For the sake of its redemption, they implied, law would once again have to become a child.

With the Elizabethan William Lambarde as their most recent model, but given a tradition stretching back to Littleton, Bracton, and Glanvill, the Stuart lawyers composed textbooks aimed at standardizing the law and at methodizing its study, though in a context that celebrated the traditions of that law. In *Archeion, or, a Discourse upon the High Courts of Justice in England*, Lambarde had traced the need for the careful administration of sacred common law from the children of Adam and Eve through Britain's own Druids. He also had emphasized that such a standard always needed circumstantial and conscientious equity; for if law were a steel rule resistant to various applications, equity was comparable to that famous 'leaden rule of the *Lesbian Artificers*, which they might at pleasure bend, and bow to every stone of whatever fashion.' Only by clearly delineating jurisdiction might English lawyers exorcise that bogey rejected by civil law – 'Antinomia (or *Contrarietie* of Law).'[20]

In Selden's day, Coke's offerings of a perfected legal rationality in his *Institutes, Reports,* and *Little Treatise of Baile and Maineprize* met with stern disapproval from Ellesmere, who found them indicative, not remedial, of a common law degenerating into uncertainty and mischief. Above all, Ellesmere accused Coke of deliberately biasing the law against the right and proper jurisdiction of the king and Parliament, the ecclesiastical and other civil courts, and equity. As Knafla explains, some lawyers privileged the warrant of an office itself, while others assessed the authority of an office on the basis of the officer's law (160–1). In other words, the common-law standard was shaken not only by its own imperfections but by the claims of rival, often civilian, legal standards and courts. A major factor in this rivalry was the question of which law was meant to regulate English religion: the civil lawyers to whom Laud would increasingly turn for help with the enforcement of conformity in worship, or the common lawyers whose view, inspired by Selden, of the positive-law basis of tithes was attacked variously as irreligious and non-conformist.

This melee of conflicting priorities, attitudes, and methods was met with equally strong attempts at order and calm in the common-law standard. John Dodderidge (a common-law judge) and William Fulbecke (a civil lawyer with common-law training) intervened with textbooks offering light, encouragement, and direction for those practising lawyers who, for all the voices singing their praises, had to contend with just as many satirists sending them up as greedy, puritanical 'ignoramuses.' As Wilfrid Prest characterizes them, texts such as *The English Lawyer* and *A Direction or Preparative to the Study of the Law* were meant to assist the scholar with 'pioneering handbooks or guides to method.'[21] The authors of these books sought to render the law more accessible, systematic, and unified. Influenced by the civil law in their methodological enterprise, in these 'first legal monographs' they also strove to accentuate the legacy of Fortescue in appropriating from civil law the sanction of a moral and devout class of barristers.

Contrary to the commonplace that 'a good jurist is a bad Christian,' a number of lawyers sought to promulgate a palatable version of the godly lawyer. Among those whose works and libraries evince a 'more than formal religious commitment,' Prest includes Finch, Coke, and Selden. Although Prest challenges any simplistic equation between godly and common-law interests in early Stuart England, he agrees nonetheless that among the common lawyers, 'zealous protestants, or puritans, constituted the largest single identifiable bloc; thus George Ruggle had good reason to specify "great Puritania" as the birthplace of his archetypal common lawyer, Ignoramus,' a satire that Selden feared pertained to him.[22] To their critics in Selden's lifetime, common lawyers were either too zealous or extremely impious but rarely possessed precisely the right measure of spirituality in their legal bag of tricks.

Although they were accused of demoting the claims of the church on behalf of the state, Selden and other leading barristers saw themselves as shoring up the legal foundations that ensured the continuing prosperity of the English Reformation. Laud recognized – and vilified – this legal stronghold in complaining to Wentworth that, 'as for the Church, it is so bound up in the forms of the common law, that it is not possible for me, or for any man, to do that good which he would ... they which have gotten so much power in, and over the Church, will not let go their hold; they have, indeed, fangs with a witness.' Prest notes that, in addition to 'the various ideological and material forces at work to bring lawyers and puritans together,' not least 'their literalism and particularistic attitude towards authority,' defenders of the common law celebrated both the sanctity of that law's 'ancient customs and forms of government' as well as the power and brilliance with which those customs protected the innocent and strengthened the faithful under a just God's watchful eye.[23]

For John Dodderidge and William Fulbecke, however, the particularity and antiquity of the common law generated as much perplexity as they hoped the law could remedy: the common law had to be converted into an efficacious norm. As Dodderidge says, God might always bestow order on variety, but that order would emerge within common law only by means of an assiduous distribution of specifics into 'Grounds and Rules.' Otherwise, the memory of the lawyer would be overwhelmed 'with infinite singularities' and the law student himself burdened with 'vnspeakable toyle,' especially once it is remembered that an equitably modified law must sometimes put down the 'inflexible stiffe Iron rule' and take 'in hand the Leaden Lesbian rule.'[24] Fulbecke also conjoins the double reform of the law, one reform aimed at method, the other at holiness. Indeed, he opens his 'preparative' to legal study with the claim that law ranks second only to divinity in the scales of righteousness. What is more, 'religion, justice, and law doe stand together, & are together trodde vnder foot by such as neither care for God, nor goodnes.' In this pious vein, he warns lawyers always to remember that 'though the charge and calling be secular, yet it must be religiously handled. For God is the author of the Law, and the reuenger of the abuse thereof.' As it is for those Jews for whom 'no man of any religious habit or vocation [is] in higher place or greater reckoning with God,' the godly handling of law demands remarkable skills of interpretation.[25] Without rules, Fulbecke advises, the law remains obscure, unstable, and protean – in short, an enormity.

According to Fulbecke, the Hebrews had God to thank for the 'square and measurs of their actions.' Legal students need an Old Testament

reverence and faith in the justice of their own law, especially since the
pious civilians shame the common lawyers whose 'daintie eares ... cannot tollerate any naming or mentioning of religion.' But Fulbecke
admits that compared with Old Testament laws and their divine master,
English common law is vulnerable to the charge that human beings
have made it ambiguous, illogical, and haphazard. He would dismiss
those charges on the grounds that grave legal substance has nothing to
do with delicate courtly eloquence; that is, the 'emphatical and significant' conventions of the law would be destroyed or hidden by either
sensuous rhetoric or sophisticated logic.[26] This approach requires that
the law always reveal its 'reason and truth' in a plain, even ugly, self-
evidence. Apparently not fully satisfied with this conclusion, Fulbecke
returns to the discontents of language and interpretation in the study of
law. If the verbalization of the common law is flawed, he protests, such is
the condition of all the arts. Fulbecke is also apt to credit language with
the practical business of accommodating readers, to which end the
interpreter must own and obey a manageable slate of rules; keep in view
the common good; seek the essential reason of a law; put faith in the
sages who have devised the law and sometimes obscured it; encourage
equity as a helpmate to law; and remember that lawyers and Christians
share a conscience.

Fulbecke's rules of reading law contain even more grit. He guides the
common reader into the mediation of those circumstances from which
a probable sense can be gathered out of words, and he offers strategies
for recovering the intentions of the lawmaker in lieu of twisting his
words in a 'Jewish or misticall interpretation.' Intention is 'a childe
vnborne'; legal certainty and simplicity must be hard won by labour, in
contrast to decadent, lazy cabbalists bored with unambiguous sanctions.
The childhood of the common law begins to resemble that of poetry
when Fulbecke emphasizes the value of imagination in the discovery of
legal intent. The legal imagination must 'buyld and destroy' fictions,
test circumstances, and 'compounde thinges,' yet it always must be
ruled by the mission of 'disposing of the Lawe against a matter of truth
in a thing that is possible, grounded vpon iust cause.' Wary of entrusting
the poet's faculty too far, Fulbecke wedges a 'great difference betwixt
imagination and presumption,' cautioning the legal student that while
all arts need to employ a carpenter's square in their measurements,
each should either have its own level or handle the shared instrument
in its own fashion.[27]

In his scholarly endeavours to recover and to celebrate the common
law, Selden subjected its claims and characteristics to incisive critique,

without which that law could accrue only an empty dignity, its judges
similar to those 'Pageants in Cheapside, the Lyons & the Elephants, but
wee doe not see the men that carry y^m' (*Table Talk*, 60). A number of
scholars – especially Ziskind, Sommerville, Christianson, and Tuck –
have explored the sophistication and scepticism with which Selden
approached the piety underwriting the common law and purveyed by
men such as Coke.[28] For Selden, Coke's *optima regula* was as vulnerable
as it was venerable, so that in Selden's view the claims made for the law's
infallibility were, in turn, desirable, impractical, and – given the tyranny
of such claims in civil and canon law – at times even despicable. For
instance, Selden was drawn to the celebrated myth and mystique of
the judicial Druids; but his own scholarship kept leading him back to
an alternative image of the law's perilous history, the Janus. In the Norman invasion Selden saw both continuity and conquest, while in the
larger history of the law he found both constancy and change. For him,
the history of the common law was not mythic: it comprised records and
cases, traditions and fitfully invented principles, and it was lived out by a
people as often savage as they were dignified in their sense of liberty and
privilege.

With common law as the best but not the only example, the history of
England's judicial and legal institutions presented Selden with a complex picture of how humanly devised laws might oversee and secure the
welfare of a religious society. As Tuck shows in discussing Selden's
search for a legitimate mixture of sovereignties, the common lawyer
'appears to have seen the history of England as a series of conflicts
between various groups of English society, and in particular between the
King and his nobles, alternating with settlements agreed to by the parties. The settlements constituted the law of each epoch ... to determine
what was legally valid one had to look at what was precisely and clearly
laid down in current law, and not at some speculative history on the
general principles of political sciences.'[29] Even when he turned to natural and rabbinical studies, however, Selden did so with an eye towards
deepening and fulfilling Fortescue's boast that the institutions of positive law might possess the sanctity to operate as the hub in the regulation of the whole of religious society. Even if he resisted what Donald
Kelley calls the absurdities of 'chauvinism and credulity' in the myths
underwriting that warrant, Selden sought long and hard for the basis
and antiquity of the law's authority. His search for the sanctity of positive
law was made all the more difficult by two factors: his sophisticated
sense of history as 'more of a crazy-quilt than a seamless web'; and the

fault lines in contemporary understandings of whether a pristine antiquity, a natural font, or an artificial rationality accounted for the credibility of the common law.[30] Above all, the normative authority of the
common law of the land required that its arbiters have goodness and
righteousness as much as they need clarity and method. Such a criterion
Selden eventually located in the judges of the Sanhedrin.

Like poetry, so common law: Selden believed that the very spirit of
the Reformation demanded a rebuilding of sacred norms from the rub-
ble made of ridiculous myths by their learned critics, and he also
believed that critics were accountable for helping to rebuild. Accordingly, in his *History of the Common Law*, Selden's colleague Matthew Hale
attempted to transmit to posterity a reconciliation between the two faces
of Selden's approach to common law: between the loyal sage for whom
that law is simply, unquestionably sacred, and the analytical sceptic for
whom the honesty and the sanctity of the law must be newly and critically fashioned. In his own last work on the common law, however,
Selden offered evidence that he embraced both these roles but in a
scholarly apparatus that makes no pretensions at a coherent final word
on the status of English law.

A commentary on that classic legal text named for the grim scene of
its composition (the Fleet prison), Selden's *Ad Fletam Dissertatio* (1647)
is focused on a question that Pocock's insular common lawyer is said to
have neglected, the bearing of Roman civil law on the history and shape
of English law. Selden concludes that the heyday of the civil law in
England belonged to Edward II, but his attitude towards carrying out
this scholarly work is decidedly mixed. In the light of his insistence that
he has undertaken the commentary during a period of illness when
unable to work on his Judaic studies and only at the editor's request, the
Fleta is to Selden's English legal studies what the *Historiae Anglicanae
Scriptores Decem* is for his English historical work: a commissioned and
not entirely wholehearted piece of scholarship. Like the *Historiae Anglicanae*, however, it vents some nostalgia for a time when the sanctity of its
subject and of its practitioners was largely unquestioned.

Selden shows great pride in the autonomy and enlightenment of the
common law, whose sages long ignored the civil law and then used it as
one instrument in their arsenal. He still admires 'the original law con-
sisting wholly of the Druid cult, which, as we learn from Julius Caesar
and the very credible opinion of investigators, held sway in all things,
sacred and profane, in Britain and in Gaul'; and he protests that the
civil '*norma*' or 'criterion' never superseded common law, whose purity

remains largely unsullied. At one point in the commentary, however, the
source of his pride is a bygone phenomenon, one that we have reason to
believe Selden did not wholeheartedly support: those early days of the
post-conquest English law during which the legal sages were monks and
priests one and all (*Ad Fletam*, 45, 96–7).

Even though in his concurrent Judaic work he emphasizes the strictly
accidental connection between sacerdotal and legal vocations, Selden's
commentary on the *Fleta* pauses in order to celebrate the ascetic lawyers
for whom ecclesiastical sanctuary abetted legal excellence. First, he
maintains: 'In earlier times men, otherwise skilled in good learning,
applied themselves to the study of old English customs and laws as
affecting public administration, and from their number were selected
advocates and judges.' He adds: 'These men, according to their education, rank and opportunities, lived in monasteries, academies, house-
holds of famous bishops, colleges or elsewhere' (129–31). As a bachelor
who lived in the quasi-monastic settings of the Inner Temple and Whitefriars, Selden shared considerable sympathy for the protection afforded
by these vaguely various hermitages; for against all institutional pressures to the contrary, these monks were dedicated to the secular English
common law as the premier guarantor of welfare in English Christian
society: 'They made no public use of the law of Justinian or Theodosius,
but used those ancestral customs and native jurisprudence then, as now,
called English common law, *i.e.* the secular law of the Anglo-Saxons, as
contrasted with the divine law' (129–31). These medieval monks-cum-
lawyers understood – as did the Jewish legal sages on whom Selden was
concurrently working and as had Selden since he wrote the *History of
Tithes* – that secular law was charged with benefiting the whole of a religious society. So it was that these legal monks strenuously defended the
church and officiated so pervasively in legal matters that William of
Malmesbury was prompted to conclude, 'nullus clericus nisi causidicus'
[no cleric who is not a lawyer'] (130). When the pope prohibited the
lawyer monks from teaching profane matters outside the monastery,
they simply moved their law schools inside its walls.

It is likely that Selden's Judaic studies confirmed his earlier, shakier,
conviction that the lay authorities in the laws of a holy commonwealth
were themselves invested with sanctity. This deepening of conviction
becomes clear if the commentary on the *Fleta* is compared with Selden's
earlier account of how the common law had maintained an autonomy
from the civil law over the centuries, that found in 'A Reuiew' of the *History of Tithes*. In this addendum to his controversial work, Selden was, of

course, on the defensive against attacks from those prelates who considered the *History* nothing short of sacrilege. In turning to discuss the common law's control over all foreign laws, he offers, first, a careful disjunction between common and canon law, the latter derived from the Roman civil code: 'For euerie Christian State hath its owne *Common Laws*, as this Kingdome hath. And the *Canon Law* euerie where, in such things as are not meerly spirituall, is alwaies gouerned and limited (as with vs) by those *Common* Laws' (478). The allowance of a purely spiritual realm – 'which hath properly Persons and Things *sacred* only and *spirituall* for its obiect in practice' (478) – gives Selden little pause here, though it will become crucial to his later, Erastian vision of the holy commonwealth. Rather, he emphasizes two points: that the Roman civil law has made little impact on the common law; and that the common lawyer is distinct from the sacred person; for whoever 'knowes any thing in Holy Writ knowes the vse of the word *Common* to be so distinguisht from *Sacred*' (478). In keeping with the secularity of its minders, the common law is clearly a mortal, changeable creature of 'accession and alteration' (479), an interaction between customs, parliamentary statutes, and judicial decisions that is powerfully and flexibly capable of governing in the commonwealth within the circumstances that have a tendency to mix the religious, moral, social, and legal dimensions of experience.

In the commentary on the *Fleta*, Selden purveys the same pride in the autonomy of the common law; but his stress is not on the distinction between the sacred and the legal person, even if, in the work on the Sanhedrin, he makes the crucial distinction between legal sages and priests. The legal monks are indeed not priests officiating at the church altar; rather, they embody for Selden a tenacious and learned love for the common law that prevented the invasion of absolutist, even papist, codes of law in England. For the author of the *Fleta* as for Selden himself, the walls surrounding the common lawyer, indeed the walls of the common law itself, had not kept some of its very best advocates out of prison. Near the end of his commentary, Selden considers the question of authorship of the *Fleta*. In the vein of the *Fleta*, Selden informs us, great judges and lawyers were often imprisoned in those days, and although he makes no mention of the fact that he himself has recently received reparations for having twice continued that grisly tradition, he could have counted on his readers' making the connection. Selden had begun his decade of parliamentary involvement in the 1620s in jail at the behest of James I, and he ended that decade languishing in prison after spearheading the opposition to Charles's abuse of prerogative. The dissertation on the *Fleta* contained within its learned commentary one last consecration of Selden's vocation and something of a miniature book of martyrs. His Judaic work may have moved very far from the traditions of English common law, but at the centre of Selden's understanding of Jewish society remained the basic assumption that legal sages were more responsible than any other human being for the overall health of a people.

Typically, however, he downplayed heroes and martyrs and looked to the fashioning of institutions, a Sanhedrin acting in large part as a court of law but also in the capacity of a senate. For Selden was much more prepared to grant a parliamentary body a legal control over the holy commonwealth than he was to leave that control to the judges of His Majesty's courts. Those judges might well teach honesty, Selden opines in the *Table Talk*, but if his comments on such judges are any indication, they might just as often teach human beings their religious duties by way of negative example. What is more, while the common law could lay claim to sanctity and to the promulgation of those religious duties that human beings owe to one another, parliaments, in Selden's view, were in large part responsible for the doctrinal constituents and devotional customs of the English Protestant church itself.

—— 4 ——

In the early seventeenth century, a controversial case was made for intimacy between the sanctity of common law and the essence of godly religion. By their staunch supporters, both common law and godly religion were perceived to be under duress, and both were perceived as growing stronger thanks to that duress. Both had incisive and powerful critics, Ellesmere for the common law, and Laud for that putatively godly religion that he believed was a cover for insubordinate Puritanism. Yet claims made for the essential kinship between legal principles and godly religion were complicated as well as emboldened once the parliamentary component of both positive law and fervent Protestantism was introduced into the forefront of debate. On the one hand, Stuart parliaments had a fitful, even contentious relationship with common law claims; on the other, common lawyers such as Selden resolutely led the defence of those parliaments called into being by Charles I when conflict came to a head over the respective yet overlapping grievances involving true religion and lawful liberty.

From the 1620s through the 1640s Selden took it for granted that parliaments have always and predominantly sponsored and framed the English Reformation. In the 1640s and 1650s his involvement in the Long Parliament, his work on the Sanhedrin, as well as the contemporary outpouring of republican and apocalyptic theories of parliamentary government kept open the question of exactly what the future of English Parliaments might be. For Selden, however, the past of Parliament was clear on the question of how the reformation of religion came about. Reminding his guests at table that the English service book had become a matter of law well before the Reformation, then was afterwards re-instituted by the law's 'elder Brother,' Parliament, he concluded that the 'State still makes the Religion & receives into it what will best agree with it' (*Table Talk*, 118). As becomes clear in his massive work on the Sanhedrin, such a claim means not that the state cynically manipulates religion from afar but rather that its legal sages constitute the social ligatures of religious faith and worship in a fashion maximally beneficial to a religious commonwealth. 'State,' of course, is vague, but at other times Selden is more specific about the governing agencies whose responsibility it is to oversee the overseers of the church. For instance, 'whatsoever Bipps [bishops] doe, otherwise than what ye Law p[er]mitts, Westminster-hall can controwle' (20); or 'There must bee some Laymen in the Synod to overlooke ye Clergie least they spoile the Civill worke' (126). What is more, the guarantors of lawfulness in English society as a whole provide religion's very best foundation: 'But the Church runs to Jus divinum, least if they should acknowledge what they have, they held by positive Law, it might bee as well taken from them as it was given them' (61). Sometimes Selden adopts a much more defensive posture: 'The papists call our Religion, a parliamentary Religion, but there was once, I am sure, A parliamentary pope' (98). Such a stance is hardly surprising from a scholar whose troubles with the Stuart monarchs and their clergy began with the massively mounted argument that tithes have been (and really ought to be) determined by the ordinary legal instruments of society.

In 1624, 1626, and 1628–9 Selden directly experienced and fervently contributed to the best and the worst of times for the intervention of parliaments in the defence of true religion and of traditional lawfulness against a perceived upsurge of crypto-papists and corrupt advocates of an excessive royal prerogative. As Stephen D. White has argued, the Parliaments of the late 1620s were noteworthy for their holistic understanding of England's grievances. Speeches upheld the 'certainty in law' as a measure for both habeas corpus and reformed religion, while parliamentary opponents of abuses in royal prerogative doubled as, or spoke the language of, those critics of Arminian worship and doctrine. These M.P.s converged in 'a feeling of confidence that [they] had access to inexpensive, uncorrupted, and definitive legal remedies' for all the grievances afflicting their people. Not only were grievances in religion and politics constitutionally united for these M.P.s, but those abuses came to be seen 'not just as sporadic violations of fundamental legal and social principles but as serious threats to these norms.'[31]

From the early 1620s Selden was treated as an incarnation of legal and procedural standards available to the Houses of Parliament for consultation. First, in the wake of his early and influential textbooks and editions, he was called upon in 1621 to assist M.P.s in resurrecting one of their long-neglected legal privileges, the jurisdiction of the Commons over impeachment and of the Lords over trial and judgment in the cases of those impeached. That is, Selden was charged with clarifying how and when Parliament should serve as a judicial court. As Colin Tite explains, Selden undertook a serious risk in advising Parliament, yet he 'devoted outstanding scholarship and a committed point of view' in assembling *The Priviledges of the Baronage in England.*[32] The evidence of these texts clarifies just how trusted Selden was to recover and to fashion the proper norms of procedure and the boundaries of jurisdiction, especially when the delinquency of highest officers of the Crown was in question.

In 1624 this excellent monitor of the normative claims made for English positive law assumed his own membership in Parliament. Paul Christianson summarizes the progress of Selden's parliamentary activities in the 1620s: 'In 1621, the Lords hired Selden to codify and establish their privileges, including the revival of judicature; as part of this task, he also helped to establish the standing orders of the Upper House. Such actions impressed influential patrons and secured his selection to borough seats in the parliaments of 1624, 1626, and 1628–9.' Once selected for the Commons, Christianson explains, Selden impressed colleagues with his work on committees, his knowledge of precedents, and the expertise and energy he devoted to high profile cases. 'By 1628' Selden had risen to 'a powerful leadership role in the Commons.'[33] Thus, it came to be that in the final Parliament of the 1620s he was in the vanguard of the mission to promulgate the Petition of Right, to protect the liberties of the subject, to hold the officers of the Crown to the rational and just measure of English law, and to guarantee the continuation of religious reform. In the *Table Talk* Selden emphasizes that all the people of English society are wrapped up in the doings of Parliament (89); in the concluding years of the 1620s it was also true that the moral, legal, and spiritual integrity of that society depended on the very words of the speakers in Commons.

As Christianson stresses, Selden gave impetus to the parliamentary critique of abused prerogative by confidently asserting the accessibility of 'normal channels' and legal standards, and his speeches elevated the excellent value of codified procedures.[34] Even as his friend Ben Jonson lauded Selden as 'the law-book of the judges of England,' the lawyer himself bolstered the precision to be gained from 'the careful examination of constitutions and customs, their received interpretations and their force, in the state and ages of which any civil disquisition is raised.'[35] Fighting, according to Berkowitz, for 'the fulfillment of the promise of history' in Parliament and 'the rule of law,' Selden spoke of the scholarly scrutiny of legal records as 'the very compass to direct in all judicial proceedings; and of singular use also in whatsoever is deliberative.'[36]

In Selden's parliamentary speeches, not only is the methodical procedure of law accessible to free subjects; its customs are also so 'settled' and established as to seem almost part of the very land itself. One of his favourite phrases, the 'parliamentary way,' makes the laws and judicial procedures of England seem far other than a barbarous, degenerate, and obscure monstrosity that the common lawyers were accused of purveying. Whereas advocates of the royal prerogative attempt to convert Selden's compass into a mathematical line too rigidly and awkwardly applied, the common lawyer offers a passionate version of the plain folk wisdom for which he is famous in the *Table Talk*: laws are as 'constant and settled' as bodies or properties. As a lawyer, he says, he has defended habeas corpus for hire, but as an M.P., he claims to protest 'according to [his] knowledge and conscience,' while the officers of the king's court put up such smoke screens as the charges of 'sedition' or the claims for 'matters of state' (*Opera Omnia*, vol. 3, cols 1937, 1954). As a common lawyer, Selden suggests, an advocate for the sanctity of positive law or for the virtually priestly role of lawyers in the securing of true religion can never quite make it above the compromises of parasitism and the all too human imperfections of legal arbitration. Certainly, one can write textbooks or collect records. In the 1620s, however, Selden detects in Parliament the opportunity for the lawyer to remedy the political and religious grievances of a people by formulating a conscientious standard of positive law against which the moral honesty of even the king and his advisers can be measured.

Out of his notes, then, he pulls histories of sedition; out of his experience he offers the M.P.s simple guidelines for the assessment of precedents as 'good *media* or proofs of illustration or confirmation, where they agree with the express law.' When Selden appeals to 'all the several ways of just examination of the truth' with which the members engage, his tone is one of opportune mastery, not perplexity – no small matter in facing what he characterizes as a legal problem of unprecedented gravity (col. 1958). Where there is potential for categorical confusion – between civil and common law jurisdictions, between acts of war and the affairs of peace – Selden counters what he considers sophistry and equivocation with the simplicity and normalcy of 'ordinary justice' (col. 1959). He also reigns in any potential hubris on the part of the Commons when he limits their role in the moral honesty and religious faith of English society to whatever can be judicially deliberated.

Selden's share in the intervention of Commons against the abuses of the late 1620s was not exclusively concerned with ostensibly secular matters. He agreed with the other leaders of the Commons in their conviction that the English guarantors of lawfulness faced an unprecedented opportunity to reform and safeguard their religious society as a whole. As the king reminded the M.P.s in 1628, their office 'to maintain this church and commonwealth,' 'to maintain ... the true religion, the laws, and liberties of the realm' was a self-evident truth. But the putative rise of Arminianism at home, the misfortunes of Protestant warfare on the Continent, and the egregious abuses of royal prerogative provoked the M.P.s with an urgency that the holy commonwealth itself was in desperate peril from uncommonly powerful and multiple enemies, not least the 'pride of Rome' and the 'Austrian Eagle.' To increase the pressure, Coke was not alone in crediting England with a normative centrality for all of Europe: 'the eyes of all Christendom are upon us,' he warned. Speaking to the Committee for Religion, Sir Benjamin Rudyard first gave advice on how 'to establish true religion,' then explained the 'rule' of the holy commonwealth: 'It shall ever be a rule to me that where the church and commonwealth are both of one religion it is comely and decent that the outward splendor of the church should hold a proportion and participate with the prosperity of the temporal state, for why should we dwell in houses of cedar and suffer God to dwell in houses of skins?' Rudyard concluded with his clarion call for the Parliament to protect the holy commonwealth from its demise: 'although Christianity and religion be established generally throughout this kingdom, yet until it be planted more particularly I shall scarce think this a Christian commonwealth. [And] seeing it has been moved and stirred in parliament it will lie heavy upon parliaments until it be effected.' If Parliament looked out for God, he added, then God would doubtless 'bless [their] proceedings in this place the better for ever hereafter.' On another occasion, Rudyard was more specific about the ways in which the royal abuses of murky claims such as 'reason of state' had 'eaten out almost not only the laws, but all the religion of Christendom.'[37] 'Reason of state' was simply an obscure way of allowing the king to act as he pleased in matters of war, taxation, imprisonment, and religion alike.

Sir Dudley Digges found his precedent for the extraordinary 1620s in the Old Testament: 'My Lords, I shall, I hope, auspiciously begin this conference this day with an observation out of the Holy Story. In the days of good King Josiah, when the land was purged of idolatry and the great men went about to repair the house of God, while money was sought for, there was found a book of the law which had been neglected and afterwards, being presented to the good King, procured the blessing which your Lordships may read in the Scriptures.' As Digges proceeded to draw the analog, English M.P.s had also undertaken simultaneously the purgation of the church, the collection of funds, and the legal recovery of 'many and fundamental points thereof neglected and broken.' The justice of freeborn property was of 'sacred' stature, the cleansing of the church was of vital civil significance, and money epitomized a trust that tied king and people together by what Wentworth called in a Homeric flourish 'the golden chain.' At times the M.P.s argued that a legally dispensed 'justice is the life and the heartblood of the commonwealth.'[38] The heart of the holy commonwealth would beat or falter, then, over the issues of habeas corpus, forced loans, the billeting of soldiers, and the integrity of advisers to the king. If the king continued to exert the prerogative to detain bodies, goods, and estates without legal cause or justification, then the consensus over the division of authority under which James had ruled would simply collapse.[39] Debates over the legality of the Petition of Right never doubted the essential points – only the transmission – of the subjects' grievances with the king. On 24 March 1628, however, Sir Henry Mildmay argued that 'religion is the stay of the kingdom. The flourishing of religion doth not only concern our souls but the commonwealth.' Pointing out religious dangers at home – those divines Richard Montagu, Thomas Jackson, and John Cosin, for instance, who were thought to be driving the Church of England back to popery – M.P.s such as 'Mr Sherwill' liked to fortify their colleagues with the conviction that 'So much is to be ascribed to this House that it brought in religion. Were there not acts of parliament for the Articles in H.8? Was not our religion established in E.6 time? How can we make laws and not debate religion? Never was there more need for this House to be careful in religion, for religion cannot be divided from the state.' Sir Edward Coke pithily united the two essences when on 21 May 1628 he remarked that 'Order is the essence and virtue of a commonwealth. Job says that in hell *nullus ordo.*' In 'order,' then, Coke united law and righteousness at the very core of the holy commonwealth. Sir John Eliot was far more elaborate, however, in compiling a catalogue of dangers that ranged from the 'want of true devotion to heaven' and 'our insincerity and doubling in religion' ('doubling' is 'doubting' in some manuscripts) through the failure of royal advisers, the incompetence of the military, 'the impoverishing of the Sovereign, the oppression and depression of the subject,' and the waste of funds, ships, and men. Foes abroad they have many, Eliot admits, but 'if in these [many grievances] there be not reformation, we need no foes abroad: time itself will ruin us.'[40]

Some M.P.s in the 1629 Parliament protested that religious concerns must take precedence over all other grievances. John Rous engineered the prominence of religious grievances in those sessions and encouraged the other members to believe that a remedy of specifically religious abuses will be attended by redress against those violations of 'our goods, liberties, and lives.' For Rous, too, the various grievances were all of a piece, and he attributed to the devil the persecution of those Caroline Jobs who were deprived of their property as a means of weakening their faith. English subjects, he continued, must hold fast to their faith, and proprietary liberties would follow suit. Sir Francis Seymour agreed: 'If Religion be not a rule to all our actions what policy can we have.' Sir Walter Erle was more torn over the priority of religion and liberty, but joined the two causes in protesting 'that the cause of justice is Gods cause as well as the cause of Religion.' Religion must come first, he cautioned, without which English subjects have no life and liberty to protect: 'For I dare boldly say, never was there (in the point of subsistence) a more near conjunction between matter of Religion and matter of State in any Kingdom in the world than there is in this Kingdom at this day.'[41] Erle acknowledged, moreover, that if liberty owed its existence to religion, English Protestant religion traced its very provenance to law.

By June 1628 the metaphor of the heart has captured the M.P.s. Time and again, they refer to their own hearts, to the 'perfect English heart,' to 'all true Engllish hearts,' and to hearts at once rational and loving, all as a way of declaring a unity of purpose in remedying 'that great disorder in state' whose ravages seize the whole of the commonwealth, not the secular with the sacred or religion without property. Indeed, the sermons of Maynwaring and Sibthorpe come to epitomize the conjunction of religion and politics in the parliamentary campaign to prevent 'the apparent ruins and destructions of this kingdom.' So, too, the much hated Buckingham, who is said to comprise within him 'the grief of the kingdom. He is admiral of our seas, and general at the land ... Religion and all is at hazard by his means now.' As the grievances over religion come increasingly into the debates in June 1628, Mr Whitaker complains that the papists have established their own commonwealth within the Protestant one. Then Coke adds: 'We shall never know the commonwealth flourish but when the church flourishes. They live and die together.' Queen Elizabeth did better, he says; for 'at all times ... she maintained religion and justice,' not least in the great year 1588.[42]

Selden's leadership in the Caroline parliaments was neither so zealously religious as that of his contemporary Erle, nor so exclusively secular as the modern scholar Berkowitz maintains.[43] Even if his activities were predominantly concerned with legal grievances, it is also the case that he was included on a subcommittee dealing with the sermons of Maynwaring on 14 May 1628, urged a vote on the Eliot resolutions against Arminianism on the last day of the session in 1629, and guided the M.P.s in their understanding of what part parliaments had played and should play in determining orthodoxy in English Protestantism. He not only gave precedents; he took responsibility also for explaining a precedent and how it should be used: 'Precedents, my Lords, are good *media* or proofs of illustration or confirmation when they agree with the express law; but they can never be proof enough to overthrow any one law, much less seven several acts of parliament, as the number of them is for the point.' In working out the legality of the king's actions involving, say, martial law, he even gave little lessons on the nature of English law itself, for instance, 'all that law that you can name clearly is either ascertained by custom or established by act of parliament,' a formula that he applied to ecclesiastical law as well. He helped his fellow M.P.s sort out the relationship between 'temporal' and ecclesiastical crimes, for example, in his remark that Maynwaring's was 'a temporal crime to have parliaments thus scandaled in pulpits.' Or more broadly: 'As for Magna Carta the Church has many liberties, but those liberties by many acts of parliament are lessened and varied.' In the same comment, he gave a thumbnail sketch of the trajectory according to which the clergy came to be more and more fully under 'lay jurisdiction ... and since the 21th

of H.8 they have been totally.' A report of the same speech showed how
carefully Selden reasoned in matters of lay and church jurisdiction: 'Mr.
Selden says he is against the bill' – that is, 'An act to restrain some disorders that are or may be in ministers of God's word' – 'but says that an act
of parliament may alter Magna Carta: that ministers and clergymen are
already subject to lay jurisdiction and may now be punished by justices
of peace. But the reason why he is against the bill is because this is a law
without all example; for by this law the minister for being drunk shall
lose his benefice, and yet both the justices of peace and the jurymen
that are to judge and pass on a clergy shall pay but 5s. for being drunk,
which holds no proportion.' Thus, alterations in Magna Carta could
limit the liberties of the clergy in keeping with the Protestant spirit of lay
authority. But this restriction of the clergy had to be carried out, Selden
insisted, without prejudice against clerical persons. Even when Selden
was not speaking, his influence was felt in the way in which M.P.s spoke
to relations between religious and civil concerns, for instance, when one
M.P. ridiculed Maynwaring – and the griping clergy with him: 'They [the
clergy] will not suffer us to question tithes, whether they be *jure divino* or
no, and now they will not give us leave to enjoy our goods, *jure humano et
positivo.*'[44] For this speaker, Richard Spencer, Selden's research into the
legal history and basis of tithes was synonymous with the Commons'
own query.

Far from getting lost in legal intricacies, and even though his manifest grasp on the whole body of the English law was extraordinary,
Selden worked to convey to his colleagues the 'fundamental' implications of their business, how at one 'little gap every man's liberty may in
time go out.' Selden made use of his learning right across the spectrum
of problems in the holy commonwealth, from the levying of soldiers
and the legitimacy of martial law to the corroboration of which documents could be considered the legal cornerstones of religious orthodoxy. As he explained his role on 27 March 1628, his appearances in the
matter of the habeas corpus at first had been for hire; but now they
became a matter of 'my knowledge and conscience,' in short, a legal
sage's devotion to the common law as well as his heartfelt sense of what
is godly and sacred. Like so many of his colleagues in the Commons,
Selden believed that the matters before the body '[were] of so high a
nature that never any exceeding it in any court of justice whatsoever, all
the several ways of just examination of the truth should be used.'[45] Here
in small was the upshot of Selden's own authority in and purpose for
the holy commonwealth, to examine all the just means of redressing the

unprecedented civil and religious grievances that threatened to tear apart its very fabric.

When in May 1628 the Commons considered 'an act concerning subscription' of ministers, Selden led the way in exposing the problems with the bill. For, while the bill promoted a return to an Elizabethan state of affairs in which subscription was made solely to the Thirty-Nine Articles of 1562, Selden informed the M.P.s that such action would conflict with those Jacobean canons demanding much more of subscribers: 'The 1 article: that the minister shall acknowledge that the King is only [i.e., the King alone is] supreme governor. 2, that the *Book of Common Prayer* contains nothing against the word of God. 3, that they should conform to the former articles.' Selden's insistence on the Jacobean canons ensured that ministers were obligated to the commonwealth, not only to theological propositions. Indeed, as this debate continued at length, a question of protocol arose over whether Selden could speak again. But the debate all around him centered on the very nature of a religious commonwealth. Sir Nathaniel Rich declared: 'Alter our religion without act of parliament, and alter our liberties.' By contrast, Sir Humphrey May worried that the bill 'much disturbs the Church.' Christopher Sherland complained that religious conformity could never meaningfully be coerced by 'cruelty and tyranny,' while John Crew argued for the superiority of the Elizabethan over the Jacobean subscription to the extent that a situation imposed by act of Parliament was better than one 'made only by the clergy of the Convocation.' Others defined the criteria of unity, both in the commonwealth (Coke's 'order') and in a church derived from Parliament. Thus, Francis Rous maintained that 'Unity is the strength of a church, and without subscription that unity cannot be maintained'; and that subscription should be limited to religious documents established by Parliament; for otherwise one is confronted with the Arminian innovations of recent times.[46]

When members of the 1629 Commons appealed to the sixteenth-century parliamentary establishment or confirmation of the Articles of Religion, they sometimes sought out Selden as their measure. John Eliot expressed their critical need for a legal square that might be held up to contemporary religious controversies, one that would replace abstruse theological debate so that 'we may avoid confusion and distractions' in order to 'go presently to the ground of our Religion, and lay down a rule on which all may rest.' In keeping with Charles's own distaste for theological subtleties, Eliot, in contrast to the king, was intent on finding a reliable instrument 'against [which] rule' Arminian 'breakers and offenders' might be indicted.[47] It would be worse than pointless, Eliot knew, to apply a legal measure to religion if the legal measure itself were bent, broken, or misconceived. Thus the value of Selden; for he was credited with an uncommon ability to assess and to rectify actual legal measures.

Because Selden was crucial to the parliamentary recovery of true religion, he was enlisted in heated if not always enlightening controversies over the rival bogeys of the 1620s: the king's bogey 'Puritanism' and the staunch Protestant's bogey 'Arminianism.' For instance, he was charged with investigating and deciding the question of 'whether Mr. Montague be a lawful bishop or no,' Mr Montagu being the same Richard Montagu who almost single-handedly ignited the combustion of the Church of England that took place from 1624. Montagu it was whose books had putatively undercut every last conviction dear to English Protestantism, its apocalyptic war with the Romish Antichrist, its vilification of human will, its iconoclastic penchant in habits of worship. Charles I did not like the controversy generated by Montagu, but he continued to elevate the man's ecclesiastical office. Selden's charge of pronouncing on the Montagu scandal would have necessitated that he also take a position on the king's actions.

Selden appears for the most part to have sided with the 'godly' or zealous Protestants in his work for Parliament, or where there is no evidence for his conclusions, he clearly was a legal authority to whom those Protestants felt comfortable turning. He supported the refusal to license those 'bad books' held by the likes of Rous and Eliot as subversive of the basic tenets of English Protestantism, and he denounced the Caroline censorship perceived to be preventing the publication of those books that indicted the outgrowth of popery and Arminianism. At a time when Charles's queen was believed to be softening the court's execution of laws against recusants, Selden was asked to report on the treatment of Jesuit priests. He corroborated the view of the subcommittee on religion that orthodoxy had been settled by an Elizabethan parliament's confirmation of the articles of faith.[48]

On the question of how it might be determined what these articles signified or permitted, however, Selden only partly agreed with his colleagues in the Commons. In anticipation of his authoritative role in the Westminster Assembly's review of the Thirty-Nine Articles as the embodiment of English orthodoxy, Selden corrected those members who offered an extensive list of textual warrants 'received publicly, and taught as the doctrine of the Church of England in those points wherein the Arminians differ from us and other of the Reformed Churches.' In response, Selden narrowed the list considerably, agreeing only 'that our Catechisme is a publique Act of the Church; and the booke of Homilies, the book of Ordinacion of Ministers, the booke of Comon Prayer; the articles were agreed unto in the Convocacion house A.1571: which was alsoe a publique act of the Church.' Since the clergy in Parliament were sitting in judgment of the clergy in Convocation, he concluded, Parliament was empowered to confirm or oppose any resolution in convocation. Whatever he might have thought about the orthodoxy of this theological precept or that, Selden was committed to the notion that either Parliament or Convocation was supposed to institute or corroborate the vehicles of belief, and this commitment excluded documents such as the Lambeth Articles, the Articles of Ireland or Scotland, and the reported results of the Synod of Dort, even if those articles had been published and 'albeit our men were sent over by pub[lique] authority' to the Synod.[49] These writings included some of the very best ammunition for the M.P.s that there was absolutely no place for Arminianism in the Church of England or on the Continent, where (these members believed) there had never been a clearer divide between Protestant truth and Roman corruption than the gaping chasm in the massive German war. Nonetheless, even if there was no question that Selden was an invaluable standard of true religion for M.P.s condemnatory of creeping popery and Arminianism in the court and church of Charles I, Selden made it equally clear that his standard of law might well prove honestly critical of his allies in the parliamentary assaults on religious corruption. For Selden, the recovery of true religion simply could not be sheltered from the requirements of law: the church was part of the commonwealth, as surely as the lawyers, judges, and M.P.s of the commonwealth were obliged to the demands of their consciences and to the protection of true religion.

The bold leadership of Selden in the Caroline parliaments was not lost on King Charles, who incarcerated the scholar so indefinitely that famous scholars on the Continent traded news about Selden's condition and longed for any evidence of his release.[50] For when it came to convincing the obdurate Charles of his deflection away from true religion and honest English liberty, the oratory and researches of Selden and his associates in Parliament proved as politically ineffectual as the delightfully rendered river sprites of the *Poly-Olbion*. Indeed, given the king's own love of myths and masques, it is not surprising that when next Selden collaborated with the legal profession for royal attention, he was involved in the production of Shirley's *Triumph of Peace*. However much Selden may have reduced his always cautious commitment to the common law as a sacred norm for English society, he nonetheless grew to believe ever more strongly in the possibility of a parliamentary religion. In working out the best of all possible institutions in the Sanhedrin, Selden would elevate his strong commitment to the guardianship of legal sages and senators to a closer intimacy with the divine, and he would take it as his primary responsibility to design just how legal institutions and magistrates should be coordinated with, responsible for, yet also separate from and respectful of, the purer labours of a zealous ministry, their preaching and praying for the purposes of saving souls. Not his time in prison but the experience of a civil war and participation in a national synod would lead him to the conviction that if rightly invented and calibrated, a legal and senatorial monitor for religious practice might enable a religious society to achieve holistic prosperity at long last. But the Sanhedrin also raised the level of integrity and godliness that would be required of the lay magistrate and lawyer.

—— 5 ——

As is suggested by the nostalgia for ascetic lawyers in *Ad Fletam Dissertatio*, Selden concerned himself not only with the assets and liabilities of positive law as a measure for English faith and manners, but also with the qualifications of its practitioners. Those arbiters of English law could be heroic yet remote, as in the case of the ascetics; glaringly flawed if Selden's several quips about judges are to be believed; and sometimes both at once, especially in the case of those aristocrats whose oversight of legislative and judicial matters in the House of Lords could be blurred by the arrogance and violence of personal honour. With Jonsonian poetics, practitioners as well as poems were also very much under scrutiny; for the moral integrity of the poet was thought to have a direct bearing on the truth and quality of the poetry. Jonson usually treated the assessment of personal worth as if were straightforward and transparent; even if Selden and he were worried about poetic parasitism, Jonson set himself up as the unimpeachable standard of honesty. In Selden's work in the 1630s on the history of the Judaic priesthood, the criteria for admission into this sacred order were reasonably clearly enumerated in the Talmud, even if interpretations and applications of those criteria were debatable. In his work on natural law in the same decade he attempted to dispense with the problem of personal agency altogether, yet his scepticism about the rational universality of that law implied the inevitability of biasing circumstances in human perception, and such ancient heroes of natural wisdom as the Druids brought with them their share of compromising associations.

Regarding English law, however, Selden concerned himself from the outset of his scholarly career with the qualifications of legal agents whose duty it was to administer justice. He knew firsthand, of course, as Christopher W. Brooks has said, that the profession of law itself was divided into higher and lower groups of practitioners. 'The first of these, "the upper branch,"' Brooks notes, 'was composed of serjeants at law and barristers, the lawyers who enjoyed a monopoly over advocacy in civil cases heard before the high courts in London.' Beneath this group were the men 'concerned primarily with organising cases, handling the procedural aspects of litigious work and providing other miscellaneous legal services such as conveyancing.'[51] In such a diverse group, moral integrity could hardly be taken for granted. In 1616, then, Selden's Fortescue edition served as something of an educational manual in ethos for budding lawyers.

Selden's early treatise on duelling focused the problem of moral character on an especially volatile group; in it he attempted to systematize the violent and arbitrary impulses of those better sort of Englishman whose responsibilities would very likely include the administration of law in the provinces as well as the protection of and judgments according to law in the House of Lords. For Selden as for other serious students of the law from the middle level of English subjects, the aristocracy presented itself both as its own peculiar Janus, since its members were the natural, venerable patrons and guardians of the laws and customs governing their society, and as an irrational, violent, and arrogant bane on their community's piety, virtue, justice, and order.

For legal students in the Elizabethan and Stuart years, Fortescue could be credited with a powerful image of the aristocratic lawyer as surely as he had set forth the ideal of a priestly one. In Selden's edition, a reader would find Fortescue's profile of the four great Inns of Court that excluded the middle and lower ranks while advertising the instruction 'of all commendable qualities requisite for Noblemen' (114v). Those seventeenth-century barristers contributing to the masques of the Inns might well imagine themselves as heirs to the medieval lawyers who, in residence there, would 'learn to sing, & to exercise themselues in all kinde of harmony. There also they practise dauncing, & other Noble mens pastimes, as they vse to doe, which are brought vp in the

Kings house' (114v–115r). A reader of Selden's Fortescue might well come away with the notion that English lawyers were meant to resemble Judaic priests, pure blooded as well as consecrated. For readers raised on panegyric poetry, however, such a celebration would be understood as presenting the aristocratic lawyer as he ought to be, not at all as he usually was.

No doubt as part of their cultivation of an often compromising noble heritage, the early Stuart law schools and their cultural brokers were intrigued by those controversial forebears, the Knights Templars. In 'The Masque of the Inner Temple and Gray's Inn' (1613), for instance, the main masque features priestly, martial knights just years before the adoption of the heraldic symbol of the Templars in the Middle Temple, sometime between 1615 and 1638. But the Templars are rarely mentioned in Selden's work, even though those ascetic knights had occupied the properties that would become the two Thames-side law schools known as 'temples.' Perhaps Selden was repelled by the scandal surrounding the trial and execution, some would say the royal persecution, of these crusaders-cum-financiers, their charges ranging from sex crimes to heresy.

Readers could find out all about the Templars and their connection to the Inns of Court in George Buc's *Third Universitie of England*, added to the 1615 edition of John Stow's *Annals*. In declaring the temples the most ancient of the Inns, Buc traces their foundation to the order of religious soldiers known as the Templars and explains the origin of the name in their residence next to the Temple in Jerusalem. Having explained their ascetic and martial vows in protection of pilgrims to Jerusalem and in opposition to infidels, Buc notes the synagogue-like circularity of the temple church in London and the noble honour and magnificence of their lives and lands. His account of their downfall in the thirteenth century is wholly sympathetic: the Templars were victims of papal and royal persecution by leaders fearful of their power, envious of their prosperity, and unmoved by their righteousness.

So it is, Buc concludes, that the knights came to suffer from trumped-up charges detailing in a papal bull their many horrific crimes, including heresy, idolatry, and sexual transgression. According to Buc, the Templars died the death of martyrs at the hands of griping princes, and even one of their emblems of solidarity – two men on a horse – was subjected to scurrilous interpretation. Buc continues his tale with the assumption of the temple properties by another ascetic and chivalric order, the Knights of the Order of Saint John of Jerusalem; but his main purpose is to accentuate the similarities between the venerable professors of the common law and the knights whose noble and pious device the Middle Templars have recently recovered for their own.

The Inner Temple, however, kept its heraldic Pegasus. In texts from Stow's *Survey* to Thomas Fuller's *Historie of the Holy Warre* (1639), English readers could discover ample reason for keeping a distance between the modern practitioners of law and the controversial medieval crusaders. Stow includes Matthew Paris's indictment of the arrogant Templars, 'who being at the first so poore, as they had but one horse to serue two of them, (in token whereof they gaue in their Seale, two men riding of one horse) yet sodainly they waxed so insolent, that they disdayned other orders, and sorted themselues with Noblemen.'[52] Stow proceeds with his account of the charges against the Templars, their trial and punishment, and the aftermath during which the lawyers took up residence in their stead. Yet Fuller's treatment is harsh, depicting the Templars as spoiled knaves on the knee of the King and Patriarch of Jerusalem – as children who impudently inflated into sluggard 'Lords' holding in scorn the 'valiant' pretexts of their own institution. In short, the Templars might have intended noble designs in protection of true religion, but they degenerated into greedy aristocrats as their ideal of knightly monasticism rotted into idleness and pride.[53]

On many occasions, some quite extensive, Selden explores the complex question of whether military aristocrats – the knights already prominent in some ancient accounts of British society – tend to benefit a virtuous, just, and godly rule of law. In both the civil- and common-law traditions, there was ample precedent for his close attention to the effects of violence on law. In Bracton and Glanvill, for instance, one finds a conventional assertion of the complementary pairing between arms and laws in the royal repertoire.[54] At the outset of the ninth chapter in Selden's *Jani Anglorum*, however, such complementarity is jettisoned for '[t]hat Antipathy betwixt Arms and Laws' (67), a not surprising development given the evidence that all around him Selden would have seen instances of aristocratic honour's erupting into violence and social disruption. From the volatile nobles on the order of the second Earl of Essex to the continuing tradition of what Prest calls 'a high level of interpersonal violence' among the law students themselves, Selden had every reason to get an intellectual and historical handle on the bloody, honour-bound wilfulness to which an aristocratic heritage ostensibly entitled certain young men in Selden's London.[55]

In his early efforts to stabilize and promulgate the legal restrictions on duelling Selden took a middle ground on a surging controversy over the theological legitimacy of personal revenge. Legally, the case of the duel was rendered all the more difficult because the leading claim on jurisdiction was made by the High Court of Chivalry, one of the remaining civil courts in England. Despite the tendency of the civilians themselves to derive from various levels of the social order, the Court of Chivalry was its most aristocratic branch, concerned as it was with 'military matters which are not governed by common law' – for instance, acts of treason committed overseas – as well as 'heraldic disputes,' some trials by combat, and, increasingly in the Stuart century, 'complaints regarding insulting acts and words.'[56] Having outlawed duels in 1613, James I directed men to the Court of Chivalry for a resolution of their disputes over honour. By the 1620s the Court of Chivalry itself was under attack, but it was defended by the king and the earl marshal, Thomas Arundel, Selden's own patron. It was, James protested, 'the fountaine of all honor,' and an ancient, dignified means of preventing bloodshed – this from the monarch who had cheapened the outflow of honours by widely selling them.

Over the course of his life, Selden returned to a moral and spiritual evaluation of duels. Early in the *Jani Anglorum*, he groups them together with ordeals as impious customs, at least as impiety is determined according to the Roman church. In the *Table Talk*, he conflates duels with wars in making the informal case that if war can be lawful, so too can duels. In both cases, he argues, God is the judge where the law otherwise has no remedy. But assessments of moral and spiritual credit cannot be separated in the case of duels from the demands of social duty. The role of the legal sage, in fact, is to work out the circumstances in which inner, transcendent, and social warrants are likeliest to converge. Thus, he remarks in the *Table Talk*, dukes have the obligation to fight those gentlemen whom they have insulted, a duty that helps to make sense of the most apparently senseless of wars (41–2). For the point is applicable (he adds) to a civil war in which the people have legitimately opposed an injurious king. In such cases, there is no 'other measure of Justice left upon Earth but Armes,' a bloodshed overseen and judged by God (*Jani Anglorum*, 84–6).

By the 1640s Selden's focus was steadily on ancient Judaism, which for him meant that God was a more reliable overseer than divine presence could ever be with common lawyers and members of Parliament. The younger Selden took no such recourse out of the perplexing requirement that it is the responsibility of human law alone to isolate and clarify the legal status of aristocratic violence. Like so many precocious yet defensive young wits in late Elizabethan and early Stuart London, who disguised their bold forays into public discourse behind jokes and a bluster of indifference, he opens his treatise on duels – *The Duello, or Single Combat* – with a feckless apology that his is no manual for duelling, but rather is a pithy account of the traditions, procedures, and ceremonies formalizing its violence (*Opera Omnia*, vol. 3). Much as he will do with titles of honour, tithes, inheritance, or calendars, Selden offers a history and legal analysis of organized if unofficial violence between men of honour. As is often the case with his early style, however, he shows a saucy, polysyllabic, and desultory allusiveness of approach, again in the manner of that same Thomas Nashe who is prepared to deflate an alderman with his literary prowess or to laugh at one of his heroes – Jack Wilton – for pretending to be an earl. Meanwhile, that style tries on fanciful etymologies, even as Selden invokes Camden's favorite text, Plato's *Cratylus*, for a model of meaningful, as against barren and unstable, verbal analysis. Selden has clearly begun to be interested in the history of aristocracy, a subject that will occupy him much more extensively in the *Titles of Honor*; but suspecting that by social definition he lacks the authority to enter into an analysis of noble codes and behaviours, he obscures and protects his search for normative meaning in aristocratic violence with a mask of *sprezzatura*.

Selden does not always conceal the difficulty of his historical problem. Like words or titles of honour, so the conventions of violence: time 'both establisheth and abrogateth'; words get uprooted and practices outgrow their formulae (*Opera Omnia*, vol. 3, col. 58). The wilfulness and fragile sense of honour that render aristocratic behaviour so vexingly abnormal are ironically recast in Selden's Platonic framework and critical methodology as epitomes of the very nature of historical institutions themselves, each one so mutable and freely floating as virtually to mock any attempt to recover its standard. From the outset of the *Duello*, Selden assembles the traditions of judicial violence in search of a definition, but the duel itself encapsulates an aristocratic resistance to the ordinary dictates of positive law that can be extended to the realm of all human behaviour and inventions, including positive law. Words slip from their moorings, logic gives way to subtlety, noblemen shed blood only because they wish to, common and civilian jurisdictions collide, and the human condition makes madness of any method. Indeed, in his methodological chapter Selden retracts what he asserts, offers judgment for our direction then abandons direction to our fantasy. Duels exemplify how the leaders of a people are steeped in the ritual codification of their behaviour and values; but duels just as effectively illustrate how those leaders in the codification of human behaviour have the greatest tendency to resent or ignore the laws that they have made, like so many petty and wilful gods, offended that there are norms of good and evil. With divine dispensation or at least natural law transparently available, human beings are always afflicted by the ridiculous arrogance, inconsistency, and brutality that heady aristocrats write large.

With his turn to the antiquity of duels in chapter 2, Selden settles down into analysis and illustration, noting the allowances and arguments for this honorific violence. Yet duelling continues to slip from the stability of law into a flimsier basis in supposition: chivalry is a code and an impulse, a formula and a pun, a judgment and a fantasy. Along the way, Selden mentions those armorial and genealogical disputes between Lord Grey of Ruthen and Sir Edward Hastings, to which he himself contributed a separate treatise. As with aristocratic violence, so too with aristocratic titles: Selden devotes his scholarly energy to normalizing those noble legacies securing and defending a social order, its manners, and beliefs. Like Jonson, however, he has only a fitful commitment to those legacies. Selden believes that aristocrats can be undesirable not simply because they so arrogantly rescind their legal obligations or make parasites of talented young men from the middle ranks. For Selden more than for Jonson, aristocratic honour also mocks the rule of law as ultimately hapless within all the many violent and amorphous forces of history.

From Selden's life and body of work, there is ample evidence for his suspicion that aristocrats often detracted from the very sacred-cum-moral measures of a religious society to which they ostensibly offered stability, propriety, and protection. In his early works, Selden followed classical leads in imagining knights or barons at the head of British, then Anglo-Saxon, government; and, unlike civil law, the common law itself was deeply rooted in land and inheritance. Selden went even further in ensuring that his readers saw barons and aristocratic rule in the earliest acceptable records of the past. For instance, at a late point in the *Jani Anglorum*, he underscores the non-monarchical status of early lawmakers or 'kings': 'Wherefore we have no reason to make any question, but that part wherein we live, now called England, was governed by several persons, and was subiect to an Aristocracy' (93). The same point is made repeatedly in the *Analecton*. No doubt Selden, like Jonson in his poetry of praise, was committed to reclaiming the goodness and rightness of that state of affairs when he assisted the Lords with understanding their judicial privileges or when he advised Bacon on the office of the lord chancellor. At their best, the aristocracy embodied a republican guardianship of a positive law that was as flawed as it was securely contractual and solidly accessible.

Selden did find it hard to ignore the dangers and disappointments waiting for a people who entrusted purely born aristocrats with the just administration of sacred faith and manners. Like Jonson, Selden himself was of mixed stock: his mother was from a socially dignified family, while his father, a musician, was not. Selden took his own maternally derived gentility into the law schools, which, as Prest has demonstrated, were not at all simply Fortescue's urban finishing school for the privileged. Despite King James's command in 1604 that only gentlemen be admitted to the Inns of Court, the law schools continued to fissure into serious scholars and amateur propertied men, and this divide in turn exacerbated social tensions.[57]

Throughout his life, Selden benefited from excellent aristocratic patrons, including Henry Grey, eighth Earl of Kent, his wife Lady Elizabeth (whom Selden is rumoured to have married once she was widowed), and Thomas Howard, Earl of Arundel. No doubt Selden would have accepted Camden's tendency in the *Britannia* to etch aristocratic families and their properties into the landscape along with woods and streams. Yet for Selden, as for Jonson, Camden himself embodied the clear attractions of a meritocracy. There is clear evidence in Selden's works that the scholar saw fit to demythologize the poetic myths of the aristocracy; Christianson is right to argue that in *Titles of Honor*, Selden eroded 'the mystique of blood so favoured by some Renaissance European nobles and their apologists,' and that he 'subverted any claim to a hereditary nobility independent of the state.'[58] In his parliamentary career, Selden was committed to ensuring that legal procedure exposed the transgressions of leading aristocrats; and in 1640 he was chosen to sit on a committee that investigated the abuses in the Court of Chivalry. In the *Table Talk*, under the category of 'gentlemen,' Selden considers the malleable nature of that status; prefers a gentleman-by-manners to a gentleman-by-birth; attributes more temperate reason to the religion of the gentle than to the religion of the multitude; then indicts the parliamentary Lords who are flattered into blindness about their vices, have their titles cheapened by their multiplication and novel invention, and look foolish in their self-interested protestations.

At times Selden appears ready to take as far as possible Nashe's measurement of the great by a standard somehow irrelevant to their greatness. In the second and third decades of the seventeenth century, of course, the standard of positive law, in Selden's scheme of values, clearly outweighs Nashe's touchstone of an excellent blank verse. But their critiques of puffed-up greatness overlap. Nowhere is it more apparent that Selden embraces what Prest calls 'a central humanist tenet, which defined true nobility as learning applied to the public good,' than in his notion that 'if common lawyers were not in fact gentle by birth, they might nevertheless be ennobled by their virtuous calling.'[59] That is, the editor of Fortescue knows that in legal sociology as well as legal history, Fortescue was simply wrong about nobility and law. Indeed, in his Judaic studies Selden makes it quite clear that there is a necessary relationship between noble birth and vocation, but only in the case of the priesthood, not in the case of the law sage. This difference makes more sense of Selden's remark in the *Table Talk* that ministers of the word and sacraments had better not be contemptible outside the temple if they hope to be respected inside – a commonplace criticism of the Laudian clergy's tendency towards the lower or middle areas of the social spectrum, and one delivered virulently in the early 1640s by Robert Greville, Lord Brooke.[60]

Throughout his early works, Selden stages an intermittent battle between his aristocratic loyalties and meritocratic convictions. The latter convictions emerge no less clearly than the former loyalties. In a panegyric for women and their fitness to rule, Selden concludes in the *Jani Anglorum* that 'Vertue shuts no door against any body, any Sex, but freely admits all.' In this vein, he recalls the pagan tradition of conceiving the supreme God as a hermaphrodite with 'the mystical name of Male-Female,' a blurring of distinction that he pursues in *De Dis Syris* and, at a more mundane level, in his defence of cross-dressing in the letter to Jonson (*Jani Anglorum*, 20). Also in the *Jani Anglorum*, he traces the ancient and medieval debate over whether marriage between nobles and plebeians should be permitted. Selden elaborates the affirmative position in a musical metaphor that posits a harmony in the marriage between a decayed aristocrat and a prosperous commoner or between a wealthy aristocrat and a poor commoner: 'and thus let *Love*, which was begot betwixt *Wealth* and *Poverty* suite this unlikeness of conditions into a sweet harmony; and this disagreeing agreement will be fit for procreation and breed' (30). With his father's music converted into cosmic *nomos*, Selden invokes comic playwrights in lieu of law for advice to future husbands. Eventually in his career, he studied the Hebraic laws of marriage and sexuality for their positive formulae; but in his youth, the sexual desires complicating a rigidly maintained social order were prone to as many poetic myths as the brutal violence of Arthurian knights.

In *Titles of Honor*, however, Selden's attitudes towards aristocratic and meritocratic claims on normative authority are woven into a highly complex pattern. In this prodigious work of archival history, he attempts to trace and to stabilize the lineage of the very titles in which aristocratic rule is vested, yet within a framework singularly devoted to personal merit and in a narrative attentive to the distinction between personal and inherited titles.

In the second edition, no fewer than four prefatory items destabilize if not subvert the birthright and honour of aristocratic blood. First, there is an epigraph from Boethius warning that high office will not honour a bad man and, in fact, will expose the man who has stained the office. Only a good, wise, godly man is worthy of high office. In both the first and the second editions of the *Titles*, the reader next encounters Selden's dedication of the work to his friend and fellow law student, Edward Heyward; in the second, the author celebrates their 'most sweet Community of Life and Freedom of Studies.'[61] Since Heyward was of the gentry, a group that Selden included among the lower nobility, Selden's emphasis on merit stops considerably short of rejecting rank as a factor in leadership; that, too, was Jonsonian; for the poet liked to link goodness with greatness in the qualifications of England's heroic regiment of natural monitors and governors. It follows that such a friendship would be based on shared values and minds, not on flattery or self-interest, and it would resemble those rare friendships heralded in Jonson's address to a man who would be 'sealed of the tribe of Ben.' Like Jonson, too, Selden highlights the basis of his dedication, a true friendship that signifies far more than patronage or advancement. More boldly, he charges that 'the Title of *Patron* is grosly, though commonly, abused, where no Censure or Power at all of Suppressing, Correction, or Monition, is left to him that is styled so' (a2r). That is, patrons receive praise without performing their duties of measuring and correcting the normative discourses of their clients. Over the course of history, he reminds Heyward, titles once 'grounded either in an Active and stirring Wit and other such Worth, or in that which was Grave and more Settled' eventually degenerates into what Jonson calls the 'cork of title' (a3r).[62] If these decadent spirits avoid 'Wildness and Levity,' the reason is simply that they prefer 'Lazie Dulness' (a3r). They do not possess even the energy to be actively evil.

To this dedicatory epistle, Jonson himself adds commendatory verses, the climax of which celebrates Selden's refusal of an aristocratic patron for the work for the sake of honouring a worthy friend. Here and elsewhere, Jonson clarifies that the ills of poetry and the corruption of social lineage infect normative discourse with much the same swollen rot. Given Jonson's metaphorical habits, his praise for Selden's comprehensive circle of knowledge resembles that centred yet dutiful Stoic sage remarkable for 'keeping of [his] State,' his essential virtue, whether emperor or slave (a4r). Such a sage is indebted to natural, not human, law for his moral honesty; and whether or not his society attends to his example, its wiser heads are delighted that the model exists.

By the time he reaches his preface to the reader, Selden virtually apologizes for a massive work on civil rather than moral honours, remarking of the ancients that 'although these wrote as Philosophers, and so spent much of what they said doubtless upon *Natural* and *Moral Nobility*, or on that which was as proportionable to what in the later times we call *Nobilitas Christiana*, as the height of virtue, in Paganisme, could be to the best exercise of Religion; yet there can be no question but that they handled also *Civil Nobility* or *Gentry*, which is part of our Subject here, and by the *Academiques* or *Platoniques* and the *Peripatetiques* was specially reckoned among *External* things that are *good*, and by the *Stoicks*, among such as are *Indifferent* only' (b2v). Offering an ancient taxonomy of different types of nobility, Selden settles into his massive assembly and learned analysis of pan-European and even Asian titles for monarchs, princes, and aristocrats. He endeavours to sort out laws, customs, stable formulae, and proper senses from eccentricities, deviations, and ambiguities. If aristocrats are to serve as legal compasses for a people, one needs a 'very Compass' for their part in '*Judicial* proceedings' (b3v–b4r). The measure needs its own measure, even though reliance on the second unsettles full dependence on the first. Selden is sufficiently sceptical that he understands that the potentially infinite regress through the criteria might well require two radical leaps of faith – one in the beneficent will of God, the other in the practical order sustained by human institutions. Even if he devotes much of his work in the 1630s to legitimizing the law of nature, his tome on that law constantly factors in God's will and human invention.

As the research of the *Titles* unfolds, Selden is apt to remind us why aristocrats – like poet laureates – are needed for a normative discourse that they also commonly damage. The simplest truth about the human artifices of custom, law, and forms of government is that they should and must metamorphose through several guises, as one after another becomes appropriate for the circumstances of a society. At times, however, changing custom establishes titular warrants of authority in promiscuous or arbitrary ways, in which case the sages of the law must re-evaluate the merits of custom.

Despite or in response to such changes in social norms, poets and genealogists gratify a people's need for continuity in the history of their values, but the fictions of these same inventors share the responsibility for much of the promiscuity afflicting the sanctity of law. The many 'circumstantial fancies and cadencies of language' converge with a fabulous and self-interested chivalric imagination in corrupting a positive and contractual law that somehow still requires the masks of genealogical and poetic myths (247). In *Titles of Honor*, Selden reclaims and stabilizes the authorities of fanciful poets and of violent, arrogant aristocrats; but in a manner typical of his scepticism, he also rejects, or at least complicates, those romantic fancies in which aristocrats and laureates collude within the immoral arts of parasitic bards.

Between the second and the fourth decades of the century, Selden also shows signs of wanting to extricate the lawyers from the poets. In his notes on Fortescue, Selden proffers his most severe attack on the ancient poetic parasites: 'And though the *Bards* knew divers things by tradition, which they onely sung, and so a specious argument is made usually for that common story [of the Trojan Brutus], because they sung it, yet I see not why any, but one that is too prodigal of his faith, should believe it more then Poetical story, which is all one (for the most part) with a fiction.' Quoting Athenaeus and Ammianus, he lowers the blade: 'For what were *Bards* but such as sung the praises of old suppos'd *Heroes* at their pleasure' (notes, 15). In this condemnation of the parasite, the pleasures of the poet and the delusions of the aristocrat have converged to deceive the future arbiters of English norms, those sages who must persist in seeking out sacred and reliable measures for those passions, conflicts, eccentricities, mysteries, exertions of will, and fantasies that no religious society can ever manage – or even simply afford – to jettison. In the 1631 edition of the *Titles*, his preface is far more emphatic about his expertise in law than the preface to the first edition in 1614. In the earlier one, he envisions himself as a member of Mercury's '*ingenuous* favorites' (b3v) fighting a cultural war against the multitude of ignorant readers, a version of Jonson's desire for 'understanders.' Indeed, Selden recalls a visit to 'the well-furnisht Librarie of my beloued friend that singular Poet *M. Ben: Ionson*, whose speciall

Worth in Literature, accurat Iudgment, and Performance, known only
to that *Few* which are truly able to know him, hath had from me, euer
since I began to learn, an increasing admiration' (c1v). Selden even
refers to his own 'vnderstanding Reader.' Like Jonson, too, he makes a
moral case against the degeneration of the nobility from its 'pure
Spring' of ancient virtue (b4v), and he quotes the Roman poets Juvenal
and Lucan on the misery of such decay. He prizes the tendency of the
ancient Romans to yoke honour and merit in impressive 'Trophies of
Virtue' – in temples, for instance (c1v). And in his dedication to Heyward, he stresses that books should concern themselves with virtue or
goodness as much as learning. Their 'instructing purpose' should speak
to 'either of the two objects of Mans best part, *Veram* or *Bonum.*' In that
same dedication to the first edition, Selden refutes 'the Prouerbiall
assertion, that *the Lady Common Law must ly alone*'; a student of law can
legitimately be promiscuous in his studies, lying (for example) with
both philology and poetry.

In the second edition, brought out at the end of Selden's great
decade as a lawyer in Parliament, the emphasis has shifted to the documentary sources of law, to the charters, patents, rolls, and legal codes,
all often neglected (he laments) when historians claim to study the '*Constitutions* and *Customes* of Seuerall States and Ages (that is, the *Lawes* of
them)' (S5v). He elaborates on the point: 'And plainly, in all this kind of
Learning, concerning either Things or Persons, as they are part of any
State, there is nothing more conduces to a right iudgement then the
carefull examination of *Constitutions and Customes,* their *receiued Interpretations,* and their *Force,* in the State and Age of which any Ciuill disquisition is raised. For they are the very Compasse to direct in all *Iudiciall*
proceedings' (¶1r). From 1631 to the end of his life in 1654 Selden
directed his efforts to searching out some higher authority with which
to underwrite these workaday proceedings, some authority in nature or
in the God of Noah and Moses. No matter where he went for his directing compass, however, Selden never abandoned the conviction, forged
in the fires of controversy in the 1620s, that a holy commonwealth must
rely in its every aspect on the processes of justice and the legal sages that
operate them.

In the digressions and analogies of his work on the titles of honour,
Selden hinted at a standard that purported to transcend the imperfec-

tions of mature positive law yet that could also avoid the infantile vacuity of poetry and so oblige the conscience if not the purse. That standard was nature, with arbiters ranging from Pythagoras, the children of Noah, the Druids, and the Stoics to Roger Bacon and modern intellectuals such as Copernicus and Grotius. In the *Titles*, Roger Bacon was singled out for having profited the studies of laws as well as stars; in both cases, he was considered a pioneer in search of precepts that are transcendent but not fabulous. Yet Selden's attempts to normalize England's institutions of positive law – whether in the courts or in Parliament, whether past or present, whether arbitrated by the well born or the learned – showed another impulse on his part: to stake down norms in historical particulars, to insist on documented contracts rather than elusive dreams, to practise in parliament what he might preach in consultation, and to actualize *nomos* imperfectly on earth rather than to sublimate human practice in some ideal of cosmic harmony or some fortress of divine right.

Among his contemporaries writing in the first half of the seventeenth century, Selden found a wide spectrum of presuppositions, methods, and theological justifications regarding the study of nature. Especially in the 1620s and 1630s, just as he was turning to the completion of his great work on the biblical corroboration of the religious tenets of natural law, students of Bacon's Great Instauration were struggling to decipher whether that six-part program is amenable to, or wholly at odds with, the Neoplatonic, Hermetic, and Cabalistic alchemy of natural theologians such as Robert Fludd. In turning to consider at length the great potential of natural law, Selden sought a measure for the ideal religious society that might permit more intellectual and moral rigour than poetry yet possess more innocence, holiness, and universality than English common law or Parliament. His interest in natural studies owed equal debts to Pythagoras and Copernicus, as much to a spiritually animate cosmos as to a quantified and demonstrable set of axioms. In sum, for his notion of natural law Selden wanted neither the vague and mythic fraudulence of the Bards nor the workaday frailty of the specific body of legal artifice in which he was trained at the Inns of Court. Yet natural law possessed its own problems: rival notions of 'nature,' a tendency towards elusiveness, and an inability to make things happen in the holy commonwealth. Above all, natural law needed its human arbiters and vehicles, its heroes and its means. Unlike the heroic Equites and Bards, the legal ascetics celebrated in the commentary on the *Fleta* could be entrusted with erasing their own egos for the sake of law. It was not yet clear to him in the 1620s whether the same might be said for those heroic philosophers so crucial to Francis Bacon, and inclusive of the Druids, Pythagoras, Roger Bacon and Copernicus in his own writings. Indeed, Francis Bacon himself understood that the ego of the magus had helped to prevent the advancement of learning.

As early as his edition of Fortescue, Selden was faced with establishing how natural law might produce and underwrite positive law. As J.G.A. Pocock has argued, there was a tension in the *De Laudibus* between the English law's straight custom – a matter of trial and error, of simple obedience and disobedience, without a universal guarantor of justice – and the promise that the study of law would produce in the prince a 'reason in the fully reflective and ordered sense of the term.' Pocock adds: 'But the prince of the *De Laudibus* is now seen to have been cheated by his chancellor. He was assured that if he would only learn the principles of English law, he would know enough to understand what his judges and other professional lawyers were doing when they applied these principles to concrete cases. It has turned out, however, that the cognition of concrete cases and the discernment of how principles are to be applied to them is a sharply different intellectual process from the cognition of principles and the deduction of their logical consequences.'[63] If Selden was confronted with the need to mediate these rival orientations in Fortescue's work, his motivation for turning to natural law in the 1630s involved, in part, a disenchantment with the merits and the efficacy of positive law, not least with its ability to educate a prince in a wide range of concerns integral to the prosperity of the holy commonwealth. The natural law of Neostoicism, in particular, with its recipes for surviving intact a politically perilous and inconstant world, appealed to men such as John Eliot at the end of the 1620s and outset of the 1630s. As Markku Peltonen has shown, Eliot's acquisition of Lipsius's *De constantia* during the time of his imprisonment was connected to 'a sense of frustration with politics,' on the basis of which Alexander Leighton could remark: 'When all things were so farre out of frame, that we are becom the prey of our enimies, the mockerie of our friends, a shame to our selves, and the fotestoole of a favourite: then nothing but a Parliament, Oh! a Parliament would men all; But Parliament we had after Parliament, and what was amended?'[64] Natural law was a motivation behind the public duty of the M.P.s, of course, but it could also justify a penchant for self-preservation when human institutions fell short.

Nevertheless, Selden never gave up on parliamentary religion and the positive institutions of the legal sages; for he held onto the firm conviction that some form of senate, together with the laws of the land, was the linchpin of the holy commonwealth. That linchpin needed an arch, however, and beyond the arch a temple complex in which natural law and poetry could assist the dispensations of the Hebraic God to the sages and the senators. Accordingly, Selden spent the last decade of his life trying to rework the institutions of human law in the idealized and rabbinical form of the Great Sanhedrin. Indeed, even in his work on natural law, nature tends to give way to a more divinely warranted human invention, to Judaic laws as well as the law of nations. He devoted his last years to a model of the kind of parliamentary and judicial regulation of religion that only sages like Selden would be equipped to oversee. At the beginning of the 1620s he was living his dictum that one must grow up from the childhood of poetry; by the beginning of the 1630s he was looking for another paradise for sacred norms, in nature and even in Eden. Yet through the 1640s and into the 1650s he kept returning to the inevitable humanness from which even the holiest societies must be raised. That recurrence made possible the very early misconception that Selden had stood for the purely civil nature of social organization all along. It also left in the minds of some mid-seventeenth-century readers the sneaking suspicion that Selden's failure to devise and legislate the best of all possible religious societies implied, if ironically, what for seventeenth-century thinkers was an uncommonly bold conclusion: that societies are by their very nature comprehensively civil.

chapter four

Natural Law and Common Notions

Whenever Selden surveyed the records of British antiquity, he liked to linger on the Druids. In his notes on Fortescue, he discusses the Roman persecution of the Druids whose responsibilities included settling legal disputes and officiating over religious rites. Appealing to Suetonius, Seneca, and Caesar for the Roman perception of the Druids, Selden accentuates Ammianus Marcellinus's recollection that these judges-cum-priests were also heralded for their 'study of the mysteries of nature and a Pythagorical learning' (*De Laudibus Legem Angliae*, nn.11–13). The Druids brought a hieroglyphic natural theology to their arbitration of law and religion. Believed to have witnessed ancient British culture, Caesar is Selden's leading authority on the natural studies of these lawyer-priests. In the *Analecton*, it is true, Selden prefaces his Caesarean narrative with other, often unsympathetic, sources for a study of Druidic wisdom and habits. First is Gildas, celebrating the salvation of Britain from monstrous idolatry, though even on this score Selden alludes to the Druids as famous priests and philosophers whose duty it was to pass judgment on the same monstrosities. Annius de Viterbo provides more information about these early priests, but none of what this 'Berosus' claims about lineage in post-diluvial Europe is any more reliable than the most egregious fables. Diogenes Laertius offers a brief but evocative analogy between the Druids and the Persian magi, Assyrian theologians, and Indian gymnosophists, all of whom (Selden notes) 'were most skillful in human and divine law and ... were deeply devoted to religion' (cols 880–90). But together with Pliny, Strabo, Lucan, and Diodorus Siculus, among others, Caesar affords Selden good reason to believe that the Druids guided the early Britons in their understanding of law, ritual, and nature alike.

Quoting Caesar's division of British leadership into Knights and Druids, Selden omits the emperor's claim that the British common folk were abused like slaves. Instead, in the *Analecton* he compiles the evidence that the Druids normalized and clarified religious belief and practice; held schools to which hordes of young men flocked; and served as judges in legal disputes, whether civil or criminal. All of human experience, excepting war, constituted their domain. Early on, Selden introduces some testimony to the claim that the Druids were somehow linked to the Pythagoreans and even to the ancient Jews in religious doctrine, cultic practice, and judicial habits, but for the most part he keeps Caesar's putatively first-hand history at the centre of his compilation. We read, then, about how parties refusing to accept Druidic verdicts were prohibited from participating in sacrifices and how they were shunned as unclean by their fellows. We read of the Druids' own chain of command and its succession; of evidence for the transmission of Druidic doctrine between Britain and Gaul; of their exemption from taxation and military service; of their instruction by means of memorized verses together with their refusal to commit wisdom to script. On the last point, Selden again introduces evidence linking the Druids to Pythagoras, but this analogue assumes significance only once the content of their religious philosophies is made clear (cols 882–6).

According to Caesar, the Druids taught the doctrine of spiritual immortality as a means of emboldening courage against the horror of death. As Lucan says, theirs is a doctrine of transmigration from body to body, not of final bliss or damnation.[1] This link between Druidic and Pythagorean theology – metempsychosis – fascinates Selden, especially given two addenda: the Pythagorean legacy of mathematical nature and Pythagoras's reputation for supporting good aristocratic government and just law for the peoples with whom he interacted. The similarity between Pythagoras and the Druids can be extended even to the Old Testament patriarchs, especially since Selden would project true religion on the earliest Britons. For Selden, the Druids combined godly religion, the just administration of law in all human endeavours, aristocratic government but with the power to pacify violence, and a mathematical-cum-spiritual understanding of nature. In their similarities to the sages of so many other peoples, especially the Jews, they slake a thirst for philosophical commonality from which seventeenth-century supporters of a natural religion were seeking relief. Also, their strange doctrine of transmigration redoubled the prospects for universality because it was a widely held doctrine that posited the unbounded shar-

ing of souls. For those to whom such a trade in souls was impious, indecorous, or simply incredible, transmigration might be enlisted as a
metaphor of that rational citizenship of the world against which the
early modern revivers of ancient Stoicism contrasted contemporary
schism, persecution, and scepticism throughout Christendom.

In the 1630s and especially after 1640 Selden emerged as one of the
leading experts on and revivers of natural religion, with its minimal slate
of universal theological beliefs and moral duties. His work on natural
law, however, a reaction against the follies and failures of the clash
between royal prerogative and parliamentary privilege, bore two crucial
characteristics in addition to a Stoic-cum-Scholastic belief in the universality of right reason as it is instantiated in the peoples of the world.
First, Selden followed Grotius, Francis Bacon, Copernicus, and (well
before them all) Roger Bacon in attempting to instil in the study of
nature a sophistication that disarmed scepticism, a sharply honed critical edge, and a penchant for the quantified and experiential methods of
induction with which the 'new philosophies' of early modern Europe
were variously associated. Second, with his Great Instauration and vision
of a New Atlantis, Francis Bacon, in particular, unleashed on the readers
of the 1620s a program for the radical overhaul of a godly society
according to a newly methodized and mundane investigation of phenomena, carried out by pious labourers in the garden of creation with
freshly purged minds. The concept of how a study of nature might serve
to refashion and redeem English Protestant society would still definitely
include those heirs of the Renaissance classicism – Lord Herbert, the
Cambridge Platonists, and Selden himself – whose scholarly work would
be given over to the reconstruction of the common religious and moral
ground among pagans, Jews, and Christians. Yet with Galileo's tele-
scope, Bacon's induction, the wars of religion, and the threat of scepticism ever in their sights, the new generation of natural theologians
would have to factor in, or ignore at their peril, the manifold pressures
on the bald assertion that a deductive right reason comprehends under
its knowledge-yielding umbrella all the faithful and honest people of the
world.

In the early to mid-seventeenth century, then, the question of
whether natural law makes a suitable measure for a religious society was
made all the more complex once the Baconian project to reform philosophy, to rebuild the human mind, and to redefine the theological warrant of learning issued a demand for the divestiture of theology and the
human imagination from the divinely constructed language of nature.

Bacon believed that the more inductive, accurate, and somatic the study of nature, the more it would be in a position to remedy the ills of Protestant English society across the board. There is ample evidence in Selden's works that he admired and emulated the precision and rigour of advanced natural philosophy, but just as often, he explored the macrocosmic-microcosmic network of analogies according to which God's providence and breath are infused in all phenomena – the cosmos of his contemporaries Robert Fludd and Henry Vaughan. Selden was in close correspondence with his contemporaries who were most involved in a deep-seated and far-reaching conflict over the contents of and approach to nature itself. Doctored and supposedly saved from death by Fludd, Selden considered Bacon one of his most important patrons. As he explores the constituents of natural law in this context, Selden's natural imagery tends to swerve back and forth between transmigration – with accent on the spiritual crossing of material boundaries – and optics, with accent on the precision with which distances can be measured. Bacon's was a nature whose motions and structures could be induced from particulars into axioms – a nature far too long misunderstood by the debased and narcissistic imaginations that invent their own soothing versions of God's creation. Fludd's was a world in which God's spirit infused the cosmos and the human imagination, rendering induction a vacuous exercise for weak minds. Both believed, however, that their natural philosophies would save Protestant England from its degeneracy. Selden lived in an England in which both Bacon (who emphasized materializing spirit) and Fludd (who emphasized spiritualizing matter) offered what they held to be the millennial key to the holistic prosperity of their society.

This challenge of navigating these two interactive yet increasingly divergent ways of understanding nature motivated Selden to fasten on the work of Roger Bacon, the medieval philosopher who most embodied for Selden a conglomeration of inductive, mathematical, and magic views of nature within the framework of an apocalyptic vision of how Christendom might conquer evil. But as he developed his own arguments about natural religion, Selden added his own complicating factors to those introduced by his contemporaries. If he came to natural law at a time when its rhapsodists were being subjected to a dissonant chorus of critics, he helped to pioneer an experiment in that universal law, one that sublimated and concretized that law at the same time. Selden italicized the divine will behind and numinous warrant of his natural law by seeking it with Maimonides in the ancient stories and codes of the Jews. In so doing, he made sure that his reaction against the hapless institutions of English positive law never strayed far from the law of nations and the positive laws of a people. What is more, his revamping for Charles I of a treatise on the ownership of the seas written for James I opened Selden to the charge that his appeals to natural law masked the most obvious parasitism in the face of punishment. As his work on the Jews and natural law kept pushing that set of universal truths towards the history and institutions of a specific people, the attacks on his integrity incited the Selden of the 1650s to shift the pneumatic rationality of Stoic cosmology towards an equally Stoic stress on personal autonomy. Nonetheless, the natural religion of the pagans was still allotted a room in the temple complex that found its normative centre in the Sanhedrin.

The idealized image of the Druids was, of course, selective and manicured. It downplayed those classical sources that conceive of that class as idolatrous and bloodthirsty savages rabidly inciting their people to atrocities. Like the rabbis, the Druids worried Selden on account of the enchanting poesies with which they conjured the spirit of justice, godliness, and wisdom. Even if the Druids held a mythic promise as legal arbiters of a godly society, their savagery, idolatry, and fabulousness amounted to cargo of a specifically British natural religion that Selden might have to sacrifice. Like the Bards and knights of early British society, the Druids attracted and repelled Selden, but they appealed to him more than the other two, because they subsumed poetic and aristocratic authority within a wisdom to which the other classes had far less claim: the mysteries and laws of nature.

Like normative poetry, which often appeals to the authority of nature, natural law purveys a relatively unworldly measure of religious beliefs and moral virtues. But in the case of nature, the measure is ostensibly unmediated by human art, and so its very supposition is that law is inseparable from the religious beliefs and honest virtues that it self-evidently measures. Even less than normative poetry, however, which at least benefits a community with the shame imposed by satire or the virtue stimulated by praise, natural law carries with it nothing like the contractual obligations on which a far more worldly positive law stakes its claim for governing a religious society. Positive law brings with it the concrete details of obligation, but also the power of coercion together with rituals of shame. Clearly, natural law is more sublime and holistic, tidier and more universal than positive law; natural law's advocates are prone to argue that its moral and religious truths shine in the conscience of every sane human being. In a time of pan-European religious warfare after all, incitements within a community might appeal to those hawks who are urging on the fight, but the peace-lovers are more likely to approve an inner and universal ligature in human affairs than a rousing poetics or a litigious positive code. In the 1620s and 1630s, however, the work of Grotius made it plain that natural law must grapple with, rather than escape from, the quagmire of international violence, and Selden himself located the best source of natural law in a biblical history replete with violence and founded on a basic division between God's people and the reprobate others. If natural law is supposed to retreat from a world at war over faith, Selden planted his philosophical foot squarely in a world that was simply at war over faith, and, furthermore, he explored in detail the ways in which the Jewish tradition conceived conversion across the divide between the godly and the godless. He was also aware that natural law, far from escaping the imperfections of human artifice that afflict poetry and positive law alike, is always implicated in the woefully fallen fancies of its claimants; for it needs vehicles of persuasion as well as agents of enforcement. If the Pythagoreans imagined a planetary harmony that could not be heard by human ears, Selden's Druids accompanied Drayton's Bards in enchanted groves from which the music of their law must be recovered with clarity and credibility.

Early in his writing career, Selden confronted head-on the extraordinary revival of Stoic natural law in the researches of Justus Lipsius. With Lipsius's guidance, the young English scholar attempted to clarify the historical legacy of that universal *pneuma*, spirit, or cosmic rationality by means of which the moral natural law is supposedly disseminated. But Selden's reading of Lipsius's recent tomes on ethics and physics prompted a more focused discussion in the *Analecton* of a more specifically British historical question, the problem of whether the Druids received the doctrine of transmigration from the Pythagoreans or vice versa. Rather than follow Neostoicism into a citizenship of the world, Selden began his studies of that trend within the context of a survey of British history and later produced a great opus on natural law in which that concept of universal religion is staked in the specifics of Judaism.

In the *Analecton*, Selden points out that in the *Physiologia Stoicorum*, Lipsius ponders the Talmudic avowal of transmigration together with the Judaic supposition in the sixteenth chapter of Matthew that Jesus might be Elijah or Jeremiah. Like Caesar, however, Selden situates the doctrine of metempsychosis within the context of the Druids' other natural studies: 'They also hold long discussions about the heavenly bodies and their movements, the size of the universe and of the earth, the nature of things, and the power and properties of the immortal gods; and they instruct the young men in all these subjects.'[2] These cosmic and theological discourses represent yet another link with the Pythagoreans. Immediately, however, Selden adverts to the savage sacrifices of the Druids that, according to Caesar, most clearly embody their religious zeal. Citing Lucretius's famous indictment of religion's evil persuasion, Selden also quotes Cicero's disgust at the notion that the gods are appeased by human brutality (*Analecton*, col. 885).

In defence of the Druids, Selden supposes that such barbarous acts might have pious motives; complains that Cicero ought to acknowledge the widespread practice of human sacrifice among the Greeks and Romans; and directs the reader's attention to those passages in the Old Testament where even God's chosen people drew human blood. Invoking the vegetarian Pythagoreans for the strange possibility that human blood might be preferable to animal blood for religious sacrifice, Selden rehearses the logic according to which nothing pleases the gods more than the vital spirit of the immortal human nature, especially from the wisest representatives of that species. He contrasts the idolatrous savagery of Druidic sacrifice with Christian illumination, but protests nonetheless that the divinatory and sacrificial rituals were more holy than the rites carried out by filthy Roman emperors.

In the *Analecton* and elsewhere in his early works, Selden looks to the Druids for an ancient British version of the various Platonic, Pythagorean, and Stoic cosmologies in which spirit, harmony, and law are indistinguishable from one another in the providential design of creation. In order to maximize the lure of a mystique that comprises a theory that is shared, but also the implications of the sharing itself, Selden minimizes the savagery of their legacy both by generalizing that savagery and by advertising the presumed kinship among the Druids, Pythagoreans, and Jews. He treats their Judaic measurement of days by nights and, as a corollary, their fundamental accord with a hexameral astronomy that applied to the shadow of night originally cast across the face of the abyss. He studies their association with the Pythagoreans who posited numerical proportions behind the processes of creation; Caesar's testimony to their administration of law; Diodorus Siculus's claim that the Druids mesmerized the fiercest warriors out of their violent passions so that Mars might give way to the Muses; Pliny's account of how the Druids practised their magic with fervour and ritual (though Selden omits Pliny's praise for the Roman termination of those savage rites); and the civility and moral discipline of those ancient Britons whose piety led them to a belief in the soul's perpetuation. Among its emphases, in the *Analecton* he devotes substantial space to the oak groves in which the Druids were thought to have prepared for and carried out their rites; again, Selden omits Pliny's condemnation of Druidic superstition but instead seeks analogues in the Old Testament, some more effective than others. The *Analecton* measures Judaic and Druidic mysteries and rites against the 'carpenter's level' of Pythagoras ('ad amussim Pythagorica') and finds matches in natural philosophy, religion, and law. It offers cabbalistic and other theories of how such wisdom was shared among the three parties, including their fraternal institutions of learning and their mediation between divine and natural levels of meaning (col. 882).

If, as Selden later confirms, natural law is transmitted through the children of Noah by primary means of Talmudic commentary, the Druids offer the promise of a direct British link to that legacy; and they triangulate law, religion, and natural philosophy with a minimum of poetic fables and aristocratic violence. Yet they threaten at times to lapse into both poesy and savagery, the one most ridiculous in Annius's 'Berosus' with its post-diluvial chronicle, the other most gruesome in scenes of Roman encounters with the Druidic charisma of bloodlust. In the *Analecton*, however, the latter meetings double as instances of the British gusto for liberty.

In the *Jani Anglorum* Selden also investigates the Druids: how they explicated and preserved the laws; how Caesar recorded their 'Religious Rites, the Laws and the Philosophy; how they had authority over excommunication and shared exemptions with the Levites' (Num. 1:49; Ezra 7:24); how they refused to write down their views, preferring that students memorize verses; how they reckoned time by the moon, were persecuted by the Romans, were replaced by the Christians, and shared beliefs and practices with the Pythagoreans in matters of transmigration and law. Indeed, in the *Jani Anglorum* he emphasizes that both the Druids and Pythagoreans were guardians and dispensers of just government and law, both groups having a penchant for some version of a custodial elite. As elsewhere, Selden defends an otherwise impious transmigration on the basis of its incentives for selfless public service (15).

It is not surprising that the commentary on the *Poly-Olbion* comprises

Selden's most extensive and searching considerations of the Druids. Praising 'the knowledge of those great Philosophers, Priests, and Lawyers,' he boasts about British precedence over Gaul in the transmission of their judicial-cum-natural-cum-religious wisdom; hypothesizes about links among the Druids, Pythagoreans, and Jews; and warns readers away from the 'infinit Fables and grosse absurdities' that have attached themselves to the legacy of the Druids. One illustration highlights the irrelevance of a distinction between 'learning Profane and Holy' in their case. For their lawful wisdom sanctifies all of human life in a holistic vision that anticipates Selden's rabbis, the latter shorn, however, of those sacrificial rituals delegated to Jewish priests. 'They sate as Judges,' Selden explains, 'and determined all causes emergent, civill and criminall, subjecting the disobedient, and such as made default to interdicts, and censures, prohibiting them from sacred assemblies, taking away their capacities in honorable offices, and so disabling them, that (as our now Outlawes, excommunicats, and attainted persons) they might not commence suit against any man.' In their philosophical and religious studies, Selden allows, they suffered from the generally pagan uncertainty about the 'one true God,' but their proximity to that truth was closer than any attributable to leading Greek and Roman thinkers or to other ancient peoples, the Jews always excepted.[3]

So it is that the Druids invoked the 'one *All-healing* or *All-saving* power,' and that they effected a moral suasion so powerful as to eradicate 'the most fiery rage of *Mars* kindled among the people.'[4] As Strabo comments, the effect of this persuasion was musical, if by that term we understand an Orphic and Pythagorean cosmic and hyper-rational harmonics. With such a cosmology under attack in their time, Selden and his contemporaries – including his friend Edward Herbert and his former adversary Hugo Grotius – seek out other vehicles and modes for natural law as a universal remedy for human conflict, violence, and partisanship. Yet in the illustrations for Drayton's poem, Selden still longs for a peaceful grove and hieroglyphic cosmos in which natural law, fervent spirituality, judicial administration, and the music of culture can converge.

In order to minimize the labour of his apology for Druidic practices, Selden opts to spend time glossing the ritual significance of mistletoe while leaving out (he admits) the human sacrifices. He declares that the Druids taught law, religion, and natural philosophy 'in a multitude of Verses and *Pythagorean* precepts, exactly imitating the *Cabalists*' in their refusal to commit learning to writing. Their oral traditions were tantamount, Selden stresses, to the 'diligent hearing' of the Rabbis. It goes almost without saying that both sets of sages, Druids and Rabbis, suffered persecution at the hands of the Romans. For if we learn anything from critical historians useful for our study of the Druids, Selden argues, it is, ironically, that we cannot trust those Romans who massacred 'our wise *Druides* ... Like whom, great Natures depths no men yet ever knew.'[5] In keeping the Druids and Rabbis in the same imaginative space of his work on natural law, Selden betrays his discomfort with the notion of a natural law that is disembodied of human institutions and inventions, that trades in specific legal and religious traditions for a vague latitude that blanches all human history with the white light of a universal rationality, and that pretends not to require poetic or rhetorical vehicles of communication when no one's take on natural law can ever convince a sceptical critic that such a law is anything but will and fancy in disguise.

2

A natural basis for religion and law was a desideratum that Selden shared with contemporaries such as Lipsius, Grotius, and Edward Herbert; but it was a basis to which Selden brought as much scepticism as reverence. One sees this mixture of attitudes especially pronounced in his frequent considerations of the various magic and pneumatic theories of his day, whether Paracelsian, Cabalistic, Stoic, Druidic, or '*Rabbinique.*' He greeted such theories of emanating, pervading, concocting, and transmigrating spirits with equal parts fascination and disdain. His doctor, Robert Fludd, claimed that Selden had perused and approved Fludd's work on the macrocosm-microcosm dynamic, and we learn from later testimony that Selden revered Fludd's chemical and spiritual philosophy. Indeed, Thomas Hearne claimed that 'Selden was a follower of such sort of learning as the Dr. [Fludd] profest himself, & used very frequently to dive into the Books of Astrologers & Soothsayers,' a tendency that, according to Hearne, accounted for Selden's obscure style.[6] Fludd's works abound with discussions of cosmic music, astrological, magical, and divinatory portents, macrocosmic sympathies, statues 'filled with spirit,' and numerical theologies expressive of the fundamental matrix of nature. Presupposing that the inhalations and exhalations of God's breath account for all natural phenomena, Fludd's philosophy holds out the promise that the spiritual order operative in the cosmos at large is governing the little human world, the sins of that world notwithstanding.

Like Fludd, Selden traces intercultural connections among occult philosophies, with Moses as something of a hub in the wheel whose spokes branched to the Persians, Indians, Greeks, and Gauls. In his last major work, Fludd boldly declares his philosophy 'Mosaical.' In mapping out its design in the cosmos, Fludd condescends to ocular proof, but he shows a distaste for it at every turn. If Selden entertains the pneumatic theology of Fludd and other occultists, he has an equally deep investment in their more empirically minded critics, and he manifests his disgust for the filthy spirits of sorcery from whose shadow a rigorously discovered natural law must be reclaimed. Selden is committed to advances towards precision and a sophisticated inductive method in natural philosophy, so much so that as Feingold says, 'in an early version of his will Bacon named Selden, together with [Edward] Herbert, as executors of his papers and the persons to decide which of the manuscripts should be published.' What is more, Selden's idea of method, his approach to evidence, 'was most compatible with – and derived much inspiration from – the "new science."'[7] Selden the historical critic has his counterpart in the realm of natural philosophy, and both personae seek to clear the way for a more reliable perspective on inmost truth, in nature as in history. Also, he uses the search for an accurate perspective in natural philosophy as an analogy for the same search in history.

Selden's confrontation with natural law, then, was not simply a matter of deciding whether at all to pursue its universalized version of the sacred norms on offer to societies throughout Europe. In the decades in which he undertook to write on natural law, that concept had accrued an extraordinary range of templates, presuppositions, and methods; sometimes these different natural philosophies were clearly contrasted, while sometimes they were mixed and meshed. Selden was eclectic in his uses of natural philosophies, but he was also severely critical of their errors and confusions. From time to time he would declare that some of them tended towards 'Poeticall authority onely,'[8] others lapsed into the worst idolatry, while still others replaced fables with experience, form with materiality, and the vagaries of human perception with mathematical or instrumental precision. His omnivorous consumption of natural philosophies took a number of shapes: the campaign to keep theology and natural law together, the opposite impulse to wedge them apart, the resulting eagerness to avoid the classic extremes of superstition and profanity, and the innumerable permutations in which relatively critical and magical habits of thought were entangled.

As Feingold makes clear, natural studies extensively contributed to

Selden's wide-ranging search for impartial sources of truth. In simplest terms, he was a patron of natural and mathematical branches of learning and undertook his own natural studies in computing chronologies, in describing the geography of Syria, and in cataloguing birds. But Selden had an epistemological investment in natural philosophy, too, one that found its main expression in the analogies or images by which he characterized his method. If, for John Milton in the 1640s, Selden's writings on natural law corroborated the intellectual, moral, and spiritual benefits of laborious trial and error, the scholar's penchant for analogies to optics and geometry conveys his Baconian insistence on forging beyond the naivety of bare empiricism as well as removing the many impediments to knowledge that derive from foolish dogmatism. Like Bacon, Selden struggles for release from the very scepticism that renders his research so cautious and exacting, and an alignment with optics or geometry allows him to promote a method at once confident in its perspective and careful in its processes. Thus, 'Selden's writings are rich in mathematical imagery,' and his library was filled with mathematical, astronomical, medical, and optical texts, ancient and modern, eastern and western. As a testimony to his involvement in the practice of mathematical studies, he himself was asked to help to arbitrate 'the claim of Marmaduke Nelson that [Nelson] had discovered the long sought after method of calculating longitudes.'[9]

If Selden (like Fludd) was committed to a cosmology in which magical spirits permeated and fashioned the phenomena of nature, he also participated in the contemporary advancement of precision in the quantification and mechanization of the world, a program with which Selden associated a number of heroes, from Roger Bacon to Copernicus to Francis Bacon. In order for a theory of natural law to work for Selden, it was expected to integrate the claims of two very different mentalities, one based on numinous forces, occult qualities, and magical correspondences within the layers of a beautiful cosmic fabric, the other on rigorous distinctions and mechanical dynamics within a far messier field of decidedly somatic phenomena.[10] In the former, the student of nature glimpses God's image or detects a divine spirit and providence in the workings of the cosmos; in the latter, the student confirms the power or majesty of a divine creator but respects the actualities of creation as contingent on God's will rather than reflective of God's image. Both 'mentalities' are convinced that they know the way to redeem a lapsing Christian society on the threshold of apocalypse.

In one guise or another, natural studies show up early and often in his works. In *Titles of Honor*, Selden confirms the need for new methods in law, astronomy, and chemistry alike (preface, b4v–b5r). In the notes on Drayton, he purveys an interest in studies of climate, astrology, cosmic harmonies, optics, Pythagorean geometry, and Arabic math.[11] He projects an ideal historical perspective (and defends the superiority of his own) with an analogy to optical principles. As illustrated by his 'receptivity to the various occult traditions during the 1610s and 1620s,'[12] however, Selden especially admires those natural philosophies that graft religious conviction, lawful order, ancient authority, and modern precision into one surveyor's perspective.

It is not surprising that the Druids and Pythagoreans are too remote, out of focus, barbarous, or mythic to fill the whole bill. For Selden, a normative natural philosophy fulfilling the demands of precision, law, and afflatus is exceedingly hard to find or, if found, harder still to guarantee or demonstrate. On the one hand, this philosophy needs to be as amphibious as the idol Dagon in Selden's *De Dis Syris*, the idol that was believed to be the source of all learning in the arts, from poetry and architecture to law, politics, agriculture, and religious ritual (262–79). That is, natural philosophy must operate equally well in all the metaphysical and cultural domains in which human nature, also amphibious, is required to operate. As a *figura mixta*, natural philosophy has to be less a Janus than a hermaphrodite, like those pagan gods that imitated the true God in combining male and female and so fully benefiting human life. In the 1640s and 1650s, Selden follows the Talmud in foisting this requirement on legal sages themselves; but natural philosophy promises to situate the ideal mixture within the fabric of the cosmos itself. Thus, Selden's frequent recourse to theories of *pneuma* and of transmigration serves to naturalize two ideals obviously elusive to even the most heroic and capacious legal sage, one according to which a single entity can encircle all wisdom at any one time and place, the other according to which an entity can mutate into the beliefs and practices of all times and places.

In the 1620s and 1630s, when Selden was turning to natural law, intellectuals were pursuing various practical means and methods of humanly achieving such a '*pansophia*.' A stubborn corollary to such philosophical ambition, however, is that natural religion must reduce all the specific religions of the world to a minimum of universal tenets, for otherwise religious society can never achieve even a modicum of peace and unity.

Such was the upshot of Lord Herbert's essays on the common notions of all religions, as well as Selden's own very different claim that such notions are crystallized in the Talmud. When understood as yielding a maximum of knowledge, *pansophia* tends towards the kind of partisan Protestant millenarianism central to the vision of Samuel Hartlib, John Dury, and their associates. When understood as a doctrinal minimum, natural religion leans towards an emphasis on a handful of basic principles in theology and worship, valuable to the notion of Protestant unity, which Dury was also promoting, but even more integral to that boldly church-less theism and paganism promulgated in the writings of Lord Herbert.

One way or the other, natural law held out promise for the generation coming of age in the war-torn 1620s that there might exist an exit from persecutory factions and irreligious sceptics. According to Selden, English law as a vessel had changed so thoroughly in its historical journey away from the natural source of positive laws that it offered only a slight access to the numinous purity and universal rationality available at that font. By the 1630s Selden was operating on the premise that another method and some other mediator must support English legal procedures and institutions if English society was to benefit from a normative authority as sacred as it is precise. However, he powerfully indicted the imprecision in most perspectives on natural law. In search of greater precision, he supposed that some intermediary position must exist according to which the distance of a remote object might be measured with a high degree of accuracy. In *Titles of Honor*, for instance, he opines that 'the severed Parts of good Arts and Learning, have that kind of site' so that a scholar in law might use what is nearby to gain access, say, to natural philosophy (a2v). It is one thing, however, to argue that there must be a way simply to connect the dots and thus to secure what Francis Bacon called the Prime Philosophy, in Selden's terms 'the vast Circle of Knowledge' (a2v). It is another, Selden knows, to find a historical and concrete vantage point from which to gain entrance into a field of natural law whose purity receded into the bosom of God at the beginning of time.

Selden claimed a medieval vantage point in fellow Oxonian Roger Bacon, and indeed it is from Bacon's works that Selden came to understand the problems of optics and their solutions. As Feingold states, these thinkers offer a 'combined effect' among law, religion, and a natural philosophy at once numinous and precise.[13] Both place a high premium on the regulation of the spirit and the animation of law.

—— 3 ——

Some of Selden's greatest contemporaries enlisted natural studies in defence of their version of true religion, whether it underwrote a specific church governance or the common notions of all religions. In late Elizabethan times, Richard Hooker had based his defence of the practices of the English church on an appeal to natural law; in the 1630s and 1640s, that defence continued in the hieroglyphic approach to the Book of Nature epitomized by Thomas Browne. At the same time, Samuel Hartib, John Amos Comenius, and John Dury were supporting the advancement of natural learning as a cornerstone of an apocalyptic Protestant unity, and Edward, Lord Herbert of Cherbury was trying to move religious truth beyond scepticism and partisanship by locating the five common notions of all systems. On the Continent in 1612 Francisco Suárez included in his *De Legibus, ac Deo Legislatore* an extended analysis of natural law. Couched between his treatments of eternal and customary law, the sections on natural law considered questions such as whether natural law is also right reason, whether God can exclude someone from an obligation to natural law, what is comprised in the 'subject-matter' of this universal law, whether its dictates are unified and whole, and whether natural law binds the conscience.[14] However, even if the *Table Talk* includes his declaration that the Jesuits can be ranked with Dutch and French lawyers as the 'men [who] have engrossed all learning, the rest of the world make nothing but Homilies' (71), Selden was eager to advance natural law beyond the tenuous guarantee of its universality offered by theologians such as Suárez and to emphasize the authority of God's will over righteous rationality in the human obligation to natural law. As Richard Tuck maintains, 'Selden had to show that [natural law's] equation with the law of "right reason," the necessity to follow which was intuitively obvious (the view of Suarez, among others), was false.'[15]

In Selden's view, however, Friar Roger Bacon had devised one of history's most comprehensive natural studies for the purposes of securing Christian society. It infuriated Selden that Bacon's reward for this accomplishment was ill repute.

Selden often ridicules those censorial cultural brokers who have made a bogey of Roger Bacon. In *De Dis Syris*, for instance, he maintains that only time and prudence can rescue the reputation of Bacon's brilliant natural studies from ignorant abuse. In a poem praising the mathematician and land surveyor Arthur Hopton, Selden wonders aloud

whether his contemporary reincarnates, among others, a triad of thir-
teenth-century natural philosophers, Robert Grosseteste, Adam Marsh,
and Roger Bacon (104–12).[16] Far from deserving a shady reputation,
Selden protests, Bacon advanced three notions of greatest value to the
reclamation of religious societies from their lapses into stagnation,
schism, and uncertainty: that the study of nature and of mathematics
ought to be carried out in a sophisticated, experiential, and enlightened
fashion; that such natural and mathematical studies should provide the
linchpin of a holistic philosophy; and that this philosophy should serve
the Christian God in combating the Antichrist and his forces of evil.
Bacon's *Opus Majus* begins, then, with a proposal to reconsider knowledge itself according to the premise that 'by the light of knowledge the
Church of God is governed, the commonwealth of the faithful is regulated, the conversion of unbelievers is secured, and those who persist in
their malice can be held in check by the excellence of knowledge, so
that they may be driven off from the borders of the Church in a better
way than by the shedding of Christian blood.'[17]

In anticipation of his seventeenth-century namesake, Bacon begins
with a full taxonomy of errors, making the case that experience of all
kinds must supplant the human addiction to authority, habit, and prejudice. Then he establishes the theological wisdom to which all other
learning owes service; like canon law, philosophy must unfold the wisdom of theology, but this service, in turn, legitimizes the servant. The
true aim of philosophy, Bacon stresses, is best attained in mathematical
and natural studies, moral philosophy, and law, all of which help to complete that integrated philosophy by which the world must be regulated,
with canon law playing its part as well. 'But the whole aim of philosophy,' Bacon rhapsodizes, 'is that the Creator may be known through the
knowledge of the creature, to whom service may be rendered in a worship that gives him honor, in the beauty of morals, and in the integrity
of useful laws, because of the reverence due his majesty and the benefits
of creation and preservation and of future happiness, so that men may
live in peace and justice in this life.'[18] All of what Selden comprehends
in his simple and commonplace taxonomy of religion – that which we
owe to God and that which we owe to our fellow human beings, God's
creatures – is woven together in Bacon's paean.

As Selden understands the progression of Bacon's learning, math
quickly leads the scholar into geometry and onward into optics, that science of light and perspective. In turn, these studies are credited with a
powerful applicability to sacred reading and action. Along the way,

Bacon aggressively distances his studies from the evils and illusions of magic and divination, and it is precisely the failure to appreciate this fact, Selden believes, that has sullied Bacon's reputation. Above all, optical and geometrical sophistication will arm the Christian church against the Antichrist, whose deployment of burning mirrors and other destructive machines must be anticipated and countervailed. In the meantime, math should enable the sage guardians of a godly commonwealth to gain foreknowledge of future dangers and to cultivate practical works for meeting those dangers head-on.

Given the wisdom to be gained from the Old Testament, as well as the return of the Jews at the apocalypse, Bacon advises a knowledge of Hebrew that, so closely set in the context of his natural studies, affords Selden with a model for his own conjunction of natural and Talmudic law. Maimonides clinches this marriage of Hebraic and natural studies. Bacon, however, stands out among Selden's heroes as the thinker for whom advanced optical and natural science was integral to the regulation of morals and the prosperity of religious faith. In his *Opus Majus*, complex explanations of optical accomplishments are brought to bear on the challenge of magnifying a spiritual vision of the remotest truths, and he insists that work on light and perspective be carried out first hand, whether the resulting experiments are intellectual or physical.

In the seventh and final portion of the *Opus Majus*, Bacon gathers his optical and geometrical findings and turns at last to the moral philosophy that must govern human relations to God and to one another. That his treatment of moral philosophy gives way to extensive quotation from the works of Seneca would make sense to seventeenth-century intellectuals like Selden; for the latter often credited pagan, especially Stoic, philosophy with the responsibility of linking natural law, religious devotion, and virtuous obligation for humanity at large. Indeed, Bacon's recourse to Stoic wisdom edges his vision of a godly philosophy away from the apocalyptic militarism that was so contentious in Selden's day and towards the greater emphasis on commonality in religions among the citizens of the world that so attracted Selden's friend Edward Herbert. With its promise of a cosmic harmony between the potentially rival claims of duty and of autonomy, Neostoicism was an uncommonly potent factor in the theories of natural law promulgated throughout Selden's lifetime. Its pneumatic basis in natural law, often otherwise known as right reason, had an immense, wide, if sometimes contradictory impact on irenic arguments for religious common notions. Neostoicism also underwrote newly sophisticated attempts to work out the limits of obligation and permis-

sion; the normative and classicist poetry written by Jonson in advice to
happy men; the everyday moral guidelines for constancy in a tumultuous
world; and even the mechanical recasting of the occult philosophies. At
times, Stoicism was enlisted to support specific creeds and rival politics,
just as it could be used to privilege the separate integrity of the honest
individual. But the Stoic celebration of natural law was a fundamental element in seventeenth-century endeavours to move a war-torn and sceptical world beyond partisanship.

In the first half of the seventeenth century, natural law and philosophy
were newly vibrant and offered sweeping remedies for religious warfare,
doubt, and fragmentation. Indeed, men like Hobbes believed the positive law philosophies of a Coke to be (in W.S. Holdsworth's words) a form
of 'obsolete medievalism;'[19] they also believed that a new formulation of
natural law, physical principles, and natural liberties was desperately
needed to right the violent wrongs of European society. If natural law was
newly sophisticated and intensely pursued, it was also newly vulnerable to
scepticism; very much embattled among theologians for whom 'nature'
was often a sinful commodity; and torridly divided among its various
advocates. Even as Selden turned from positive law to natural, he himself
led the chorus of sceptics who understood that the natural law tradition
needed a major overhaul. It needed a level of certainty, stability, sophistication, and force that it had probably never had before. Otherwise, its
supposed universal warrant was a chimera, and its promise of normalizing the religion, morality, and civil affairs of human society no more than
a shepherd's piping.

In the years during and just after his sustained engagement with natural
law, Selden made it perfectly clear to his interlocutors that it was an elusive yet appealing moral authority in dire need of readjustment and
focus. 'I cannot fancy to my Selfe,' he poses in the *Table Talk*, 'what the
Law of nature meanes, but the law of God, how should I knowe I ought
not to steal, I ought not to comitt Adultery, unless somebody had told
me, or why are these things ag[ains]t nature?' (69–70). According to
this definition of natural law, we must be told how to act morally – that
is, the content of moral law – rather than simply to act morally. The criteria of honest living are not rationally self-evident. Yet if we must be
told not to steal or sleep with our neighbour's spouse, the teller cannot
be human; for then the source of natural law is no better than the

source of such artificial or customary laws as arbitrate transgression in separate communities. Worse still, such a telling might reflect our neighbour's all too fanciful conscience or passionate self-interest, a danger that Selden mocks with his opening nod to 'fancy.'[20] So the teller is God, who wills the strictures and permissions found in divine law. But what is the medium or location of that law? If the medium is the Bible, then of course its interpretation might depend on localized custom or amorphous fancy. Natural law requires a divinely warranted enforcer who will prevent the many recipients of that law from laxly unbinding themselves or wrongly binding others. Who or what is this enforcer? Is it some spirit or guardian angel, one's conscience or one specific tradition? Does it elicit fear or zeal or reverence? How do we recognize it and how is it spread to all human kind? In his comments on the scholastic notion of moral right reason, Selden repeats the emphasis on 'a Comand from above,' without which we have only the foolish fancy of self-evidence and no means of enforcing obedience (*Table Talk*, 116). If God is that enforcer, however, it is not clear what the content of the 'natural' dictates are or whether the obligation in this world – this side of heaven – is only voluntary. For if God is the source of the obligation, Selden attempts to answer, how shall we 'incurr the detrement?' (116).

To Selden, the remarks on natural law found in the *Table Talk* are as committed to reestablishing its suasive authority as they are sceptical of all the wrongheaded ways in which that authority has been formulated. It reflects the Selden of the 1640s, the author of the massive *De Jure Naturali* and a man who is well on his way back in the direction of a reconstituted positive law. At some level, of course, Selden never leaves positive law, even in the work on natural law, whose full title is *De Jure Naturali et Gentium Juxta Disciplinam Ebraeorum*, 'On the Law of Nature and of Nations according to the Teaching of the Hebrews.' Nonetheless, in the 1640 volume he devotes immense scholarly effort to finding out the moral and religious norms of nature once and for all. And still, once he has turned decisively to the Sanhedrin in the 1640s and 1650s, Selden finds a place for nature within his conception of its institutional complex, even if that place has shrunk to the courtyard for natural religionists in the temple or to the Stoic's haven of the autonomous self as the only true site of cosmic holism.

Before he arrived at what he considered an innovative Talmudic perspective on natural law in *De Jure Naturali*, we have seen that Selden had spent a long courtship with the venerable doctrine of a universal moral law instilled in the whole cosmos and distilled in the right reason that guided human beings in their moral decisions. The Fortescue commentary, for example, had invoked natural law as the universal yet adaptable guarantor behind all positive codes of law. In the 1640s, however, after the publication of *De Jure Naturali*, Milton recognized that for Selden, natural law offered an unsurpassed opportunity for both intellectual-cum-spiritual trial and moral certainty alike. In keeping with Selden's claim in his *Table Talk* that 'the business of Nature' encourages men to change their opinions in the face of a convincing 'experiment,' Milton argues that Selden's approach to natural law 'proves, not only by great authorities brought together, but by exquisite reasons and theorems almost mathematically demonstrative, that all opinions, yea errors, known, read, and collated, are of main service and assistance toward the speedy attainment of what is truest.'[21] In Milton's words, Selden's method vis-à-vis natural law is geometrical, the content in that method is experimental, and the ready offshoot of that trial is truth or even divine light. What Milton understood was that Selden's turn to natural law was an attempt to accommodate the requirements of trial and error against foolish, tyrannical dogmatism, yet to serve the desideratum of certainty against the rash scepticism of the age.

It was Selden's engagement with the works of Grotius that catalysed his full-scale attention to theories of natural law. What had started as a Jacobean debate with Grotius over the narrow question of the ownership of the seas turned, during the Caroline revisions of the *Mare Clausum*, into Selden's admiration for and imitation of Grotius's 1625 *De jure belli ac pacis*. Thanks in large part to Grotius, Selden undertook massive research on comparative religion and persisted in his wrestle with the enigmas of true method; for both of these burdens were necessary if Selden were to have any hope of approximating the goal of such labours: a sweeping vision of a naturalized social regulation whose religious authority and critical rigour were concurrently and unimpeachably heightened.

The argument in *Mare Clausum* for British ownership of the seas divides its attention between questions of law and records of fact. With the former, the author's main problem is to sort out precisely how the law of nations compares with the law of nature. For at times in the civil law tradition, Roman law lays claim to a naturalness that its opponents take as a guise for imperial will or, at best, for artificial custom. Alternatively, the law of nations can be identified as the overlap between separate codes of positive law, the shared portion having some claim to embody natural law. Finally, the law of nations might be construed simply as a contract devised between separate but legally equal states. As Christianson explains, it was Selden's attempt to work out this problem with a comprehensiveness similar to that of Grotius that motivated his 'shift in focus towards a foundation in the natural-law tradition which would become increasingly evident in later tomes such as ... *De Jure Naturali et Gentium Juxta Disciplinam Ebraeorum* (London, 1640).'[22]

In *Mare Clausum*, Selden's theory of law shapes up as follows. All law is either obligatory or permissive, devolving into either general or particular law. Eventually, the general and the particular meet up once again, but before that line in the schemata is drawn, general law divides into divine (the will of God) and natural law, the latter also known as the primitive law of nations. Now natural law, while stable, is not static: its obligatory dispensations permit addition but not alteration, while its permissive side can be altered. Out of this flexibility – additions to obligatory natural law and alterations of permissive natural law – derive those positive laws whose status branches into those laws peculiar to a society or a nation and those received by divers nations. Selden leaves unexamined those positive laws that bear no relationship whatsoever to natural law, so that the *Mare Clausum* rehabilitates the theory posed in the notes on Fortescue that the positive laws of various nations begin equally and evenly with natural law.

As the scheme in *Mare Clausum* unfolds, however, Selden appropriately ignores the positive laws peculiar to one society and elaborates those laws found in divers nations. This overlap divides into the (in this case irrelevant) laws binding nations equally but accidentally – that is, not to one another – and the more pertinent laws that bind nations equally in a shared obligation. That common obligation bifurcates into an imperative law imposed on divers nations by a higher authority (an emperor, say, or God), and 'intervenient' compacts or customs shared between or among divers nations in matters of war, peace, embassy, or commerce. These laws amount to a secondary law of nations: the ownership of the seas (Selden argues) is such a secondary law.

There are two emergent problems with Selden's theory. First, its schema stretches so far that the natural basis of the positive law of nations recedes from view. The latter phase of the argument – regarding records of fact – only magnifies that recession as Selden sifts the kind of documentary evidence so prominent in the *Analecton* and the *Jani Anglorum*. To adapt his own metaphor, the ship of natural law is rebuilt so thoroughly that its very naturalness becomes ghostly compared with the concrete carpentry of positive law. Perhaps Selden cannot escape from his own scepticism about the law of nature – the view that even if it existed, natural law would offer us no sure or immediate access to its universal rationality or that, even if we have access, natural law has no instrument of obligation outside the conscience itself. In any case, Selden's critics are bound to notice the erasure of nature and the emergence of custom over the course of the work.

For indeed, the second problem with Selden's theory is that it can hardly conceal its gargantuan English self-interest. Along this line, critics might well object that Selden does not actually answer the arguments for open commerce; that his sensibilities are more Grotian than propaganda will allow; and that, worst of all, in the *Mare* natural law is brashly reduced to a bargaining chip for Selden's release from prison. The danger here is that natural law, like normative poetry, might well be enlisted to festoon a hideous parasitism. When Selden comes to answer these charges two decades later in the *Vindiciae*, he has worked out, then partly moved beyond, his own innovative version of Grotius's *De jure belli ac pacis*. Arguably, the *Vindiciae* replaces a natural law of duty and holism with an alternative, more self-protective, natural law of rational autonomy and personal constancy. As he revises the *Mare* at the request of Charles I, however, whose policies stand to benefit from the learning that the great scholar lends them, Selden is vulnerable to the critique offered generally by Grotius's sceptical persona Carneades, who maintains that when it comes to naturalizing law, each interested party can say whatever it pleases. In the *Table Talk*, Selden feminizes the whimsical tendency to manipulate natural claims, much as Jonson deems effete those kinds of poetic wit that have no basis at all in natural law. Yet more than the epistemological weakness of a basis in fancy is at stake in mounting arguments on natural law. There is also the risk that the natural lawyer will prove a wretched parasite at worst, and a partial loyalist to state interest at best. With the help of Grotius, Selden comes to understand that natural law can be set forth as the ligature behind the beliefs and practices of far-flung humanity and therefore serve as a warrant for charity, toleration, and peace. Conversely, it can also be wielded as an instrument of severing one interest from another, one honest self from a corrupt world, or one political interest group from another. Indeed, in the mid-1630s Meric Casaubon's edition and translation of Marcus Aurelius conflates both these tendencies: the work celebrates a cosmic holism as the foundation of sociability and charity, but its sociable-charitable religion is framed by the editor and translator as a defence of conformity and submission in Caroline England against the 'Puritan' insubordination that the king and his chief prelate, William Laud, are striving to quash.[23] It is worth noting, then, that along with the royal patronage of the *Mare Clausum* in the 1630s, Selden dedicates to Laud the 1636 and 1638 editions of his work on the Hebraic laws of property and priesthood, and his *De Iure Naturali & Gentium* 'was licensed for the press by Laud's chaplain in 1639.'[24]

Both Grotius and Selden betray conflict over the rival natural claims of charitable sociability against ownership, propriety, and self-interest. Each is torn between the irenic position that common notions should induce us to love one another and the eventually Hobbesian view that common instincts, fears, and interests must prevent us from killing one another.[25] So it is that for Grotius and Selden alike, natural law offers not one but at least two ways of understanding how its transhistorical standard might maximize the welfare of early modern Christian societies. In the *Mare Clausum*, this tension arises in regard to the question of whether there was community or ownership in Paradise. Selden is largely dismissive of what he now considers golden-age poesies, preferring to focus on God's apportioning the world to the children of Noah. On the one hand, he maintains that the Noachidae revived Adam's 'private Dominions or Possessions'; on the other, he concedes that the human perspective on Adam is severely limited. That is, in Paradise no natural obligation bound human beings either to community or to propriety, nor was there any prohibition on either. In large part, the matter was left to Adam's discretion (20).

Whereas his opponents tend to characterize the seas as by their very nature indeterminate, Selden opts to compare them to wild animals waiting for a claimant or hunter. These hunters, he stresses, were the children of Noah, so that all the world came to be owned 'either by distribution or occupation' (24). As ownership replaced community, the former was modified and particularized 'according to the various Institutions of several people,' some of which opted to limit 'the free and absolute power of the Proprietor.' What this means is that both the will of God and that of the various peoples have to be taken into account in assessing what happened to the law of nature once it embarked on its travels through time. With reference to his schema, Selden accounts for the complex development of propriety by concluding that the permissive natural law was changed into a positive law, and that this change was supported by the obligation of all nations jointly to observe 'Compacts and Covenants' (24–5). All in all, ownership of the seas was either naturally permitted (as the occupation of 'things vacant and derelict') or nationally contracted by those civilized peoples who 'in judging matters of this nature, [are] the best Interpreter of the *natural Law* which is *Permissive*' (26–7).

As does Grotius in *De jure belli ac pacis*, Selden adverts to Old Testament examples alongside his theoretical analysis, in some measure no doubt as a rescue from the complexity of that analysis. According to Selden, God's law and its sage commentators are 'very plain' on the inclusion of seas within borders. The wealth of biblical support is meant to evince a 'Universal Permissive Law' for ownership. Nonetheless, in following the rabbinical 'Exposition of the divine Assignation,' Selden retains a vestige of his long-standing distrust of rabbinical fictions (41). In so many ways, it is hard to keep claims for natural law free of the suspicion that they are little more than poetic praises for hire.

One motivation for his greater acceptance of rabbinical tradition is Selden's scepticism about the right reason putatively embodied as natural law. When he cautions his readers not immediately to conflate 'a right use of humane Reason' with the overlapping 'Customs of several Nations,' it is crucially unclear whether the problem lies with custom as an index of reason or with reason 'as an Index of the natural Law,' especially (he notes) in assessing 'things Divine' (42–3). So a simple appeal to the universal and certain foundation of natural law might be meant as an escape from all the human liabilities of positive law. But the natural law theorist encounters a welter of problems in trying to stabilize and systematize the dynamic among nature, reason, divine will, human custom, and consensus, above all when there is a specific controversy to be arbitrated. No poet's formula – such as Jonson's 'consent of the learned' and 'consent of the good'[26] – will do for determining when the convention of natural law is legitimately normative and positively enforceable. Selden himself decries those sloppy attempts to juxtapose natural, divine, and human laws 'without exact and convenient examination,' those 'for the serving of their own Interests' or suitable only to 'the humor and disposition of the people whom [the legal authorities] are to rule and keep in order' (*Mare Clausum*, 42–3). For all its supposed commonality, Selden complains, even reason cannot be entrusted to the many-headed multitude.

As he begins to make plain in the *Mare*, Selden is arriving at the position that reason in or by itself is not to be trusted very much at all. In the supremely, divinely lawful society of Judaism, he maintains, reason 'hath often been most deservedly restrained, by certain set-Maxims, Principles, and Rules of holy Writ, as Religious Bolts and Bars upon the Soul;

lest it should wantonize and wander, either into the old Errors of most Ages and Nations, or after the new devices of a rambling phansie. And truly, such a cours as this hath ever been observed in Religious Government' (43). This passage moves in two directions. For one, it insists that natural law can achieve the status of sacred warrant only if it is grounded in scriptural and Talmudic maxims censuring and imprisoning the wildly fanciful faculties of human knowledge. In such a case, there must be a higher intellectual agent than human reason, much as there is in Lord Herbert's *De Veritate*. For another, the passage hints at Selden's dalliance elsewhere in the 1630s and 1640s with some version of Archbishop Laud's commitment to the regulation of religious society by canon laws and ecclesiastical censors. Those bolts and bars are hardly 'natural' in their force and jurisdiction.

In the *Mare*, however, Selden settles for far less: for conclusions about human relations rather than theories about the relations between God and the creation. What this compromise entails is that natural duties and permissions are gauged 'by the Laws, Placarts, and received Customs of divers Ages and Nations, both antient and modern' (43). Selden tries to naturalize these customs, laws, and edicts, but in the *Mare* he raises the possibility that new natural law is but old positive law writ large. Even his imagery – which likens customs and edicts to those plants gathered in husbandry from various countries – blurs the line between the commonality ensured by nature and the variety cultivated by human invention. Worst of all, Selden has to admit that if nations have agreed on maritime propriety for many ages, then it is at least theoretically possible, if also unthinkable, 'that so many and those the more famous Nations, have for so many Ages erred against Nature' (44). Recourse to natural law might relieve a holy commonwealth struggling with scepticism, persecution, faction, and warfare, but as Selden understands it, any quest for nature's universal perspective is sorely encumbered with human error. Natural law, however, is so much empty air without the interpretation and application of human law by which the universal is concretized and empowered. Each holy commonwealth must find the best constitutional means of elaborating divinity as well as nature in legal institutions, positive laws, and enforceable contracts.

—— 5 ——

In answering the objections to an ownership of the seas, Selden seeks to reconcile the claims of 'Law and Right,' on the one hand, with the obligations of duty and charity, on the other. As a reference to Bodin makes clear, however, he is eager to branch out from the matter of the seas alone to the question of how to normalize the practice of war, that spectre of violence so troubling in his work on aristocratic codes and privileges. More than ever, not simply any theory of natural law will do: Selden ridicules Heraclitus's reduction of all being to mere flux as an example of a natural philosophy that offers nothing but vain poesy. From time to time in the *Mare Clausum*, even as they disagree on the specifics of maritime law, Selden turns to Grotius for leadership in recreating a natural law as an unimpeachable yet a serviceable normative authority in the most difficult of human affairs.

Invoking the improved precision of navigational instruments as his standard of excellence, Selden suggests to the readers of the *Mare* that whatever the two authors' conflicts over the matter of the sea, Grotius's *De jure belli ac pacis* serves as an extraordinary guide for sizing up errors in law. But errors of law are not understood in a vacuum. In chapter 26 of Book 1, the English author celebrates the Dutch scholar in the context of drawing an analogy between the discovery of errors in law and the reformation of mistakes in natural philosophy. In both cases, Selden argues, 'observation and experience' must uproot addictions to outmoded authorities and dogmas. In this respect, he continues, Grotius possesses 'great learning, and extraordinarie knowledg in things both Divine and Humane,' a level of admiration that Grotius also showed for Selden (171). In the *Mare Clausum*, Selden devotes substantial space to a reconstruction of the political world in which Grotius found himself a political and religious prisoner. This kinship between the two prisoners is obvious when Selden concludes 'that persons in power usually take a libertie to aspers men as they pleas when they are in question' (174). Even in making their cases about the oceans, Selden implies, the two men are imprisoned not just physically but intellectually by their sovereigns and by the contentious religious politics of their times. In the 1630s, however, Selden is invested in exploring the possibility that a newly grounded natural law might show the way out of that intellectual prison – for religious society at large as well as for the gifted legal sages at the mercy of that society.

For Selden, the natural law at the heart of Grotius's *De jure belli ac pacis* might help to spring Europe from the intellectual prison that was made more brutal by rampant warfare and more embarrassing by the taunts of scepticism. However, Grotius's way to success is paved with great difficulty; for the version of natural law that Selden receives from him undertakes to argue down the sceptics, to reconcile charity and self-interest, and to normalize the morality of that most bestial of human actions, war, the very goal of which might be refashioned as a godly peace.

First published in 1625, seven years into the thirty years of bloodshed in European Christendom, Grotius's great work on the law of war and peace promises a full and methodical account of international law that would mediate among nature, custom, and divine will; answer the hypothetical scepticism of a persona dubbed Carneades; and reverse the trend that prizes power and expedience over justice, charity, and law. The sceptic challenges the very existence of natural law, believing that all law is customary, expedient, and mutable. To this claim, Grotius responds with a Stoic stress on 'sociableness,' a retort to religious factionalism that in England was captured in the decades of Selden's work on natural law by texts such as Meric Casaubon's edition of Marcus Aurelius (1634, 1635).[27] But whereas in Casaubon's Marcus the quality of sociableness is integrated with duty and charity, the relations among the three virtues are more fitful in Grotius's *De jure*, and sometimes they are divisive. If Casaubon readily links charity and sociability in his translation of and notes on the Stoic emperor, Grotius holds specifically Christian virtues like charity to a far higher standard than Stoic duty. Indeed, that standard is so high that its virtues are legitimate only to the extent that they are immeasurably bountiful; and no such uncontrolled *copia* could ever work as a rule of any kind, never mind one charged with regulating violent human tendencies.

At first Grotius's 'sphere of law' contracts to a few highly self-interested and self-defensive requirements: 'abstaining from that which is another's, the restoration to another of anything of his which we may have, together with any gain which we may have received from it; the obligation to fulfil promises, the making good of a loss incurred through our fault, and the inflicting of penalties upon men according to their deserts.'[28] But the law of nature signifies more to Grotius than such a ministry of self-interest might allow. At the very least, it judicially tempers our fears, pleasures, and violent impulses; at most, it derives from the will of God, even if its formation of man's very essence is unequal to those laws whose very essence is God's will. The Grotian law of nature does protect the relatively weak individual or state from aggressive neighbours, but it also prompts a love for the family of man.

War, Grotius argues, must be guided by natural directives towards peace and moral righteousness, a state of affairs made easier by the constancy of natural law. The constancy of natural law was by no means taken for granted in the early seventeenth century. In the *Mare Clausum*, Selden himself reused the imagery of his notes on Fortescue in order to argue that 'even those things which naturally are thus flitting, do notwithstanding in a Civil sens remain ever the same; as the ship of *Theseus*, a Hous, or a Theatre, which hath been so often mended and repaired, that there is not so much as one part or plank left of the first building' (133). Like any non-contractual law, natural law might well suffer from drastic mutations according to human fancy and the shift of times; but Grotius holds fast to his conviction that natural law is stable and that its constancy lends itself to systematizing much more readily than 'the elements of positive law, since [the latter] often undergo change and are different in different places' (21). Also, the principles of natural law boast a self-evidence eluding only the obtuse, though Grotius nonetheless elicits substantial testimony in order to corroborate a natural law whose principles are supposed to be clarified by his system.

As his prolegomena unfolds, then, Grotius offers his readers a hope and a challenge: hope in the very real and clear presence of a universal moral norm, and the challenge of distilling, arranging, and legitimizing its contents and modus operandi. But he also offers careful interpretive guidance. In the matter of whether the Old Testament offers a reliable source for natural law, Grotius leads and directs the discriminating reader: 'I frequently appeal to the authority of the books which men inspired by God have either written or approved, nevertheless with a distinction between the Old Testament and the New. There are some who urge that the Old Testament sets forth the law of nature. Without doubt they are in error, for many of its rules come from the free will of God. And yet this is never in conflict with the true law of nature; and up to this point the Old Testament can be used as a source of the law of nature, provided we carefully distinguish between the law of God, which God sometimes executes through men, and the law of men in their relations with one another' (26–7). On the one hand, the certainty of Grotius's treatment of law is comparable to the abstractions of math; on the other, he acknowledges that regarding natural law, clarity must be attained rather than assumed. Order in natural law must be fashioned rather than reflected; and one must always remember 'to distinguish clearly between things which seemed to be the same and were not' (29). Indeed, much later, in the twenty-third chapter of Book 2, he agrees with Aristotle that moral certainty can never pretend to a mathematical invulnerability, the concrete circumstances of life being as complex as they are.

In the three books in which he lays out his system, Grotius mediates between natural right and natural charity by means of a traditional definition of natural law: 'The law of nature is a dictate of right reason, which points out that an act, according as it is or is not in conformity with rational nature, has in it a quality of moral baseness or moral necessity; and that, in consequence, such an act is either forbidden or enjoined by the author of nature, God' (38–9). He is careful to point out that these prohibitions and injunctions are dispensed by God as essentially moral – as moral in themselves – and so, as functionally independent of God's will, which might devise or cancel other dispensations at any point in time. Indeed, Grotius extends the theological authority and reliability of natural law as far as they can reach: 'The law of nature, again, is unchangeable – even in the sense that it cannot be changed by God' (40). The essential morality of natural law ranks in predictability with the simplest sums of mathematics; and providentially, right reason affords human nature with the capacity to gain ready access to nature's general principles. It is typical of Grotius's combination of faith in and sophistication about natural law, however, that he chooses to enlist its putatively simple sums in devising a casuistry for determining the rights and wrongs of war, that most savage creation of fallen humanity.

Grotius's main conclusion about the natural law of war is simple enough: natural law prohibits only those uses of force that either damage or ignore the welfare of society. On the one hand, he has in mind a benefit by means of which 'each individual be safeguarded in the possession of what belongs to him' (53). One sees this guardianship of rights everywhere in history, he shows, but crucially among the children of Noah, who were guided by natural law well before the Jews received their own special code from God. On the other hand, Grotius knows that he must answer the requirements of charity. Having tested his claims against the supposed opposition of the New Testament, he appears to have clinched what he names 'the law of a well-ordered love' according to which 'the good of an innocent person should receive consideration before the good of one who is guilty, and the public good before that of the individual' (75).

Yet love is as hard to normalize as violence – a problem to which Selden himself turns in the *Uxor Hebraica* and in the treatment of agape in the work on the Sanhedrin. In Grotius's *De jure*, the pressures exerted by sociable charity on the natural law of war are never quite laid to rest. Grotius's systematic analysis of the legitimate parties and causes of war is well under way, his explanation of ownership, rights, and contracts is learnedly established, and the guidelines even for religious warfare are brilliantly drawn, when, in the opening chapter of Book 3 – 'General Rules from the Law of Nature Regarding What is Permissible in War' – he introduces a leitmotif featuring love, moderation, and the mitigation of legal rigour into his discussion. 'But, as we have admonished upon many occasions previously,' Grotius cautions, 'what accords with a strict interpretation of right is now always, or in all respects, permitted. Often, in fact, love for our neighbour prevents us from pressing our right to the utmost limit' (601). Although Grotius has argued that the New Testament offers no opposition to lawful war or, if it does, that this opposition transcends the normative boundaries of nature, he worries that when it comes to decisions about the potentially brutal means of war, good and evil will contest one another more confusingly than was the case in the matter of ends. What standard should guide us then? 'The decision in such matters,' Grotius allows, 'must be left to a prudent judgement, but in such a way that when in doubt we should favour that course, as the more safe, which has regard for the interest of another rather than our own' (601). In short, love is the ready and easy way out of brutality as well as the supernatural and superfluous ideal to which few human beings can aspire.

The charitable bias of this casuistry regarding the means of war reappears when Grotius distinguishes between the law of nations allowing slavery and the law of nature to which 'slavery is contrary' (690); or when he decides to revisit the requirements of honour. 'I must retrace my steps,' he begins, 'and must deprive those who wage war of nearly all the privileges which I seemed to grant, yet did not grant to them. For when I first set out to explain this part of the law of nations I bore witness that many things are said to be "lawful" or "permissible" for the reason that they are done with impunity, in part also because coactive tribunals lend to them their authority; things which, nevertheless, either deviate from the rule of right (whether this has its basis in law strictly so called, or in the admonitions of other virtues), or at any rate may be omitted on higher grounds and with greater praise among good men' (716). As the law of nations and its strictly legal contracts give way to the more soft and flexible intuitions of humanity, Grotius attempts to delineate the authority, source, and accessibility of the latter. Like conscience, honour, or charity, the kinder face of natural law accentuates that standard's elusive and unenforceable tendencies.

Perhaps the law of nature serves as the rule of right guiding human beings to love their neighbours and to moderate desire. Perhaps the rule of right results from the shame and approval meted out by the community, ideally within the domain of natural law. Perhaps righteousness descends from a divine source much higher than either nature or community, inspiration or zeal, but not finally to quasi-rational human beings. Grotius does not say. In *Natural Rights Theories*, Tuck summarizes the problem of the relationship between natural law and righteousness as Selden inherited it: 'Why should rational individuals possessed of a full complement of natural rights be under laws at all?'[29] Better yet, why or how should they know when the spirit of charity is present or needed no matter what either natural law, positive law, or communal attitude might allow? Repeatedly, Grotius preaches human moderation and equity in the brutal activities of war, since 'the rules of love are broader than the rules of law' (722–82). But at what point does the broadening of measure leave human measures well behind, even that most inaccessible but most morally authoritative law of nature?

In Grotius's *De jure*, then, natural law tends to abandon the realm of mathematical certainty for the amorphous fancies of honour, conscience, and charity: it is unsettled by, but very much in need of, the righteousness of those warrants. Prompted by Grotius, but with Moses Maimonides as his chief perspective on inmost antiquity, Selden attempts to forge a normal and maximally beneficial interplay among natural law, community dynamics, contractual law, and zealous righteousness. Yet the authorities on which he most relies for the legitimacy of this ensemble – the Bible, the Talmud, Judaic institutions, and (behind those texts and customs) the will of the Judaic God – are expressly distinctive from the culturally non-specific minimalism of natural religion. As Tuck emphasizes, God is Selden's arbitrary enforcer behind the universal rationality and piety of natural law; Selden's key claim is that the pressure exerted on souls and societies by their apprehension of the divine is alone sufficiently great for keeping human beings in line with the law of nature. In short, the law of nature attains the obligatory force of a positive contract, and our obedience to that contract is ensured by the shame, fear, and love that are generated between neighbours, by poets, priests, and magistrates, and within the zealous or timorous human heart itself.[30] In *De Jure Naturali et Gentium*, Selden is obviously and elaborately attempting to realize Grotius's hope for a universal authority in natural law. But if, with Lord Herbert, he is fully prepared to delineate the common notions of religion without regard to Christ, he is not prepared with Grotius to imagine a natural religion whose warrant would remain constantly powerful were God to be effaced from the minds of its participants. Selden's challenge is to derive and to situate the natural law so that its universally moral and godly rationality prevailingly jibes with the wilful dispensations of the divine spirit, the ritualized and customary interactions of the community, and the positive jurisdiction of historical courts.

—— 6 ——

In the *Mare Clausum*, Selden reverts to a favourite optical analogy that he fashioned largely with the assistance of Roger Bacon. In order to view a wall, say, at a considerable distance, one requires a surveyor's device that permits the measurement from the viewer's position to the wall by reference to an intermediary point or set of points. Throughout his works, Selden investigates the legitimacy of a number of intermediary points between the members of an actual community and the ideal of the well measured religious society. Unlike poetry and human law, however, natural law makes a greater promise of removing the viewers beyond the need for instrumental devices even if, more than is the case with the artifices of human manners, access to nature's moral and religious trove requires considerable improvement of mental acuity. If nature is an intermediary between divine dispensations and human societies, those societies require intermediaries between themselves and nature.

In the case of the *Mare*, the ancient ownership of the sea is calculated by reference to the intermediary point of 'the continued and more certain usage and custom of later times' (189). Yet such a claim, that English historical records deliver the very perspective that one needs in gaining access to the law of nature, is self-evidently liable to the politics of self-interest that Selden's critics satirized in both the author and the government that he was serving. In *De Jure Naturali et Gentium Juxta Disciplinam Ebraeorum*, Selden has projected the intermediary point far beyond the domain of English politics and policy, so far, in fact, that it might be considered impossibly distant from contemporary readers. For Selden's intermediary point is nothing less than the Talmudic transmission of God's dispensation of moral rules first to Adam and Eve, then again to Noah and his children once the world was washed of its sins. For a European Christendom in search of certainty, peace, and harmony, nothing could be more desirable than these minimalist guidelines, believed to be flush with God's very spirit yet ever steady and constant in the measure that they afford the complicated and mutable affairs of human life. Selden knows, however, that one traditional aspect of natural law is bound to collapse the distance between the contemporary reader and the exotic rabbinical writings: for setting aside for a moment the obvious point that the Old Testament is an integral part of the Christian Bible, it is also the case, according to Stoic wisdom, that natural law is intimately incarnated in every human being's right reason. The intermediary point between early modern readers and natural law is, on the one hand, far to the east, far in the past, among a people no longer even allowed to live in England, and as intimate with the immediate revelation of God as that experienced by Adam, Noah, and Abraham. On the other hand, early modern readers can find a personal distillation of the exotic Talmud within their breasts.

Lest one conclude that Selden has abandoned the Caroline and Laudian pursuit of utter conformity within the boundaries of English worship, a vision to which he contributes in his work on the Judaic priesthood in the 1630s, the *De Jure Naturali* is habitually skewed away from its focus on natural law by its equally prominent study of the laws according to which the ancient Jews dealt with aliens and proselytes. At its most conciliatory, idealistic, and irenic, then, Selden's massive recovery of natural religion looks both to Adam and to each honest soul for the purest guidelines available to all religious societies. He also ventures through the world of learning in search of an intermediary between nature and modern society that is neither so distant as Eden nor so proximate – and suspiciously biased and fanciful – as one's own heart. Like Grotius, Selden must answer the charges of the sceptic that it is humanly impossible to certify the truth-value of ostensibly natural norms of behaviour and belief; like his patron Laud, however, Selden expends a great deal of thought on the ways in which societies have managed the cultural and religious impurities of an alien presence. The minimal slate of truths and duties embodied by natural law offers a recipe for widespread harmony among the warring factions of the European religious scene; but *De Jure Naturali* never strays too far from a recipe of another kind, the Judaic laws for converting otherness to, or for expelling it from, the sameness of a strictly regulated orthodoxy into which one can most genuinely be born. In the first instance, pagan culture, whether Greco-Roman or Philistine, is perfectly pious in its common notions; in the second, pagans must be reborn and leave behind all vestiges of their alienage.

In *De Jure Naturali*, Selden takes a number of approaches to the affirmation of the certitude of natural law. As in the *Mare*, he offers a taxonomy of its dispensations, especially as its guidelines to human manners are variously permissive and obligatory. He looks to pagan writers for evidence that the natural norms of honesty are universal. He appeals to the venerable notion, both biblical and pagan, that natural law is inscribed in human hearts. And, at the risk of pushing nature into the realm of artifice, Selden touts its comparability to geometrical lines, angles, and planes, the measure of which can be taken by some intellectual or moral carpenter's rule (*amussim*). Not fully content with that metaphor, he shifts it to a related geometrical truism, to the perpendicular line that assures the parallelism and so the rectitude of two lines that it crosses. But his oft-repeated image of the carpenter's rule implies the requirement of some artifice outside of nature that might guarantee not so much nature itself as claims made on nature. Selden does tend to resurrect the well-worn convention that nature takes the measure of humanly positive laws, not the reverse. Yet the whole thrust of his orientation towards Judaism in *De Jure Naturali* has a way of supplanting nature with God's dispensation of positive laws to his chosen people. Positive law is the centrepiece of Judaic society, their complicity in the transmission of a universal natural law notwithstanding.

Selden points out that in the face of artificial and culturally specific authorities of law, right reason can be understood to react in two ways. In keeping with an ancient, largely Stoic, tradition of insubordination against autocracy, right reason can be heralded for refusing to heed any local or human authority and for declaring its only citizenship in the whole of the cosmos. But in the vein of Cicero's *De officiis*, right reason can be understood as carefully guiding human beings in their execution of obligations to local and human authorities. In facing the wilderness of the fallen world, Milton's Adam and Eve must learn from the archangel Michael that divinity is everywhere in the cosmos, not limited to specific holy places or rites. As Selden understands Paradise, however, Adam and Eve received the minimal guidance of nature from the very beginning and then transmitted that guidance to their children. Yet the conditions of the fall, the history of the Jews, and the casuistic tendencies of the rabbis tell a story of human rationality far more entangled in specific obligations as well as in bewilderment over its own discrepancies – witness the fragmentation of philosophy into hundreds of sects. Pagans who have spoken the same language of normative nature have, in fact, often agreed only in the name of their guide. No wonder, Selden says, that the sceptics have been able to undermine the authority of natural law. At the very least, right reason is simply and purely a genetic legacy inaugurated by Adam and Eve; indeed, its dictates and habits are so thoroughly mediated by cultural specificity and historical change that, as Selden and Lord Herbert agree, the religious warrant of the common notions of world religions should claim a higher ontological status than discursive reason.

It is imprudent, Selden concedes, for natural religion to lean heedlessly and naively on the strength of reason alone; for reason is inevitably multiform, narcissistic, political, and distorted. The fanciful addictions and corrupting politicization of reason are especially disappointing if the premier benefit of natural law is some certain and harmonious recourse from the polemical and military discord of the 1620s and 1630s. Yet the *De Jure Naturali* is torn between rival moralities: a Stoic's imprudent devotion to universal religion and to the honest self that instantiates that universal; and a more worldly-wise prudence whose advice is geared towards the local and often contentious politics of specific religious societies with a vested interest in the offices of conformity. With Lipsius as their model, Selden knows, the early modern heirs of a fervent yet irenic Stoicism are weary of the wars between Arminians and Calvinists and Lutherans, between Catholic emperor and Protesant prince, between 'Laudians' and 'Puritans,' as those caricatures are generated in the mill of polemics. These seventeenth-century revivers of natural law must somehow gain access to the early days of the Creation during which right reason and natural law were fully and fervidly awake in human hearts, at which time that law was intimate with the divinity that dispensed it and obliged human beings to obey it. As Selden portrays the dilemma of method in natural religion, however, there are at least three ways to pinpoint the intermediary between early modern readers and Noah, and each way comprises difficult questions of ontological status, of epistemological reliability, and of practice in a world that exacts duty and conformity within specific polities.

Down one way, Selden projects an intermediary for natural religion that comprises the whole tradition of Jewish law and rabbinical commentary before, during, and after the Roman period of crisis for the Jewish people during which the Talmud of Babylon and the Talmud of Jerusalem were composed. As Selden is apt to point out, however, such a tradition is highly uneven in its reliability, in its internal conflicts, and especially in its entanglement of Noachian general principles with specifically Judaic strictures, customs, and rites. In a second way he revisits the numinous, occult, and often pagan vein of his Neoplatonic and Pythagorean interests; for the intermediary between early modern readers and the universal truths of natural religion is identified as the 'intellectual agent.' Insofar as this guardian spirit is neither identical to fallible human reason nor cleanly divorced from human faculties (*De Jure Naturali*, 109–17), Selden recapitulates the medieval debate over whether the *intellectus agens* amounts to an angelic assistance emanating from God or an inner monitor implanted by God and concludes that the difference is negligible.[31] His unwillingness simply to resolve the debate is indicative of his desire to elevate natural law above its ordinary rational warrant yet to check the cabbalistic or mystical vagaries into which an obsession with emanation often leads. Selden's recurring discussions of transmigration in a spirit-filled cosmos find their potential for enthusiasm checked once the *De Jure Naturali* begins its dominant program of containing that spirit in a handful of Platonic forms, natural laws, or common notions. For these forms, laws, or notions convert the wandering Pythagorean spirit's transgression of normative bounds into framed and formalized universals; thanks to this conversion, human beings might receive the benefits of divine imperatives and angelic assistance as more accommodating and trustworthy moral intuitions stimulated to the awareness of the conscience by Selden's other textual intermediaries. But even if Selden's intellectual agent shies away from the unstable power of a boundless cosmic *pneuma* and from fully indulging the speculations of Jewish, Christian, and pagan mysticism, he refuses to imprison the spirit of that agent in human rationality itself. Whatever the intellectual agent might be, Selden notes, we can say with certainty that it shines on reason in the manner in which the sun – Robert Fludd's densest cosmic embodiment of the divine breath – blazes on the eye, plainly and dazzlingly all at once.

Selden's third intermediary is neither a tradition nor a spiritual force. It is one especially wise man. Yet Moses Maimonides promises the distillation of both tradition and divine spirit. As Selden's chief authority on the Talmud, Maimonides works to transform the formidably complex Talmud and Mishnah into a finite number of precepts; to rationalize each precept according to the touchstone of moral utility; and to reconcile the philosopher's penchant for rational and general principles with the requirements of voluntary obedience to and faith in the not always rational or general will of God.

For Selden as for modern scholars, Maimonides' two greatest works are very different despite their overlaps. Unlike the *Moreh Nebuchim* (or *Dalalat al-Hairin, The Guide for the Perplexed*), the *Mishneh Torah* was offered to a broader audience as a distillation of the Mishnah and Talmud into workable, rationalized, and general principles, each of which comprised a portion of Judaism's 613 precepts (by Maimonides' count). Both the Talmud and the Mishnah themselves were divided into six rubrics: agriculture (including benedictions); holy seasons; women; civil and criminal justice; sacred things; and ritual purity. But these categories did not prevent the rabbinical tradition from becoming conflictive, voluminous, and at times maddeningly obscure. In the *Mishneh Torah*, Maimonides sought to reorganize, reduce, and clarify rabbinical wisdom so that the people of God might be able to live lawfully with the guidance of that redaction. As Selden understood this project, Maimonides was not simply edging a recalcitrant code of positive law towards system and clarity; the great rabbi was also making it possible to find natural, constant, and rational guidelines for behaviour within the dynamic mass of the Talmud.

In his own version of the distillation of Hebraic into natural law, Selden looked to the *Mishneh Torah* far more often than to the *Moreh Nebuchin*, a fact that testifies to the practical aims of his often exceedingly scholarly and digressive presentation of sacred norms. Indeed, Milton recognized Selden's intention to afford his readers a light by which to live.[32] The *Guide for the Perplexed* also fascinated Selden as a torch for those elite lawmakers entering the labyrinth of Talmudic methods and texts in search of a rationalized and clarified set of moral and religious norms. Maimonides demonstrates that, before the labyrinth is exited, such lawmakers must encounter that monstrous question of how to reconcile the commonality and rationality of natural law with the non-rational, wilful, and tribal demands of the faith of Abraham.

In his introduction to the *Guide*, Maimonides promises to assist that reader whose impasse between legalistic piety and philosophical reason has led to 'perplexity and anxiety': 'The object of this treatise is to enlighten a religious man who has been trained to believe in the truth of our holy Law, who conscientiously fulfils his moral and religious duties, and at the same time has been successful in his philosophical studies.' Maimonides continues: 'Human reason has attracted him to abide within its sphere; and he finds it difficult to accept as correct the teaching based on the literal interpretation of the Law, and especially that which he himself or others derived from those homonymous, metaphorical, or hybrid expressions.'[33] Even the sage will be tempted into extremes: 'If he be guided solely by reason, and renounce his previous views which are based on those expressions, and if, instead of following his reason, he abandon its guidance altogether, it would still appear that his religious convictions had suffered loss and injury. For he would then be left with those errors which give rise to fear and anxiety, constant grief and great perplexity' (2). Maimonides recommends that the wise strengthen their grasp on God's laws for regulating human actions by familiarizing themselves with God's wisdom in nature. More complexly, he edges Judaic law in the direction of rational principles and, along the way, works at the problem of how Judaic and natural laws pertain to one another.

For instance, in claiming that human nature is as various as it is sociable, Maimonides maintains that the welfare of human life consequently depends on a normative director; this leader 'must complete every shortcoming, remove every excess, and prescribe for the conduct of all, so that the natural variety should be counterbalanced by the uniformity of legislation, and the order of society be well established' (233). From the desideratum of this uniformity, Maimonides summarizes how law relates to nature: 'I therefore maintain that the Law, though not a product of Nature, is nevertheless not entirely foreign to Nature' (233). In order for human society to persevere in well being, God wisely instilled in human beings properties of governance that, if not fully belonging to a natural domain, are harmonious with the inhabitants ordering that domain.

Later in the *Guide*, in turning to rationalize the moral utility of God's 613 commandments, Maimonides prefaces his efforts with the general exhortation that law seeks our physical and spiritual prosperity. For the body, it proceeds first of all 'by removing all violence from our midst; that is to say, that we do not do every one as he pleases, desires, and is able to do; but every one of us does that which contributes towards the common welfare' (312). Again for the body, the law instils 'good morals as must produce a good social state' (312). For the soul, however, the law transmits 'correct opinions ... to the people according to their capacity,' the *Mishneh Torah* serving as Maimonides's attempt to adapt the law to more limited capacity (312). For Selden it is crucial that Maimonides stresses the distinction between religious duties owed by human beings to God, and those owed among human beings themselves. If moral honesty in religious society is a primary goal of a normative spirituality, then it should be remembered that even the laws pertaining to a man's relationship with God 'in reality ... lead to results which concern also his fellow-men' (331).

Even when the moral utility of a precept is opaque, Maimonides is eager to establish its rationale along the lines of justice, goodness, and true belief. Concerning rules about clothing made of linen and wool or about the process of killing a calf, he seeks to situate a difficult precept within one of those three domains in benefit to society. In allowing that the precepts cannot suit every rare circumstance, Maimonides likens the Judaic law to natural dispensations; for the best law 'must be certain and general, although it may be effective in some cases and ineffective in others' (329). Even as he always keeps Judaic and natural laws apart, he experiments with versions of a companionable intimacy between them. For instance, in his discussion of the Passover season, he writes: 'It is also known how great is the importance of this period in Nature, and in many religious duties. For the Law always follows Nature, and in some respects brings it to perfection' (352). When he turns away from this theme, Maimonides explains why Nature, which by itself 'is not capable of designing and thinking,' might be completed in God's law for the Jews, which 'is the result of the wisdom and guidance of God, who is the author of the intellect of all rational beings' (352). In short the Mosaic code was given not to overthrow the Noachian law but to fulfil it.

Maimonides clearly wants Judaic codes to lay claim to the benefits of natural law – its constancy, lucidity, universality, and orderliness – without jettisoning the singular assets of a unique and positive dispensation from the biblical God, or for that matter the special mediation of the rabbis. So, too, for the rabbinical Selden: Noachian law promises to distil the best of divinity and human artifice without sacrificing the naturalness that ensures its defence against the wilfulness of God or the contamination and variation in human invention.

7

As David Novak explains in *Natural Law in Judaism*, 'Natural law ... is the idea of a reality that is less exalted than direct divine revelation and more exalted than merely local human arrangements.'[34] For Selden, however, the Judaization of natural law shifted that ostensibly rational and universal standard in directions more supra-rational like divine revelation yet also more culturally delimited than its ordinary conception. Like Maimonides in the twelfth and early thirteenth centuries, Selden believed that in the 1620s and 1630s his people had reached a critical turning point with regard to the welfare of their lawful religious society. Whereas the Jewish rabbi borders on naturalizing his people's law without ever really doing so, however, the English lawyer verges on Judaizing natural law, but does not do so. Whereas Maimonides attempted to give some order and rational legitimacy to the often perplexing positive laws of the Jews, Selden looked away from the English common law towards a natural universality whose origins were tied up with the Hebraic narrative of creation and civilization. In his work on the Great Sanhredin, Selden came to terms with the realization that natural law, while still of limited use, is, for the most part, neutralized by its position between the transcendent authority of divine inspiration and the efficacious jurisdiction of contractual legal institutions. In addition, he confronted the difficulty of what he knows he must discover, a way for contemporary Protestants to be convinced that the ancient Jews possessed a heritage of rich and zealous spirituality, one in keeping with their devotion to God's law and at odds with their undeserved reputation for arid legalism. When Jesus came to earth, Selden believed, it was in an attempt to make traditional Jews and reformed Jews – that is, Christians – understand that they must embrace one specific coordination of law and spiritual largesse in order for religious society to thrive. In *De Jure Naturali*, however, Selden posits that Jews and Christians must be saved from the perplexities and inadequacies of their separate customs by being swept together with pagan cultures into a comprehensive commonality of religion and manners. Yet he is repeatedly found moving back into the domain of Jewish positive law, as though his study were sizing up the place of natural law in Judaism rather than the place of Judaism in the purveyance of natural law.

Selden understood that the major proponents of natural law in his day – Grotius, Lord Herbert, and, before them, Lipsius and Du Vair – were mounting a philosophical resistance to the adverse circumstances of their times, including religious warfare and fragmentation, the persecution of fellow Christians, whether they be boldly conscientious or simply peaceful, and an ever more rampant scepticism. No doubt his sense of the dire conditions motivating the invention and perpetuation of the Talmudic tradition attracted Selden both to the ancient texts and to Maimonides. Like the composers of the Talmud, who raced to preserve their traditions as the Romans destroyed the temple and forced them into exile, Maimonides had looked around him and seen 'severe vicissitudes ... [and] the pressure of hard times.' Worst of all, he feared, 'the wisdom of our wise men has disappeared; the understanding of our prudent men is hidden.'[35] Rather than take their wisdom with him to the grave, Maimonides sought to accomplish a distillation of all normative morality so that his people might gain access to its basic guidelines and so that the elite might find their way through its labyrinth.

In his preface to the *De Jure Naturali*, Selden stresses that his anchoring of natural law in the seven Noachian principles intervenes in a dispute among moralists, politicians, lawyers, and theologians. Distinct from the covenant between God and the Jews alone, the Noachian principles match the precepts given Adam and Eve in six of seven cases – against idolatry, blasphemy, murder, incest or illicit sex, and theft or deceit, and in favour of obedience to some judicial apparatus – with the seventh (concerning the consumption of animal limbs) added in due course. No doubt Selden was attracted to the Talmudic interpretation of natural law because the rabbis assert an earliest point, historically and logically, for rooting nature's universality in the formation of the holy commonwealth. The rabbis also provided him with a particularized vehicle for the transmission – for the adaptation and preservation – of natural law. By contrast, the law of nations on which Selden also spends considerable time in the text pertains to contractual, marital, military, and other relations between the Jews and the proselytes, the latter understood both as gentile inhabitants of Judaic lands and as gentile converts to Judaism.

The natural norms dispensed to all human beings spell out their obligations to God and each other and, as such, offer the very constituents of human happiness. But Selden emphasizes their functional power by comparing these natural laws to those wedges, levers, or pulleys on which other bodies – that is, positive laws and governments – must depend for their operation, balance, and support.[36] He wants a natural law that can somehow help specific societies accomplish their happiness and not simply dream of it. By centring his analysis on the principles of Talmudic and other Judaic writers such as Philo and Josephus, he hopes to move the foundation of natural law into the realm of the divine will and beyond the human contestation of which scepticism takes such advantage. For if natural law is to function as a machine engineering the happiness of religious societies, it must be afforded some secure Archimedean ground, one free of the earth and its always tremulous institutions; from this blessed ground, Selden suggests, the natural machine might hoist the burdens of human perplexity, conflict, and scepticism that otherwise will manage to subvert its authority every time. Yet the Talmud itself is a triply contested ground: its tradition involves debate among its own rabbis; is challenged by scripturalist and priestly factions within Judaism; and is subject to a Christian hostility sometimes expressed even by Selden himself, especially throughout the first half of his scholarly career. Lest his approach prove more narrow and contestable than, say, Lord Herbert's more pagan-heavy common notions, he prefers to speak of his approach as 'eclectic' or selective and often forays into pagan literature (6). Whether its main warrant is a lineage from the divine creator of Genesis, a judicious selection of textual moments from the great cultures of history, or a precise and mechanical bolster for positive laws and courts, Selden's natural law can never quite claim the success of escaping his own strongly sceptical sense that there is no Archimedean ground, at least no efficacious one, for the norms responsible for the godly regulation of human societies.

In preparation for the reception of his natural law, Selden presents his readers with a demanding protocol. He exhorts them to cultivate moral and interpretive discipline; to resist those evils responsible for making individuals unadaptable to common notions and to a '*vitae normam*'; to ignore those censorial forces of the modern age that have demonized the Talmud (and, for that matter, Roger Bacon); to recognize the checks and balances built into the Talmud itself; to repudiate those sceptics who reduce the very existence of a natural justice to excuses for power, will, and utility; and, above all, to disarm those same sceptics by embracing a course to nature that does not depend on erroneous human rationality. All the while, Selden intersperses analogies to optics, geometry, and mechanics, though, as in the case of Archimedes, he seeks a certainty of principles that derives only from having solved a conundrum. For Selden, the Noachian laws promise a hard-won but holy and unimpeachable certainty about the patterns according to which a religious society should be measured. Given the best scholarly filter, the impurities of their transmission should not prevent the common patterns from emerging with sufficient clarity for the seventeenth-century reader. If Selden hopes that the historical distance between Eden and his England will be closed by the ontological continuity of the natural law itself, his elaboration of the peculiarities of ancient Jewish culture tends to plunge readers into the messy process of filtering out natural tenets rather than simply to present the readers (as Lord Herbert sometimes does) with the neat and universal results of the sifting for common notions.

Indeed, the largest difficulty in attaining the Noachian principles comes from having to sort the universal from the peculiar in the Pentateuch. Obviously a key but often unclear span of narrative is the account in the Bible of the world from Noah to Moses, that same span of time for which Selden had such ridicule when it was forged by Annius de Viterbo, the pseudo-Berosius. In *De Jure Naturali*, the payoff for following the rabbinical line of perspective back to inmost history is nothing less than nature's uniform law and pattern of living ('pro jure

Normaque vivendi' [44]), the carpenter's rule ('Norma & amussis' [45]) devised by the divine carpenter. Without these few common notions of the licit and illicit, obligatory and permitted, of justice, honesty, and piety, human thought and action are, finally, vain, groundless, and erroneous, whatever the circumstances. Without natural law, human beings lack a shared measure that might rectify their ideas, impulses, and deeds; they have no square framing their intellectual, spiritual and material being, without which their being must disrupt the ligatures of religion. Contrary to his dismissive synopsis of natural law in the *Table Talk* – without the fear of an imperious God, natural law has no basis or weight, he remarks to his guests – Selden claims in *De Jure* that adaptation to the square of nature is not simply a response to fear. Rather, human beings acquire an affection for justice and obligation through the revelation of principles that their own reason distorts – and they do so by means of an intellectual agent that transmits the divinity shaping the ends of natural law to the faculties of the soul.

As Selden's own penchant for scepticism leads him to insist, reason needs a superior authority according to which learning can be steadied and obligation secured. What remains unclear is whether that higher authority is a raised and awakened reincarnation of reason itself. Like Lord Herbert, Selden largely removes Christ from his account of the redemption of human morality; like Herbert, too, Selden knows that ordinary reason cannot save itself from evil and uncertainty. Unlike Herbert, however, Selden's guarantor of common notions is the God of Adam and Abraham: embodied in the Old Testament, distilled by Maimonides, recorded by Josephus, and allegorized by Philo to add a spiritual dimension to text and tradition. Yet this spiritual presence must remain lawful, the spirit moving a lawgiver. For Selden, God's spirit appears to prisoners of human rationality and folly as it were some ur-Lady Philosophy appearing to the earliest Boethius: inspired vision is meant to clarify perspective, adjust method, and ensure the ligatures between those instruments of measure and that immeasurable zeal operating at once on behalf of human redemption. It is not surprising that, on the one hand, Selden shows an admiration for the Jewish sect of the Zealots, and on the other, he appeals to geometry for the value of the third line that crosses two others and sustains their parallelism. Without the crossing of the third line, the other two will deviate towards the bias of their own pleasures, delusions, and interests. In *De Jure Naturali*, that third line is God the father, creator, and governor; but the two points of intersection are nodes at which angels, Judaic texts, Christian commentary on those texts, an idealized Stoic and pagan rationality, and the fallible thought processes of human beings must somehow converge in a newly steadied and clarified perspective on the norms of human living. Selden leaves it unclear which of those many threads is mostly responsible for securing the knot. Instead, he enlists metaphors of light to suggest a continuum among the agents; deems negligible the debate over the exact identity of the *intellectus agens*; and expresses what, for him, is a rare impatience with the sceptic who rashly will not wait for an answer (109–17).

Still, it is a concession to scepticism that he would rather think the intellectual agent a radiation of divinity or a divinely dispensed and ministering angel than reduce it to reason. With a clear understanding that he is treading into controversial, perhaps even heretical territory, Selden summarizes the key distinction made by admirable philosophers between numinous or angelic versions of the agent and the humanization of the same: 'Sanè quod habent sic de Intellectu Agente, eum nempè non omninò esse animae humanae potentiam seu partem magis atque ipse Sol est Oculi, sed sive Numen ipsum sive ministrum Numinis (quod heic in idem recidit) separatum, velut Angelum seu Intelligentiam generi humano assistentem, novum aut ipsis singulare non esse scimus omnes [Certainly, what they thus have in mind regarding the intellectual agent is that assuredly it is not at all a portion or potential of the human soul, any more than the sun is a portion or potential of the eye, but rather that it is either divinity itself or a distinctive attendant of the divine (which results in the same thing), either an angel or an intelligence lending assistance to humankind, all of which we know not to be new or singular in and of itself]' (111–12). In opting for the ministering angel on the numinous side of the spectrum, Selden accepts the safer, less pantheistic version of the theory, namely, that some being far greater than we are inhabits or at least accompanies our faculties in order to correct them. This angel is not interchangeable with a familiar supernatural force such as divine grace – and indeed, it is hard to express precisely what this agent is – but somehow its remedial influence on human knowledge conveys the immediacy of the divine as effectively as any created being ever could. Selden does not address, as Thomas Browne was currently doing in his composition of the *Religio Medici* (1635–42), what it is like or what it implies to hold a belief in guardian angels. He does not work out whether guardian angels tend to lend their assistance to individuals more than communities or nations, or whether the belief in such an agent is rational or natural. In making the case that myopic human beings are enlightened in their vision of natural law by a higher intelligence, Selden is encouraged by the fact that Roger Bacon agrees, even if he is also unsettled by the disrepute into which his medieval model has fallen. After all, by the time of the publication of *De Jure Naturali* in 1640, even critics of the established episcopal church, and of its Laudian excesses in particular, are eager to convince their own critics that the future belongs to those Antinomians claiming a complete personal overhaul by the habitation of the Holy Spirit. Meanwhile, learned Anglican divines like Henry Hammond are intent on enlisting the rational holism of the Stoics while protesting that their revised understanding of the spirit filling the cosmos does not go so far as to identify divine with human nature.[37]

Accordingly, Selden is defensive about his position on the intellectual agent – one that renders that agent comparatively divine rather than decidedly human – and he attacks those medieval authorities who deemed it heretical in the days of Roger Bacon and Adam Marsh. Tenaciously, if also at times stealthily, these men tried to preserve the doctrine of the intellectual agent that Selden also locates in Arab, Hermetic, and Stoic legacies and finds well served by the imagery of light. Some of these legacies attempt to fuse natural law and divine illumination in their visions of a *pneuma* permeating the universe, and Selden remarks in passing that even those writers – for instance, Paul, the Church Fathers, and Aquinas – who oppose the idea of a particle of divinity enclosed in all human beings have a tendency to lapse into the language of such a view as though they wished it were true. Yet the desire for divinity in humanity might suggest two very different possibilities: that right reason credits such an angelic presence because it intuits that such is, in fact, the case, or that fancy conjures divine presence as poets dream ideals to which they exhort their readers. Selden is encouraged by what he deems a consensus among Jewish writers that divinity inhabits all of us, and his method is informed by the belief that divine radiation was maximal during the period between Adam and Noah. Lest his view of the intellectual agent incur the charge of encouraging sectarian and illuminist fancies, however, he stresses over the course of the *De Jure* that the sun (divinity) and our eyes (reason) require a reliable measure, a sundial that he finds in Judaism. As our measure of the sun, Selden argues, the dial relieves us from squinting or, worse, from closing our eyes in search of some inner measure, and the Noachian version of natural law keeps that law as closely related to history, textual criticism, and positive law as it can be without becoming simply human artifice.

Like poesies of ancient Bards, so the angels of Hermetic, Jewish, Neoplatonic, and scholastic strains of mysticism benefit from collaboration
with criticism and scepticism. What remains a little unclear is whether it
matters to Selden that such angels exist in nature or that human beings
in search of natural norms for belief and practice believe (thanks to a
poetics of emanation) that they do.

Having prepared his readers and invoked his guardian Muse, Selden
turns to the more straightforward if elaborate charge of laying out the
common notions of religious societies. According to Ambrose, Selden
writes, the upshot of natural law is threefold: honouring God; living
morally and modestly according to God's law; and using the knowledge
of divine creation as a means of teaching the order of things and the
place of humankind in that order.[38] Whether the Noachian tenets are
clear or intricate, Selden starts his study of the seven headings within
the framework of Ambrose's three rationales. Of the seven principles,
two directly regulate the honour paid to God, while four rectify human
relations and one prohibits cruelty towards animals. God dispensed the
first six to Adam and Eve at Creation, after which the six were invariably
transmitted to their children by the various means of texts, speech, right
reason, and divine illumination. The seventh arose later once human
beings were permitted to eat meat, but it is no less natural than the others, Selden concludes. It was simply concealed until needed.

Selden emphasizes that the great rabbis agree on separating the Noachian principles from statutory Jewish obedience to God, though they
differ at times on where exactly to draw the line, say, regarding the Ten
Commandments. It is harder, however, to work with Maimonides
towards rational principles according to which the licit and illicit can be
sorted within each Noachian heading. Concerning idolatry, Selden
mediates between the undeniably clear prohibitions against images and
the didactic and accommodative value of visual aids (232–9). Given the
heightened conflict in the 1630s between Laudians and iconoclasts over
this very question, he hopes to find a way out of the impasse of the controversy in a Judaized natural law. The Jews, he maintains, had a profound understanding of the educational value of images, as surely as
they abhorred idolatrous misuse. They understood that it is one thing to
worship an astral image and quite another to teach astronomy or to calculate holy days by means of an astral diagram or model. They recognized that, in the temple itself proportionate architecture might convey
the idea of cosmic order while the artifice of a great golden vine might
legitimately serve to remind the worshippers of metaphors in the Bible.

With the interdiction against blasphemy, Selden confronts the problem of whether natural law prescribes any specifics for the practice of worship. In the 1620s and 1630s English Protestant society was wracked by virulent disagreement over precisely what God prefers in human acts of devotion; over precisely what canon is supposed to resolve such disputes; and over the grounds for corporal punishment once an infraction has been assessed. There are, Selden believes, three ancient considerations in the question of blasphemy and the positive prescriptions for worship: What is known about habits of worship up until the time of the giving of Mosaic law? What happened to worship after that gift? How was religious practice modified by the laws governing the relations between the Hebrews and their proselytes?

Regarding the prohibition against murder, Selden returns to the domain of Grotius's *De jure belli ac pacis libri tres*, with a careful consideration of the circumstances under which violence is licit. Seventeenth-century religious society, they agree, has transformed what appears a simple interdict into a hugely complex casuistry involving Christians' killing one another. Selden's responsibility is not simply to offer etymologies and records of one custom, such as the duel, but to settle the dispute over the morality of violence full stop. This challenge extends to the case of abortion; to the matter of those vigilante zealots who destroy transgressors openly contemptuous of God and of the Noachian laws; and to Jesus' harsh ejection of the moneychangers from the temple. Here and in later texts, the Zealots are especially significant for Selden; for they clinch the presence of singular, extreme spirituality within the comprehensive law of Judaism. Theirs is a zeal for the law, but it is an extralegal force all the same. As Josephus makes plain, their violent resistance to open blasphemy and sacrilege has often been abused as an excuse for shameful acts; and Selden cites Grotius's example of Saint Stephen's being stoned in the name of zeal, alongside the Dutch lawyer's review of the tradition in which private Hebrew men have violently defended God's law and the true religion. One of the latter zealots, possessed with the Holy Spirit, was Jesus (*De Jure Naturali*, 487–98).

Selden follows Maimonides as well as Grotius in sorting out the legitimacy of violence, as well as in deciphering the instances in which deception might be sanctified, notwithstanding the strictures against theft and the violation of contracts. These intricate analyses of the contexts and circumstances of the Noachian precepts tend to reorient Selden's distillation of natural law in the direction of positive laws and the human institutions that arbitrate those laws within or between specific peoples.

This redirection evolves in a number of forms. Most pervasively, Selden studies the details of Jewish-proselyte relations. Insofar as these relations centre at times on the conversion of gentile to Judaism, he returns his attention to further explorations of cosmic transmigration. That is, a belief in the total regeneration of the convert – which conceives of the convert as if he or she had newly dropped from heaven – is associated with cabbalistic, Platonic, and Pythagorean theories of how a soul newly enters a body and transforms the very nature and identity of the person. For Selden, Judaism is not simply a religion of law in contrast with the spirit of Christianity; rather, it accentuates the presence of both legal codes and unbounded spirit in its comprehensive vision of God's choice society.

Yet for Selden metempsychosis remains something of a poetic fable, perhaps even a cheat. What matters more to him is that this new soul – a Jewish one – is escorted by means of the specific rites of sacrifice, baptism, and circumcision.[39] Selden's ongoing attention to the problem of proselytes jibes with his studies in the 1630s of the priestly vocation and with the Laudian emphasis that coherence and unity in religion must resort to an 'us versus them' mentality. This mentality serves not only to set one church apart from the others but also to establish reverence for holy things by ritualizing their purity apart from the profane. Indeed, in this context, Selden refers us to a work that he has already written on the priesthood (his patron in this work being Laud himself), but also refers us to a work that he has yet to complete, on the Great Sanhedrin, whose role in the regulation of a religious society (as Selden understands it) is obviously still unclear. Yet what is clear is that Selden returns time and again to the specific ecclesiastical and civil institutions according to which a specific people were governed at specific times.

In *De Jure Naturali*, however, the polarizing mentality of Jewish laws involving proselytes continues to run at cross purposes with the unification of religions under the tenets of natural law, even if (at times) the Old Testament stresses that the Jewish people should treat the proselytes as equals under the law. Selden intensely scrutinizes the changes in social status, cultural affiliation, and legal privileges of the convert; the positive grounds for permitting the habitation of unconverted gentiles in Judaic territory; the ritual formulae of conversion; the guidelines for international war; the difference between mixture or commerce in times of legal stability against times of Roman aggression; rules about intermarriage; rules about the children of converts; the pressures of commerce with an especially idolatrous people; and formulae regarding a change of status between sacred and civil materials. As much as Selden seeks the universal warrant of natural law for the norms according to which human beings live, in his *De Jure Naturali* he never strays far from the laws ensuring the separateness and purity of particular religious societies, the kind of segregation to which, in the 1630s, his patron Laud was fervently committed in mounting a ceremonial hedge or canonical moat around the fortress of the English church. In keeping with Laud's deep commitments to lawfulness and conformity in the English church, as well as to the special authority of priests, Selden in *De Jure Naturali* conveys a clear interest in exploring the history of what in his time was considered the domain of canon law, of priests in their temples, and of divines in their synods and councils. Selden has been engaged with the laws and practices of this clerical domain since the second decade of the century with his massive and controversial *History of Tithes* and since the 1620s with his edition of Eadmer. The separate jurisdiction of the clerics occupies a considerable share of his attention – and of his layman's criticism – in Selden's work on inheritance and the priesthood in the 1630s, in his writings on marriage and divorce in the 1640s, and in his participation in the Westminster Assembly in the 1640s. Yet even in *De Jure Naturali*, he studies the qualifications for priesthood in everything from the factor of sexuality to the criterion of wealth. In sum, an emphasis on the laws regarding proselytes shifts Selden's text away from nature to nations, and in particular to the ways in which uniformity is preserved among God's chosen and isolated people. The discussions of the canons pertaining to priests takes Selden's focus even further into a cultural logic of separation, of spiritual distinction within a society already spiritually distinguished from the rest of the world. As he attempts to create a ligature between the religions of the world, he also suggests that the only meaningful and well-regulated religious unit might well prove a very small community.

As the culmination of the clerical vein running through the *De Jure Naturali*, however, Selden attempts to reverse the thrust towards separateness by concluding his massive survey of the natural rules for religious society with a study of the canons of the Jerusalem synod celebrated by the Apostles in the fifteenth chapter of Acts. With Selden's emphasis on the fact that this synod worked for peace and unity between Jews and gentiles, what emerges from his scholarly study of the various permutations of the passage is a complex, dynamic, and hopeful model of Jews, Jewish Christians, and gentile Christians resolving to live among one another with the assistance of the synod's canons.

The main concern of the Jerusalem synod, Selden argues, is not so much to emphasize a core of natural truths as it is to offer guidelines for social behaviour that will prevent scandal and maximize piety and goodness. In keeping with the aims of natural law, the synod's goal is to overcome the hard and fast divisions between Jew and gentile; but its modus operandi is not natural but canonical. Far from the flat prohibitions of the Noachian principles, the synod's canons navigate complex intercultural circumstances and facilitate interaction between those peoples who eat, converse, and marry together. That is, the early Christians realized that they had to proceed largely ad hoc, considering the mixture of cultures and peoples in their faith; but they also realized that a reliance on elusively natural commonality was liable to fizzle (838–47).

In his discussion in the *De Jure Naturali* of the fifth Noachian precept – against stealing, dishonesty, and the violation of contracts – Selden has extended the basic interdict to include in its scope the highly difficult dilemmas of when a lie is conscientious and legitimate, an issue of great concern to recusants and non-conformists in the England of his time. He expressly states that natural law is of minimal benefit for parsing conflicts over the ownership, possession, acquisition, and transfer of goods. By contrast, the laws peculiar to the Jews retain the universal compulsion towards justice distilled in the natural interdict, yet they apply that compulsion in a manner more supple, subtle, equitable, and useful than natural law ever could accomplish alone in the face of actual problems. Casuistry can be too subtle, as everyone knows, but the right court would move beyond the airy thinness of casuistry without resorting to the ham-fisted generalizations of nature. Again, Selden promises his Sanhedrin, without having worked out whether that institution is a synod in which certain laity support the priests, or a parliament in which the clergy might be allowed to join the laity.

The more Selden reverts to positive laws, rites, and courts, the more the reader is left to struggle with what to make of the promise of natural law, the hope of a warrant that would be universal, spiritual, precise, and historical. As he does in the notes on Fortescue, Selden gestures towards the idea of natural law as the foundation for positive laws; but he persistently comes up against the problem of serving two masters in one's normative investments. Is natural law a viable alternative to positive law? Is it the more purely divine basis or font for that law? Or is natural law finally, like poetry, a gossamer decoration for the much too obviously flawed artifice of human legal institutions? At times, for instance, in his discussion of keeping the Sabbath, Selden considers the possibility that such a practice is natural as well as customary, only to leave nature behind.

When, in *De Jure Naturali*, Selden characterizes the court for gentile worship placed within the Temple complex, he reminds readers of the narrow space for the non-Jews and their natural laws within the architecture of Jewish worship and judgment. He does include a section on the universal belief in a heavenly justice, but this belief removes human commonality from its presence in the world and resituates it in a transcendent paradise. Of the ways in which the gentiles can permeate the boundaries of Judaism – by natural commonality, mystical transmigration, and cultural imitation – the first tends to be subordinated to the other two.

At one point in his discussion of the Noachian rejection of idolatry, Selden edges his solution of a textual crux towards the argument that Judaism secures its norms through the protective ritual and legal practices of segregation more readily than through the historical transmission of natural universals. The passage in question occurs in Claudian's 'Against Eutropius,' in which, among a list of comical impossibilities, the poet alludes to 'all the vain imaginings of India depicted on Jewish curtains.' Selden glosses the key phrase, 'vain imaginings,' as those monstrous prodigies – men with eyes on their shoulders or with serpentine heads – that Claudian assumes can be glimpsed on Jewish textiles and tapestries (239–48). According to Selden, the Jews decorated their fabrics with an imagery that they differentiated from that of the pagans, but they chose their images carefully so as not to idolize natural phenomena. In order for Judaic art to be licit, that is, the artists had only one choice: the distinctively and fancifully unnatural. No doubt, the Jews living under Roman rule understood that adherence to the law against idolatry entailed a separation from the gentiles, but also a circumcision of their art against the natural world made by their God.

Even after the publication of *De Jure Naturali*, however, Selden's hope for a natural guarantor of religious truth and moral honesty persisted. One major tendency of that persistence was a movement away from the conformist and pneumatic holism featured in some versions of Stoicism, an example of which Selden found in Lipsius's treatment of transmigration and spirit over the course of the Dutch scholar's *Physiologia Stoicorum*. Instead, Selden adopted the Stoicism of Epictetus, with its emphasis on personal autonomy and the internalization of right rational norms in the face of the uncontrollable and adverse circumstances of life. The clearest expression of this inward and protective Stoicism –

sometimes virile, sometimes fetal – emerges from the pages of Selden's *Vindiciae*, but it appears on occasion in *De Jure Naturali* as a *vitae norma*. For honest members of a corrupt society, this argument runs, the first step is to recognize that evil derives from an unwillingness or inability to adapt the common notions of theology and virtue to the circumstances of one's life. The second is to try as best as one can to act dutifully and reverently all the same.

When Marcus Aurelius is quoted in the treatise on natural law, the chosen passage is not one of the many in which the emperor urges duty and conformity to the cosmic whole – the emphasis of Selden's friend Meric Casaubon's translation of Marcus.[40] Rather, the citation showcases the Epictetan subtext of the *Meditations*, which stresses the divine spark lighting the individual soul and productive of a personal contentment with 'carrying out the will of that "genius," a "particle" of himself which Zeus has given to every man as his captain and guide – man's reason and intelligence' (*De Jure Naturali*, 112).[41] This *pneuma* might prove socially cohesive or disruptive; but in essence it is the divinely created steersman in each soul as human beings face life's enormous and ceaseless adversities. Even if they manage to gain positions of power, the best that *pneuma* allows them is that they navigate their own way through the perils of the wrong mentality. For many seventeenth-century commentators, however, there are severe limits to the good that the heroic resilience of the Stoics can perform for a godly and lawful society. Selden corroborates the human vestiges of natural law when he spotlights Job, but the agonized if faithful Job is the biblical figure most problematically as well as most commonly likened to the Stoic sage under duress. Stoicism provokes the honest man to duty but often affords little beyond an inward liberty from the bonds of passion, desire, and humiliation. The ascetic autonomy of the Stoic takes as far as possible a notion that spans the time from Selden's membership in Jonson's tribe of Ben to his work on the Judaic tribes on which Jonson's coterie was loosely based, namely, the notion that the value and coherence of religious societies expand to the extent that their membership contracts. The danger of following the logic of the slave Epictetus is that the sage abandons all prior and external human obligations, an exclusively personal version of the logic of conversion that the ancient Jews and early Christians apply to their newest members.

With great enthusiasm nonetheless, Selden digresses from the laws regulating wartime slavery to celebrate Daniel Heinsius's argument that the famous Stoic paradox – only the wise man, even if enslaved, can be free – resembles the rabbinical conviction that true freedom derives from a zeal for the study of law. With the law memorized in rabbinical hearts and minds or engraved in the reason of the Stoic sage, even the prisoner or the exile is truly free. If positive law cannot spring a man from prison, the student of Epictetus knows, then natural law can spring the traps of life provided that one is convinced that stone walls make no prison. Selden leaves off his quotation of Heinsius's *Aristarchus Sacer,* the 1639 edition, with a simple phrase, 'Perpulchrè sanè [certainly very beautiful].' It is an epithet that Selden's editor will apply to his digressive scholarship in the work on the Sanhedrin when the great scholar has run out of time for building his final model for the coordination of religious societies. It is hard to know how much stock Selden placed in such beauty, harder still to gauge the 'sanè' in his attribution of aesthetic comfort to a Stoic natural law. Perhaps the modifier indicates sobriety, perhaps certainty; or perhaps it signals that a concession is being offered to a seductive illusion. As the persecuted subject begins to pretend that the horror of his world is unreal, natural law begins to converge with poetry, exquisite in its mode of instruction, consoling to the otherwise afflicted, but unable to bring either holiness or measure to a world run amok with impiety, violence, dishonesty, lasciviousness, and idols in the temple and the mind alike (*De Jure Naturali,* 777). Noah's principles require an ark in which to wait out the storm that might not end.

By 1640 whatever halcyon calm English writers might have claimed for their society in the 1630s could be reasserted only with the feigned pastoral naivety of a masque-making poet. The king had undertaken an unpopular and a dishonourable war with the Scots in a miserably failed effort to demand conformity in the kirk to the liturgy, ceremony, and polity of the English church. In order to fund these campaigns, he had followed the advice of Thomas Wentworth, now the Earl of Strafford, to invite parliamentary assistance once again after eleven years, and this decision produced a rancorous collision between a king impatient for money and a Parliament anxious to present and to have redressed their grievances over the religious and political abuses first vetted in the 1620s but made worse by the divisive official policies of ship money, the Book of Sports, church beautification, altars and rails, the suppression of any show of non-conformity among laity and clergy alike, and notorious cases of corporal punishment inflicted on godly authors such as William Prynne, Henry Burton, and John Bastwick. In 1640, then, English religious society stood in great need of encouragement in believing that all God's people are united in a few precious truths governing belief, worship, and morals. Much as they longed for peace and unity, however, the arbiters of belief, worship, and manners in that very same society were more than ever convinced that the welfare of English Christianity could be secured if and only if the corruption and weaknesses of its normative institutions were redressed once and for all according to the criteria of God's word, English law, and proper liberty. His membership in the Long Parliament and his imminent assignment as a lay participant in the Westminster Assembly thrust Selden back into the midst of a battle over the past and future of English values. Yet even if he left behind the grander claims of natural law, he continued to find a place for those claims within a larger imaginary reconstruction of the Jewish institutions regulating God's chosen people. Selden was still not content with the limits placed on his normative thought by a complete focus on English institutions, and as civil war broke out across the British Isles, he was more committed than ever to making his learned contemporaries think outside the box of their own circumstances. Ironically, one of the roles that he continued to assign natural law involved the rational integrity in which that law was believed to seal the honest but beleaguered sage.

—— 8 ——

Of all his texts, including the *History of Tithes*, the *Mare Clausum* was most thoroughly turned into a political and polemical weapon. For, while the *History of Tithes* was attacked and defended, the *Mare* was conceived, revised, and translated for the purposes of scholarly leverage in a controversy. James I wanted it, then Charles I; republicans claimed it during the Interregnum, then royalists after the Restoration. Even in the royalist appropriation of the text, the J.H. who presented it in 1663 struggles to work out Selden's personal involvement in what the former judges the wretched old cause of the Parliament and regicide during and after the civil war.

In the *Vindiciae*, Selden seeks to save his legal arguments in the *Mare* from their implication in national bias or courtly sycophancy.[42] In the course of this apologia, he revisits his two incarcerations in order to prove that he has never bought his way out of jail and in fact that he suffered his afflictions with unswerving integrity and patience. During that first incarceration under James, Selden tells us, he found strong support in his friend Ben Jonson, himself a cultivator of the Stoic ethos in which personal fortitude, constancy, and honesty were so highly prized. Selden is proud to recall that he received additional help from the magnanimous Lancelot Andrewes, another of his prominent friends among the clergy. In his second imprisonment under Charles, Selden's term of affliction was more protracted and, in his view, even more unlawful. It was during this imprisonment that he opted to settle into his Talmudic studies, though he had difficulty in getting books and all his writings were strictly censored.

That plague so dreaded by normative poets – court sycophancy – he complains, managed to supplant the rule of law in these years. Even with the help of great men, even with a plan to revise the scholar's understanding of ecclesiastical and natural law, Selden's mainstay was the advice offered by Prudentius that, even in the grip of bondage, the soul repudiates the corruption of the body. In representing the sordid conditions in which the king's justices landed him, Selden suggests that he might find some distraction from melancholy in his studies of external laws. Yet only the inner law of nature might free him to stand alone, however abused, as a normative pattern, one at which his own topsy-turvy England only marvels but never follows. In such a sage, the law of nature is instantiated in such a way as to elude the grasp of common humanity, to shroud itself in the obscurity of what nature prescribes but seldom reveals.

At times during the 1630s, 1640s, and 1650s Selden took refuge in various domestic hermitages as emblems of the inner refuge: in the dwellings of a country house at Wrest, of the Inner Temple, and of White Friars. If the *Vindiciae* expresses the consolations of retreat into the honour of the self, it overwhelms any focus on Stoic autonomy with the seventeenth-century presupposition that, in polemics, attacks on one's ethos are essentially attacks on one's cause. It is appropriate, then, that Selden composed his apologia in between what must have been a maddening rush to complete his construction of the Jewish Sanhedrin. If taken as a defence of ethos, Selden's vindication befits his ideal of the legal sage whose authority must be entrusted with regulating the manifold affairs of living in the holy commonwealth. Thus, the Latin vindication is addressed not to himself but to the international community of scholars whose respect and attention he desired.

In the *Vindiciae*, natural law is at times converted into the well-composed soul, one learning to live without or beyond compromise, a soul forbearing worldly involvement and bearing up against pain. Such a soul would have no need of external measure, though it would never be able to convince anyone else of its own measure. It would inhabit a Boethius among the barbarians, or a Roman slave for whom liberty's price cannot be met. The chief spiritual norm of such Stoicism is an honest equanimity, the virtue assumed in one's mind for survival against the rewards and abuses doled out in the fortuitous world. Just so, Selden remarks, he acts no differently if another person is fat or thin, tall or short, white or not, drunk or sober. For no matter how far into the world the law of nature takes hold, perhaps all one can claim in a world torn by polemics, civil war, and treachery is that the natural fusion of the supreme moral law with a divinely dispensed spirit provides comfort and fixity from within ('Aequanimum mihi semper fuit, sive mecum quis sentiat, sive dissentiat ... Perinde fere esset, si aliter facerem, anxius urgeri, quoniam quis me brevior, procerior, crassior, macilentior, voracior, bibacior, mihi discolor, aut quid eiusmodi esset' [col. 1438]). Yet the Stoic legacy of natural law can also urge the sage always to remember that the whole of the cosmos is far more significant than any one part; and that each and every part should always strive to remember its place in and duty to the whole. In the 1630s Meric Casaubon deployed his English translation of Marcus Aurelius as a vehicle for resisting zealous fragmentation and for honouring the 'charitable-sociable' citizen of the world.[43] When he published a Latin edition of the great Stoic emperor a few years later, he dedicated that volume to Selden as an apt embodiment of Stoicism's broadest reach into universal natural law. Selden's dalliance with a private honesty was fleeting; he was far more invested in situating Stoic natural law within the holistic context of religious history.

Accordingly, in the 1650s Selden was dutifully and monumentally constructing the temple complex in which the legal sages of the Sanhedrin might make their judgments and in which poetry, natural law, and the spiritual labors of prayer and preaching all might take their proper places. If natural law is sometimes privatized in the *Vindiciae*, such diminution is no indication that Selden has reverted to a fetal position in an imaginary paradise. Rather, it intimates two refinements in his sense of duty: that the legitimacy of his scholarship requires a defence of his character; and that the holy commonwealth needs God's will above nature and human law beneath nature more than it needs nature itself.

In the *Table Talk* Selden leaves it somewhat unclear whether, along with his friend Edward Herbert, he believed in the existence or value of common notions in a natural religion. 'Religion is like the fashion,' he quips; 'one man weares his doublett slashed, another lac'd, a third plaine, but every man has a doublett.' The lesson seems obvious: it matters more that we share the basic apparatus of dress than that we exactly agree on style; but even if the artifice of fashion and dress is forgotten, Selden's payoff for this analogy is not fully lucid: 'Every man has his Religion, wee differ about the trimming' (117). It is easy to see that trimming is nugatory, but less easy to understand whether it matters that the religion is each man his own. Similarly, in another recorded remark: 'Men say they are of the same Religion for quietness sake but if the matter were well examined, you would scarce find three of the same Religion in all points' (117). So, is it better to contribute to quietude by suppressing one's difference from another? Is the ruse of sameness a true and godly remedy for the problems of a religious society ? Is it good to examine religion well, and are important points contained in that 'all'? Clearly, unlike Lord Herbert, who persists in his articulation of the natural notions that should unify all religious peoples, Selden never allows the loftier natural law – the one promising the pneumatic integration of the cosmos – to claim a stature as the best prevention against faction and bloodshed in contemporary Europe or England. Far from it: the idea of such a natural law, like his own *Mare Clausum*, has been passed between partisan royalists and parliamentarians as though it were a fiction for hire.

Between the private Boethian sage and the ambitious engineer of a complete human society, however, Selden continued throughout his life to imagine ways in which smaller or select societies within the holy commonwealth might help the scholar to resist the extremes of the escapist womb and the all-too-dutiful parasite. Early on, he prized the intellectual coterie associated with Jonson and grounded in the classical world of academies and symposia, of Epicurean gardens and the Stoic porch. Such a coterie might retain the common values distinguishing a community but minimize the vice, ambition, contingency, and conflict that communities have a tendency to produce. Jonson's metaphor for his own little group, the 'tribe,' was Hebraic in its resonance, of course; and in the 1630s, 1640s, and 1650s Hebraic sects, families, tribes, and small communities played an increasingly significant role in Selden's own understanding of how a religious society might best coordinate the rule of law and the effusion of spirituality. The inner tranquillity of the Stoic sage had a limited attraction for Selden, and an idealized, ahistorical, and universal law of nature was more seductive than credible or demonstrable. In his studies of the Judaic priesthood and of the Hebraic customs surrounding inheritance, marriage, and government, then, Selden sought to make sense of the levels at which, and means by which, Judaic society managed to retain its adherence as a complete and integrated holy commonwealth. Yet within that Judaic society, he located and praised the smaller groups of those persons zealous in the law who might adhere together when even Judaic society was caving in to centrifugal pressures.

In *De Jure Naturali*, Selden would diminish the specificity in Judaism as a way of naturalizing a sameness in religion; but that project very often gave way to the specificity of Judaism as a religion, law, and way of life apart from the rest. As he worked on the Great Sanhedrin and on Jewish treatments of marriage, property, the calendar, and the priesthood, Selden committed himself to the notion that Judaism in its own right has something to offer the reformation of contemporary and Christian societies. It would not be enough to cull a moral law from the rest of Judaic law and then to naturalize that law so that it might be compatible with Christian morals. Judaism offered a law, a justice, and a social dynamics of its own. It was the opinion of some of his contemporaries that the religion of the Jews was far too mixed with civil or profane affairs to serve any purpose in the purification of the English church in the 1640s. Accordingly, Selden was compelled to demonstrate that, if rightly understood and applied, Judaism was not simply a legalistic adulthood from which the Christian must return to the childhood of grace or, conversely, the ritualistic childhood of superstition out of which the Christian must mature in the riches of spiritual sacrifice and love. Rather, Judaism was the religion of Jesus, Jesus was a reformed Jew, and the religion of the Jews had worked out what God appeared to have supported as the very best fusion of legal strictures and spiritual zeal.

Selden believed that Christianity in contemporary England was tragically veering between the zealous and the canonical components of ancient Judaism, between antinomian enthusiasm and Laudian hyper-regulation. In response, he devoted the last years of his life to refashioning an ancient way in which seventeenth-century Christians might save their religious society from its hapless history of extremism. They would have to save themselves with the courage to think beyond their current impasse, with a foresight that the Jews and their reformed sect, the Christians, had failed to attain by refusing to embrace one another. The need for such an embrace reveals that in the governing complex of the new Jerusalem there must be proper room for natural law as well as for poets, legal sages, and the priests, prophets, and preachers whose labours are separately spiritual and ritualistic.

The last of those separate but coordinated constituents, persons entrusted with specifically spiritual or religious offices, was in many ways the hardest for the often anti-clerical Selden to place. But this difficulty meant that he worked long and hard at the problem of how to protect the spiritual without unduly segregating it from the normative authorities in the holy commonwealth, not that he cast the spiritual labours aside with a Hobbesian peevishness. Beginning early in the 1620s with his edition of Eadmer, then continuing through his formulation of the purity of spiritual labour in his work on the Sanhedrin, Selden considered the possibility that the unworldly sanctity of church practices, persons, and labours might best prosper behind some carefully constructed but permeable border separating the holy from the profane. In the 1640s and 1650s Erastianism did not provide Selden with an argument against the value of spiritual labour; rather, it afforded him a bold, clear, and careful mode of construing England's way beyond the havoc of Laudianism, Presbyterianism, and Antinomianism to a holy commonwealth in which zeal and conformity might lie down together.

chapter five

The Canons of the Church

Throughout *De Jure Naturali et Gentium*, Selden distinguishes the natural, Noachian precepts from the laws divinely dispensed to the Jews alone. When in the 1640s he returned in *Uxor Hebraica* (see J. Ziskind) to one of the Noachian precepts – that involving sexual transgression – it was the latter, special, set of laws that came to occupy centre stage. It is clear that in the 1640s Selden prized the law of his own people as much as he ever had – his pride in the common law's autonomy from Roman civil law in his commentary, *Ad Fletam Dissertatio*, leaves no doubt about the matter. And, no doubt, Selden persisted in his belief that English common law, like all other codes of law, derived in the final analysis from natural law and so from the author of the law of nature, God. Like English common law or any law especially developed for and by one people, Judaic positive law must be adaptable to the many changes in historical circumstances as well as suitable to the peculiar needs of the people whom this law would govern. Yet Selden became obsessed with understanding exactly what it meant to say that Jewish positive law, however arbitrary it might seem, had a far greater intimacy with divine will than any other code of law in history. He believed that Jewish sages, too, were singularly open to the special vehicle of God's commands, the *intellectus agens*, even if it was notoriously hard to say exactly what the nature of that vehicle was.

For Selden, a divinely generated Jewish law raised three administrative possibilities. As a canon law for the regulation of religion, manners, and property, it might be administered solely by the Jewish priests. Or, as a sacred law, it might be administered by priests and rabbis acting together within a 'synod.' Finally, as a sacred-cum-civil code, Jewish law might be administered by a rabbinical court in which qualified priests –

priests zealous about and competent in the law – could serve in the capacity of rabbis. By the time in the 1640s that Selden had participated in the Westminster Assembly and had progressed considerably in his work on the Sanhedrin, he was clearly resolved on the third option, that the Sanhedrin was a comprehensive court and senate in which priests took a place only for some other qualification than their priesthood. Even so, the more Selden was resolute on the rabbinical magistracy of Judaic society, the more he counterbalanced that power with a separate domain for the purely spiritual labours of the ministry. Always operating on the principle that civil magistrates must have some degree of control over and involvement in the administration of the social instantiations of religion, Selden became increasingly committed to delineating the extent to which the church should be liberated by virtue of its own special domain comprising spiritual labour, belief, and worship. This liberty was the dramatic centrepiece of his early 1620s edition of Eadmer; the special norms for Judaic priests occupied his attention in the 1630s, when Laud was his patron; but during the 1640s he attempted to intervene in the revolutionary contest over the identity, jurisdiction, autonomy, and future of the Church of England.

In several ecclesiastical projects, Selden tested the extent to which the church and its spiritual labours were best served if left to their own devices and laws within their own sanctum. He was especially intent on apportioning a pure, if restricted, area for spirituality when he invented his ideal of Erastianism to replace the caricature with which some contemporaries had attacked him; but he was an inveterate lay interloper in the affairs of the church and was on record repeatedly for his cynicism about the clergy's tendency to spoil civil affairs in settling religious ones. Were the laws of the church most favourable to the church in anything other than worldly self-interest? Does spirituality thrive best if segregated from civil jurisdiction? How might a lawyer best serve true religion either outside or inside the religious domain? In *De jure belli ac pacis*, Grotius often reiterates the truism that Christianity holds its followers to a far higher standard than natural or national law. In the *Table Talk*, Selden accentuates the obvious in remarking that 'The Text (Render unto Caesar the things that are Caesar's) makes as much ag[ains]t Kings as for them, for it says plainly that something is not Caesars' (62). But given what he calls the tendency of the priesthood to flatter itself with this verse and of kings to forget the 'something' plainly owed to God, Selden's greatest challenge consists of actually determining what is owed to each master. For, in the words of his amanuensis Richard Mil-

ward, Selden's 'sence of various matters of weight and high consequence' pertained most 'especially to Religion & State' (1). Far from
settling an autocratic authority on the state over the church, Selden
laboured to understand how best to liberate the church from the state
yet maximize the welfare of the entire holy commonwealth.

Selden's earliest, and most controversial, attempt to calibrate the debts
owed to and laws supporting the church was the *History of Tithes*. In its
prefatory matter, he conceives of his work as that of a lay lawyer entering
into sacred territory so as to bolster the defences of that territory. The
'Historicall Truth' that he produces is said to derive from 'the inmost,
least known and most vseful parts ... both of Past and Present Ages.' Lest
we miss the metaphorical temple suggested by 'inmost,' Selden ridicules
his lazy, ignorant readers as 'raw Nouices' who tend to be unsettled
'vpon their first admission to the sacred Mysteries of the Gentiles.'
These novices have haunted themselves 'with a world of false appari-
tions while they thought of what they should see in the inmost Sanctuarie at the vnknown presence of their Deitie.' The guiding priest for
these novices must teach them how to disperse the bogeys of their
superstition without violating the sanctity of the temple: 'And doubt-
lesse, the Priest had not a litle work to perswade them that what they
should there meet with, was not an vnluckie *Empusa*, not a formidable
Mormo, not a wanton *Cobalus*, not a mischieuous *Furie*, not indeed any
thing that their idle brains, being such meer strangers to the abstrusest
parts of Truth, had fashiond out.' According to Selden, his malicious,
jealous, and ignorant opponents have conjured spectres 'equally fear-
full, but equally false' (preface, A3v).

For the first of many occasions, Selden thus assumes a persona that
might either assuage or alienate the men who have official ordination in
the church. He plays a priest: 'And I must here first play the Priest also,
and so cleer, if it were possible, those Fancies, by protesting that [the
History of Tithes] is not written *to proue that Tithes are not due by the Law of
God*; not written to proue that the *Laitie may detaine them*, not to proue
that Lay hands may still enioy Appropriations; in summe, not at all *against
the maintenance of the Clergie*' (A3v). Assuming the part of the priest, he
seeks to enter the temple of church history, exorcise the ghosts, and
erect a legal and historical scaffolding that will leave the church more
strongly supported than before.

In his words, scepticism itself – wielded gravely, sincerely, yet boldly – offers the best way into the temple of truth; for thanks to 'their Libertie of Inquirie,' sceptics find 'the only way that in all kinds of studies leads and lies open euen to the Sanctuarie of Truth, while others, that are seruile to common Opinion and vulgar suppositions, can rarely hope to be admitted neerer then into the base court of her Temple which too speciously often counterfaits her inmost Sanctuarie' (preface, xii–xiii). Citing Quintilian's praise for the lawyer who succeeds because he has approached a case with the greatest scepticism, Selden is convinced that entry into the temple of ecclesiastical history offers unprecedented support for the payment of tithes in the actual temple of the English clergy.

The clerical fear – both perceived and actual – that a common lawyer's very entry into the temple will pervert the church into a lay estate is the scariest bogey that Selden must disperse. Perhaps deciding that role-playing will appear feckless at best and deceptive or insulting at worst, he does not sustain the persona for very long. By the end of his preface, he is acting the part of the simple historian whose 'meer Narration' (preface, A3v) studies honours in the way that Pliny or Theophrastus explored animals, without an obligation to make the case that the creatures receive their being and sustenance from God. So in his case, Selden avers, God and his expectations for the ministry can be taken for granted. His tone and aim, however, are rather hard to gauge: it is possible that he is sincerely concerned about offending the clergy, but also possible that he is mocking the ignorant and hapless clergy whose means of sustenance a layman understands far better than they do.

Selden is especially critical of the position that holds that the practices of tithing are securely anchored 'in any old *Canon* of the Church, as if euery thing so ordaind, necessarily had also a following vse.' Indeed, church canons often bend 'directly contrarie to ... Practice,' in addition to which the laws and customs of each people inevitably modify canon law (preface, v). History shows, Selden continues, an insufficiency in the church's own standards, 'euen in the proceedings of the Canon Law, which (as the body of it is) was neuer receiued wholly into practice in any State, but hath been euer made subiect in whatsoeuer touches the temporalties or maintenance of the Church (which come from Lay men) to the varietie of the secular Laws of euery State, or to Nationall customes that crosse it' (preface, v). Christianson has argued that essentially all Selden's scholarship through the 1630s corroborates the views that he held in his version of a common lawyer, including a moderate scepticism, a commitment to middle-level patterns, and an emphasis on the changeable nature of particulars.[1] Just so, Selden's accent on the prevalence of various 'secular Laws' and 'Nationall customs' indicates that even as he plays the priest, he plays to the Inns of Court and the English law that they oversee as guarantors of the institutions of true religion (preface, v).

Selden goes further to generalize the unreliability of the canon law as a measure of practice, remarking that one might as well refer practice to 'some consonant Law of *Plato's* common wealth, of *Lucians* men in the Moon, or of *Aristophanes* his Citie of Cuckoes in the clouds' (preface, vi). Canon law, then, has all the fanciful attractions of a *locus amoenus* and all of its ridiculous inefficacy; but its fancies attempt to be penal rather than pastoral. By contrast, Selden's history is offered to 'such as inquire about this Ecclesiastique Revenue' as 'a furnisht Armorie,' and he makes his intentions clear that the power of this armory might well be secular to the extent to which it is coercive, as surely as it is sacred to the extent to which it is true (preface, vi). He reiterates that in his survey of Judaic, gentile, and Christian practices, he has limited the field of study to tithes only as they have been dedicated to sacred uses, not those collected as commercial imposts, in landlord fees, or by imperial exaction. Given these boundaries on the subject, Selden presents his thesis: those defenders of divine-right tithing who ignore positive law and customary practice leave church revenue vulnerable and unreliable in some non-coercive utopia.

In all Christian states, Selden argues, tithes paid in accordance with positive law are 'subiect to some Customes, to Statuts, to all ciuill disposition' (preface, xiv). It might well be up to divines to decide whether their own office is a matter of '*Iure Divino*,' but positive law waits on no such argument and demands the tithes for sacred use whatever the divines might conclude. Summing up the reasons why positive law anchors sacred tithes more securely than divine right, he repeats the call to disperse the superstition that clouds the pure air of the sanctuary; for 'what brain then except one bewitcht can think that Human positiue Law and common Practice which vsually either declares or makes also a positiue Law, are not most carefully to be sought after in inquiries touching this sacred Reuenue, which is no otherwise enioyed in any State then as that Law hath ordaind and permits' (preface, xv). Comparing his argument to those mounted by pioneers such as Roger Bacon, Selden offers a restoration of the temple that resembles Francis Bacon's great instauration in their mutual desire to move beyond the 'commonly receiud Nihil ultra' and in their mutual analogies to the path-

clearing work of the Protestant Reformers (preface, xvi). Like Francis
Bacon, too, Selden is committed to assuring his readers that the sun of
divine right will not lose its heat and light simply because the fires are
stoked to heat the houses on earth.

Whereas Bacon resists the charge that he has removed nature from
the domain of the sacred, Selden wards off claims that he is setting up
camp for poaching within the sacred domain itself. In making the case
that divines have no proper familiarity with or competence in the legal
history of the Judaic and Christian churches, Selden is even more ada-
mantly opposed to the claim that civilians (Roman lawyers) and canonists have such entitlement. Rather, it is the 'farrre more generall Study'
of 'true *Philologie*' that, with the assistance of industry and diligence,
escorts a common lawyer like him into the inner sanctum of historical
truth. More boldly, Selden claims that common lawyers are philology's
'chiefest Darlings,' given their ability to assess variations in how customs
and ordinances 'permit or restraine the Canons in legall exaction of
them' (preface, xix–xxi). Yet philology gives Selden something more,
namely, a sage authority in the interpretation of scripture that warrants
attention from James I himself and, twenty-five years later, makes him so
awesome among the divines with their little pocket Bibles in the Westminster Assembly.

Whatever his hostile clerical foes might say, Selden protests his commitment in the *History of Tithes* to securing constitutions that would remedy
'the playnest part of sacriledge,' that is, any 'vsurpation vpon the
Offrings solemnly consecrated to the Priests at the Altar' (85). In the
'review' attached to the work, he more extensively assails the lay profanation of revenues ordained for sacred use. Even if sacred lands and revenues have been implicated in superstitious practices, he argues, the
laity have no warrant to seize those goods for 'common vses.' Especially
in regard to the years immediately after the start of the Reformation,
Selden lambastes the violation of the sacred and charitable uses of
tithes, church property, and churches themselves: 'But I doubt not but
that euery good man wishes that at our dissolution of Monasteries both
the Lands and Impropriated Tithes and Churches possessed by them
(that is, things sacred to the seruice of God, although abusd by such as
had them) had been bestowd rather for the aduancement of the
Church to a better maintenance of the labouring and deseruing Minis-

terie, to the fostering of good Arts, relief of the Poor, and other such good vses as might retain in them, for the benefit of the Church or common-wealth, a Character of the wishes of those who first with deuotion dedicated them (as in some other Countries vpon the Reformation was religiously done) then conferd with such a prodigall dispensation, as it happend, on those who stood readie to *deuoure what was sanctified*, and haue (in no small number) since found such enheritances thence deriued to them, but as *Seius* his horse or the gold of *Tholouse*' (486). Even if the bulk of this treasury remains in the church and even though the church is responsible for having established the sanctity of the resource in the first place, Selden nonetheless extends sacred use to learning and the commonwealth. This extension overrides any special dispensation for the church and instead advocates the welfare of the holy commonwealth in its entirety.

The tone and aim of his satirical rhetoric, moreover, are once again hard to gauge: if Selden protests a little too much, it might be the case that he wants to disarm his clerical critics, or it might be the case that he wants to mock them. In the sixteenth and seventeenth centuries, after all, the laity had usurped far more than revenue. In his satirical passages, that is, Selden has a way of resembling one of his cultural heroes, the saucy Thomas Nashe, whose attacks on the Marprelates found a way to offend the prelates themselves.

Concomitant with the Reformation was a greater role and power for lay persons in the affairs of religion, full stop, from the princes who governed churches to the nobility whose privileges included the appointment (though not the ordination) of priests in certain livings, right down to the 'base mechanic' who might lay claim to the Holy Spirit's warrant in himself preaching or lecturing. It was widely held that the laity were not to consecrate churches; but ceremonies developed in which bishops even dressed a lay patron in a robe so that the patron might be confirmed in the office of investiture. Whatever the clarity of its thesis about the legal history and basis of tithes, in the *History of Tithes* Selden leaves unsettled the matter of whether he supports the priesthood of all believers, a separate ontological realm for the consecrated priest, or a sage elite determined by scholarly, not ecclesiastical, credentials. He does stress the free contributions of the laity to the material welfare of the church and shows disdain for the power-hungry and fraudulent claims of the clergy. The *History* certainly anticipates and is consistent with Selden's later and very clear assertions that magistrates and legal sages should play and have played a comprehensive role in overseeing the prosperity and practices of the church. Yet it leaves hanging the question of exactly what the people and leaders of a holy commonwealth owe specifically to their spiritual welfare, to the special guardians of that welfare, and at long last to God Almighty. Over the course of the 1620s to the 1650s, Selden attempts, first intermittently, then in a concentrated way, to clarify this debt and, in doing so, to stabilize the relationship among legal sages, the holy priesthood, and the sometimes zealously inspired laity at large.

For English Protestants in the 1630s and 1640s the involvement of the laity in the offices of religion was strenuously asserted and hotly contested. On one side, a group of gentle patrons named the Feoffees of Impropriations attempted to secure the maximum number of godly ministers in the church and objected to the arrogance of the often basely born Laudian prelates. In the 1640s the Scottish Presbyterian church emerged as what was arguably the leading model of reform among the English godly sort, a model that conjoined lay elders with deacons, ministers, and doctors in the offices of the church itself. But even those godly English folk unwilling to embrace the Scottish example were eager to modify episcopacy so as to incorporate Presbyterian elements into the Church of England. Others went further still in reform, arguing for the autonomy of congregations in keeping with the practices of the Netherlands and New England. Such Congregationalists looked to the Holy Spirit, not to the ecclesiastical officers, for the legitimacy of their preachers.

On the other, and more restrictive, hand, the Laudian clergy shut down the Feoffees and insisted on the sacred separateness of the ordained clergy from the profanity of the laity, while even moderate defenders of divine-right episcopacy such as Joseph Hall ridiculed the very concept of a lay elder as a nothingness: neither a civilian magistrate nor a proper clergyman but an amphibious thing with no appropriate place in the nature of things.[2] Paradoxically, however, in the Westminster Assembly, the Presbyterians led the charge to secure what Samuel Rutherford called 'the liberty of Jesus Christ's kingdom, for it is a free kingdom,' from the overreaching control of the Long Parliament.[3] In the midst of these debates, Selden was charged with an Erastianism that favoured such an overreaching control – for instance, when the staunch Presbyterian Robert Baillie feared that parliamentary manipulation of the divines' findings about ordination would serve to 'scrape out whatever might displease the Independents, or patrons, or Selden and others who will have no discipline at all in any church jure divino, but settled only upon the free will and pleasure of the Parliament.' As Baillie's conflation of Selden's position with that of the Independents implies, the truth about Selden's understanding of the liberty of the church was much more complex than caricature allowed, especially that found in Baillie's immediately following complaint that the 'Independents and Civilians' would connive in so subverting 'the Assembly's reputation' that 'Erastus' way would triumph.' Even as the Presbyterians are resisting the overweening influence of the Long Parliament, Baillie is unwittingly revealing the ironic situation in which believers in the basic autonomy of the congregation are seeking a parliamentary protection of their liberty against oppression by the Presbyterians.[4]

It is not surprising that, in the early 1620s, some twenty years before his involvement in the Westminster Assembly, Selden's published work on the question of the autonomy or liberties of the church had begun, just after the eruption of the mainly clerical storm over his secularizing of church revenues in the *History of Tithes*. Somewhat ironically, Selden was penalized for his supposed mistakes in this treatise when King James requested that the learned layman settle three theological disputes in as many treatises. Yet Selden's independently pursued scholarship also took a turn towards promulgating one of the great and neglected defences of the liberty of the church from political and lay control; for in 1623 he produced an edition of the Anglo-Norman Eadmer, whose *Historia Novorum in Anglia* passionately and unmistakably argued that the church should be fully in charge of its own affairs and that religion is best served and protected whenever this is the case. It is very hard to say what Selden was up to with this edition. The fact of the edition does not prove that its editor agreed with Eadmer's views. In fact, even though he admires Eadmer the historian, he is silent on the question of whether he sympathizes with Eadmer the churchman. Selden makes available for readers a cleric's interpretation of the time immediately before 1200, an account that exposes the insolence of those princes who sought to rob the church of its proper offices, revenues, and liberties. Selden's readers are made privy to a vigorous and compelling plea for protection of the holy church from the greed and corruption of politics, and he tells them that in the realm of medieval historians, Eadmer is uncommonly reliable.[5] The editor does, however, allow the thesis of the history to speak for itself.

As Antonia Gransden explains, Eadmer 'was the first Anglo-Norman to write contemporary history.' For his '*Historia Novorum in Anglia*, which he wrote between about 1095 and 1123, was ... the second part of

a bipartite biography of Anselm constructed on the Anglo-Saxon model.
It was the account of Anselm's public acts (the *Life of St. Anselm* concerned his character and private life).'[6] Selden presented his edition in
1623 to a high-ranking clerical patron, the bishop of Lincoln, John Williams (1582–1650), one whose career embodied the extension of episcopal authority into civilian offices rather than the encouragement of lay
encroachment in matters of the church. Over the course of his life in
the church, Williams evinced an 'attitude of aloofness from extreme
parties' that was equally troubling to the ceremonialists and the iconoclasts, for example, in the moderate stance that he took on altar policy
in the 1630s.[7] In the second decade of the century, Williams had
received one ecclesiastical promotion after another until in 1617 he was
appointed to serve as chaplain to James I, of whom the talented clergyman was a favourite. Soon after, he became a political adviser to Buckingham, then Bacon's replacement as the lord keeper with authority
over equity in the Court of Chancery. In the same year, 1621, Williams
was made bishop of Lincoln; by the time that Selden dedicated his Eadmer to him, Williams was very near the apex of influence in church and
state alike, advising Prince Charles and Buckingham against their ill-
fated journey to Spain, then counselling them against a war with the
same country and attending King James at his death.

The text that Williams received from Selden was a powerful defence
of the protection of the church from civil invasion and contamination, a
case for the canonical liberty of the church that would go a long way
also towards pleasing Williams's eventual nemesis, William Laud. The
Historia Novorum features Anselm as the hero of a narrative with an
unflinching commitment to and celebration of church autonomy in the
very century, the twelfth, in which the great body of canon law would be
consolidated. Although Eadmer's devotion to his monastery and to the
archbishop of Canterbury would eventually lead him into a dispute with
the archbishop of York (ironically, the position to which Williams was
translated in that troubled year 1641), the bulk of the 'new history' heralds the valour and piety of Lanfranc, Anselm, and the defenders of the
church against the encroachments of William II and Henry I, kings
whose Norman identity helps to explain their violation of sacrosanct
ecclesiastical liberties.

In his capacity as a historian, Eadmer made the most of an everyday
intimacy with his subject; moreover, in Gransden's words, he 'fully
understood the value of a document quoted *verbatim*.'[8] Thanks to this
intimacy and accuracy, Eadmer can advertise the reliability of his testi-

mony to the brave efforts made in Canterbury to protect or reclaim church resources, rights, authority, and honours from the grasp of the magistrates and the laity. For Eadmer, the new and diacritical mark of his age is, as Southern writes, 'the resistance of the archbishop of Canterbury to the royal authority over the Church.'[9] For Selden, then, the *Historia Novorum* combines the best of poetic history – it makes a moral and spiritual case by means of praise and blame – with the best of critical history. Indeed, in his own dedication to Williams, Selden praises the reliability of his author, emphasizing that the material forming the basis of the narrative is fully documented and that it contains virtually nothing along the lines of those ridiculous fables so often filling the volumes of monkish historians.

Selden stresses to Williams that Eadmer is openly favourable to the holy estate of the church yet diligent, accurate, and credible as its champion. Anselm himself is heralded for his lucid sense of the boundary between sacred and secular power; for he is fearless in his obedience to the Pope in religious concerns yet happy to obey the king in matters exclusively of state. To Selden's mind, Eadmer avoids the pitfalls of inexperience, of desire for approval, and of the rash dislike for authorities, and he writes skilfully and honestly in a grave style. Adding only skimpy notes to the edition, Selden is largely prepared to let Eadmer speak for himself on behalf of those resolute clergy who protected the fortress of the church from Norman invasion; helped to ready it for and square it with the Gregorian reinvention of church honour, liberty, and authority; and endured the pains of exile for their efforts.

In his preface, Eadmer equates the arrival of the Normans with the debased secularization of priestly investiture. 'Anselm wished to put an end to this practice of investiture by the King,' he recalls, 'as being contrary to God and to the canons of the Church, and thereby to prune away the mischiefs resulting from it.'[10] Before conflict between king and clergy had reached a critical stage, Anselm's predecessor at Canterbury, Lanfranc, managed to steer William the Conqueror into a course of service to the church and to Christian living throughout the kingdom, especially in the monasteries. Under Lanfranc, the church prospered inwardly and outwardly. With the succession of William Rufus, Eadmer continues, England was faced with a king for whom the church became part of the political machinery and marketable goods of the court: thus, William Rufus 'ruined the churches and then held them exclusively in his own hand. He refused to appoint anyone except himself to take the place of bishop or abbot so long as he could by his officers extract from them anything which he thought to be of any value' (28). Only Anselm, according to Eadmer, was willing boldly and persistently to oppose the royal insolence according to which a subject cannot serve his master, William, if the subject is also serving God.

With his Eadmer, then, Selden presents to readers in the 1620s a credible historian whose narrative and viewpoint support the purity and self-governance of the church against the Norman invasion of the sacred domain. His patron, John Williams, is a bishop whose career is a throwback to the distant time in which clergymen were deeply involved in the legal and political affairs of the kingdom more than the king and his court were apt to dominate the Pope's universal church. This editorial project emerges in the wake of the controversy over Selden's *History of Tithes*, in which the author himself is accused of raiding the church of its revenues and divine sanction. In choosing Eadmer for his scholarly attentions in the early 1620s, Selden might be offering the protectors of the church a new weapon for warding off the lay profanation of the church that his own historical work might have inadvertently granted. But Selden never once says that he is offering such a weapon. The Eadmer evinces his concern with the arguments for liberating the church from undue lay encroachment, but Selden is as yet either unprepared or unwilling to advance a thesis about exactly what this liberty should involve.

—— 3 ——

Given the context of the period between the first edition of the *History of Tithes* and Selden's edition of Eadmer, James I's request that layman Selden compose three theological tracts as correctives to doubts raised in the *History of Tithes* is double-edged: admonished by James for profaning and scandalizing the church, Selden is also entrusted by his royal master with setting the church right again. Even as Selden protests in a 1620 letter that in his study of tithes, he left any theological consideration 'wholly to divines to whom it properly belongs,' his theologizing king recognizes him as a learned and acute religious scholar who might thwart 'scandal in the church' and leave cruxes 'more clearly either rectified or explained' than divines might manage.[11] It is, of course, a further irony in a controversy over relations between laity and clergy that the kingdom's highest magistrate is also its theologian-in-chief and ecclesiastical head.

In the first tract, regarding the interpretation of the apocalyptic number 666, Selden apologizes to James for what has appeared to be his attack on numerical exegesis in general, then proceeds to confirm that the standard of numerical interpretation must be measured 'according to the analogy of scripture and church story' (col. 1402). He notes further that, as the career and attitude of Calvin illustrate, the greatest exegetes have approached such interpretation with caution; like Calvin, too, no doubt, they have spent their early years largely in the study of human letters and law, that is, in learning that facilitates their theology. In the second theological crux, regarding the celebration of Jesus' birthday, Selden moves directly into the scholarship of calendar studies, an area that, together with his work on inheritance, priestly succession, and marriage, represents his closest involvement with subjects traditionally covered under canon law. In the third and final tract, explaining his purpose in writing the *History of Tithes*, he not only professes his reverence for the clergy but also expresses his intention to be useful to divines and canonists as well as to 'every ingenuous Christian' (col. 1453). He adds that, even had he formed an opinion about the question of right (as against fact) in his research on tithes, his respect for church authority and doctrine as it is 'licensed by publick authority' would have prevented him from foisting that view on the reader (col. 1455). In short, the learned layman depicts himself as little more than a handmaid or an intellectual acolyte to the clergy. As the 1620s give way to the 1630s, however, Selden undertakes those major Judaic studies that will catalyse his efforts clearly and forcefully to delineate the debts that are owed to a coercive magistrate – one in some measure responsible for regulating religious and moral practices – and those owed in a more spiritual currency to priests, the church, and God.

In the 1630s William Laud spearheaded a powerful effort, one fully supported and in many ways conceived by Charles I, to restore the dignity, wealth, and autonomy of the consecrated clergy in the Church of England. In that same decade, Laud became a key patron for Selden's Judaic work. Yet if Selden's views of Eadmer's churchmanship remained mysterious and his tone in the condemnation of lay profanation remained elusive, Selden's assessment of the archbishop was at once very simple and highly complicated. At least by the 1640s, when Laud was imprisoned, his program of recovering and bolstering the ceremonial and canonical uniformity in the Church of England, together with the authority and reverence of its clergy, was repugnant to Selden. He did appreciate Laud's fervent support for the kind of oriental scholarship that had become so central to Selden's own vision of the holy com-

monwealth; and Laud had assisted Selden in regaining the favour of
Charles I – no small feat. Accordingly, Selden dedicated his work on the
jurisdiction and character of Jewish priests to Laud, and one can imagine that the prelate himself might accept the gift as a learned contribution to his own program of securing the protected territory of the
English priesthood by means of elaborating the catholicity of its lineage
and offices. In the prefatory matter, Selden depicts himself as a pioneering minister on behalf of the Church of England under Laud; but he
never says that he supports the specifics of Laud's program, even if biog-
raphers of Selden in the years just after his death chose some of the
words that he addressed to Laud as the epitome of his religious views.
These words emphasized that the Reformation in England had never
abandoned a commitment to the catholic traditions and full-scale history of the Christian church in general; and that the character of Reformation in England had nothing to do with the insolent innovations of
base mechanic zealots.[12] In the 1640s, however, Selden was clearly articulating a vision of the holy commonwealth far more complex than
Laud's focus on the privileges of the clergy, a vision in which spiritual
labour was more evangelical in its protected sphere yet nonetheless
coordinated with the judgments and governance of legal sages and institutions. For Laud, neither the control by magistrates of the church nor
the uncontrolled zeal of the 'Puritans' was acceptable; in the 1640s and
1650s Selden was thinking his way towards a holy commonwealth in
which both the rule of law and the power of zeal could thrive.

In its penchant for reverence, decorum, and uniformity, Laud's construction of defences around the clergy and rites of the English church
received full support from King Charles, who invested his own royal
authority with a priestly sanctity. The upshot of Laud's archepiscopacy
might be seen as a Protestant version of the work of Anselm – to ensure
that the church remained its own mistress, controlled its own resources,
and regulated its own practices and creeds. The potential insubordination of such clerical aggrandizement was not lost on those critics of
Laud who warned the king that he had far less to fear from honest 'Puritans' than from bishops with a divine-right chip on their shoulders.

Laud's ideal for how a religious society should manage the potentially
rival claims of spiritual zeal and lawful conformity was advanced in the
1620s and 1630s at two levels: with regard to English governance and
society as a whole and with regard to the church as a sacred subset of
that society. In a sermon preached at the opening of Parliament in 1625,
Laud announces his strong desire for reciprocity in his Jerusalem

between civil government (the 'city') and the church (the 'temple'). He argues that the church must have its residence in the civil domain or lose itself in the wilderness of the world, and that the civil domain cannot prosper without the church. As the civil government relies on justice as its mainstay, the church has its own buttress, religion, and requires its own 'holy unity in faith and charity.'[13] This unity demands that authority in the church be settled and separate from the civil, as surely as the temple building itself is secured and consecrated. As his key analogy for the conformity that should unite all the preaching performed in the temple, Laud celebrates the Jewish premium on obedience to law.

The model of 'the Sanhedrim of the Jews' assists Laud in explaining how the civil and ecclesiastical arenas relate to one another within the Jerusalem of his England. Whereas the Sanhedrin comprised a mixture, ecclesiastical and civil, of judges and causes, kingdoms since that time have seen fit – rightly, Laud believes – to divide 'the seats of ecclesiastical and civil judicature.' His main point is this: even though at times the ecclesiastical authority has overwhelmed the civil, the case is very much altered now; for 'the civil courts are as much too strong for the ecclesiastical, and may overlay them as hard, if they will be so unchristian as to revenge.' God was so committed to ecclesiastical order and judicature, Laud maintains, 'that He set the High-Priest very high in the Sanhedrim,' a point that Selden would eventually modify and even dispute. Even now, Laud concludes, God wants powerful bishops, not anarchy or parity, overseeing 'the trial and ending' of 'ecclesiastical and Church causes.' The commonwealth prospers, then, if clerical leaders have the authority in the civil domain to protect the church in her own domain. But a well guarded religion repays the commonwealth. As Laud warns in another sermon before Parliament, a loss of strength and unity in the church weakens the order overseen by civil government and its laws: 'For there can be no firmness without law; and no laws can be binding if there be no conscience to obey them; penalty alone could never, can never, do it. And no school can teach conscience but the Church of Christ.'[14]

In Laud's sermons, then, the mutual support of commonwealth and church is premised on the sacred distinction of the church from secular control. Religion has its own proper unity, its own pillar of strength, its own judges and foundations, always held in close proximity to and in mutual support of civil affairs, but a different order all the same. If the civil domain can be said to contain the church, it can make this claim as a body might about the soul, or as human nature might about the con-

science. The civil government has the greatest reasons for protecting
from profanation its precious core.

In his official speeches, Laud focuses on the specificity and legality of
church authority, defining 'the public Acts of the Church in matters of
doctrine' as 'Canons and Acts of Councils' (this, in instructing the
House of Commons in which Selden sat in 1628–9); the authority of the
church in expounding the Articles; and the extent to which 'the Church
derive their authority from the King, as well as the civility.' Laud considers it an egregious offence when a man of law violates church authority;
for 'as it is a great offence in a divine to infringe the law of the kingdom
wherein he is born and bred up, so it is also a great offence if those of
the profession of the law vilify the poor laws of the Church.' He converts
this analogy into a warning for men of law who hold the church, its canons, and officers in their grasp: England has known a day when the
clergy were as powerful as lawyers have become; 'and let me be bold to
prophesy, there will be a time when you will be as low as the Church is
now, if you go on thus to contemn the Church.'[15]

Given such a dire warning and Laud's sense of rivalry between priests
and lawyers, the prelate's patronage of Selden speaks even more highly
of how much the former admired the learning of the latter. Laud clearly
wanted to encourage the scholar to remove himself from the contentious and insubordinate tendencies of his constitutional- and common-
law work in the 1620s to a scholarly focus on topics traditionally of concern to priests and canon lawyers: inheritance, priestly succession, and
marriage. Laud would later complain that no one could tell what the
fundamental laws of England were, since 'the common laws of England
have no text at all,' and he no doubt hoped that shifting Selden's attention away from the common law would render the scholar more serviceable to order and conformity in the holy commonwealth, that is, to
a strictly regulated spirituality in which prosperity of the Church
depended on the priestly 'upholding of the external worship of God in
[the church], and the settling of it to the rules of its first reformation.'
For thus Laud reprimanded men whom he deemed prominent lay zealots for taking the affairs of the church into their own hands. In pushing
for clerical autonomy and ritualistic conformity, Laud believed that the
devotional richness and the legal authority of the church were mutually
constitutive of one another, that the state and the church stood or fell
together with this belief, and 'that with the contempt of the outward
worship of God, the inward fell away apace, and profaneness began
boldly to show itself.'[16]

In the 1630s Selden simply did not play Eadmer to Laud's Anselm, a role that would be played by Peter Heylyn, and in the 1640s he moved decisively away from his association with Laud. He did dedicate to the archbishop a pair of apt works on the Judaic priesthood and on an aspect of Judaic law (property and inheritance) that dovetailed with the traditional domain of canon law. The two works were *De Successionibus in Bona Defuncti ad Leges Ebraeorum* and *De Successione in Pontificatum Ebraeorum*, the first published alone in 1631 and the two published together in 1636. In his prefatory matter Selden sought to establish a common ground between client and patron, in which the best coordination between Reformed spirituality and normative control is appreciative of tradition and learning and occupies a moderate ground between insolent papist clergy and wild sectarian fancies. But it is entirely possible that Selden was attempting to move Laud beyond the repressive and xenophobic tendencies of his ecclesiastical policies, to escort him towards a more latitudinarian and oriental understanding of the holy commonwealth than the archbishop had heretofore achieved.

For the 1636 edition of his analysis of the transfer of goods and the succession of priests, Selden explains to Laud that two types of resourceful, skilful readers have reverted to the study of Hebrew affairs. One is a deserter to the fractious enemies of church unity and order, the other an explorer, spy, or scout on behalf of church interests: 'In genere sunt duplici, Antistes Eminentissime, homines qui, è coetu Christianorum, studiis rebusque Ebraicis aevo nostro solertiùs versantur. Instar Transfugarum alii, alii tanquam Exploratores [In our age there are two kinds of men, most eminent high-priest, who are the more skilfully engaged in the assimilation of Christians with Hebrew studies and affairs. One group bears a resemblance to a deserter, just as the other group can be likened to scouts]' (dedication). Among the first group are those sectarians who erroneously extend the Hebrew Sabbath to Christians and in general wreak lay havoc on the order and reverence of the church. But the second group comprises those faithful men who facilitate worship and clarify the faith by making proper use of the wisdom of the ages, and these men are obliged by their initiation into the fortress of sacraments.

Selden offers his services to England's premiere overseer of church order and canonical authority as just such a scholar-scout boldly journeying from the fortress of the English church into the foreign intellectual territory of ancient and medieval Judaism. From that territory, it is the responsibility of the scout to retrieve both clear normative guidance and rich spiritual resources for the empowerment and improvement of the native church left behind. In turn, Selden praises Laud for earnestly, prudently, and assiduously vindicating Christian doctrine and discipline from the justly hated sectarians with their bogus claims on the Holy Spirit, and for so magnanimously supporting the scouts (not least with his manuscript collection) in full recognition that they incur spiritual and public danger in their discursive journeys ('Vt verò Genus anterius impensè habes, Praesul Reverendissime, idque meritissimò invisum, utpote prudentissimus, amplissimus, assiduusque Doctrinae & Disciplinae Christianae assertor & vindex; ita Posterioris generis Fautorem, Patronum, etiam & Instigatorem summum te palàm exhibes' [dedication to Laud]). It helps the sojourner in Palestine, Selden insists, if there are very good maps – that is, scholarly resources – regarding that land in the treasury of the church fortress itself. The scout, however, must make sense of those maps, refine them, and discern the best use for them in the Church of England. That is, Laud must look to Selden for a new understanding of what is best for the church that Laud must govern, as surely as those aristocratic leaders praised by Jonson were being seduced into a new understanding of their own noble virtue.

Indeed, Selden prefaces this, his inaugural work on Judaism, with a prolegomena offering guidance to future scouts in the Talmud. In this context he criticizes not the sectarian abuses of Judaism, not simply the neglect of that territory, but rather those scholars who seek an escape from contemporary troubles in the exotic world of Judaica. Such holiday scholarship avoids the disgust and tedium of the present day, but singularly reneges on the grand opportunity to reform present day faith and manners with help from the ancient Jews: 'Ita scatent passim feruentia eiusmodi Studia & impetuosi in ea feriatorum hominum affectus; siue quia, praesentis aeui taedio ac scelerum odio, ad annos praeteritos, qui tamen à Scriptorum reticentia meliores maximè videntur, recurrere libet; siue quia nostris, ut sit, neglectis, aliena potiùs vt Exteros terrarum Tractus, Mores, Status, Actus, Domestica in super habentes affectamus, non sine graui animi vitio & solenni [Here and there ardent and impulsive studies of such a kind gush forth in that human inclination for holidays; either because, out of a disgust for and weariness from the ills of the present age, one wishes to return to ancient times, which only appear to be so especially better, thanks to the silence of the Scriptures; or because, from our own neglect as it were, we prefer having in mind above the familiar all things foreign, such as the foreign districts of land, the manners, constitutions, and laws – not without moral damage to our sober and serious souls]' (prolegomena, i).

The more judicious scholar understands, Selden maintains, that ancient Palestine is not some idle wit's substitute for the delights of Arcadia. Instead, the scout bears the responsibility for diligently investigating those resources that might instruct, and thus reshape, the Laudian project of elevating, normalizing, and enriching the church at home. For the ancient remains of a godly and lawful Judaism can help England to prevent religious error, not least that blindness foisted on the unsuspecting worshiper by the apparently learned leaders of factions. With a careful search into the Talmud, the scout can discover the clarity and integrity of set forms in such a way as to magnify, not undermine, the fervent spirituality of the community. Among the Hebrews, then, English theologians, clergy, and their supporters can and should lay hold of norms for adjudicating church controversies in such a way as to cultivate both conformity and holiness.

In forestalling the charge that his own scholarship is merely an inglorious and a recondite curiosity, Selden offers his studies of property and priesthood as help to both the legal and the clerical judges whose office it is to assess and to settle the conflicts of their own times. Whenever veneration of the ancient and foreign Judaic culture bolsters the discernment of divine and human affairs as they are operative in present circumstances, then the panegyric mode of scholarship is appropriate. In addressing Laud, however, Selden emphasizes the utility of his studies over its poetics. Both clerical and legal minds should benefit from the disclosure of those Judaic norms and warrants that still pertain to the adjudication of controversies. He argues, moreover, that England is all the more shameful for neglecting the Hebrew '*normam*' insofar as other European countries in which Jews still live – Belgium, Italy, Poland, and Germany – have not neglected it (prolegomena, ii). He further accentuates English neglect by pronouncing the authority of the Talmud as the embodiment of the unwritten Mosaic Law. The two Talmudic collections – Babylon and Jerusalem – are chequered sources, he concedes, replete with fables and follies about Jesus and the Virgin Mary, for instance. Scouts must be as vigilant with the rabbis as they are with church fathers, canon laws, and medieval histories or councils. Yet the Talmud is no more fabulous than those medieval chronicles that amass miraculous tales, and they are incomparably greater in truth and use value.

Finally, in the prolegomena, Selden attacks those scripturalists who oppose the assistance of any such received and oral tradition as the Talmud, no matter how prudent that tradition, and who trust only their own rash wits to explicate the Bible, inevitably disturbing the peace of their religion with their impious and ridiculous innovations. For Selden, the contrast between approaches is crystal clear: how much more reverent were those Jewish compilers of the Mishnah and two Gemaras than any scripturalist; for the former were compelled to assemble their traditions or else lose them in the diaspora created by Roman persecution. Thus, the rabbis captured traditional wisdom, court decisions, and strains of exegesis as they had accumulated since the days of Moses on Sinai. Even today where Jews are free, Selden marvels, they exercise legal judgment according to the Mishnah norms ('*normas*') as explicated by the Babylonian and Jerusalem Gemaras (prolegomena, ii).

Even as he turns to the rabbis or law sages for his model, however, Selden is also addressing the specific concerns of contemporary and medieval clergy. That is, by opting to write on the transfer of property and on ordination, Selden selects topics associated in his own day with the jurisdiction of canon law. By addressing the work to Laud, he conciliates an archbishop whose attempts to restore church authority, uniformity, reverence, and prosperity Selden would redirect and redefine. In his work on the Sanhedrin, Selden brings to fruition his own vision of how best to coordinate the lawyers and the clergy – a vision of how a holy commonwealth might entrust the law sages in a comprehensively normative way yet preserve a proper domain for those ministers devoted to holy living and spiritual labour. But by the time he comes to publish his work on the Sanhedrin, Laud has been executed and his designs on the church discredited even by many supporters of (a more moderate) episcopacy.

Since the twelfth century, in work carried out most prominently by Gratian, advocates of canon law could claim a legal corpus characterized by its comprehensive scope, sophisticated method, and minimization of contradiction. The body of canon law owed debts to the legacy of civil law, but that legacy was subsumed in the church's legal system. As R.H. Helmholz has written, the comprehensive and analytical canon law sought 'to regulate the whole life of the church' and 'to place the authoritative texts in usable form, arranging them around basic subject matter categories.' And it aspired to 'an independent discipline' with 'an existence separate and distinct from both theology and Roman law, even though it overlapped with both in its coverage and sources.'[17]

The development of canon law formed a basic part of a larger push by the clergy in the eleventh and twelfth centuries to secure or reclaim the offices and liberties of the church from lay control. Selden's dedicatee,

Laud, was very much a reformer along the same lines. Like the case of Gregorian reform, so the case of Laud: a 'salient objective' in isolating and protecting what has been called the 'spirit of classical canon law' is the aim 'to improve the morals, the status, and the education of the clergy' and 'to secure the independence of the clerical order from the control and perhaps even the influence of lay men and women' (Helmholz, 61). In the search for *libertas ecclesiae,* a certain type of church reformer from Gratian to Laud emphasized canonical regularity and its enforcement as the chief means by which the sanctity of the church might be protected from contamination in the world. The clerical maintenance of legal authority worked on behalf of God's presence among Christians, not at cross-purposes with that presence.

Even in his work on natural law, Selden had encountered the reminder issued by Grotius that the norms of Christianity demand much more than those of the nations and of nature. These higher norms would be best served, a Laudian would conclude, were the church to reclaim its own 'juridical community' together with the elevation and regulation of its own officers, means, and ends.[18] Selden's earliest forays into Judaic studies were not prepared to say exactly how the scholar would articulate the conditions of autonomy for spiritual labour, or to aver exactly how that labour would be controlled by civil magistracy. But in this work on the priesthood, then increasingly in the scholarship of the 1640s, Selden explored the ways in which ancient Jews and Christians had dealt with the kinds of religious conflict sorely plaguing the people of England in the reign of Charles I.

In his treatise on priestly succession Selden examines the way in which the ancient Jews established fixity in and reverence for the priesthood and its clerical offices. The work is organized simply into a first book surveying the history of priesthood from Aaron until the destruction of the second temple, followed by a second book on the laws governing succession. More important than his efforts to rectify the names and numbers of the Old Testament lineage, Selden's study portrays Jews as a people who grow all the more tenacious to preserve their laws, traditions, and rites when times and conditions become more lawless, corrupt, and hostile. Their high priests served as especially zealous leaders in such times, he says, and did so at least until the time of Herod, when lawless corruption produced hysteria, lawless men became their leaders, and customs were so imperiled as to provoke the creation of the Mishnah and Gemaras.

During his discussion of the priesthood, Selden takes up two especially knotty questions: Were there ever two high priests at once? What relation obtained between High Priests and the leaders of the Sanhedrin? The latter question, of course, is more far reaching in significance for Selden's later work. Having laid out a number of interpretive guidelines and having drawn analogies to the church in his own day, he concludes that high priests were, precisely speaking, officers separate from any office in the Sanhedrin, that their lineage from Aaron was peculiar to their sacred office, and that any civil use of a similar title is inexact. The two chief officers of the Great Sanhedrin, the chief and the father, could only incidentally be high priests, much as Laud was not a political officer in Charles's court by virtue of his status and duties as archbishop per se (*De Successione*, 185–94). In his later work on the Sanhedrin, Selden makes the same points as a way of insisting on the civil status of the legal sages overseeing the whole of Judaic society; in the work on priestly genealogies, however, the only accidental link between priests and civil offices might just as easily serve to accentuate the separateness and sanctity of the priests.

Having established the priestly lineage to the best of his ability, praised the Jewish people for their defence of tradition and law, then attempted to settle the matter of why priesthood as such was only incidentally mixed with civil office, Selden turns in the second book to his analysis of the legal components of eligibility for the Judaic priesthood. Such a normalization of participation in the ministry is one of Laud's chief concerns, against those unofficial or renegade 'Puritans' who in the 1630s are looking to lay patrons or to the Holy Spirit for their sanction. Among the qualities of the priestly person in Judaism, Selden considers matters of kinship, pure family blood, age, physical condition, spiritual integrity, and reputation, each with its own part to play in elevating the authority of the ministry both inside and out. Along with the extensive list of blemishes to be considered, in this section he moves in the direction of his later study of Hebraic marriage and sexuality, another area that was considered proper for canon law in his day. But he is also led to catalogue many other factors in support of priestly dignity: those vocations (bath attendant, barber, butcher) not permitted entrance into the priesthood; the sins that can and cannot be mitigated by penitence for those wanting to enter the priesthood; the rites of consecration with their vestments, anointing, and sacrifices; the difference between the accoutrements of the first two temples; finally, the jurisdiction, power of judgment, and interpretive authority of the priesthood, especially in matters of controversy.

As a scout, Selden can bring his scholarly riches to the intellectual fortress of the church, then leave them in the care of the properly qualified and consecrated clergy. Having insisted that Hebraic scholars train their focus on the utility of their studies, he modestly plays his role as a pioneer who boldly ventures out for foreign resources, then, having fetched them home, leaves their employment to the officers and guardians of the religious society. However, his reticence about deciding the specific uses of his scholarship leaves a trail of ambiguity. It is unclear how Selden envisions the relationship between the jurisdictions of his two topics, property and the priesthood. Both have belonged within the conventional domain of canon law, but Selden does not say how he would have lawyers and priests sort out their jurisdiction in seventeenth-century England. Much the same ambiguity arises when Selden concludes with an assertion of the Great Sanhedrin's authority in settling controversies over priestly succession. Insofar as he does not yet define the Sanhedrin in any detail, it might still be a clerical synod with selected members of the laity working therein in support of the clergy in charge; or it might be a parliament with clergy working therein; or it might be some wonderful mix of different elements into a union far greater than the sum of its sacred and civil parts. Whatever the Sanhedrin might finally be, Selden's commitment to reconstructing that institution shows little intention of simply leaving the church to its own ostensibly pure devices. So, too, in deciding which oriental materials to bring back from his forays, and in presenting those materials for consumption, the legal sage has gone a long way towards determining how the leaders of the Church of England might rethink their own role in the holy commonwealth. After all, a bachelor archbishop is unlikely to find a flattering image of himself in the hereditary priesthood of the ancient Jews.[19]

—— **4** ——

In the decade following publication of the volume dedicated to Laud, Selden's studies continued to pursue the Judaic traditions behind the rites and offices often associated in medieval and early modern Christendom with canon law and the clergy. Together with his work on the rituals and rules of marriage and sexuality, his scholarship focused on the calendar, chronology, and temporal organization of religious rituals and holy days. Given the profound influence of Joseph Scaliger on him, Selden had long before understood full well that chronology was not the exclusive preserve of a clergy in charge of an ecclesiastical calendar. Indeed, in the *Arundel Marbles*, the layman Selden had applied his chronological learning to the construction of pagan history; and the more he studied the Talmud, the more he knew that the Jewish calendar had been rectified in the Sanhedrin, whatever that great body was. Indeed, his own work on the laws of nature qualified him as much as anyone to think out the intricacies of a ritual time whose obligations were owed as much to the cycles of nature as to the holy days determined in church history. In the 1640s, then, Selden's Judaicized revision of the jurisdiction of the Christian canon law, together with his participation as a civil law sage in the Westminster Assembly of Divines, led him ever further into the contentious ground on which ordained lawyers and ordained priests faced off and clashed for authority in the regulation of the habits of living in a religious society. Rather than simply reject any notion of church autonomy, however, Selden worked hard at constructing a scholarly temple complex meant to clarify and to model a mutually beneficial interaction among legal magistracy, spiritual labour, natural law, and normative poetry.

In *De Anno Civili et Calendario* (1644), Selden studies the ancient Jewish methods for the best way to calculate time through the lens of the sectarian conflicts between scripturalists (Karaites) and legal traditionalists. In 1644 he is still very much committed to research on the kinds of festival and ceremonial rites whose decency and reverence have owed so much to the vigilance of Laud and to a holistic myth of merry old England epitomized (and enforced) by the reissue of the Book of Sports in 1633, a document the poet Herrick refers to as the 'proclamation made for May.' Unlike the work on the succession of estates and priests, however, Selden's study of the calendar no longer repudiates the more zealous, adversarial, or 'Puritan' contributors to the understanding of Judaic culture. Laud is in prison, a civil war is under way, and the Westminster Assembly is in debate over changes to be made in the polity and liturgy of the church. The Long Parliament is in charge of those religious debates but is concurrently engaged in the reformation of civil government as well, and powerful cases are being made for even sectarian experimentation in texts such as Milton's *Areopagitica*, along with the growing alarm among the conservatives of the reforming side that they have unleashed a monstrous pestilence on themselves. In this heady, adventurous, yet blood-soaked and divisive time for England, Selden's scholarship is expressly mediatory among the traditional ceremonialists, those Presbyterians whose aim is giving new but specific form to the extemporaneous warrant of the Holy Spirit, those Congregationalists for whom a loosely organized national church is acceptable yet less important than the gathered community of faithful with scriptures in hand and prayers in their hearts, and the sectarian iconoclasts who resist their own proximity to the antinomian fancies threatening the most basic proprieties of English society. *De Anno* is a work without a patron, no king to require a predetermined answer about the controversy over the celebration of Christmas, and no prelate with very strong views about and enormous power over the conflicts arising from the celebration of the Sabbath. Consequently, *De Anno* comes closer than Selden's scholarship did in the 1630s to offering expressly normative guidance in redress of the grievances and impasses of modern religion. In the preface, he even edges towards Milton's position in *Areopagitica*, also published in 1644, that truth tends to rise more effectively from the conflict of sects, a lesson that (Selden claims) one can see in the history of Roman law as well as in the Protestant Reformation and in ancient Judaism;[20] indeed, Milton himself applauds Selden's support for the insight that truth thrives in an atmosphere of free and charitable difference far better than it does under the forced conformity of censors. If carefully mediated, Selden argues in *De Anno*, the scripturalists can teach the traditionalists about the sacred uses of irregularity, while the traditionalists can bestow a greater normative stability on the cantonizing tendencies of a purely spiritual warrant.

The two chief aims of Selden's study in chronology modify the Laudian potential of his work on the Judaic priesthood: the overarching purpose is to direct the English imagination away from its addiction to cyclical thinking and towards a sensitivity and comfort with living and worshipping according to lunar vicissitudes; the underlying purpose is to work out the relative merits of an often irregular scripturalism and a sometimes stultifying traditionalism in his own day. With both purposes, Selden intends his English readers to gain insight into Judaic means of coping with, even of sanctifying, the abnormal constituents of cultic experience in the process of reasserting a consensual normalcy over their religious society. Some of these abnormalities arise in nature itself, for instance, those lunar irregularities unsettling the rituals of time. Some derive from the singularity of human beings themselves, especially from those interpreters of divine law who shirk the assistance of tradition. Whatever the source of abnormality, it is the Karaite sect – the one most responsible for interpretive singularity in Judaic history – that best understands how and why to live according to the vicissitudes of lunar time. The tragedy of sectarian conflict arises when, as is so often the case, the sects fail to realize that their very conflict with the other side – not the hegemony of one side or the other – can supply a religious society with its beneficial complement of normative and ineffable elements. The Karaites have so much to offer a holistic understanding of consecrated time that their views, Selden asserts, ought not to be relegated to the fanatic ravings of fractious spirits, in either ancient or modern times.

When the Talmudic rabbis and the Karaite scripturalists are locked in an irresolvable conflict, Selden acknowledges, the former are to be trusted as the sturdy and ordinary foundation of tradition, one on which the Karaites themselves, ironically and unintentionally, have tended to rely. It is one thing, Selden knows, to support a spiritual flexing of the highly restrictive and ritualized Laudian canon, quite another to oppose a legal uniformity – and to do so zealously on behalf of individual inspiration and interpretation among the sectarian groups. Selden is not prepared to embrace the Karaites at the expense of the legal traditionalists, especially since the Talmud comprises within itself such a variety of voices, positions, and resources. Instead, he touts Judaic studies as the best means for moving beyond partisan conflict, a means that attempts to harmonize (as he has newly appreciated) the norms and variables of religious belief and experience.

He points out that, even if the Karaites have jettisoned tradition understood as the oral transmission of divine law, at the very least they made considerable use of written and traditional interpretations of the law. Much the same state of affairs obtains, he adds, among Christian groups; for some sects might reject the carnality of tradition as such yet venture to confer with the history of exegesis. Conversely, Talmudic rabbis have a strong sense both of the value of debate and of the spiritual zeal owed to God's word. Selden remains a scout in search of new foreign treasures, but he is now also playing ambassador to those domestic factions that fail to recognize how much they share within the confines of a single religious society.

More than the Talmudists, however, the Karaite or scripturalist Jews have sought to find ways of living piously according to singular lunar variations. For, like the fluctuations of an island or the inconstant motions of a comet ('Insulae fluctuantis aut Cometae motum' [*De Anno*, preface, 1]), Selden argues, the lunar year is not restricted to bygone patterns. Yet Karaite efforts, he laments, have been studied too superficially and carelessly. In restricting Judaic scholarship to the Talmud, seventeenth-century Hebraic scholars have addicted themselves to the comforts of whatever is fairly constant in both the natural world and the temple. The Karaites, however, accept – even embrace – uncertainty in nature and unpredictability in worship (4–11). Selden's appreciation of their notions suggests a disenchantment with any rigid Laudian insistence on set forms, canons, traditions, and ritual cycles, or with its associates in the world of poetry, the celebrations of merry old England and its naturalized calendar found in the verses of Robert Herrick. The fact that the Karaites make considerable concessions to tradition might be used to ridicule their hypocrisy, but Selden maintains that it is far more productive of true religion to convert this irony into grounds for a reconciliation with traditionalists.

When Selden argues that Karaites and their modern Christian counterparts end up conferring with non-scriptural traditions more than they would like to admit, his point is not primarily that these groups should be indicted for their hypocrisy, but rather that their approach has a natural prudence built into its narrow-minded tendencies. Selden emphasizes that the Jewish treatments of time reveal a consistency between the rival groups, notwithstanding their subtler disputes about how to calibrate years by means of inter-calendar months or about how to determine the phases of the moon. What is more, clerical and lay officials – those who are best for the job – work together in the Sanhedrin on calculating ritual time; it is only when that court ceases to exist, he maintains, that sectarian conflicts and the lay-clerical divide take hold in this and other judicial concerns. In *De Anno*, then, Selden argues for a quality in Judaism that he epitomizes in one statement of table talk: the Jews have a penchant for sticking together, for cohering in their habits of religious thought and practice.

In 1644 Selden is at work in the Westminster Assembly on the reinvention of English worship and he is planning a study of Presbyterianism. In both cases, the model for a mix between lay and clerical authorities is the synod rather than a parliament or court, the synod ideally serving as a body in which supporters of bishops, presbyters, and autonomous congregations can unite in refashioning the laws of ecclesiastical polity. In this body, law sages might serve and guide the clergy whose assembly it remains, and religionists who look to tradition for help might work together with those who look only to scripture. In keeping with his hope for such a synod, Selden concludes *De Anno* with a discussion of the twenty-first chapter of Acts (20), in which Jewish converts to Christianity who have remained zealots for the law meet as 'presbyters' in the Jerusalem synod with the Apostles (100). In *De Jure Naturali et Gentium* Selden

notes this synod's efforts to decide the essentials of Jewish law so that
gentile Christians can be enticed to respect them. So, too, the Westminster Assembly is faced with the challenge of determining, on the one
hand, those essentials of the episcopal church that Presbyterians might
fairly be asked to retain and, on the other, those essentials of the Presbyterian church that supporters of episcopacy might fairly be asked to
embrace. With its incorporation of rival Judaic approaches, then,
Selden's investigation of ritual time attempts to model ways in which factions in his own day might unite in order to achieve the ideal coordination of spiritual liberty and legal norms.

In another Judaic work that he completed by the mid-1640s, the *Uxor
Hebraica*, Selden persists in his exploration of the laws and rules according to which the chosen people of the Old Testament and their successors infused order, normalcy, and formal reverence into the passions,
fancies, and vagaries of the sexual body as against those of the worship-
ful soul. In fact, for Presbyterian heresiographers such as Thomas
Edwards, whose *Gangraena* catalogued an explosion of sectarian errors
in three parts over the course of 1646, sexual libertinism and anarchic
zeal were mutually constitutive within the raving Antinomians of their
perilous times. If, moreover, sexuality represents another hard-to-nor-
malize area of experience belonging for centuries to the jurisdiction of
canon law, Selden is prepared once again to play the priest but with an
eye towards removing amours from the clerical realm altogether. Like
the controversial rituals of the festival calendar, marriage had become a
contested rite in the 1640s on the grounds that, according to Milton,
the civil liberation of marriage from the clutches of a censorious
national church would maximize the spirituality of the union. Thus,
controversy over how to formalize marriage, sexuality, and divorce doubled in the mid-1640s as a debate over the proper relationship between
civil and ecclesiastical authorities. When Selden returns in the *Uxor
Hebraica* to the conflict between the Karaite scripturalists and the rabbinical traditionalists, he links his study of marriage with his study of the
calendar and even to his work on property in the 1630s; for, when it was
first published in 1646, the *Uxor Hebraica* was coupled with the fourth
edition of *De Successionibus*.

Selden had already covered the Judaic standards for licit sexual relations in *De Jure Naturali*. In Book 5 of that tome, he studied the question
of marriage between Jews and gentiles along with the growth of the six
Noachian prohibitions against incest into twenty-six more propositions in
Leviticus. In addition, he examined the rationale behind the universal

prohibitions; rabbinical reasons for excluding certain persons from marriage; the natural obligations within marriage; the arguments for and against polygamy; and the natural legitimacy of divorce from the marriage contract. Because his main aim in that text was the discovery of natural law, Selden expanded his discussion from Judaic rules to pagan cultures. But in returning to marriage and sexuality in the *Uxor Hebraica*, he captures in his very title the reduction of his scope to the rituals of one people with their own laws and religion. As Jonathan Ziskind has noted, the *Uxor Hebraica* clarifies Selden's 'focus on the area in which Judaism profoundly differs from Christianity – its juristic character.' This focus was in keeping with Selden's direct participation in recasting the church in its relationship to civil jurisdiction in the Westminster Assembly of Divines; for 'who or what constitutes a court, especially where excommunication is concerned, was a burning issue in Selden's day, and as a lay delegate to the Westminster Assembly, he was deeply involved in attempting to resolve this amid other religious controversies.'[21]

As Jason Rosenblatt argues, the *Uxor Hebraica* is offered as a counter-argument to 'the rigors of canon law on divorce.'[22] Once again, Selden invokes Judaism as a religious society that coordinates scripture and tradition; the claims of spirit and law; and an original proximity to God with a commitment to the perpetuation and adjustment of institutions according to the difficult and unpredictable circumstances of experience. As in *De Anno*, the structure of the study is simple: in Book 1 Selden is concerned with those marriages that are forbidden or required; in Book 2 he examines the protocol for betrothal and marriage; and in Book 3 he works out the ramifications of the marriage contract. Like John Milton's work on divorce, Selden's challenge is to decipher a hermeneutic dilemma according to which interpreters must struggle to understand how much flexibility and rigour God intended for the marriage contract from its very inception. Thus, Ziskind shows, Selden attempts to demonstrate 'the inability of the Karaites to maintain coherent and workable rules on incest' as evidence of 'the problems inherent in making scriptural fundamentalism the basis for a program of social and political action' (21). Yet Selden is also intent in this and other studies of this time period on ensuring that the Karaite voice is recovered as a counterbalance to the normative rabbinical emphasis on oral tradition. More than before, he is attentive to Karaite modes of interpretation as an assembly of 'the biblical text itself, argumentation by analogy and the hereditary transmission of interpretation' (21). And he is more impatient with the Karaite failure to concede their convergence with the

Talmudists or, for that matter, to admit the conflicts produced among themselves when it came time to recognize that 'practicality must sometimes prevail over exegetical rules if the survival of a society is at stake' (22).

In the *Uxor Hebraica*, then, Selden takes a major segment of classical canon law and uses Judaic traditionalism and scripturalism as means of prying marriage loose from overly rigid law without depriving sexuality of a sturdy normative scaffolding. He clarifies that this scaffolding is made not from the materials of natural law, not from the law of nations, but rather, from 'civil' law, a term that appears also in the title of the work on calendars. By 'civil,' Selden says that he means the laws of a 'particular Church or commonwealth' (33). The 'or' here is hard to read. On the one hand, Selden suggests some indecision about whether the ideal coordination of law and spirit is best left to a synod including qualified laity or to a parliament-cum-court including qualified priests. On the other, Judaism offers a model of a holistic religious society in which the senatorial court and the rituals of priesthood proceed within the same complex of the temple.

If Selden's ulterior aim in synthesizing the Karaites and Talmudists is to harmonize the positions of scripturalists and traditionalists in his own religious society, his work in the 1640s is also committed to leading English readers to reconceive the family dynamic between ancient Judaism and the early Christian church. His main point is that Christianity was 'like a reformed Judaism' retaining 'Hebrew customs and rituals'; for such an intimacy or identity between the two groups is the keystone of Selden's attempt to reconcile law and spirit, law and love, law and grace, tradition and inspiration, sacred rites and sacred word, norm and zeal, the judgments of the civil court and the labours of the church (222–3). According to Rosenblatt, Selden shared the conviction with Milton, indeed helped to teach Milton, that the Hebraic mindset was monistic – and Selden had always been interested in largely monistic and pneumatic theories of cosmic interchange. Following the work of Helgerson, Rosenblatt stresses that for Selden monism was as much an ideal for negotiating 'a plurality of discursive communities' as it was an ontology; each community had its own calibration of the rigours of law with the liberty of spirit. As both Helgerson and Rosenblatt show, the great Judaic phase of Selden's late career affords a bold and brilliant way of forging the unification of communities whose tendency is to stray variously towards too much rigour or too much spirit.[23] On the one side are the hyper-Laudians, who care only about canons, rites, conformity, and clerical order; on the other side are the antinomian groups for whom any religious experience or authority aside from that of the Holy Spirit is the grossest carnality. If a monism between law and ineffable spirit cannot be left to the natural order and if God exacts from religious societies their own devices for coordinating the rival claims, then Hebraic scholarship stands a very good chance, or so Selden believes, of pioneering the territory in which English Protestants of the law and English Protestants of the spirit might discover their membership in the same community.

Outside the confines of his study, Selden sought to effect the marriage of Judaism and Christianity in the Westminster Assembly and, withal, to reinvent the norms of spirituality within the English church itself. It is clear that Selden emerged from the Assembly with a very bad impression of the Presbyterian version of lay and clerical authorities working together in one synod, but it was an attitude that he derived from, rather than brought to, that synod. Like Milton, Selden glimpsed a possibility for the recovery of true religion in the Presbyterian pattern of religious society, then quickly became disenchanted with the modern proponents of that pattern, though he continued to retain, and to redefine, some of its terminology. In the Westminster Assembly, Selden was invited to play priest with practical matters of polity in the balance. The goal of the Assembly was to refashion English religion into an ideal marriage between the uniformity provided by law and the ineffable spiritual largesse afforded by the also Hebraic 'daughter of the voice.'

Whatever his eventual disregard for the Presbyterians clutching their 'little pocket bibles with gilt leaves,'[24] Selden considered, if only briefly, the possibility that their synods of divines working together with lay elders might constitute the modern approximation of the Great Sanhedrin, with its commission to regulate the whole of religious society. In *Aërius Rediviuus*, the biased pro-bishop Peter Heylyn utterly scorned the Presbyterians for their zealous contention that they could 'fain intitle them to a descent from the Jewish Sanhedrim, ordained by God himself in the time of Moses.'[25] In Selden's much earlier musings on that body in the *History of Tithes*, he tends to think of it as a parliament, much as in *Paradise Lost* Milton would describe it as a senate of elders; but in the *Uxor Hebraica*, as well as in his 1642 edition of a passage written by a patriarch of Alexandria, Eutychius, Selden focuses on the categories of presbyters and elders as though there might be some promise in the church polity associated with them.

Ziskind has rightly shown that in the 1640s Selden envisioned the Sanhedrin as regulating the whole of religious society, including temple matters, matters of family, tithes, and calendars, of civil and criminal transgressions.[26] He understood that the Sanhedrin combined rabbinical and priestly judges in its one body, but it was much harder to say exactly what this combination involved and entailed or, for that matter, precisely what an ancient 'presbyter' might have been, or under what dispensation and circumstances those diverse parties were united, one with responsibility for law, the other with responsibility for temple sacrifices and rituals.

In the *Uxor Hebraica*, Selden mentions that the cases involving a brother-in-law's marital obligations were brought before 'elders or presbyters' according to the Hebrew and 'senate' according to the Greek. Then he adds that the Great Sanhedrin was an assembly of elders and presbyters in some passages of the Pentateuch, and that these men were among the wisest Israelites in the study of law. Referring us to his edition of Eutychius, Selden clarifies: 'talmudists understand presbyters or elders to be not only those duly elected as members of a Sanhedrin or not yet chosen but also private individuals of any kind who are not incompetent, as it says, in the manner described for a judicial proceeding or an action of this type' (127). So the Sanhedrin is 'a college of elders' competent in legal forms and norms covering the whole spectrum of Judaic life and cooperating 'with one spirit as citizens.' These presbyters are consecrated by the laying on of hands, a ceremony that (Selden reminds his readers) is also used in England 'with Doctors of Law (such were all the members in the individual sanhedrins)' (128). In his summary of the matter in the *Uxor Hebraica*, Selden stresses that the terms 'presbyter' and 'elder' were commonly used among the Jews; that these officers were assembled in one body whose jurisdiction was so wide as to comprise the whole of religious society; and that otherwise brilliant scholars have mistaken the assembly's jurisdiction as regarding only religious issues, whereas 'the court for religious and sacral matters was one and the same as for secular and non-sacral matters' (129). It is hard to know when these words were written, for Selden was working on the *Uxor* as early as the publication date of *De Jure Naturali*. It is impossible to know how much his conflation of all judicial authority into one body was affected by his experience of the Westminster Assembly with its obligation to report its findings to the Long Parliament.

In the *Uxor Hebraica,* Selden promises to elaborate his thoughts in a *History of Presbyters and Presbyteries,* a promise that scholars have often assumed to have been fulfilled in the treatise on the Great Sanhedrin, which began to appear in instalments in 1650 but was under way much earlier. Yet even as he moves towards the unification of the judicial authority holding all the jurisdiction available in religious society, Selden never abandons – rather, he refines – his belief that there is a domain belonging to the church or, at least, belonging to labourers in the love, grace, and power of the divine spirit. Eventually, Selden's clue to the best means of coordinating these domains comes from an unlikely source, from the condemnatory and reductive charge that he is an 'Erastian.' Prior to and even over the course of his work on the San-hedrin, 'Erastian' is a term or position that Selden must recover from the murk of polemics and reinvent to his satisfaction. In the early 1640s, however, his understanding of 'Presbyterianism' is still very far from clear.

What does emerge clearly from his work of the early to mid-1640s is that Selden was intently participating in debates over the prospect of a new Presbyterian hegemony in English religious society. But his role in this revival was no more to secularize the sacred than it was to conse-crate the secular. He was interested in finding out through the history of Presbyterianism whether its offices and institutions had managed benef-icently to reconcile the conflicting demands of conformity and extem-poraneous spirituality as well as to maximize the contributions made by magistracy, lay spiritual leaders, and clergy in the project of this recon-ciliation. Under the bishops, England had been torn between the car-nality of a royal-cum-parliamentary religion, the excessive rigour of Laudian ecclesiastical courts, and the reeling fantasies of zealots in flight from carnality and tyranny. Selden sought to find in the early 1640s if there was historical evidence for the contemporary claim that a Scottish Presbyterianism, itself without bishops since 1638, was likely to heal the errors and rifts in England.

All the while, Selden was considering how Presbyterian institutions compared with the Judaic Sanhedrin and its charge of integrating nor-mative and mystical warrants. In the *Uxor Hebraica,* for instance, he turns his gloss on the conflict between the Hillelites and Shammaites into an opportunity to explore the leadership of the 'seventy-one judges on the tribunal or Great Sanhedrin,' the so-called Chief and Father (383–7). With the quiet Hillel as its chief and the irritable Shammai as its father, the Sanhedrin erupted into a conflict that, according to Talmudic writers, proved productive 'for the sake of God.' Their key dilemma was this: What should be the role of heavenly inspiration – a heavenly voice or *bath qol*, 'a daughter of a voice,' in settling legal or interpretive disputes? As the Talmudists came to insist upon consultation with such a voice, spirit, or oracle, they also sought to discern the relationship between prophets and elders. Quoting the Jerusalem Gemara at length, Selden relays a similitude with which the rabbis sought to clarify the warrant of the Holy Spirit alongside the warrant of law, especially as they are invoked in turbulent times. The upshot of the similitude is that, whereas prophets needed special, ad hoc, insignias from God, elders were sufficiently familiar in their authority to require no such thing. Yet the elders needed guidelines from the man directed by the voice of God before they could move beyond interpretive and legal impasse (388).

Selden's decision to translate and edit a section of Eutychius's *Annals* in 1642 demonstrates that he was seriously engaged with the history of Presbyterianism and with its singular mode of coordinating the claims of spirit and law in religious society as well as the roles of clergy and laity in the church itself. Published two years prior to the *De Anno Civili* and at a time when major efforts were being made to forestall civil war and reconcile the opposing political and religious affiliations grouped often unwillingly around Parliament and the king, Selden's edition is forthright about its contemporary relevance and hopeful that a balancing act can prevent (rather than painfully spring from) torrid conflict over the make-up of law and religion in England.

Eutychius lived from 877 to 940 and was a patriarch of Alexandria whose history included the world but focused on the church. Writing in Arabic, the patriarch offers his readers a treatment of the early days of his own church, an account in which Selden found much of relevance to the conflicts between bishops and presbyters in his own day. In his preface, Selden remarks that a grave and vexing wound has reopened among his contemporaries concerning the question of the priestly order and its rites of ordination; for supporters of bishops and of presbyters mutually claim their own origin in the early church, and they debate whether the two ranks are similar.[27] Like the calendar, so also clerical offices: Selden purveys his own rigorous scholarship, in this instance steeped in philology, as the vehicle for rectifying the grievances of his own religious society.

Praising Eutychius as the Egyptian Bede for his reliability, the translator-editor-commentator culls a passage that commences its narrative in the ninth year of the emperor Claudius, when the evangelist Mark was dwelling in the city of Alexandria in order to propagate the Christian faith. Having miraculously healed a faithful shoemaker, Mark makes the man the first patriarch of Alexandria, then establishes twelve presbyters, so that when the shoemaker Hananias vacates his office, the next patriarch can be chosen from those twelve, with the remaining eleven consecrating him by means of laying on their hands. Over time, Eutychius reports, presbyters lost their exclusive privilege of choosing and consecrating the patriarch; and bishops were introduced in the Alexandrian province, first three, then twenty. As Selden italicizes in his commentary, however, Eutychius's main point is that at one time the church of Alexandria bestowed on presbyters the authority of ordaining the lead clergy, and that this authority derived from Mark. It was only over time that bishops were established in Egypt as intermediaries between the patriarch and other clergy; for patriarchs (Selden stresses) were decidedly not bishops in that early church, confusions in the nomenclature notwithstanding. 'Because Selden adduced evidence which imputed historical importance to the presbytery,' Ziskind writes, his Eutychius 'was bitterly attacked by church authorities,'[28] since the edition appeared only one year prior to the Westminster Assembly and at a time when there was great support for a national synod as a means of preserving (by reforming) the Church of England. The problem facing Selden in his assessment of a presbytery was not simply whether it might succeed in normalizing spirit and in spiritualizing uniformity. The question remained of exactly what or who a presbyter might be and, moreover, what the Presbyterian organization of the church might entail for the practices of worship.

   In the edition of Eutychius, Selden is not simply adducing evidence for the early existence of 'presbyters.' He is also eager to trace the titles of 'patriarch' and 'episcopus' for information on those fraternities of head priests. For, in their capacity as religious fathers, nurturers, and overseers, they deserved reverence whenever they fulfilled their sacred offices apart from the attractions and compromises of the world. Similarly, he wants to clarify the Arabic and Hebraic etymologies of 'presbyter,' which linked the term to old age, eldership, or senatorial status. Thus, in his commentary on Eutychius, Selden exemplifies the careful recovery of meanings for contemporary terms that require substantial relief from the partisan accretions they have gathered. With its instrumental role in discovering the truths in the inmost part of history, the critic's philology might help to forge the prosperity of English religious society without the extremes of its more insubordinate and conformist factions.

Throughout his commentary on Eutychius, Selden pushes the terms of ecclesiastical debate towards ancient Judaic notions and practices. Among the Jews, he argues, anyone with a superior understanding of the law and its application might be elevated to and consecrated as a presbyter, with the laying on of hands linking initiates into the Great Sanhedrin with the bestowal of doctorates of law in Selden's own day. Selden studies in considerable detail the origin, quality, consecration, number, and effect of ordination vis-à-vis these Jewish judicial presbyters, and he maintains that early Alexandrian Christianity as portrayed by Eutychius was fundamentally Judaic, having its beginning in the thirty-seventh chapter of Numbers (18) where Moses ordains Joshua by divine command (*Eutychii*, commentary, 18).

Along the way, Selden reiterates the simple but vital point that for the Hebrews, lawyers and theologians were essentially the same: thus, presbyters were at once legal sages, consecrated judges, and divines sitting in the large and smaller courts of the land, servants to both the law and to the Holy Spirit resting calmly on them during ordination. For these doctors in the law, the Holy Spirit is a calming influence thereafter too, a spirit of wisdom in judgment rather than a licence to indulge in Antinomianism. The best sacred order for a people, then, comprised not lawyers playing priests, but lawyers truly consecrated in the spirit of God and gifted theologically as well as civilly. Such sages were not identical to the Aaronic priesthood, though a priest might incidentally become a consecrated presbyter. The Aaronic priesthood was an order into which one was born, while eldership was an order into which one was adopted. Joshua was a presbyter, Aaron a priest, and priests qua priests were confined to altar service at sacred functions; in the 1630s Selden had already studied the criteria for the priesthood in the work dedicated to Laud.

Thus, the Great Sanhedrin was not a church, and it was not run by priests; rather, it consisted of a judicial court filled with law sages, though the latter were consecrated in the Holy Spirit for their knowledge of the law governing a religious society. In identifying the Sanhedrin in this fashion, Selden sets aside for the time being the matter of what the 'Holy Spirit' might be, though he will take up this critical matter in his work on the Sanhedrin. In the Eutychius, meanwhile, he does not fully rule out the possibility that the Sanhedrin might be approximated by a synod of divines. Indeed, rather much is left uncertain about the Sanhedrin: Selden is unprepared as yet to set forth his views on that court, never mind his speculation about the cultural and ontological room that it might reserve for spiritual liberty and prophetic zeal.

If Selden is unready to coordinate the Sanhedrin and the Holy Spirit, he is more narrowly concerned in the Eutychius with specifics of religious worship involving the relationship between orthodox formulae and the irreducible workings of the divine spirit. At one extreme, formula converts into oppression; at the other, the warrant of the Holy Spirit is lost in the wanderings of human fancy. With his focus on the phrase 'Eumque benedicerent' (commentary 35), Selden devotes one of his longest notes – about a sixth of the entire commentary – to resolving a controversy that figures centrally in contemporary debates about how to delineate the pure domain and the unworldly labours of spiritual liberty. 'Formulae certae' can hold the church together, but only superficially if the agency of one's own choice or authority – the 'arbitrium' of the individual worshiper – is prevented from venturing interaction with God's divine and gracious spirit within the vicissitudes and circumstances of everyday life.

In debates over the criteria of prayer, Selden knows, this domain and these labours must be readjusted and refashioned within the context of the new modes of lawful uniformity towards which the Church of England was heading in the 1640s. Selden's note strenuously and confidently intervenes in the debate over whether extemporaneous or liturgical prayer better serves true religion (commentary, 35–62). Lamenting the ignorance in evidence on both sides of the contemporary impasse, he examines the Judaic benedictions used by priests in the temple, the formulae, gestures, responses, and other prayers uttered by the Jewish people on a daily and occasional basis. But his aim is to show that the violent controversy over the forms and the spirit of prayer is altogether pointless, and that organized rites and personal wills can be reconciled.

Selden clearly seeks a middle ground between spirit and norm in the matter of prayer, a balance at the centre of the turmoil between extemporaneous zealots and conformist censors. It is easy enough to see how each extreme manages to discover support for its position in the Jewish Bible. On the one hand, Selden notes, the rabbis legitimized prayer without set formulae, numbers, or times in the age from Moses to Ezra. Prayer itself was required in the twenty-third chapter of Exodus (25), and it was considered the chief means of serving God with all one's heart, but it was, indeed, the heart that mattered most in the execution of prayer. On the other hand, Judaic tradition also established formulaic guidelines for prayer – that daily orisons should recount the glory of God's blessings, humbly implore God's help, then praise God's goodness. Jews prayed while standing and directed their prayers towards the temple, yet they did not genuflect, and they offered their own new prayers on a daily basis together with those fulfilling normative stipulations.

Then, in the time of Ezra, Selden explains, custom and tradition were converted into established prayers by those excellent men in the Great Synagogue and Sanhedrin who undertook to rebuild Jewish practices at the end of the Babylonian captivity. At that time, many Jews were uncertain about how to undertake or understand their own ancestral customs, their sacred language, and their holy offerings, all distorted or effaced during their years of intermixture with gentiles. As Selden portrays the matter in his commentary on Eutychius, the Jewish leaders fashioned prayers so that their people might not stammer like children in their efforts to praise God. Selden believed that it was the Great Synagogue of 120 men with Ezra as their leader that did most to remedy that ill. Clearly, he conceives of this body as the ancestor of the national synod called in 1642 as a means of rescuing the English creed, liturgy, and church polity from the slough in which it was largely agreed to be stuck. Even if, as Ziskind says, there is considerable uncertainty over the existence of such a synagogue,[29] it was commonplace in the Jewish tradition that liturgy derived from its wisdom.

In the Jerusalem Gemara, Selden continues, one rabbi maintains that the 120 'presbyters' established these forms for praying from eighty prayers used by the prophets. So the 'daughter of the voice' of God is the source of inspiration for the prayers. To ensure, however, that prayer would flow forth regularly, if variously, after the captivity, the presbyters established set hours as a standard, aiming to raise the minimum supply of prayers. Selden stresses that Judaism always encouraged the addition of new prayers for emergent occasions, even new or altered formulae. In short, two standards operated at once and in harmony: the guidelines for prayers offered according to individual initiative or inspiration, and the slate of required prayers. Of the eighteen prayers devised by the Great Synagogue, the first one and final three were inflexible, but the intermediate fourteen could be augmented or arranged according to the devotion of the heart and soul, in keeping with the vicissitudes of life. In the case of calendars, Selden introduces the Karaites as a model for acknowledging the inconstancy of nature; but for the Great Synagogue, he conceives of a model for encouraging the inner and zealous worship of the scripturalist yet also for rectifying that worship within the normative traditions of a public church (commentary, 42–4).

If the length of his commentary is any indication, Selden's concern with uniting standard and spirit in prayer was deep-seated. From the

beginning of his career, especially in his affiliation with Jonsonian poetics, he was involved in the Stuart search for a normative discourse that
would benefit from both imitation and deviation. Yet the question of
prayer raises the stakes: it is putatively the Holy Spirit, not simply the
human fancy, that must be accommodated within the strictures of set
forms. Selden also was intervening in the debate over prayer at a time in
England's history when there was more than one viable paradigm for set
forms and many more than one inflection of the mysterious ways in
which God's Holy Spirit operated. Most crucially, his Eutychius offers a
scholarly dignity and perspective to a society spiralling out of control
into bloody trauma. Once he developed his views of the Sanhedrin in
the wake of the Civil War, Selden would be more inclined than before
simply to locate all strictly spiritual labours in a domain apart from magistracy, still leaving open the question of the extent to which prayer is a
social ligature or an inner capacity.

Beyond the specific habits of prayer within the church, in the Eutychius Selden explores the prospect of a new church order in the possibility
that some form of Presbyterian organization might be best suited for
rebuilding the Church of England. His discussion of this prospect coin-
cides with the inauguration of that Great Synagogue of the 1640s, the
Westminster Assembly of Divines. He drives home the contemporary relevance of his scholarship on Judaic prayer by tracing the interplay
between formula and invention in modern Judaic communities – in
Spain, Poland, and Germany, among others. At the inmost chamber of
the temple of history, however, Selden does not find nature in the Eutychius but rather the careful and artful coordination of canons and spirit
in the practices of worship. This state of affairs is overseen by presbyters
in a Great Synagogue, and their numbers feature consecrated law sages
whose own fusion of *nomos* and oracle must be internalized in the
prayers of the citizens. In sum, Eutychius helps Selden to translate rabbi
into presbyter on the eve of the Westminster Assembly, at a time when,
in his commentary on the Patriarch, he can quote with approval Avi-
cenna's conviction that set forms of prayer motivate the people to benefit from the memory of God's spirit imprinted on their souls. Without
such commemoration, Selden agrees, devotion is a fleeting thing. Yet he
posits the origin of this coordination of spirit and formula in a fleeting
institution, the Great Synagogue, about which he has little to say. He has
promised a work on the history of Presbyterianism; he is already at work
on the Great Sanhedrin. And he is poised on the brink of his contributions to the Westminster Assembly of Divines.

More than the *De Anno*, the notes to Eutychius offer what is clearly a
form of guidance to his own religious society. His goal in the earlier text
is to curtail conflict, in the later to make use of the undeniable fact that
horrible conflict is occurring. The very selection of a single passage
from the Patriarch is clear and compelling evidence that Selden is seeking to intervene directly in the religious controversy over clerical offices
and church liturgies. But if he is confident in his own ability as a lay
authority to make an impact on the concerns of the church, this optimism is prompted in no small measure by the shift from the bishops'
hegemony to the consideration of Presbyterian notions of church polity,
and to the prevalence of such thinking among participants in the Long
Parliament as well.

Even in 1642, however, Selden was more sceptical and scholarly than
he was dogmatic; he did not leave the evidence to speak for itself, but
neither did he exactly pronounce upon it. As pioneer and ambassador,
his role was more one of seeking out material, of fashioning a vehicle
for that material, of helping select readers to understand it, and of ges-
turing towards the remedial uses of history. Yet just as Selden was compelled to distance himself from holiday scholarship in the work for
Laud, even the commentator on Eutychius faced the dilemma of how
far to elaborate constructs of religious society for the sake of historical
accuracy, and how far for the sake of actualizing the hope that the long-
lost Canaan of a lawful yet boundless spirituality could be regained in
England. It is true that his translation of Eutychius's Arabic into Latin
expanded the domestic and international audience of that history considerably, but Selden's Latin kept the arbitration of religious conflict
within the domain of the legal and clerical scholar, in contrast to his
work in the Westminster Assembly that was carried out in English
among men of highly varied levels of education. It is not surprising that
in that Assembly Selden's authority derived almost entirely from his languages and his learning. Even while the scholar commited himself to
the recovery of Judaic rites, institutions, and formulae, he and his contemporaries were faced with the more immediate problem of what kind
of person must embody the rescued abstraction within the circumstances of a peculiar society.

—— 6 ——

Although the Westminster Assembly began its work as a review by three
committees of the articles of the church, it soon received orders from

the Long Parliament (to which it was answerable) for its divines and laymen to undertake an overhaul of English church discipline. According
to Benjamin Warfield, its charge was to advise Parliament 'in its prosecution of the task of reconstituting the government, discipline, and worship of the Church of England.'[30] Even though the status quo prelacy in
the church had recently been abolished, many of the assembled advisers
held out some hope that a reformed episcopacy might replace the old,
degenerate one. But once the Covenant was signed with Scotland and
the Scottish commissioners had arrived, the divines began to shift their
discussion away from bishops in the direction of Presbyterianism, that
church polity in which preachers, teachers, lay elders, and deacons
divided the offices of Christianity among them. More controversially, it
was a polity according to which single congregations were represented
locally in classic presbyteries, the latter again in synods, and those
synods in a national assembly. Perhaps most problematical of all, the
English Presbyterians of the 1640s, their allies in the Long Parliament
notwithstanding, came to understand their crusade in the Westminster
Assembly as one in which the freedom of the church must be saved from
the clutches of civil intervention, even as these same Presbyterians
began to clamp down on the religious toleration that (it was feared
among them) they themselves had unleashed.

Many staunch critics of the bishops' church put stock in the future of
Presbyterianism, even if they soon withdrew that stock. In the early 1640s
they cherished its apparent grant of autonomy to the congregation; its
strong scriptural authority; its congruence with the reformed churches
on the Continent; its accent on lay participation in the governance of
the church; and its broadening representation of the flock the higher up
the chain of command one went. But as the divines in the Westminster
Assembly began debate on the viability of this polity, the Presbyterian dispensation of judicial authority and coercion in the church led former
sympathizers such as Milton to comment that '*New Presbyter* is but *Old
Priest* writ Large.'[31]

Although the participants in the Assembly did not state the case so
baldly, their options for the coordination of lawful uniformity and
capacious spirituality in the new English church were reducible to four:
(a) reform the prelacy so that it wields its authority with the spiritual
warrant and Christian motivations of the overseers in the early church;
(b) shift the power of, say, ordination and excommunication to the Presbyterian polity, so that congregations are united by means of an
overarching structure without the tyranny and carnality of the bishops;

(c) permit each congregation to take care of all the Christian offices, whether they be preaching or excommunication; and (d) bifurcate civil and spiritual realms so that all public judgment, regulation, and punishment – including excommunication – are deemed appropriate for civil authority, and all spiritual labours for the church. The irony of the Westminster Assembly is that in the increasingly normative view of the Presbyterians, the enemies of true religion were, together, the Independents (option c) and the so-called Erastians (option d). So it was that the caricatured 'Statists' or 'Civilians' (including Selden) and 'Congregationalists' or 'Independents' (men resembling Milton's position in the 1640s) were lumped together by Presbyterian sympathizers as inflicting civil tyranny and religious anarchy on the true religionists of England. For the Presbyterians, whose initiative had been gained from that most dishonourable war carried out by Charles I against the Scots, true religion was understood as embodying the consensus of the European reformed churches on how lay persons and clergy should cooperate in the achievement of a righteous ecclesiastical polity most agreeable to the predestinator whose gracious but wilful dispensation was laid out exclusively in the scriptures.

Before Selden became one of the chief bogeys plaguing the Presbyterians, it is easy to see why he was welcomed as a law sage to convene with the divines in their crucial synod. A cursory reading of the notebook of John Lightfoot makes it plain that Selden was viewed as a touchstone of scholarly authenticity for the Assembly's learned exploration of church history, scripture, the church fathers, and the liturgical tradition. Early on in the proceedings, Selden was 'appointed to search for the most authentic copies of the thirty-nine articles'; reported on 'seven translations of the Bible' regarding how they render Jesus' supposed descent into hell; provided expert testimony on Hebraic institutions; glossed difficult terms in ancient languages; and proposed methodical approaches to convoluted questions.[32]

As the debate over church government became heated and protracted, Selden's name was transformed in the rhetoric of the Presbyterians from the watchword of scholarly legitimacy to a code term for the folly and profanity of secularizing the judicial authority and coercive powers of the church. And even though the usage was a reckless one, they liked to call him and his ilk 'Erastians.' According to Robert Baillie, the Erastians and the Independents made strange bedfellows in the Assembly as those parties eager to evacuate the church of any regulatory and coercive office. It was Selden, together with the Independents, he complains, 'who will have no discipline at all in any church *jure divino*, but settled only upon the free will and pleasure of the Parliament.' Baillie worries that 'the Independents and Civilians' will undermine the English church by imposing on it 'Erastus' way'; and he blames 'especiallie the lawyers, whereof they are many,' for 'believing in no Church government to be of divine right, but all to be a humane constitution, depending on the will of the magistrates.'[33]

Ironically, it was the conflation of Selden with the Independents that clarified his position in the Assembly more than the tag 'Erastian' that Selden himself did not yet fully understand. Selden resembled the Independents, however, only if one slant is put on an ambiguity in the Independent position itself. For Independency can entail either that a congregation wields any judicial, censorial, constitutive, and condemnatory powers with which the church holds any truck, or that the church holds no truck whatever with any such worldly power. It is the latter position that Selden would corroborate – the church must be kept pure by being concealed apart from the flesh and force of the world – but as with any position of segregation, this one could be read as either protecting or emasculating the spiritual labours of the church.

Congregationalist rhetoric is often quite subtle in its representation of Christ's magistracy. When Katherine Chidley separates the power that magistrates wield over the 'bodies, estates, and lives' of their subjects from the authority that Christ owns over their consciences, the neatness of her analysis is meant to free the Saviour himself from having to 'sit at the Magistrats footestoole.' But this clean rendition of the separate debts owed to Caesar and to Christ leaves open the question of whose office it is to ordain a minister or to excommunicate an egregious sinner. To declare that Christ has bestowed on each congregation 'all that power and authority which is in any way needful for the carrying on that order in worship and discipline' is to leave unclear or unsaid what the scope and mechanism of those 'needful' powers might be. At times the Independent will stress that the labours of the church are 'purely spiritual'; but there is potentially a world of difference between what is pure and what is necessary.[34]

In *The Reason of Church Government* (1642), Milton interjects an analysis and a defence of the Independent position into what remains a case for a Presbyterianism that he would in two years time come to loathe. Most simply, he aims to explain how the church can retain its 'spiritual efficacy' only if it jettisons the 'temporal support' of coercion otherwise known as 'the false vizard of worldly authority.' The church, he argues, should owe thanks only to 'the mighty operation of the Spirit,' not to the 'way of civil force and jurisdiction.'[35] As is typically the case with Milton, however, the idealism of fundamental principles must reckon with the practical matter of means, lest actual society leave religion languishing in what Milton elsewhere calls 'Atlantic and Utopian polities, which never can be drawn into use' and so 'will not mend our condition.'[36]

In order to ground the strict division between civil and church realms in the practices of the world, Milton offers a taxonomy of punishment, the upshot of which is a dualism between 'two sorts of cure, the church and the magistrate.' Whereas the church is meant to cure the diseases of the soul, the magistrate is supposed to attend the 'outward man'; but Milton's dualism readily softens into a monistic spectrum of differences by degree. The 'outward man' is defined in biblical terms as 'the mind in all her outward acts.' What is more, the decidedly coercive strategies of the magistrate – the levels of which Milton compares to variously severe medical and surgical operations – have the potential beyond their service to the 'outward peace and welfare of the commonwealth' to send messages or light to the soul. Milton works hard for just the right metaphor – for the one that will permit civil authority to influence the soul without 'once touching the inward bed of corruption and that hectic disposition to evil, the source of all vice and obliquity against the rule of law.'[37] For to touch the soul is to force it and, therefore, to violate the true and free spirit of religion. Similarly, even though Milton separates the civil and the religious realms, he conceives of them as mutually supportive in their opposition to prelacy and tyranny – in part because the prelates and tyrants have joined forces, in part because, in apocalyptic terms, the only operative distinction is between the blessed and the damned.

Whereas Milton's magistrate contributes from a distance to the spiritual medicine of the church while attending in the main to 'the rule of law,' his lay congregations and their ministers are best equipped to censure the soul without lapsing 'into civil force and jurisdiction.' But he must make the case for such local and spiritual censure so cautiously that he prevents the carnality of force from creeping in. At first boldly, he likens the pressure applied by the church community to the shame experienced by epic heroes when they acted ignobly before their peers. Thus, just as Hector could not abandon the Trojan battlefield for fear of 'honorable shame,' so, too, Christians hold 'the reverence of [their] elders ... brethren, and friends' as 'the greatest incitement to virtuous deeds and the greatest dissuasion from unworthy attempts that might be.'[38] In a similar vein, Thomas Goodwin distinguishes between excommunication as a 'political power' and a censure more appropriate to the church, by means of which 'one presbytery may take recognizance of the miscarriage of another, call them to account, and declare it, and withdraw from them.'[39]

Milton, however, is always suspicious about, if not fully hostile towards, any herd mentality with its extraneous, carnal, and even tyrannical customs. The pressures of fame and shame appeal to nobler minds, he notes in 'Lycidas,' but they are nonetheless indicative of mortal 'infirmity.' So, too, in *The Reason of Church Government*, Milton retreats from the merit of external, communal valuation in order to internalize its censure. As God is the source of true conscientious fame in 'Lycidas,' so God and conscience are the monitors of internal shame or 'esteem' in *The Reason of Church Government*. Esteem depends on whether Christians bear an 'inward reverence toward their own persons'; its basis is the rational image of God in which they are created and the price paid for the reclamation of that image in the sacrifice of Christ. Its outgrowth is the autobiographical impulse found in *The Reason of Church Government* itself and in Milton's sonnets, other prose, two epics, and tragedy. Lest we think that in moving from shame to esteem, Milton has simply abandoned the communal pressure of congregations for the purified authority of the Holy Spirit interpreting the Bible to the individual conscience, he exchanges the dualistic language of 'two sorts' for the monistic notion of difference in degree. In arguing that esteem is 'a more ingenuous and noble degree of honest shame,' Milton pursues what Rosenblatt considers his Judaic, as against his Pauline, insistence on keeping law and spirit ontologically proximate.[40]

So, too, in his sonnets, Milton praises the Independent Henry Vane for possessing the rare wisdom 'to know / Both spiritual power and civil, what each means, / What severs each ... The bounds of either sword to thee wee owe.' Still, what this rare sense of profitable segregation means for Milton is that 'Therefore on thy firm hand religion leans / In peace, and reck'ns thee her eldest son.'[41] It is the same in his sonnets to Cromwell and in his praises for the Long Parliament in his prose: the separation of church and civil power depends at long last on the wisdom and support of statesmen. Yet, in turn, his statesmen are only as wise as the extent to which the Holy Spirit interprets the scriptures to their individual consciences or repairs the ruins of the fall in their right reason. In effect, the proper coordination of civil jurisdiction, communal pressure, and right rational autonomy is exceedingly difficult to stabilize, even if the Erastian and Independent models can be neat in taxonomy.

Whereas the Presbyterians meant only to abuse the Erastians and Independents by lumping them together, they were closer to the truth of what was becoming Selden's case in the 1640s than their caricatures would have allowed or revealed. In his work on the Great Sanhedrin, Selden devotes massive scholarly effort to coordinating yet separating the various warrants of civil jurisdiction, spiritual labour, and, somewhere in the middle, the dynamic of communal support and shame. But Selden's construction of the Judaic court and the religious society around it steers as far clear of Milton's rejection of custom, tradition, and censorial judges as it does of the Laudian insistence on the supreme and almost solitary authority of canonical rigour. Selden finds in ancient Judaism a model for reinventing the relationship among judicial courts, the ministry, the conscience, and the local community as each plays its appropriate part in the establishment of a godly and lawful society.

In the mid-1640s, then, it is not surprising that Milton recognizes his kinship with 'our illustrious Selden,' especially given the *Uxor Hebraica*'s liberation of divorce from the clutches of canon law. Milton celebrates the author of *De Jure Naturali et Gentium* for his 'exquisite' and 'almost mathematically demonstrative' argument 'that all opinions, yea errors, known, read, and collated, are of main service and assistance toward the speedy attainment of what is truest.'[42] That is, the poet-cum-propagandist interprets Selden's commitment to liberty as belonging fully on the side of the sectarian and apocalyptic reconstitution of the body of truth in the wartime of the 1640s. No doubt Milton approved of the recompense received by Selden at the time for the damages that he had suffered under Charles I.

Although Selden's tendencies in the Westminster Assembly sometimes dovetail with Milton's radicalism, and both men would agree on the benefits of a Sanhedrin as a governing body,[43] they were by no means identical in their views of what it meant to reach a Canaan in which spirit and law could lie down together like the lamb and the lion. At long last Selden had found his way into a proper office in the temple, as a prominent lay and non-partisan assessor in the synod for reinventing the Church of England; but he was also beginning properly to reinvent Erastianism, the name with which he had been attacked. His key model for this invention would be his own scholarly fiction or invention of the Great Sanhedrin. Thus, in the record kept by John Lightfoot of the proceedings at Westminster, one can see his concerns emerging concurrent with, yet distinctive from, the arguments of such Independents as Thomas Goodwin and Philip Nye.[44] Simply, Selden's last known position on how to coordinate law and spirit held that the spiritual labours of the church, the lawful peace of the commonwealth, the liberties of the conscience, and the productive dynamics of the community can thrive together only if all legally coercive power (as against neighborly shame) is relegated to the civil authority. But the recovery of the Sanhedrin would prove an impediment, as well as the key, to transferring this position from the polities of New Atlantis and Utopia to the topsy-turvy society in which English Protestants actually lived.

———— 7 ————

Looking back on the seventeenth century, modern scholars such as John Neville Figgis and Robert S. Paul have understood that Selden was groping towards, rather than confidently presupposing, the dimensions and dictates of his so-called Erastianism.[45] Above all, they have grasped that neither Erastus nor Selden sought to subsume the church or religion within civil authority. Opposing the Presbyterian jurisdiction over excommunication, Selden and the so-called Erastians are rather less clear than the Independents about what labours remain for the church after such jurisdiction is gone.

The Erastian position held that officers of the church might use persuasion and even something like shame on its members, but not force or excommunication. In dubbing Selden the vain 'head' of the Erastian party, one contemporary attempted to clarify this distinction when he noted its basis in the argument that the Jewish state differed from the church, and that the two realms divided the Sanhedrin between them, one court being civil, the other ecclesiastical. Selden disagrees with splitting the Sanhedrin into a civil and a church court; at the Westminster Assembly, he tends to speak of a greater and a lesser Sanhedrin, both of them civil but one national and the other local. Yet his contemporary Robert Baillie captures the notion – not shared by all their contemporaries – that Judaism featured a split between the power of the judge and the labours of the priest; and, as Figgis points out, Erastus himself 'does not touch doctrine, and therefore gives the magistrate no power over truth.'[46] This division was precisely the one that Selden had to refashion into a holistic religious society overseen by the one Great and many Small Sanhedrins.

In the *Table Talk*, Selden would complain that 'presbiters have the greatest power of any Clergie in the World, & gull the Laytie most' (113). With regard to Selden's intellectual development, the paradox of the Westminster Assembly was that, in that forum for his greatest involvement as a lawyer in the remaking of the church, Selden began to consider the possibility that there can be no satisfactory or normative fusion of law and spirit. The two might be coordinated in their separate spheres but not fundamentally constitutive of one another in any onto-logical sense. As Figgis says of Erastianism, truth and policy would inhabit their distinctive domains; for 'It is the impossibility of two co-equal jurisdictions in a State which strikes Erastus.' Pastors could use means of persuasion on man's conscience, but not jurisdictional force on his body or property; as Richard Baxter stated the point (quoted by Figgis), the power of pastors was 'only persuasive, though authoritative and by divine appointment; and ... pastors were officers of God's institu-tion, who were not only to persuade by sermons general and special, but by particular oversight of their particular flocks.' Baxter adds for clarifi-cation that 'as pastors they had no secular or forcing power; and that unless the magistrate authorised them as his officers they could not touch men's bodies or estates, but had to do with conscience only.'[47]

As he came to understand the sixteenth-century Erastus, Selden would have agreed to some extent that 'The main object then of Erastus was not to magnify the State, nor to enslave the Church, but to secure the liberty of the subject.'[48] After all, Selden's motto elevated liberty above all other goods and in all considerations; but increasingly in the 1640s Selden, like Milton, was committed to the idea that liberty in-volved the moral-cum-civic duties and religious obligations of the self as much as it loosened the false political, customary, and ecclesiastical bonds imposed on the self. Liberty demanded precisely the right bal-ance between the rigours of justice and the flexibility of charity; it required that each self be simultaneously tied to and untied from the ligatures of a religious society. For liberty was not licence in either the restrictive sense of censorship or the libertine sense of debauchery.

At first, Selden's interest in Erastus was provoked by caricatures of his own views in the Westminster Assembly as 'Erastian,' but once he under-took an exploration of Erastus, he became an advocate and purveyor of the genuine meaning of the sixteenth-century physician's body of work. To some extent, the tumult of the 1640s was at odds with Erastus's premise that his polity is best suited for a commonwealth in which reli-gion is settled and unified: in the records of the Assembly, we are constantly reminded of the war and chaos outside its Westminster hermitage, and the debate within the Assembly was often heated and intricate. Even though his explanations to the Assembly of the Sanhedrin's civil jurisdiction were usually presented in a spirit of honest enquiry, Selden's remarks became increasingly hostile towards the Presbyterians. Like Milton, he had come to believe that their vision of church polity was licentious – of benefit neither to the strictures of law nor to the goodness and bounty of spiritual dispensations.

The very charge of the Assembly was conflictual. On the one hand, it was instructed by the Long Parliament to secure order and peace in the national church. On the other, it was charged with finding true religion according to scripture and the analogy of the reformed churches, 'to reform the Church and to provide a theologically viable and ecclesiastically workable system of church government to take the place of the established order swept away by Parliament.'[49] To the latter end, they laboured over scriptural and traditional church officers and offices, one by one. They debated which biblical texts to use as well as the meaning of those texts. Even as they theorized the nature of church government, the assembled divines and lay assessors were often asked to practise governance on the heightened threats to the church, not least on blasphemous profanity and on antinomian spirituality. It was never made clear whether this synod of divines had power, owed power, laboured with the Holy Spirit, or enforced some canon of laws on a variety of transgressors.

In his recorded remarks to the Assembly, Selden seldom lost sight of the exploratory nature of their work and of their need for method, clarity, and accuracy. As his colleagues recognized, one of their hardest challenges was to decide how far to base their desiderata on Judaic models, whether because their knowledge of those models could never be so sufficient or because, as Lord Saye protested, the Judaic model of the church in relationship to civil authority was highly confused and flawed.[50] Pressure was heightened by Parliament, which hurried the Assembly in its work lest a diseased religion die while it was on the surgeon's table. But Selden led the way in urging the Assembly to carry out its office at once cautiously and expediently. Lightfoot notes that 'Mr. *Selden* desired that the business of excommunication might first be looked upon, for that very much may be said to prove, that there is no excommunication at all; and for that, in this kingdom, ever since it was a kingdom, Christian excommunication hath ever been by a temporal power.' Lightfoot agrees: 'This motion had good cause to be taken notice of'; it is a motion at once searching and confident, at once a recommendation for efficient method and a principled provocation to controversial scholarship.[51] As a law sage playing the divine quite convincingly, Selden gives the clarion call for what might be mutually destructive needs, the one to bring about some semblance of law and order, the other to creep gradually towards a surprising truth.

In his other contributions to the Westminster discussion, Selden adopted – or was perceived to be adopting – two very different personae. One was the adventurer in the foreign lands of Judaic discourse, a scout for religious truth admired by Laud at one end of the religious spectrum and by Milton at the other end. But the other persona might well differently justify the epithet of 'moderate Protestant' awarded to him, as well as its conflation with the Independents in the remark found in Lightfoot's journal that, according to 'one *Ogle*, a prisoner in Winchester-house,' the hope for the King and his church depended on whether 'the moderate Protestant and fiery Independent could be brought to withstand the Presbyterian.'[52] This Selden held onto the value of a reformed episcopacy and spoke the famous formulas regarding the civil administration of religious affairs found in the *Table Talk*. After all, Selden had characterized his scouting mission as a service to the conformist Laudian vision of the church, a vision that nonetheless retained considerable power over the church in the church itself.

One persona was happy to explore the benefits of a multitude of ecclesiastical permutations. The other cared more passionately about preserving the rule of law in a time when the antinomian 'fancy' could not be trusted to remain in a designated space or to cohere, however loosely, to a normative coordination between civil force and spiritual labour. The formulaic Selden triumphs over the exploratory one in the *Table Talk*, though the alter ego is still very much in evidence, but the exploratory Selden was on display at the Assembly, even if a more formulaic one was in the making. Thus, he desired 'to consider what is the effect of, or what follows upon, Ordination'; made a 'motion, that in our votes, when we come near an equality, the scribes should take account of how many negatives there be, and how many affirmatives'; offered a brief history of the laws of ordination in England; made a recommendation that 'our proposition should be taken into its proper pieces, that every one might know what to speak'; agreed with a recommendation that the divines 'leave ... metaphysical terms, and fall upon Scripture'; and argued extensively that the early Christians were a sect of Judaism and that, as such, they supported the practice of relegating excommunication to the civil jurisdiction of the Sanhedrin.[53] Indeed, in his work on the Sanhedrin, Selden sought to bring a normative coordination of civil authority and spiritual labour out of an extraordinary investigation of the truth about the Sanhedrin; and in his magisterial Judaic construct, he hoped to restore to Erastus his genuine meaning and purpose, even if this meant revisiting all his previous notions of how spirit and law might best come together. The work on the Sanhedrin offered the distant prospect of the reunion of poetry, positive law, nature, and a pure and spiritual church left to its own devices. It also offered the prospect that Selden's two personae, the scholar and the activist, might converge.

At the Westminster Assembly, Selden took seriously the role of lay assessor in a synod of the church, and he strove to articulate those essentials on which the divines would have to agree in order to justify the institution of a Presbyterian polity. Meanwhile, the 'Erastian' Selden was being forged in the polemical fire into what his friend Bulstrode Whitelock saw as the gadfly of those Presbyterians who cloaked ecclesiastical tyranny in the garb of ignorant exegesis. Selden held out the possibility that the Holy Spirit required a truth far purer than the laws of the world, and a behaviour far more elevated than the concessive dictates of positive and natural law. Yet he also sought to ensure that claims on the Spirit did not undo law, that the increasingly vocal English Antinomians of the 1640s would never realize their vision of a Canaan without its canon.

Throughout the Westminster debates over excommunication, the name 'Sanhedrin' was on everyone's lips. This speaker dubbed it a civil court, another made it spiritual and ecclesiastical, a third doubled the court so that it might divide its identity into both realms, and a fourth declared Judaic institutions so thoroughly mixed in church and state that it was impossible to make Christian sense or use of that model. Selden maintained that early Christianity itself was reformed Judaism, and thus its worshippers fell under the jurisdiction of the Sanhedrin. Attempts to make sense of the Sanhedrin grew convoluted as well as partisan, Thomas Goodwin explaining that 'The Lord hath not made the like institution to the Sanhedrim in the Christian church; for to the Jews there was a representative government, because there was a representative worship; and the government was in the place of worship; and he [Goodwin] gave this analogy: that as, in a particular congregation, the people must be present, so in the classical, should they be.' Lightfoot reveals that at this point Goodwin was interrupted for diverging from 'the argument in hand.' On the basis of the evidence in the Westminster

Assembly, it is clear that Selden's colleagues were much taken with the prospect of discovering Hebraic templates for their reinvention of English religion. It is equally clear, however, that the Sanhedrin itself must be reinvented. For virtually every time that a divine or lay partici-pant in the Assembly introduced Judaic institutions, according to Light-foot, these propositions 'cost some exceptions and debate.'[54]

chapter six

The Hope of Israel

The final decade of Selden's life, 1645–54, was arguably England's most tumultuous and experimental period vis-à-vis the constituents of a social and political order understood by its inhabitants and brokers as comprehensively religious. At the outset of that decade, the New Model Army was created, organized, and unleashed upon the military forces backing the king. In the years that followed, that new army not only won the civil war and quashed counter-revolutionary resurgence; it also grew to sponsor a forum in which the political and spiritual goals of the war were examined, radicalized, and debated. As the Presbyterians and the Scots were either paralysed by the growing radicalism or fervently committed to returning to the fold of the king, the remainder of the army once solidly behind Parliament confronted the fissures in its own, never fully unified vision for England: Levellers sought out major reform in the franchise, constitutional balance, and legal system; Grandees defended the primacy of property in nonetheless pressing for social justice, moral reform, representational government, and a zealously purified religion. In one man, Oliver Cromwell, were all these goals embodied, a complexity that prompted his leadership, seriatim, in negotiating with the king for the restoration of balanced government; in purging Parliament and engineering the trial and execution of the king; in establishing a unicameral republic whose executive was a Council of State; in dissolving that Parliament and setting up a house of nominated senators-cum-saints in an ad hoc institution compared by its advocates to the Jewish Sanhedrin and ridiculed by its opponents as the 'Barebones' Parliament; finally, in striving to preserve and advance the cause of justice, reform, and true religion by undertaking to serve as lord protector together with Parliament and the Council of State.

During the same period there were many changes: the abolition of the Church of England; largely failed attempts at setting up a national Presbyterian church; subsequent efforts to establish a loosely organized national church of primarily autonomous congregations; gathered churches such as the Baptists, both General (non-Calvinist) and Particular (Calvinist); militant apocalyptic sects such as the Fifth Monarchists; communistic movements such as the Diggers; and elusive, partly fictional antinomians such as the so-called Ranters and Seekers, for whom anything outside the grace-filled inner self was idolatrous and carnal formality. The discursive air of England was tremulous with the inventive and competitive theories of Hobbes and Harrington, Baxter and Milton, classical republicans and saintly theocrats, all of them with bold ideas about what should be done to reshape the religious and political framework of English society, indeed, to transform English society itself. Meanwhile, there was in corners, homes, and hearts a powerful longing for the *locus amoenus* that was merry old England, with its common prayers, shared rites and festivals, and its government according to king, Commons, and Lords. When Cromwell was offered the kingship, the motivation was not flattery but rather familiarity; so, too, when the Council of State was called the Privy Council, or the Protectorate government proposed a second house of parliament, the 'Other House.' The Cromwellian government also was faced with the exigencies of quashing radicalism – of putting down Leveller mutinies, resisting the lawlessness of the antinomians or militancy of the Fifth Monarchists, and penalizing the Quaker James Nayler in 1656 for riding into Exeter in imitation of Christ. The apocalyptic criterion of readmitting the Jews into England was fervently discussed but not finally delivered. In 1660, of course, the king, the Church of England, and the House of Lords were restored.

Selden's reconstruction of the Great Sanhedrin, and of the comprehensive religious society that radiated outward from that governing body, was a learned contribution to this public ferment of ideas. In private, too, at his table, he returned time and again to discussions of the various types of clerical offices known in his day and to the best possible relations between civil magistracy and true spirituality. He would try on ecclesiastical options for size, then weigh their benefits and pitfalls. In imagining what institutions and arrangements might best suit English society, he continued to play the priest, posing the question of when he 'should thinke [him] selfe most in [his] office' in the event that he were ordained in the ministry (*Table Talk*, 102). For him, playing the priest was a complex act of impersonation, for it demonstrated how fervently he wanted those sacred offices to be rectified and purified, only alongside with his aggressive lay appropriation and civil suspicion of their putative secrets. In remarking that civil authorities must oversee a synod in order to ensure that the divines did not ruin the civil works, Selden once again invaded the domain of the clergy, but he also limited the rationale for the infiltration to the interests of the magistracy.

Whatever domain the Selden of the 1640s and 1650s was prepared to surrender to the labourers in the spirit, however, there can be no question that in assuming the authority to explain tithes, inheritance laws, and marriage rites, and in setting up the Sanhedrin as the chief normative arbiter in a godly society, Selden carved away at the traditional domain of the canon law – and he did so on behalf of legal sages outside the ordination of the church. In the *Table Talk*, he is said to have judged lay intellectuals the Bible's very best interpreters (11); and, on more than one occasion, the *Table Talk* records his opinion that, rightly understood, the jurisdiction of the church is civil and that the legal warrant of the church depends on the magistrates of a Christian state. That collection of Selden's memorable bits of conversation has no dearth of anticlerical remarks.

Yet Selden never relinquished the idea – indeed he grew virtually obsessed with its significance and complexity – that the right ministerial order must be found and that, once found and properly established, it would afford religious society the seeds of holiness that no civil authority could ever plant or cultivate. Allowing, for example, that the Caroline bishops 'have done ill,' he is scarcely prepared to condemn their 'function' as irredeemable (*Table Talk*, 21). Rather, he supposes in a conversation at table that even if the episcopacy is destroyed, some office similar in nature must be devised in its place. A holy order of priests is so vital to a religious society that, in Selden's view, the legal sages of that society must do everything in their power to rectify, reinvent, or improve it. Accordingly, his remarks about the offices, arts, and aims of the clergy are as exploratory and torqued as his assertions of an overarching civil jurisdiction are calm and pat. The Judaic scholarship of his final years is given over not to erasing the holiness of the church, the autonomy of the clergy, the zeal produced by the Holy Spirit, or the powerful dictates of the conscience – and this, on behalf of the state's needs and preferences. Instead, Selden attempts to construct a model of a comprehensive religious society within which all the contributors to the prosperity of that godly and lawful unit can have their properly coordinated places. Places also are reserved for poets as well as lawyers, for natural philosophers as well as spiritual labourers cultivating the otherworldly fruits of grace. Outside his study in London there was an extraordinary experiment under way in the shape and destiny of civil magistracy, legal authority, and spiritual dispensations; and the experiment extended not only to each of these matters in turn but crucially to the question of how they articulated with each other. From the folksy quips that he made so often at table to the uncommonly learned and bold venture that he took into the history of an alien people, the Jews, Selden understood that England's religious society had never before been so promisingly malleable and never before so helpless and perilous.

In the *Table Talk*, Selden stresses that all jurisdiction is civil rather than spiritual, and he often lambastes a clergy that is all too apt to forget this simple division of responsibilities. There is no question that Selden, as he is represented in that collection of bons mots, is repelled by the vocation of the clergy as they are often exemplified in his time. He attributes the very doctrine of original sin to a clerical desire for insurance that baptism will remain popular; and he flouts the clergy with the superiority of laymen in biblical exegesis, even as he complains about the democratization of exegetical warrant (31). Conceding that 'there never was a more learned Clergie' than the present class, he quips that they also 'have worse faults' than their predecessors (32), reflecting the commonplace complaint that the Caroline prelacy had fallen away from the high standard of preaching set by their Jacobean forebears.[1] Selden punctures the source of any number of clerical inflations, including the arrogance of consular appeals to the Holy Ghost; the perverse attraction of audiences to preachers who damn them in 'long' and 'lowd' sermons; and the trickery by which the clergy 'gain upon mens fancyes' in pretending to cast out devils (*Table Talk*, 39–41).

It is hard to say whether Selden's anti-clerical sentiments fall in line with the long tradition of estates satire that he so admired from early in his studies of English poetry, or represent his Hobbesian vision of a present and a future in which the clergy are entirely disenfranchised, or both. It is possible, too, that the *Table Talk* is as much a compiler's fashioning of Selden's values as it is direct reportage of those values. The relationship between Selden's work on the Sanhedrin, the contemporary logic that conflated his Erastianism with Independency, and the

underscoring of the civil nature of jurisdiction in the *Table Talk* begins to
emerge, however, when the clerical fault that in his reported conversation trumps all the others is equally the one whose reversal might well
restore the clergy to their legitimate, entirely spiritual offices. As Constantine once discovered, Selden explains, the clergy have a penchant
'to be Judges of matters they understood not.' In response, the emperor
altered the structure of authority in his empire so that the clergy would
be encouraged to deal only in the spiritual offices of religion, leaving
excommunication to the domain of civil punishment for 'matters concerning adultery, Tythes, Wills &c.' Selden adds that the desire for
power over excommunication is the prominent blemish on contemporary Presbyterians (46). But he does not simply fault the clergy for their
meddling in civil affairs; in addition, he devotes much of his conversation to discussing the arts and duties that are far more appropriate to
warranted labourers in the spirit. If 'Glorious,' the church itself is compared to a banquet at which each guest finds something agreeable to
eat; but, Selden adds, no one appreciates the impressive variety of the
entire feast: each 'chooses out of it his owne Religion by which he Gov-
erns himselfe & letts ye rest alone' (29). It is unclear whether this per-
sonalized consumption is healthy for either the guest or the host.

Nonetheless, Selden is concerned to appreciate the gifts of the spirit
with which the comers to the feast are graced. 'If I [were] a Minister,'
he imagines, 'I should thinke my selfe most in my office, reading of
prayers & dispenceing of the Sacram[en]^{t}s' (102). This emphasis on
prayer leads him to establish a ground for the meeting of formula and
spirit. 'Admitt the preacher prayes by the Spiritt,' he supposes, it
remains the case that 'Sett formes are a paire of Compasses' by which
the people are best guided (103). As in his edition of Eutychius, however, the matter is not so simple: admit that set forms discourage people
from the laxity of saying whatever they will to God, it remains the case
that if the 'people must not thinke a thought towards God but as their
pastors putt it into their mouthes,' the clergy 'will make right sheepe of
us.' He adds: 'The English preists would doe that in English wch the
Romish doe in Latine, Keep the people in Ignorance, but some of y^e
people outdoe them att their owne game' (*Table Talk*, 103). The
extremes of unbridled spirit and inflexible formulae produce competing degrees of ignorance, yet history nonetheless tends towards these
extremes, towards fiery then sluggish humours that, according to John
Denham in 'Cooper's Hill,' have alternately wreaked havoc on the harmony and welfare of English society throughout its Christian history.

Selden himself predicts, 'Wee have been a while much taken with this praying by the spiritt, but in time wee may grow weary of it & wish for our Comon prayer' (104).

As recorded in the *Table Talk*, Selden's conversation on preaching is as extensive as his views on any other subject. Unsurprisingly so: in the last decades of Selden's life, preaching was the ministerial labour most precarious yet also most promising for dispensing both conformity and inspiration to English Protestant society. Preaching can strengthen the canonical and moral ties that bind that society together, or drive the members of that society into fancies and factions. At times, Selden's bolder comments on preaching deny the survival of its holy warrant in a contemporary England running wild with sermons. In the early days of Christianity, he argues, preaching was intended 'to tell the Newes of Christs comeing into the World,' and obviously, this task has been accomplished (104). Accordingly, in the work on the Great Sanhedrin, Selden characterizes those law sages whose chief role it was to teach in lecture settings rather than to pass judgment in the court. For he would have his English audience understand that rabbis were theologians as well as lawyers, that Jewish law and spirituality were tightly bound together if not finally identical, and that the public discourse of rabbis amounted to a kind of judicial sermonizing.

In the work on the Sanhedrin, as in the *Table Talk*, however, Selden is also eager to map out the space in which spirituality would thrive apart from the Assize and the law sages, whether it pertains to priests having temple service or to more zealous forms of religious inspiration. When he turns to fashion the continuing role for preaching in the church, Selden has considerable advice for preachers and their audiences. It is especially important for auditors to remember that any preacher's claim on revealing the 'meaning of the Holy Ghost' is, in fact, his code for demonstrating the processes by which the minister is attempting to accommodate that meaning by means of his own faculties, experience, and learning. Selden stresses that interpretations are always human 'applicacion, wch a discreet man may doe well, but tis his scripture not the Holy Ghost.' Indeed, the 'comon people' are so apt to praise the spirit in preaching and to despise learning that Selden aims to restore the balance by emphasizing the learned art of preaching (*Table Talk*, 104–5). As he turns to the Sanhedrin, Selden never doubts the value of right, honest, and zealous claims on a spirit of higher station than any ordinary human thought or invention. The difficulty lies in finding the best space for and definition of this spirit, in recognizing the element of human invention in any such claim, and in knowing how to coordinate the self-disciplinary power of zeal with the coercive, externally disciplinary power of magistrates in their courts.

When in the *Table Talk* Selden emphasizes the uncommon value of the preacher's labours, the arts of the sermon – the speaker's tone and narrative strategies – figure prominently in the discussion. Selden urges preachers to focus their themes on human duties rather than on theological niceties; to consider the audience to whom they preach; to found rhetoric on logic; and to work hard at devising a rhetoric that 'is most seasonable & most catching' (108). The artificial or rhetorical success of a sermon does not stop there. Selden accentuates the role of the most judicious laity in acting as liaisons between a suspicious people and the clergy who would drive a bargain with them. The reception of sermons requires such monitors if the discourse is to have its most beneficial effect on the community. The fact that preaching tends to elevate the standard of human behaviour above the level of mortal limitations lends it a romantic or poetic idealism, the value of which can be strengthened by the respected arbiters in theatrical religion. With the light of their judgment, the community sees its way to the value and execution of what the preacher has romanticized.

Selden's protracted advice on the reception of sermons is symptomatic of his conviction that among all the forms of religious experience, they have the tragic capacity for abuse. Preachers often emerge from the *Table Talk* as self-aggrandizing hypocrites who would serve the faith better if they erred on the side of catechisms – as parasites trading their own brand of poesy for favours. Arbiters of prayer abuse their offices too: set forms can be used to deaden the members of a religious society, but claims on the spirit of God tend to madden them. From his own 'temple' in the Inns of Court, and with an eye to rectifying the religious mania of his time, priestly Selden even goes so far as to play the exorcist in tricking a 'person of quality' into thinking that he has cast out his devils (145–6). As it has from the beginning, Selden's tendency to play the priest resembles the ancient institution of critical censure for the bards. No less than with normative poetry, the holy arts of shaping religious experience, imagination, and conviction are incomparably valuable in a society: they cannot be replaced by the lukewarm laws of ecclesiastical polity. Nevertheless, the poetic, theatrical, and rhetorical arts of religion need judicious measure and lawful purpose. Then they can stimulate the godly and lawful zeal that Christ himself displayed with the money-changers in the temple. Lawful zeal can commence in public with preaching and in the grammar of liturgy that stabilizes what is 'gen[er]ally believed' (72). If rightly generated, however, such zeal will carry over into private or solitary life, remaining lawful for those latter-day zealots who look to Christ for their model. Zeal must have its legal rectification and public, shameful checks, lest it happen again that 'They that putt this law in Execution were called Zelotts, but afterwards they comitted many Villanies' (144).

What Selden emphasizes, then, is that the arts of worship must continually change for the better in order to benefit the community of worshipers. For an instance, to which he will return in the work on the Sanhedrin, Selden notes that if under the Mosaic law God was in the habit of consecrating places, the Gospel changed this state of affairs to one in which human beings chose a place of worship 'for the conveniency of men to worship in ... God him selfe makes noe choice' (36). To ensure the benefits of the religious arts for the community, Selden wants to keep faith and works together and to keep human duties at the centre of religious experience. His emphasis on the human aims and artistic elements of worship is offered in opposition to the reckless iconoclasm of some contemporaries, who maintain that 'there must bee no humane Invention in the Church, nothing but the pure word' (59). Selden's retort – that exposition *is* human invention – edges the spiritual labours of the community towards another version of the *locus amoenus*, towards a fiction in which a religious society might dream its own ideal status, then hope to awake and find that the garden of dreams, like Paradise for Milton's newly created Adam, is real. But unlike Richard Hooker, who presupposes that natural decorum ensures the uninterrupted warrant of those human inventions so pervasive in English worship, Selden understands that it is up to him to make that fiction out of the Herculean labours of his scholarship. 'Conveniency' – an accommodating yet authoritative decorum – is not already in place for English society to imitate; it must be built in the process of recovering the Judaic materials left over from antiquity.

That fiction is far removed from the Westminster Assembly in Selden's reconstruction of the Great Sanhedrin as the judicial body that coexisted in the sacred, even Edenic complex of the temple in Jerusalem. Yet over the hundreds and hundreds of pages given to constructing the Sanhedrin, Selden rarely lets his audience forget that even if one's touchstone is scripture and even if one's models – the rabbis – prove that 'old Invencions are best' (59), it is the ongoing burden of the judicious monitors of English religion to reinvent the ways in which its laws and spiritual largesse might best serve one another while nevertheless keeping to themselves.

In the *Table Talk*, Selden's quips about the clergy are sometimes notably ambiguous; for the value of the clergy to a religious society is as ineluctable as the sins of its members are deep, widespread, and egregious. When he jokes that an unblemished minister will have the 'faults of ye whole Tribe ... layd upon him,' it is not quite clear whether this guilt by association is unjust (30). When he notes that laws made by the clergy 'are most favourable to ye Church,' his analogy to those heralds who devise 'their own pedigree' is satirical to be sure, but he leaves it unclear just why a body of laws invented in favour of the church is undesirable (29). If heralds can cheapen the true standard of nobility, what is it that canon laws might debase? Whether the thing subject to infection is (in keeping with the analogy) a standard of spirituality within the church itself, or the civil institutions that Selden fears an unmonitored synod might wreck, canon law is riven by the same kind of divide into which both normative poetry and aristocratic titles tend to devolve in Selden's thinking: ecclesiastical laws can sponsor an ideal according to which spiritual and moral offices should be carried out in a compromising world, or they can degenerate into the most gruesome forms of parasitic self-interest. Selden has a way, then, of reminding his companions of the imperfection of religious officers and their offices, even while he makes the point that the ongoing revision and reform of clerical offices are the most pressing of intellectual enterprises.

Accordingly, throughout the *Table Talk*, Selden examines a wide variety of church polities, including the leading contemporary versions of episcopacy, Presbyterianism, and a nascent Congregationalism. As an endangered species, the bishops receive his most sustained and mixed consideration, for instance, when Selden makes the case that the attention paid to the ceremonial arts of holiness does not evacuate religion of its spiritual purity. Far from it: human ceremony preserves – by containing and shaping – the human grasp on that spirit: 'Ceremony keeps up all things,' he says, 'ti's like a penny glasse to a rich spirit or some excellent water; w^{th}out it ye water were spilt; ye spirit lost' (24). This characterization of the art of holiness would be Laudian, were it not the case that the container is necessarily cheap. Clearly, God does not need artful devices on our part; but we gain access to the paltry device and ingest

the spirit by means of it. In this regard, neither Laudianism – which
champions the richly beautiful vehicles of holiness – nor radical iconoclasm and antinomianism – which relegate any human form of mediation to the trash heap of carnality and idols – understands the nature or
warrant of those accommodations that organize and stimulate religious
communities.

Far more the historian than the prophet, Selden lingers on the apparently fading custom of a church overseen by bishops. The Stuart bishops
have made many mistakes in their self-presentation, he says, but his
explanation of their errors differs greatly from the charge so often levelled against the bishops that (in Viscount Falkland's words), 'though at
first their preaching were the occasion of their preferment, they after
made their preferment, the occasion of their not preaching.'[2] On the
contrary, Selden believes that it was a mistake for the bishops to waste
their energies on preaching. Yet, like Falkland, Selden objects to the
tendency of the Laudian prelacy to foist strict obedience on the people
'without prepaireing Them and first insinuateing into their reason and
ffanceyes' (*Table Talk*, 14). The bishops relied too much on canonical
precedents, too little on persuasion, imagination, and relevance. Perhaps above all, their own fancies were tickled far too much by dreams of
divine right; they lost sight of the complex history of ecclesiastical titles,
and they forgot that the contemporary practice of religion always
trumps theoretical pretence. To be sure, Selden is convinced that bishops are the most suitable church officers for a monarchy, in contradis-
tinction to Lord Brooke's claim that they violate at one and the same
time the prerogatives of the monarch, the social hierarchy headed by
the aristocracy, and the popular basis of true religion. But Selden is very
much prepared for what seems inevitable, that the clergy will need reinvention if England's religious society is to have a prosperous future. 'A
Preist has no such thing as an indelible Character,' Selden generalizes;
for unlike Jewish priests, who were born to the class as well as made
within it, Christian priests are always designed: that is, they are designated and then made. Priests have 'made themselves unlike Laytye,' but
a minister is also such a thing that 'when hee is made,' he is 'a materia
prima apt for any forme the state will putt upon him' (78).

In the 1640s, in turbulent England, which 'forme' is best? Selden
either has less to say about Presbyterianism and Congregationalism than
he does about bishops, or his amanuensis neglects much of what he
said. As for the former, Selden has decided that its antiquity is an all too
commonplace pretence; that 'presbiters have the greatest power of any

Clergie in the World, and gull the Laytie most'; that Presbyterian ministers flourish while their lay supporters suffer; and that in the Assembly
they were patently unable to substantiate the divine right of their polity
(111–14). As for the Independents, Selden allows that their polity made
very good sense before there was a Christian state; but now, he has
decided, the new Congregationalists are but old Presbyter writ differently. For the former 'doe equally exclude the Civill power though after
a different manner.' In short, the only just motive for Independents to
claim an autonomy in their own governance arises if some clerical
officer is threatening to govern all the churches: 'for either wee must say
every Church governed it selfe or else wee must fall upon that old foolish Rock, That S^t. Peter & his Successors governed all.' Selden leaves no
doubt that those primitive days are past, and that the proper civil
authority should govern a religious society in all matters requiring some
coercive jurisdiction (57).

Given a tumultuous state of affairs in which the invention of a stable
form for clerical offices and persons is made difficult by virtue of the
fact that the possibilities are suddenly several, yet also severally imperfect, much of Selden's advice for the minister, then, is aimed at persons
occupying an unspecified form. The minister 'should preach according
to the Articles of the Religion Established in the Church, where he
lives'; apply all his studies to the circumstances of his time, place, and
people; study the fathers, church history, school divinity, and casuistry;
and acknowledge his humility in comparison to those ancient apostles
of Christ who 'had a voice from heaven ... a marke to bee knowne by,
spake tongues, cur'd deseases, trod upon serpents' (79–82).

Yet generic advice to the ministry can benefit the spirituality of a society only so much. The construction of the ideal minister needs more
definition. As a starting point, Selden is puzzled by the dilemma of
whether and how to remake the old fiction of the bishops. 'If there is
noe Bipps [bishops],' he is quite prepared to hypothesize, 'there must
be some what else wch has the power of Bipps; though it be in many and
then had you not as good keep them' (21). Other critics of the Caroline
bishops – again, Lord Falkland, for example – are as certain the current
prelacy must be refashioned as they are that the expulsion of a spiritually dutiful prelacy altogether will wreak havoc in England. Thus, Falkland stresses that 'I neither consider [the bishops] as necessary, nor as
unlawfull, but as convenient or inconvenient,' as suitable and decorous
or not. He continues: 'since all great mutations in government are dangerous (even where what is introduc'd by that mutation is such as would

have beene very profitable upon a primary foundation) and since the greatest danger of mutations is, that all the dangers and inconveniences they may bring are not to bee foreseene, and since no wise man will undergoe great danger, but for great necessity; my opinion is, that wee should not roote up this ancient tree as dead as it appears, till wee have tried whether by this or the like lopping of the branches, the sappe which was unable to feed the whole, may not serve to make what is left both grow and flourish.'[3] Falkland recuperates the climactic Ciceronian syntax of Richard Hooker as a way of preserving the spirit of an institution that Hooker defended in all its accoutrements against the Presbyterians of the 1590s. But in arguing that something like a bishop must be retained in church polity, Selden does not say exactly what that power should or must be and exactly why it cannot be dispersed. Instead, he reverts to analogy: comparing church offices to coins rather than sap – some of them might be stolen without the whole currency or its mould being nullified – Selden expresses exasperation at the considerable labour that minting and distributing a new coin are going to exact, even from him, a layman who has studied divinity as intensely as most clerics. From one vantage point, all this effort is expended for a penny glass to hold the spirit; one cannot dispense with such an artifice and remain a religious society, but it is easy to forget the fragility of any one fanciful construct. Falkland would recover the spirit or sap from the broken vessel; but Selden emphasizes that there must be a ready-made second vessel for catching it in history's mid-air.

More sturdy and more decidedly Laudian is Selden's metaphor for the basic tenets of the settled church: rails guaranteeing safe passage over a bridge. As rails on the bridge over the turbulent waters involved in the 'Severall readings of the Text,' the canons, catechisms, and liturgies of the orthodox church provide the normative devices allowing the otherwise unsteady individual to hold fast and remain balanced, yet 'dance here and there, as you please.' The arbitrary dancing is, in fact, the interior vagaries and delights of interpretation, when we 'flourish upon [our] various Lections' (*Table Talk*, 13). Between the two figures, Selden captures his negotiation between a belief that the human invention of law provides the scaffolding for the often nugatory play of the spiritual life, and his suspicion that human inventions are the necessary trivia making it possible for human beings to experience the grace that can redeem them from their own devices. Whereas his table talk captures Selden's passing hypotheses and lingering suspicions, his massive work on the Judaic Sanhedrin tests his own capacity to devise and legiti-

mize an invention of a lawful and zealous religious society at once
supremely ancient and boldly innovative. Indeed, he devotes the last
phase of his life to mounting a normative fiction whose potential for
success in guiding his war-torn Protestant society is undercut by its own
scholarly remoteness yet energized by that apocalyptic tenor of the
1640s and 1650s, during which time the people of England had to discern and decide 'the implications of the teaching of the age of spirit.'[4]

— 3 —

In the *Table Talk*, Selden mentions that the court, the Sanhedrin, serves
as the basis for his major reinvention of spiritual labour in its relationship
to civil authority. In an effort to impress his listeners with the maxim that
each entity should 'Act within [its] Comission' (100), he shows how recon-
structions of the Sanhedrin might be torn between, on the one hand, the
divines who would give civil power to the church and, on the other, the laymen who believe that such power belongs to the civil authorities themselves. 'Christ himself was a great Observer of the civill power,' he notes,
then adds that 'Divines ought to doe no more then what the State per-
mitts' (100–1). In his assertions of church subjugation to the state, Selden
focuses on excommunication, regarding which he makes the simple case
that the church controlled this act only until the 'State became Christian'
(101). More than once, the Sanhedrin serves as the model for a civil court
that controls the act of 'putting away' a wicked person. Yet its own secular
status is not so simple once one adds that the law in question is divine and
the human dispensers of that law are theologians.

Selden is wary of the clergy's tendency to usurp civil power. Rebuking
the presbyters in the Westminster Assembly who 'challenge to bee *Jure
divino*, & so to bee above the civill power,' he accentuates the value of
laymen in the synod, as monitors of the divines who, as arbiters in religion, might 'spoile the Civill worke' (126). Elsewhere he generalizes the
separation of civil power from spiritual labour in his remark on 'jurisdiction': 'There's no such thing as Spirituall Jurisdiccion, all is civill, the
Churches is the same with the Lord Mayors' (60). Chastising papal and
priestly ingratitude for the coercive expertise of civil authority, Selden
returns to the thesis that he set forth in the tithes controversy, namely,
that the church should be thankful to a forceful civil power for helping
to ensure the prosperity of the church in a sinful and neglectful world:
'If you should say you held you[r] Land by Moses or Gods Law; and would
trye it by that you may p[er]haps loose it; but by y[e] Law of y[e] Kingdome

you are sure to carry it.' In the 1640s he is newly equipped with a recent case in point: 'soe may ye Bipps by this plea of Jure Divino loose all' (20).

There is a vast difference, however, between that maxim in the *Table Talk* – 'All is as the State likes' (20) – and the three tomes in which Selden attempts to work out exactly how both law and spirit are best served if all jurisdiction is placed in a civil court, the Sanhedrin (*De Synedriis*). In its first book, published in 1650, this great work offers an extensive treatment of excommunication, corrects the caricatures transmitting the Erastian theses about that official act, and attempts to formulate the optimum mode of interaction between jurisdiction and spiritual labour. Along the way, Selden revisits each of the measures for normalizing a holy commonwealth that have appealed to him over the course of his scholarly and legal career: poetic, parliamentary and juridical, and natural. But above all, the scholarly charge recurring through each volume on the Sanhedrin reprises the chief claim of poets and lawyers, namely, the conviction that the norms coordinating restrictive laws and capacious spirituality must be humanly made, no matter how much they owe, or claim to owe, to divinity and to nature. Even if Selden largely disagrees with Hobbes in his final model for the ideal commonwealth, he is attuned to the habit of thought epitomized in the 1650s by the author of *Leviathan* – the one that stresses the fictive character of the religious commonwealth.

Early in and throughout *De Synedriis et Praefecturis Juridicis Veterum Ebraeorum* (1650, 1653, 1655), Selden invents metaphors for coordinating the domains of law and of spirit. At times he opts to imagine civil and ecclesiastical authorities as separate but equally significant entities, but his images – two suns, two souls – are palpably unworkable, and he does not dwell on them. Nor does he linger on the numinous but elusive image of the perfect continuum between realms of authority, the sun and its rays. In the first case of separate but equal entities, he admits that one of the suns or souls is bound to surpass or attack the other. In the second case, of the continuum, the notion that human legal processes could simply flow from their divine and natural source proves as utopian as its analogue – also offered by Selden – that a geometrical relation between an unstated postulate and stated demonstration might obtain in fusing a transcendent spirit with an all-too-human judiciary body.[5]

Selden tries on other metaphors inventing the ideal interaction between civil jurisdiction and spiritual labour. One crucial vein comprises images of containment, circumscription, and protection: spiritual labour and authority are enclosed within the fortress, hedge, or circle of human penal jurisdiction and legal deliberation (Book 1, preface, viii). This metaphor is not the same as that Laudian tendency to situate spirituality within the fortress or behind the hedge of church canons, ceremonies, and authorities. Rather, the church and all spiritual labour provide the core within or the pure maiden behind a barrier of civil protection. As Selden explains, the image pattern is Talmudic: among the rabbis, he reminds us, such coercive customs as excommunication are frequently compared to a fortress around the unbroken reception of God's sacred word. For Selden, the Talmud itself is a fortress that contains spiritual truth and labour.

Metaphor not only embodies the prospect of containment in Selden's reconstruction of the Great Sanhedrin. In addition, metaphor and poetry are part of the spiritual core that civil jurisdiction protects. Indeed, the Talmudic writings themselves feature metaphors, allegories, and other narrative-cum-speculative tendencies, together with law: they include *Aggadah* as well as *Halakhah*. In *De Synedriis*, Selden pays homage to rabbinical poetry and the challenges that it faces in interpreting law beautifully as well as carefully – a far cry from his much earlier tendency to lambaste the rabbis for their outrageous fictions. In one case, he adduces the Talmudic use of imagery from the Song of Solomon for the purposes of celebrating the Sanhedrin. The court's semicircular seating plan is comparable to the navel that 'is like a round goblet shaped like the moon.' As a goblet, it protects and encloses the whole world; and it contains 'mixed wine,' an allegory of the legal requirements for a quorum. The 'belly' of the Sanhedrin – or so the Talmudic allegory continues – contains the heap of wheat described in the Canticles, insofar as everyone benefits from its nourishment.[6]

Finally, the Sanhedrin is 'surrounded by Lilies'; Selden does not gloss this image of an enclosure around the Sanhedrin, itself a container, though elsewhere he provides a metaphor for the court's containment within Roman imperial jurisdiction. But Talmudic writers themselves offer the idea that the Great Sanhedrin would not injure the most vulnerable and insignificant persons and would avoid sin while helping the unclean and the sinful.[7] Selden leaves unspoken his thoughts on the lilies – on the beautiful fragile hedge around the dispensers of the law. Instead, he moves on to other Talmudic poetry: the princeps of the Sanhedrin is like the umbilical cord connecting the Jewish people to their mother, and law flows from his mouth like waters from the great river of Paradise whenever the princeps pronounces on the unclean and clean, or the absolved and condemned. But the hedge of the lilies turns enclosure inside out: rather than a part of spiritual labour enclosed within the civil rigors and coercion of law, poetry, beauty, myth, nature, and ceremony put the best face forward for law; yet they offer no protection for either law or spiritual labour and little help with arriving at the best coordination of spiritual labour and civil jurisdiction.

At one point, early in Book 1 of *De Synedriis*, Selden adapts and crafts a metaphor according to which civil jurisdiction and law are both solidly contained by and structurally responsible for the welfare of the domain of spiritual labour. Arguing that coercion, punishment, and jurisdiction must be completely removed from the spiritual domain in order for that domain to thrive, he compares jurisdiction to the keystone in an arch, the removal of which would dislodge all the other stones wedged into the structure. Selden derives the key image for his comparison from Ausonius's poem 'De ratione librae' (Of the Nature of the Pound or Balance), in which the poet explains how heavenly bodies manage to avoid decay. Those planets, Ausonius says, are made of finest atoms, but the atoms cannot be broken, and the planets of which they are made endure forever. The Latin poet maintains that if any one atom were removed, the whole structure would be undone. The cosmic balance, poise, or integrity would collapse.[8]

Selden ignores the cosmic orientation of this image, though later he will introduce Stoic cosmology as a way of challenging the otherwise crucial notion for him that the sacred domain can be lawfully contained. He believes that the architectural image offers a prefatory vehicle for representing how the force of magistracy – insignificant in size – is responsible for the welfare of holy endeavours in the world if only the keystone might retain its equipoise within the beautiful design of the arch: 'Demto enim aut non admisso Jure illo Gladii Spiritualis Forensis Divino, universa Imperii ac Jurisdictionis inde obtensae vis, ut simul corruat, necessum est, *Ut Medium si quis vellat de fornice Saxum / Incumbunt cui cuncta simul, devexa sequentur / Caetera, communèmque trahent è vertice lapsum* (Ausonius, *De ratione Librae*), seu ut Vara sequitur Vibiam [Thus with the law of the public sword removed from divine spirituality, or with that sword not admitted into the spiritual realm in the first place, it is necessary that the whole force of jurisdiction be held in place lest the structure collapse all together, "As, if we were to wrench out from an arch the keystone upon which all the voussoirs (wedge-like stones) bear, the rest will follow suit and come to the ground, their general downfall caused by the topmost stone," or just as the prop follows suit when a clasp falls]' (Selden, Book 1, preface, xi; *Ausonius*, 177). According to

Ausonius, nature itself dictates that every '*modulus*' must have a '*libra*': every unit of measurement or of time, every rhythm or structure must have its perfect balance, counterpoise, or tension.[9] For Selden, it is not nature but rather human institution that supplies the arch stone capping and securing the perilous balance between opposite and equally powerful stones and wedges, the potentially warring sects, passions, and interests constituting an ostensibly unified religious society.

With Ausonius's lapidary imagery in the preface of his first book on the Sanhedrin, Selden has come to imagine the ideal construction of a religious society as Ben Jonson conceived the invention of the perfect poem, as a carefully crafted stone structure from which no constituent can be removed without great loss. Somehow, the whole of this structure should conceal the sweat and struggle required to build it, though the poet Jonson is more committed to this deception than the scholar and historian Selden. Jonson, however, conceives poetic walls as the perfect masonry of well-placed syllables and words. Selden's arch has far more at stake, namely, all the discourses, institutions, groups, and ontological levels constituting the whole of religious society. Many of the stones Selden has fashioned before, from normative poetry and natural law to those spiritual labourers left to their own devices. Now he must fashion and then place the keystone itself, the Sanhedrin. And so long as human agents are fashioning the social artifice, no institution can hope to be as precise as the mechanism of the cosmos; like actual props, clasps, and pins, the discourse of mechanism is itself artificial, an accommodating metaphor for the coordination of a religious society – no less so than the navels and lilies of the Talmud.

As David Norbrook has shown, writers lauding the new commonwealth in the 1650s – or often in the same text, projecting their idea of what that commonwealth should be – frequently had recourse to 'architectural metaphors.'[10] If Selden's arch metaphor substitutes the abstract constituents of a religious society for the highly imperfect human agents who must design, build, and constitute that society, Andrew Marvell mingles the human with the institutional element in a similar image presented in his 1655 poem, 'The First Anniversary of the Government under His Highness the Lord Protector.' Praising Cromwell as the new and paradoxical guarantor of the young English republic, Marvell compares the commonwealth to the 'public wall': 'The crossest spirits here do take their part, / Fastening the contignation which they thwart; / And they, whose nature leads them to divide, / Uphold this one, and that the other side.' Thus far the two sides of an arch rise up in the form of those partisan

rivals of the civil war years which against their very wills prove to counterbalance one another. Yet those sides, according to Marvell, need both an
institution and a man, the former the 'basis of a senate free.' If there is a
Sanhedrin in Marvell's image, it is the foundation of the structure, significant but not constitutive of the mechanism of tension. On top of the
structure is Cromwell himself, the Protector: 'But the most equal still sustain the height, / And they as pillars keep the work upright, / While the
resistance of opposed minds, / The fabric (as with arches) stronger
binds, / Which on the basis of a senate free, / Knit by the roof's protecting weight, agree.' With his arch, Marvell captures both what is fragile
and wondrous about the invention of godly commonwealths and about
the men that come to build, make up, and secure such an invention. So
it is in Marvell's 'Horatian Ode' to Cromwell in 1650; the praise of the
poet does not override the hard truth that abstractions and ideals 'do
hold or break / As men are strong or weak.'[11]

Even as Selden's metaphors attempt to weatherproof the invention of
a religious society from the fallen human agents who live and breathe
therein, he shows considerable awareness that in human practice the
civil and spiritual domains that one might want to separate have a
decided tendency to mix, shift, and fluctuate. In the Westminster Assembly, Lord Saye finds this tendency especially pronounced in the Judaic
culture at the very heart of Selden's project: for in Judaism, Viscount
Saye and Sele protests, 'the church and state were so mixed, as that
it cannot any way pattern evangelic churches.'[12] It is Selden's hope
that refashioning Judaic institutions of law, in coordination with Judeo-
Christian labours in the spiritual dispensations of true religion, might
afford contemporary society with the best of all imaginable norms. But
the author of a commentary on the Arundel marbles and on Drayton's
Poly-Olbion has known for a long time that monuments from the past
tend to crumble or fade, and that the attempts of bards, musicians, and
natural philosophers to avert that erosion are themselves often inse-
curely founded in the civil bonds of obligation. If a coercive and mediatory Sanhedrin is to provide the keystone of religious society, it must be
refashioned as well as recovered, and then carefully situated in counterpoise with the other building blocks of the society.

In *De Synedriis*, the metaphors devised for coordinating the relative
domains of civil jurisdiction and spiritual labour are meant to prepare

the way for Selden's argument about excommunication. As it was conceived and practised in ancient Judaic and early Christian societies, he urges, excommunication held the same warrant as exile, execution, or almost any other punishment: it was invented by magistrates and disposed, augmented, diminished, and inflicted according to their judgment and will. By contrast, those priests, ministers, and lay teachers who laboured for spiritual purposes – those who exhorted and cautioned, prayed and administered sacraments – operated in a domain quite separate from penal jurisdiction; or if those persons worked in the domain of jurisdiction, they did so in a separate capacity, as elders allotted the civil task of judging and punishing according to the law.

This is not to say, however, that the ancient Jews segregated their society into matters sacred and profane. Nothing could be further from the truth as Selden sees it. God commanded the Jews to make the institutions of justice; God's spirit presided over that making; justice itself was a natural and sacred dispensation; Mosaic law was God's law; and the Great Sanhedrin considered all cases, oversaw all functions or duties, observed no distinction between secular and sacred cases, and assumed a singular custodial responsibility for the interpretation, preservation, and administration of a law at once divine and human. Selden is at great pains to emphasize that each of the elders in the Sanhedrin was a theologian as much as a law sage. Indeed, his belief that the removal of bishops from the House of Lords in 1642 had wrought damage in the English constitution reflected the conviction that Parliament, like a Sanhedrin both judicial court and legislative body, was charged with overseeing all aspects of the holy commonwealth. As Selden stresses in his study of the Sanhedrin, however, the clergy who served in the chief court of the land would ideally share the legal expertise of the lay sages.

Confirmed by Selden's reading of Erastus, these arguments are fraught with the difficulties about which Viscount Saye and Sele warned the Westminster Assembly when he rejected Judaic models for evangelical churches. It seems impossible, that is, to erect a model of coordinated yet separate realms according to a Judaism in which the realms are hopelessly, famously mixed. After all, not only does Selden award a great deal of religious warrant and scope to the Sanhedrin, but his notion of pure spiritual labour runs up against his insistence that all spiritual labour operates within the context of human invention. All the same, at its simplest level Selden's argument dovetails with the more Congregationalist views of the 1640s and early 1650s: magistrates and jurisdiction must be kept out of the rarefied domain of spiritual labour that nonetheless it is their utmost responsibility to protect, to oversee, and even to unify. His Sanhedrin is decidedly a senate, not a synod; but its realm of influence includes those prophets and priests whose labours in the spirit they must somehow regulate and measure without breaching or sullying the purity of that spirit. And together with the supporters of independent congregations and of parish communities, Selden is committed to delineating the role of tightly knit local units within a society that might serve as quasi-coercive, quasi-spiritual mediators between the civil and spiritual realms of a godly society.

From very early in the first volume through the closing pages of the third, Selden makes a case for the purity if not the full autonomy of spiritual and sacramental labour. Like Erastus, he claims that Judaic excommunication was never intended to prohibit transgressors from participating in the sacraments; rather, the transgressors were obliged so to participate; for it was believed that they could benefit more than their peers in doing so. Moreover, it was one thing to be 'cut off' by God, whether from one's life or in the afterlife, and another to be excommunicated by magistrates. One might be absolved in the eyes of God, but not in the view of the magistrates, and vice versa; indeed, Selden expends great effort in clearing up confusions in Hebraic terminology on this difference. In ancient Judaism – and again Erastus stresses this point – persons were prohibited temporarily from the sacraments only on account of some ritual uncleanness. While uncleanness was a legal matter over which the Great Sanhedrin had final authority, its status was not the same as that of the wilful transgressor against moral laws. That is, the prohibition of the unclean from the sacraments was not so much a punishment as a ritual.

Selden isolates the domain of spiritual labours in a variety of ways. He argues that the early Christian notion of a spiritual 'sword' is merely a metaphor for the labours of preaching, praying, teaching, and dispensing the sacraments, and that only the ambitious cleric would concretize or politicize that sword into civil, coercive jurisdiction: 'Et Gladium Spiritalem per temporum Christianorum, quae iam tractamus, allusionem tantùm inde haustum esse adeo palàm est ut nihil manifestius. Adeóque argumenti, quo firmari possit jus Excommunicationis, vis nulla omninò ibi reperta [And nothing is more patently manifest than the fact that the spiritual sword was a metaphor eagerly seized upon throughout those Christian times that we now treat. Indeed arguments according to which the law of excommunication could be confirmed by this image were found then to have no force at all]' (Book 1, 271). The clerical expansion of the religious domain into the civil yields chaos in an abyss that serves as Selden's evil alter image of the boundless spirit praised as supportive of a pure realm of holiness. The sword of the spirit is not wielded in courts, Selden insists, and has uses far removed from penal coercion. It should be revered as the vehicle of divine grace and holiness, not contaminated by the worldliness of legal procedure, judgment, and force.

In synagogues and prayer houses, Selden argues, excommunicated transgressors were expected, encouraged, even obliged to participate in sacred offerings, readings, and teachings, unless, of course, the transgressor was also ritually unclean. His favourite example is Judas Iscariot. Knowing full well that Judas was evil, Jesus admitted him to the Passover communion of the Last Supper, and God would expect no less for the feasts of first fruits and of the final harvest. A hermaphrodite would be exempted from the festivals; but an excommunicated man with the appropriate genitals would be required to attend. Uncleanness was not equivalent to transgression; excommunication meant separation from human community or privileges but not from God and grace. Indeed, the Jews understood that one's separation from the sacred means for the remission of sins was fundamentally different from penal coercion; and even if the penal judgment included execrations for divine vengeance – a feature that Selden often finds overly theatrical and superstitious – the remission of sin involved a broken heart, prayerful entreaty, and access to the vehicles of grace, having nothing to do with legal procedures and formulae.

Selden also denies that the metaphor of the keys has anything to do with excommunication. Invoking the standard criticism of dream imagery, he argues that the key symbolizes the inclusion of persons already in a group, as well as the exclusion or admission of persons outside the group; but excommunication ejects the insider (Book 1, 272–3). In this vein, the key can be understood as that blessed doctrine necessary for spiritual redemption. Dreams themselves will figure in Selden's delineation of a spiritual as apart from a civil realm, and he does not linger on them yet. Instead, he invokes such proto-reformers as Wycliffe and Hus in order to maintain that a truly evangelical ministry uses words and sacraments for teaching, chastising, guiding, correcting, and blessing – not legal strictures, coercive power, or civil magistracy. The metaphors of a spiritual sword and key belong to a trade in divine and eternal treasure, not in the changeable, secular realm of human politics.

To separate the spiritual labours from civil jurisdiction, Selden draws upon a long Christian tradition, best embodied in a powerful passage cited from Minucius Felix, according to which the heart religion of grace, love, and internal sacrifice is elevated over pagan carnality, altarbound superstition, ritual sacrifices, and ceremonial art (Book 3, 334–5). But Selden keeps returning to the point made so often in the *Table Talk*, that spiritual labour requires its own human arts. Once that labour takes the form of art and invention, it has edged in the direction of civil control and the invented apparatus of justice. To clarify how the art of religion can remain pure even as it becomes secular, Selden makes use of a story from Boethius's history of music, a text and field of study that play such a prominent role in his work on the Arundel marbles. According to Boethius, magistrates judge music in their capacity as arbiters of their society's mores, customs, and laws, not as music critics. Others will judge the music as music. Presumably, then, ministers and priests would approach the labours of spirituality on their own terms, not for any socio-civic ramifications (Book 1, 652–3). Similarly, Selden offers an analogy between the various uses of the term 'judgment' in religious affairs and the same slippage in poetry criticism (Book 2, 322).

The more Selden attempts to sever spiritual labour from civil judgment, the more the costs and problems of doing so appear to rise, especially with reference to Judaic society. In the Boethius analogy, for instance, the purity of religion approaches a kind of self-contained aestheticism not very suitable for making changes in those human beings who are still very much in the world of religious society. Selden's argument protects spiritual labour within the holy of holies, not so much in the temple as in the holy *pneuma* coursing between heaven and earth but not actually incarnating. More systematically, he is confronted with the fact that in Judaic culture, magistrates and priests can be one and the same person. In making the case for the separation of civil coercion and spiritual labours, Milton too had noted that one person might don two hats, one as lay minister, the other as magistrate. While the former might shame a member of the congregation, only the latter could excommunicate him. So, too, Selden examines the case of shame in the neighbourhood, which together with the difficult case of Judaic priests in the magistracy helps him to answer the question of how or whether spiritual labourers participate in the social regulation of religion.

Throughout the three books of *De Synedriis*, Selden studies the role of local communities, secret societies, and coteries in shaping the mentality and monitoring the behaviour of their members. Even the most unlearned member of Selden's England would have understood the value of this monitoring; for the dispensation of shame through customs such as 'ridings' and 'rough music' was woven into the fabric of English communal living. Such customs had analogues in the official legal system as well as links to the culture of festivity of which Robert Herrick liked to write. In a commonwealth for which every crime was considered first and foremost a sin, Cynthia B. Herrup explains, '[t]he equation of legal decisions with a moral structure contained a dilemma escapable only by allowing considerable discretion to those participating in the legal system. Since human nature was flawed, a law without room for more than occasional mercy was a mockery of justice. However, since morality was supposed to be unchanging, a law that was continually emended could not mirror morality. The retention of rigid rules alongside flexible applications was necessary for law enforcement to reflect both human potential and human frailty.'[13] In showing that the ancient Jews also appreciated the communal performance of shame, Selden was making the simplest link between present and past; but he was also elevating the present customs – which themselves could prove lewd – by way of the ancient and godly precedent. Selden's associations with Jonson in the present, as well as his understanding of the critics regulating the Bards in ancient Britain, showed further that the dynamic of communal monitoring had, in his view, its culturally higher manifestations as well. As Selden sees the ancient Jews, however, high and low alike participate in the distribution of shame, as surely as they do in Milton's vision of the Christian congregation.

In Judaic custom, Selden argues, ample room was allowed for an unofficial excommunication, for the purposes of which neighbours, friends, and family would deprive a transgressor of his daily fellowship. Indeed, a passage of interest to Selden in the Jerusalem Gemara makes clear how similar such a dynamic is to Milton's congregational shame, itself a radical revision of the aristocratic warrior code found in Homer's *Iliad*. In the words of the Gemara, this custom 'allowed that men keep [the transgressing associate] away from themselves, and that they pour sufficient shame on him.' If the transgressor persists in his sins, the community may take the matter to the officers of the court. But with examples from the Psalms, Selden reiterates the critical distinction between a private refusal to interact with a sinner and a public excommunication that would change the legal status of the sinner.[14]

According to Selden, groups such as the Judaic Essenes or the pagan Pythagoreans are remarkable for their singular zeal in obedience to God's law and word. Sometimes their zeal manifests itself in violence or

cruelty, but among Christians, in particular, its motivation is supposed to
be an extraordinary love for God as well as for one another. As a zealous
fraternity, the Essenes committed themselves to a purity of life and to
conspicuous, vigilant service to law. Their very inductions included horrific imprecations of divine justice against the inductee as warnings lest
the latter fail to abide by the covenant of the group or by the standards
set by God's law ('Sed expressius multò est in Essenorum secta seu soda-
litio Judaico illo celeberrimo, hac de re testimonium. Apud illos mos erat
ut in suos admitterentur soli qui vitae puritate, religione, jurísque tum
Divini tum Humani apicum observatione se conspicuos idque accuratiùs
exhiberent, & sodalitii rituum ac morum tandem se tenacissimos fore
profiterentur, sed interim non sine juramentis seu execrationibus ab
admittendis praestitis ... id est vindictae divinae imprecationibus solenni-
bus unà cum Separationis comminatione, id est Excommunicatione
comminatoria, si in praemissa committerent' [Book 1, 158–9]). What
amazes Selden about the Essenes is that each person so completely internalized this contract that he became his own best monitor and most brutal punisher. Should one commit a serious transgression, the Essenes
had their own court of a hundred men to inflict a wretched, gradual
death from which the others were obliged not to save the transgressor.

As it happens, however, the transgressor would ardently refuse all
help, so powerful were those imprecations and rituals, the compact of
shame, and the individual's own zealous penchant for obedience to
God's law. In short, the transgressor would rather die than be saved –
even if he were not yet absolved in God's eyes. Obligation weighed more
heavily on the Essene than any hope of personal survival or redemption.
Indeed, one option for the transgressor was his own self-excommunica-
tion, once his zealous conscience, reinforced by rituals of shame and
reverence, had taken hold of the situation. Selden is uneasy about the
impressive yet horrific ritual imprecations of zealous coteries, but he is
more at home with the power and solidarity generated in small communities by their mutual reverence, love, and faith within the directives of
law. So it is that he expends great energy reclaiming the legitimacy of
oaths in covenants and contracts (Book 2, 452–515). Lest the high standards of virtue, spiritual labour, and lawful duty wreck the workaday
happiness of a community, whether it is a parish, sect, or coterie, he softens the terrors of shame with an emphasis on the value of agape; and
given the vigilante tendencies of some zealous groups, Selden sets a
safety net on their activities by containing them within the judicial strictures and processes of the public court. Claiming that the Essenes

should be imitated only when doing so would not violate public norms is less troublesome for religious society if one is arguing, as Selden is, that the norms of the Sanhedrin – and the Sanhedrin itself – begin with God's own commands. Otherwise, Selden's praise for the spiritual zeal, abundant love, and neighbourly shame of coteries, sects, and local communities suggests the possibility that larger social units cannot, in fact, be religious at all, that institutional society should aspire to pure civility.

For Selden, the Christian instances of communal monitoring should be reformed versions of the Judaic ones. When Paul declares that anyone preaching a message at odds with the gospel should 'be outcast,' the apostle has in mind those Jews who have not yet accepted the Messiah. According to Selden, this ejection simply separates the transgressor from his familiar community or congregation. Rather more problematic (he believes) is the Pauline injunction in Corinthians that good Christians avoid the company of their vicious fellows, especially since Paul follows up what appears to be a leave-them-to-God exhortation with something more aggressive: 'You are the judges within the fellowship. Root out the evil-doer from your community' (1 Cor. 5:9, NEB, 205). Again Selden contends that such an uprooting concerns solely the tightly knit members of a neighbourhood, association, or congregation.

Working primarily with the eighteenth chapter of Matthew, Selden emphasizes the efficacy of reproach – of shame – among intimates or relatively small communities of believers (Matt. 18:17–18). Thus, any recourse to court is a last and voluntary resort for these groups, though their own warrant should be spiritual, moral, and lawful rather than the arrogant inclinations of aristocratic honour (Book 1, 291–9). Reproach, he stresses, must be eager for forgiveness and the spiritual restitution of the lapsing associate. Hence the value of agape, a better cement for a religious society than the fearful rites of imprecation no doubt, yet viable only if the transgressor has not dissembled his rigorous and active conscience. As David Baker has shown, early modern celebrations of agape tend to caution that this radical spirit of love must not lapse into a decadent Antinomianism.[15] Clearly, Selden wants agape to operate as the spiritual guarantor of a covenant or confederation in the law. For the key text behind his understanding of Christian – that is, reformed Judaic – confederation is Tertullian's *Apologeticus*, in which the church father celebrates 'a common religious feeling, unity of discipline, a common bond of hope' among his co-religionists. This bond unifies them in feeling but also in the disciplinary measures that deprive associates of 'all share in our prayer, our assembly, and all holy intercourse.'[16]

Together these friends read the scriptures and pray for peace in the world; theirs is a society whose bond is precisely not contractual but rather spiritual and mental, social and voluntary.

Selden accentuates Tertullian's most extravagant praise for this micro-community: 'When decent people, when good men gather, when the pious and when the chaste assemble, that is not to be called a faction; it is a Senate.'[17] Selden's main point, of course, is that such a communal dynamic is precisely not senatorial, and he is unwilling to cede very much to Tertullian's claim that obedience to such a compact can surpass the force of jurisdiction. Clearly, Selden says, Tertullian is employing a figure of speech: the local compact is imitative or figurative of the lawfulness and dignity of a senate – agape is not Bacchanalian revelry – but it is not and should not be coercive in the same way that a senate would be. In line with Selden's Erastian argument that public excommunication does not prevent participation in religious worship, the implications of the local shaming seem almost more severe insofar as the transgressor is cut off from at least his familiar access to the dispensations of grace.

Selden understands that Tertullian, like Origen in similar circumstances, has been provoked into such a figure by the pagan charge that Christian love is lawless, licentious, and esoteric. If in his defence of the English church polity Richard Hooker has claimed that the love feasts of the Apostles were appropriate only for them, Selden maintains that love is perhaps the greatest bond on behalf of zeal in the law, even if this means that he must omit Origen's analogy between secret Christian associations and tyrannicides. Unlike his treatment of the matter in the *De Jure Naturali et Gentium*, in *De Synedriis* Selden downplays the zealot model of the compact and prefers philosophical fraternities and self-disciplinary associations that refuse to tamper with the institutions of public judgment and coercion, even in the event that one of their own is executed. Nonetheless, his treatment of the local compact is variously imagined along the lines of Jonson's tribe of Ben with its 'understanders,' Selden's own coterie in 'table talk,' the zealots of the Jews, the love feasts of the early Christians, the shame culture of ancient warrior societies, and the modern-day microcosms of congregation, parish, sect, or fraternity. This smaller and tightly knit version of a religious society strikes Selden as a highly promising means of coordinating spirituality and lawfulness whatever the turbulence of society in general. It is also proleptic of a commonplace sentiment in the eighteenth century that, as Shaftesbury claims, 'to cantonise is natural when the society grows vast and bulky.'[18]

The danger, of course, is that such cantons might cause the very social disruptions, violence, and indeterminacy from which they were meant to offer redress and multiply Laud's nightmare of a church within a church, a religious society within a religious society. But in admiring these local communities, Selden operates on the assumption, an understandable one in a time of civil war, that 'mankind's intrinsic sociability, and with it the moral instinct, become obstructed in large societies because they have too much material to contend with.'[19] As relatively protected, loving, and morally harmonious if not uniform, coteries generate moral values rather than partisan schisms; they explore ideas but also award fame and shame. In the 1640s and 1650s, one might point to the Platonic and romantic circle of Katherine Philips, to Walton's imaginary fraternity of anglers, to the Freemasons, to the revival of the Epicurean garden. With varying degrees of rationalism and zealous devotion, of openness and secrecy, of debate and tranquillity, such circles offer a philosopher's and poet's *locus amoenus* that both imitates and rivals the segregating impulse found in the Independent congregations and gathered churches. In turn, Selden's meditations on the social subset are prompted by what he would consider the Janus-like moment of the 1640s and 1650s, a moment at which English society appeared to be concurrently disintegrating into ruin and rising from its flames. In writing of the Sanhedrin, Selden commits himself to thinking about how the whole of English society might look fresh from those flames. But the recurring motif of the coterie in that work suggests that the only hope for a meaningful and manageable fusion between lawful measure and spiritual or moral zeal might well reside in the local rituals of shame, festivals of love, and conversations at table.

Throughout *De Synedriis*, then, Selden investigates the psychosocial dynamics of small communities as an intermediary between the utterly private labours and visions of the individual soul, and the utterly public, formulaic, and often coercive dispensations of the court. But agape and shame might not work well as imitations of judicial power; after all, with regard to redressing transgression, the imitation bears in some respects too much authority (since the transgressor might be isolated from and deprived of the sacramental means of grace) and too little (the neighbours have no forensic jurisdiction). In cases of local failure, the neighbours would be free, at times even obliged, to have recourse to the courts. Nonetheless, Selden strives through his characterization of local dynamics to carve out a larger space for religious labour apart from the courts – for preaching, prayer, reproach, and sacrament – than a simple bifurcation between civil jurisdiction and an inwardly turned spirituality would allow. With his study of the work done by Judaic priests and prophets, he aims at further mapping out the domain for spiritual labour, but the evidence is even harder to digest than it is with the largely etymological and philological toils of clarifying the notion of communal monitors.

There is good reason why Selden works so hard at stabilizing and protecting the domain of spiritual labour: his main Erastian thesis can be easily mistaken for erasing that domain altogether. After all, Selden's essential point is that Judaic forensic jurisdiction observes no distinction between the sacred and the profane, that theirs is a religious society whose controversies and activities in toto are in the domain of the Sanhedrin; and that priests per se have no special place, prerogative, or entitlement in the courts. In no uncertain terms, Selden protests that scholars claiming otherwise are ignoring the evidence and probably serving their own ambitions. In their proper capacity, priests officiate in temple sacrifices, not in court deliberations. Indeed, Selden refers us to his previous work on the priesthood for a refresher on what a Judaic priest is and what he does. If priests appear to gain political power over the course of Jewish history, then this fact reflects the vicissitudes of civil power itself, with its ability to establish any judicial warrant that it so desires.

Building the archway that wedges together civil authority and sacred labour is difficult, and some of Selden's contemporaries would remark that the construction is especially tenuous if one takes Judaism as one's model. What is more, a number of factors threaten to erode his relegation of priests (as priests) to the rituals of the temple. Priests are essentially the indisputable aristocrats of Judaic society, so Selden revisits his studies of whether, how, or how much purity of blood has a sacredly normative value in ancient and contemporary societies. At one point towards the end of his first book, Selden cautions that the link between primogeniture and priesthood must be handled with care. After all, Abel and Moses were second children, the former being one whose sacrifice was acceptable to God, the latter a priest as well as a ruler. Before Aaron, the duty of sacrifice belonged to eminent men, not only to priests; and even after Aaron, the laity retained certain sacrificial obligations (Book 1, 641–56).

Nonetheless, as Selden shows, the early history of Judaism bears out the consolidation of priestly primogeniture, and many sacrifices or rites were held appropriate for priests alone. Yet, he repeats, these priests had no special claim on magistracy: they could become magistrates only if they had expertise and singular wisdom as lawyer-theologians. To illustrate this key point, Selden draws an analogy between priests and physicians: the latter would not be awarded jurisdiction in medical litigation any more than priests in cases involving sacred matters. Indeed, this notion of judicial authority would hold even if Moses had delegated that authority exclusively to priests. For this reason, law sages must have extensive knowledge in any area of learning that might figure in court cases, yet they must approach each case with impartiality and without consideration for the contents of that domain taken on their own terms. Cases involving music should not double as exercises in music appreciation.

When Selden turns to the Talmudic qualifications of the judges sitting in the Sanhedrin, the second criterion – next in line after singular excellence in jurisprudence, theology, and the many branches of learning – proves to be lineage, a quality that appears to overlap with the aristocratic tendencies of the priesthood. Those sages selected for the great or smaller courts – as one of the seventy-one or twenty-three judges – were supposed to have pure Judaic blood. What is more, in some passages priests are even mentioned as eminent examples of this criterion; for instance, in the Mishnah, fourth division (4.2): 'priests, Levites, and Israelites who are suitable to marry into the priesthood' can try capital cases.[20] Selden acknowledges this point, but answers that Levites and indeed any other Jews with purity of blood could qualify, especially if that purity were matrilineal. Moreover, no pure-blooded priest can become a sage if he lacks singular excellence in the law or, for that matter, the moral qualities set forth in the third criterion. Historically, Selden adds, any association between priests and legal excellence derives from the ample leisure for study that priests tended to have, an argument that he also embraces regarding the prevalence of priests in early English law. In other words, any connection between priests and magistracy is accidental, historically contingent, inclusive of many others aside from priests, and subject to the primary criterion of brilliance in law, theology, and other learning.

Noble or pure blood helps to ensure that the sages are not contemptible outside court, but it is no guarantee of anything else. Some of Selden's favourite authorities make him squirm on this matter, however, by singling out priests as special candidates for the Sanhedrin. When

Maimonides quotes Deuteronomy in making the point that priests and
Levites should be included in the numbers of the Sanhedrin judges and
omitted only if none is available, Selden complains that this great
author has truncated the verse that conceives of lay judges as equally
legitimate as priestly ones. Contrary to his belief in the 1640s that laymen should be present at synods, Selden resists the extensive testimony
to the singular love of the legal vocation in levitical priests, men who are
first born and of pure blood. Quoting as much rabbinical evidence as he
can find in opposition, Selden repeats the claim that priestly prevalence
in ancient law was owed merely to leisure, not to any legal privilege or
ontological status. Whereas the twenty-first chapter of Deuteronomy (5)
has led some commentators to argue that some kinds of cases – say,
regarding marriage or unclean lepers – are appropriate for priests,
Selden counters that whenever this was the case, it was the magistrates
who isolated, delegated, and oversaw such affairs.

In sum, Selden argues, the original creation of the Sanhedrin was
advised by Jethro, commanded by God, and executed by Moses with no
word about priests. Even if the priestly order, like other confederations,
was committed to monitoring itself, he maintains, all their duties, controversies, and criteria were subject to censure by the Sanhedrin; and
high priests could be tried and convicted like any men. Even when, in
his third book, he skips the priestly issues under the special control of
the Sanhedrin – omits them because he has covered them elsewhere –
Selden cannot resist offering one vivid instance of the authority of the
Sanhedrin over the functions of the priests. Seven days before the Day
of Atonement, according to the Mishnah, the high priest is brought to
the chamber of the elders or judges in the Sanhedrin, and these sages
devote the week to preparing the priest to perform his own ritual. They
read to him, hear him read the liturgy, and in general familiarize him
with the forms and procedures of his most sacred office. The priest is
not allowed to eat much, to sleep, or to fornicate. As they leave him on
the day of the ritual, the elders address the high priest with a warning:
'We abjure you by Him who caused his name to rest upon this house,
that you not vary in any way from all which we have instructed you.'
Such an oath against deviation, innovation, or forgetfulness is all the
more urgent insofar as the elders are unable to witness the ritual within
the veil of the temple.[21]

Within the veil the high priest labours alone in the spirit, although
the Great Sanhedrin has done all that it can to secure the normalcy of
this labour. It neither invades the veil nor leaves unshaped what takes

place therein. Prophets, however, offer a more challenging case for the rabbinical Selden's efforts to coordinate the domains of civil jurisdiction and spiritual labour. The problem with prophets is that they themselves censure other authorities – priests, judges, kings – on the basis of what they have experienced behind the epistemological veil of private visions, dreams, and voices. Indeed, one rabbinical category for unofficial versions of excommunication involves those judgments prompted by dreams putatively sent from God. Selden marshals evidence that the Hebrews highly valued the wisdom of dreams, but also that the rabbis approached such claims critically, since claims made on dreams might prove nugatory or even harmful. What is needed, then, is a critical, judicious, and normative approach to dreams and dreamers, prophecies and prophets – an oneirocriticism and a forensic procedure for supposed revelation. For Selden suggests that a society cannot afford to dispense with the visionary realm of experience, any more than it can afford to be fooled or torn apart by the claims made on its warrant.

If a court is to deal properly with dreams, sometimes it will need to adopt extraordinary procedures to ensure the presence of qualified judges and to bestow a special reverence on the matter. In making this case, Selden offers a humorous reminder that dreams are as distinct from normal judicial procedures as human experience can become. He alludes to a story from the pastorals of Theocritus in which a poor fisherman intending to hook a fish with his 'piece of deception' instead falls asleep and dreams of a gallant golden fish who promises him wealth if he will never fish again. Upon waking up poor, the fisherman asks his companion if he must keep the oath made in the dream. The friend assures him that the oath was no more binding than the golden fish was actual, and that he must fish again or 'die of hunger and golden visions.' Selden's own point appears to be that a naive appeal to dreams is the worst, most destructive kind of languishing in a *locus amoenus* or bower of bliss.[22]

As links to the spirit of God, however, prophetic dreams are potentially too valuable simply to be dismissed as empty shows or golden hooks. After all, the spirit of God plays a prominent role in the origins of the Sanhedrin itself, though there are conflicting rabbinical views over how to interpret that role. Selden pays careful attention to that origin in a conversation between Moses and his father-in-law, Jethro. The growing burdens of settling legal disputes and of resolving difficult cases of conscience prompt Jethro to advise Moses not to handle them alone but to set up a body of elders. In turn, God commands Moses to assem-

ble the elders at the Tent of the Presence where the spirit of God will
visit them: 'I will come down and speak with you there. I will take back
part of that same spirit which has been conferred on you and confer it
on them, and they will share with you the burden of taking care for the
people; then you will not have to bear it alone.' A key interpretive problem emerges from the description of this spiritual reassignment,
namely, that if in some versions the elders receiving the spirit are said to
have commenced a prophesying that 'did not cease,' other versions
claim that they prophesied once then never again (Num. 11: 16–30,
NEB, 150–1; Book 2, 104–44).

The question arises, then, whether ecstatic prophecy affords a normal
ingredient in the judicial procedures of these elders, or is simply an inaugural infusion of God's wisdom and grace. Selden simplifies matters
somewhat by insisting that this spirit is no Trinitarian person but is, rather,
an ineffable divine influence. As usual, Maimonides helps Selden to rationalize and systematize difficult points of Judaic thought, in this case by
delineating gradations of spirit and of prophecy in the *More Nebochim.*
Allowing that such mysteries cannot be perfectly understood according
to the level ['*amussim*,' the carpenter's rule] of any human thought, Maimonides helps Selden to alert his readers that they must never take for
granted that they already comprehend what is meant by 'spirit' in any particular passage in the Bible. After all, its meanings can range from wind
and air to life and reason, and onward to some higher agency. Regarding
the case of inspiration and the Sanhedrin, Maimonides opts at first for the
once-and-never-again explanation of the prophesying elders. In this reading, the elders resemble all those other human beings who might catch
one glimpse of truth's splendour before returning to the shadows of their
everyday perception and to the imperfect measures according to which
they make decisions (Book 2, 112–22).[23]

Maimonides explains, moreover, that there are degrees of prophecy:
'The first degree of prophecy consists in the divine assistance which is
given to a person, and induces and encourages him to do something
good and grand, e.g., to deliver a congregation of good men from the
hands of evil-doers; to save one noble person, or to bring happiness to a
large number of people.' This influence from the spirit of God takes
hold of judges such as Samson, those who are raised to free an
oppressed people, for instance. At the second level of prophecy, 'A person feels as if something came upon him, and as if he had received a
new power that encourages him to speak. He treats of science, or com-
poses hymns, exhorts his fellow-men, discusses political and theological

problems.' The elders of the Sanhedrin possess the spirit of God in this sense, as do sacred poets, wise monarchs, and oracular high priests consulting God's will via the Urim and Thummim. In every one of these cases, the prophetic elocution transpires while the person is 'awake and in full possession of his sense.'[24]

As Selden notes, however, Maimonides complicates the question of spirit even in the process of normalizing divine influence at the second level of prophecy. For without warning, the great rabbi shifts to the view of the elders' inspiration that maintains their incessant prophesying. To be sure, theirs remains a reliable and authoritative spirit of counsel and judgment. But as far as Selden is concerned, the interpretive damage has been done: Maimonides confuses his account of the inaugural interaction between spirit and legal wisdom in the judges of the Sanhedrin more than he manages to clarify it.

Perhaps, Selden explains, judges are charismatic in the commonplace way that apostles, teachers, healers, and prophets are: that is, they are gifted by God to perform a sacred duty in religious society. This wider distribution of charisma is supported by Moses's exclamation, 'I wish that all the Lord's people were prophets and that the Lord would confer his spirit on them all' (Num. 11: 29–30, NEB, 151). This conferral might simply lead to people performing their holy duties in everyday life; but in the 1640s and 1650s the notion of a 'nation of prophets' has taken on radical new dimensions for writers like Milton, who conceive of such a nation as ushering in the apocalyptic overthrow of church polity, monarchy, and custom. Selden, too, is entertaining (though not enthusiastically heralding) an alternative model for a religious society in which monarchs and bishops largely disappear from view and a senatorial and judicial court guides the people towards the most prosperous coordination between their amorphous, potentially anarchic, spiritual gifts and their measured, potentially autocratic, ligatures. However, the scholar of the Sanhedrin makes no comment in his discussion of Maimonides on exactly what sort of changes in English society would be required for his Judaic dream to come true. It is not even certain whether Selden is arguing for such a change, whatever its scope or factors might be. He rarely applies his discussion directly to contemporary issues, let alone to topical events. Yet a senatorial government without a monarch overseeing a domain of ostensibly sacred spiritual labour cannot help but speak to the future of a society embarked on just such a radical experiment in which Parliament rules without its aristocratic half and its king, aspirants to sainthood seek a fundamentally transformed dispensation of the

Holy Spirit on the verge of apocalypse (with the Sanhedrin itself a model to which they appeal), and Levellers call for a major overhaul of English legal institutions and practices. Selden's world is alive with rampant, bold, sometimes violent assertions of how English society could best liberate itself from the legal, political, moral, and religious transgressions of the past. But at the heart of that search for the truth about liberty is the matter to which Selden devotes his full scholarly attention, the matter of how prophets and zealots are to be kept lawful while legal arbiters are kept respectful to prophecy and zeal.

Having considered the extent to which the elders are inspired prophets, Selden strengthens their oversight of religious society in stressing that the indictment of false prophets ranks among the prerogatives of the Great Sanhedrin (Book 3, 72–80). Like true prophecy, so too its false sibling: a lucid understanding of how far the court's jurisdiction extends is hard to come by. By 'false prophet,' Selden contends, the rabbis do not mean one who incites the Hebrew people to form a new sect or mode of worship, insofar as human nature is apt to produce peculiar or various interpretations of doctrine. Nor do the rabbis understand by 'false prophet' those seers who inaccurately predict the future. The key factor, according to Selden, is the pretext of the prophet: the false version will counterfeit or simulate dictation either from God or from idols, or he will base a prophecy on the authority of an idol whether or not the content of the prophecy is licit ('Etiam quicquid ex idoli autoritate praemoneret, tametsi res ipsa licita aliàs esset nec à vero cultu dissona, pro Pseudopropheta nihilominùs habebatur' [Book 3, 73]). In other words, a false prophet either maintains that an idol is a true god, or fraudulently claims authority from either a true or false god's dictation.

Deuteronomy itself raises and attempts to answer the obvious question in this matter: 'How shall we recognize a word that the Lord has not uttered' (Deut. 18: 21, NEB, 202). Insofar as support in Deuteronomy for a wait-and-see strategy is mixed, Selden is happier with the Talmudic answer that prophecies should square with what Moses has lawfully established. Claims on God's spirit can and must be measured according to the prescriptions of God's law. One provision, however, restores an extraordinary authority of inspiration to the spirit of prophecy: if a prophet articulates a vision contrary to established law, the people should believe him if a dire situation requires uncommon measures and if the prophet is a sage tried and celebrated for his piety, duty, and justice. That is, the more a prophet is qualified for the Sanhedrin, the more leeway the Sanhedrin is apt to grant him when his prophecies break the law. But Selden leaves his readers without updated guidelines for dire situations and uncommon measures; there are no allusions to the Thirty Years War, the English Civil War, the persecution of individual consciences, or the execution of a monarch. For no doubt that is the problem with uncommon measures; they cannot be predicted, rectified, or systematized, dependent as they are on the spirit of wisdom that putatively speaks to the sages of law.

—— 6 ——

However much Selden might sketch the outlines of a separate domain for spiritual labours, the overriding thesis of his *De Synedriis* is that the rabbinical understanding of forensic jurisdiction observes no distinction between sacred and profane matters requiring some public dispensation. As a division within the jurisdiction of a court, a capital as against a pecuniary case makes sense to the rabbis, but a divide between sacred and profane is not practicable. Excommunication is Selden's primary example, much as it is for Erastus: the judges to the Sanhedrin decide when to inflict this humanly devised punishment. So, too, the proselytizing rituals of a pagan's regeneration into Judaism: it is the office of the judicial prefects to examine the legitimacy of their administration. Indeed these civil duties themselves are sacred, the law that they administer is holy, as are, ultimately, all aspects of living in a religious society. To this extent at least, Selden's Judaic Erastianism does not secularize the sacred; it consecrates the civil even as it asserts a disjunction between sacred civility and spiritual labour. Since ancient Judaism provides the model for a unified jurisdiction – of jurisdiction in one kind – it follows that the civil agents, theologians to a man, and procedures for the execution of justice are sacred. Their domain does not 'mingle' with the sacred because nothing can be said to mix with itself. In the Bible, Mishnah, and Talmud, justice is as dear to God as ritual purity and times, more so than any notion of personal redemption. In any case, ritual purity and times are also concerns for the deliberation of the Sanhedrin. Selden stresses what is found in Chronicles – that judges should worry about pleasing God rather than man (2 Chron. 19:6). In making a ruling over what might seem a secular controversy, judges in the Sanhedrin are vested with a sanctity regarding the law that they serve or the office that they fill, or both.

Nothing emphasizes Selden's unification of all jurisdiction into a sacrosanct civil power than his out-of-context quotation of a section from the *Historia Novorum* of Eadmer. The passage in question characterizes William the Conqueror's total control over the public affairs of the eleventh-century English church, but Selden includes none of Eadmer's righteous indignation at what the monk considers a corrupt innovation and violation of the crux of English spirituality (Book 1, 364). By removing the passage from its context, Selden subverts the passionately clear message of his thirty-year old edition; in its place, he accentuates the Roman legal basis of that medieval church as a way of making the case that any judicial authority exercised by the church was a special allotment. This allowance was precisely like those other Roman law courts practising in England – the court of chivalry made obsolete with Selden's help in the 1640s; and given Selden's minimization of the influence of Roman law on England as he presents the matter in his commentary in *Ad Fletam*, he clearly undercuts Eadmer's protection of church autonomy in the public domain with an emphasis on all jurisdiction being held in English legal institutions. The latter are conceived as surrounding and controlling the deliberations carried on by church officers whenever the civil officers see fit to consult them.

Unlike spiritual labour, Selden argues, church forensics was always made and modified, not protected as a pure core, by the arbiters of legal jurisdiction. As he points out in his discussion of Wycliffe's thought, any judgment dispensed by prelates ought to have depended on the permission and regulation of those vested with public authority according to their invented standard (Book 1, 418). Aside from its allotted public deliberations, the church was meant to carry forth the badge of Christ's humility, rejecting all manner of worldly power in labouring always for human salvation and by means of the divine spirit. Presbyterians and any others claiming a proper jurisdiction for the English church transgress against the norms of the sacred English law.

The list of cases deemed by the Mishnah to be appropriate for the Great Sanhedrin alone includes but is not limited to judgments or consultations concerning obstinate elders, whole tribes, apostate cities, false prophets, wives suspected of adultery, priests, high priests, kings, sacrifices, certain homicide cases, the calculation of holy times, and voluntary wars. But in all these cases, judicial invention is responsible for making sanctity come alive in the form of the social, in imitation of a God whose spirit made the social come alive in the form of the sacred. In emphasizing the human artificiality of what might be history's most accomplished model for protecting a lawful spirituality, Selden comes full circle to a poetics of positive law – to prescriptions for fashioning the civil norms of holy living. The maker of a template for a religious society must appreciate and cultivate the amplitude of natural law; protect and encourage the media through which God's presence is most purely and reverently dispensed to the realm of human experience; respect the rituals of shame within earnest and honest communities; and monitor as well as rectify the potentially uncivil claims made on natural law, prophetic inspiration, priestly sanctity, poetic delight, and fraternal community with a wise and at times coercive human invention.

Selden probably started work on the Great Sanhedrin in the late 1630s, and he certainly worked on the project throughout the 1640s until his death in 1654. It is not surprising, then, that his work on natural law is on display in the frame of reference for *De Synedriis*. But what role does natural law play in his invention of the Sanhedrin and the religious society that it monitors? Early in Book 1 he claims that even if there were no evidence that the ancient Jews formed judicial institutions, it could be assumed that their rationality would naturally prompt them to originate some apparatus for rectifying manners. Notwithstanding the corruption, neglect, and deviations of conscience, the Noachian peoples of the world would always have God's word reminding them that it is calamitous for a society to proceed without law and justice. This word of God would be written universally in their very hearts, not on tablets. It would tell them always and everywhere that societies must have wise judges and good laws in order, as Abraham understood, to conform to the way of the Lord in living in a just and righteous fashion.

Selden reminds his readers of the list of Noachian precepts that he has discussed so extensively in *De Jure Naturali et Gentium*. But in *De Synedriis* the list has really narrowed to the sixth, the institution of justice, so that when Jethro advises Moses to create the body of elders, the father-in-law is acting on a natural, universal, and godly obligation. At times Selden's treatment of this obligation edges it towards artifice, for instance, when he compares its force to the compulsion of a syllogism, or to natural reason crystallized in artificial reasoning (Book 1, 49–55). Obligation is forced upon us both by the law that God has instilled in each of us and by the pacts and coercive apparatus that we make for ourselves. The double bind of this obligation means, on the one hand, that jurisprudence is an immutable and a pious norm for all manner of life's actions and decisions, and, on the other hand, that human beings must fashion enforcements of natural justice. The enforcers of nature must also supplement nature with laws appropriate to the circumstances of history.

Intermittently over the course of *De Synedriis*, Selden naturalizes justice and makes it incumbent on human beings to seek out the divine-
cum-natural foundation of their legal fictions. This search is especially
valuable when the artifice – say, excommunication – is coercive. Yet
through the three volumes, natural law tends to get lost in the emphasis
on judicial artifice; and its universal authority is unsettled by two factors.
The lesser factor involves Selden's celebration of reform in natural studies. By valorizing Copernicus on a par with Erastus, he highlights the discord among natural philosophers themselves, but he attempts to restore
something of the timeless authority of new philosophies in protesting
that Copernicus and Erastus are hardly the first to advance their supposedly heterodox ideas.

The larger factor complicating the invocation of natural law arises in
the final sections of the unfinished third volume. In what appears to be
a simple matter in a list of judicial prerogatives, the great scholar is considering the Sanhedrin's leadership in determining the legitimacy of
additions made to the city of Jerusalem and to the courtyards of the
temple. This seemingly specific matter expands into a remarkably
digressive history of the rites of consecration and dedication, of the
assets and liabilities of sacred art, and of conflicting views regarding the
human fashioning of enclosures and vehicles for the holy. In this history, the very worth of human artifice in dispensing or capturing the
holiness of a higher law is suddenly in question. For the ancient Stoic
ideal of an unbounded pneumatic divinity is powerfully invoked, and
this *pneuma* in turn embodies the universality and purity of nature
against the idols, superstitions, and politics of art. According to this
often Christianized Stoicism, human attempts to contain this cosmic
divinity in beautiful temples and altars, in polities or rites, is absurd at
best and debauched or tyrannical at worst. The shrines of the cosmic
pneuma are twofold: the cosmos at large and the heart or mind of the
honest and reverent man. For Selden, the use of natural law within his
normative construct is difficult enough if one considers the heightened
contention among natural philosophers of the sixteenth and seventeenth centuries; but a place for natural law becomes almost impossible
to locate once the natural legalists themselves assail the virtues of
human artifice and urge a choice between two masters.

The final sections on the history of sacred art are virtually hapless in
Selden's attempt to include all the formulae and rites for making, consecrating, containing, and beautifying holiness. Along the way, however,
he allows ample room for the devastating critiques of the very mentality

that aims to contain the holy in a relic or ornament. In the penultimate chapter of the entire work, he quotes Minucius Felix's early Christian assault on pagan shrines and rites, which proclaims God's image in the shrine of human nature itself, according to which notion the mind is a better place for dedication and the heart for consecration than any artificial structure (Book 3, 334–5). More than this, Minucius Felix maintains, no temple can contain the divinity that fills the universe, the one celebrated in that heroic poem (Lucan's *Pharsalia*) that Selden himself has praised in a poem. How much better to sacrifice one's spirit and conscience, to live virtuously and faithfully, to experience God everywhere in nature, and to remember that God looks with most delight on the beautiful spectacle of the persecuted Christian. Pagan notions of gods who reside in altars, require votive gifts, and recline on decorated cushions are drastically impious – or so the Christian author concludes. 'What image can I make of God,' asks Minucius's Christian interlocutor Octavius, 'when, rightly considered, man himself is an image of God? What temple can I build for him, when the whole universe, fashioned by his handiwork, cannot contain him?'[25]

Octavius proceeds to reject the attempt to contain God in any 'tiny shrine' in the kind of Stoic rhetoric that made a powerful impression on Selden and his contemporaries (Minucius, 413). Selden's own rhetoric of personal autonomy grows Stoic in his *Vindiciae*, also among his very last works. In the face of political and cultural vicissitudes, he asserts in that apologia, the best fusion of righteousness and measure exists within one's own bosom, which in turn is the human instantiation of a cosmic natural law. Like his friend Ben Jonson, Selden appeals to such autonomy in resisting the substantial evidence that what he makes can never refashion the world.

Yet in constructing the Sanhedrin, Selden persists in his highly intricate history of consecration rituals, arguing that the Stoic critique of superstition makes full sense for Christians only when they are persecuted and have no magistrates. Stoicism is strategy under duress, while a heavily Judaic artifice of sacrifice must take hold once it is one's responsibility to forge a lasting coordination between law and spirit. Unlike his treatment of Judaism in *De Jure Naturali*, Selden's work in *De Synedriis* is no longer making an effort to take the specific rites and polity out of Judaism. To strive for natural universals, one is no doubt better off going the way of Lord Herbert – the pagan way – though even there considerable ritual has to be stripped away or explained. Selden is no longer apologizing for the specificity of Judaism: the challenge is rather to unite its legal religion with its spiritually renewed manifestation in early Christianity. The question at hand is not how one might reduce Judaism to common notions, but rather whether Christian agape has enough law, and Judaism enough spirit, for them to reunite.

As Selden's history of artificial holiness trails off with the author's death, however, it can hardly be said that he has sided with either nature or art. The table of contents makes it clear that he planned to come to sections on the role of the natural world in religious worship. Even if it can be said that at times he has in mind civil government as an enclosure for a purer spirituality, that spirituality is not enclosed in the government in the same way that holiness is enclosed in corporeal beauty or even a magical *pneuma* in a charm. And the keystone metaphor suggests that civil cohesion is so positioned as to allow everything not identical with the artifice of government to extend outward from its anchor.

The arch is decidedly, doubly, an artifice: it is made as a metaphor, and the content of the figure refers to a humanly fashioned structure. It is meant to welcome us to the temple complex in which Selden's Sanhedrin will assume its duties. Within these layers of artifice, he allows a courtyard for the gentiles in which natural law serves as a reminder of a great dream – of a universal presence at once wholly measured and maximally pneumatic. But as Selden runs out of time in his search for the rituals of consecration, his last great work of scholarship leaves no doubt that the courtyard of natural law is also part of an artificial structure. From start to finish in *De Synedriis,* Selden argues for the warrant of human invention and regulation, even as that human artifice must enclose and promote a spirituality and naturalness far holier than its shrine and guardian.

Indeed, the great artifice of *De Synedriis* is Solomon's temple, an architectural complex in which all of Selden's contributors to normative spirituality might have a space. The Great Sanhedrin not only oversaw the affairs of the temple; its very residence was in the temple complex itself, in the chamber of hewn stone. On one side is the courtyard of the people or the gentiles, a space where the natural commonality of religions might be respected and mediated. Thus, having cited Seneca's opposition to shrines, temples, and altars, Selden also cites Acts, where Paul tells the Greek Sanhedrin, the Areopagus, that 'the God who created the world and everything in it, and who is Lord of heaven and earth, does not live in shrines made by men' (Acts, 17:24, NEB, 165). In Selden's day, it was commonplace to think of the temple complex on a level with the Garden of Eden and to posit a correspondence between the cosmos and the temple.

On the other side is the courtyard of the priests and beyond that the temple building itself, both of which unfold gradations moving in the direction of the clergy left to its own devices. In support of their rites and prayers, Levites sing lovely songs of faith amid the ornamental splendours of the architectural complex. It is significant, then, that in the passage chosen by Selden from Acts an explanation follows for why God accepts human services, even though God needs nothing and 'is himself the universal giver of life and breath and all else' (Acts 17:25, NEB, 165). God does not need our own fashioning of the sacred, but God nonetheless expects and demands it. In the middle of the temple courtyards are the rabbis, whose responsibility it is not only to pass judgment according to law, but also to rework the truth of God's law in poetry, allegory, and narrative. As Selden likes to say, the Sanhedrin is situated between diverse worlds or realms, one in which natural law is acceptable and the other in which ritual holds sway; one that is sacredly civil and the other that is exclusively holy; one in which the laity challenge the privileges of the priests and the other in which the priests commune alone with the presence of God, those priests apart from the dynamic of shame yet instructed and exhorted by the judges-cum-senators themselves. Somehow, rabbinical fictions must cement all the realms together, both the fictions that the rabbis have made and the fiction that Selden makes of the rabbis.

For Selden, the essence of Jewish history is that God commands a people and their leaders to make vehicles for the reality and truth of unthinkable sanctity, then insists that those vehicles be appropriate, lawful, and unifying. In fact, some of the worst sins involve the malformation of such vehicles. As with excommunication or oaths, Selden would reclaim the rites of dedication and consecration in holy places as a synecdoche for the human struggle to make lawful vehicles for unthinkable holiness, whether they be laws or poems, buildings or formulae, whether they have a natural basis or not, and boast utility or beauty. At times, he isolates heroes who appear to fuse a wisdom of natural law and a commitment to artifice in their judicial duties. In this mould, his old friends the Druids make a brief but potent appearance in *De Synedriis* as wise pagans whose procedures of excommunication have been thought by some to possess a deep antiquity (Book 1, 409–17). More pervasive, however, is Selden's celebration of the Sanhedrin elders as they are depicted in the Talmud, as sages whose virtuous and godly character, birth status, and learning all contribute to their excellence in the everyday fashioning of religious society.

Time and again, Selden returns to the extensive and diverse qualifications for these judges, as if to demonstrate beyond any doubt that nature and art converge in their godliness and wisdom. It is this ideal of the sages and their institution, the Sanhedrin, that Selden must make and remake, brick by brick, wedge stones against keystone. After all, God commanded Moses to make him a body of elders; and elders were indeed made in rites of ordination. Yet from time to time, Selden hints at the burden of his own making, whether his model for the maker be the normative poet fashioning social ideals or the lawyer making forensic and legislative arguments. Such making has its strengths and weaknesses, and it has its own problems with uniting gnosis and praxis. At times, the maker accentuates the practical means of rebuilding religious society, and sometimes he dreams of an earthly paradise. To the very end, the reader of Selden's Judaic polity is suspended over whether its maker seeks to rebuild English religious society, or he indulges himself in solitary dreams of Canaan, the recovery of which the scholar never projects.

In the *Table Talk*, Selden can often be found using the language of 'making' when he considers the mandates of religion. 'But now the temporall & the spirituall power ... spring both from one fountaine,' he remarks. 'They are like two Twists that make upp the same Rope' (98). Whereas 'the Jewes ... could make no figure of God,' Christians have so benefited from the incarnation that they 'knowe what shape to picture God in, Nor knowe I why wee may not make his Image, provided wee bee sure what it is' (55). Sacred art or making must be carefully rectified but, if carefully wrought, it is fully legitimate. 'Those words you now use in makeing a Minister' (78); 'The Laws of ye Church are most favourable to ye Church because they were of ye Church mens owne makeing' (29); the Thirty-Nine Articles 'were made att three Sevrall convocacions' (8): throughout his recorded conversation, Selden reiterates his conviction that invention is no less integral to religion than it is to poetry (Nashe's point that aldermen 'cannott make a Blanke verse' [77]) or social rank (heralds 'make their owne pedigree' [29]). But biblically obsessed Protestants refuse to admit that spirituality must thrive or falter on the basis of human invention. To those who 'say there must bee no humane Invention in the Church,' Selden responds that all human involvement in religion is invention, and that 'old Invencions are best' (59), presumably those like the Sanhedrin made by a people who tended to 'thrive where ere they come' and 'keep together' (54).

The Jews, he believes, understood that the further they trailed away from the divine font of the biblical covenants, the more their hope for a measured yet abundantly spiritual society would depend on the ways in which they refashioned their institutions and traditions. If their authorization of religious artifice tended to show more severity or rigour than the iconic festivals of Roman Catholicism, it was also the case that the Jews conceded and even celebrated the value of accommodating inventions far more than the most iconoclastic Protestants. In the face of enormous oppression under the pagan Romans, Jews coped very well with the state of affairs in which the pretty glass holding the spirit was both indispensable in its function and nugatory in its constituents. It is finally unclear, however, whether Selden was of the mind that, unlike ancient Judaism, which managed the arts of law and the spirit so as to maximize cohesion even as the Jews lost direct contact with their Creator, the English Protestant society of the 1640s and 1650s had squandered both its sacred arts and its intimacy with God in one catastrophic dissolution into internecine violence. For it is also possible that Selden could see his way to propose the Sanhedrin to the learned in his society as a vote of confidence in England's progression beyond the canonical persecutions attached to Laudian beauty as well as the zany rant of the Antinomian spirit.

In *De Synedriis*, Selden's fascination with the ways in which human beings make their religious societies is evident in his discussions of biblical translations, in his study of conflicting interpretations of the Sanhedrin, and in his publishing history of Erastus. Indeed, even though Selden's view of excommunication and spiritual labour is deeply influenced by Erastus, his discussion of that sixteenth-century author is much more taken with the strange history of his publication and transmission – in short, with the distorted invention of Erastianism – than with a blow-by-blow analysis of his theses (Book 1, 429–39). Repeatedly, Selden stresses that human beings make the mandates, institutions, and partisan boundaries as vehicles for their religious beliefs and practices, then strive to efface the marks of the making. Selden not only understands this striving; he also hints at the motivations of his own endeavour in making the 'Great Sanhedrin.' In his attempt to understand the motives of sacred artifice, however, he raises the question of whether human invention preserves the traditions of a religious society once that society has passed away, or the human need to rely on invention tragically contributes to the mutation and cessation of those traditions.

Late in the second book, Selden considers Henricus Spondanus's contention that the history of the Sanhedrin involved constant change, along with the corollary that the Sanhedrin became an image, semblance, or perhaps even just a mental picture of what it was or might have been: 'Sunt autem qui Continuationi Synedrii Magni,' Selden begins, '(è cuius Maiestate adeò pependit reliquorum constitutio & autoritas) eousque adversantur, ut certi de eiusdem numero aut autoritate quidquam perseverasse sibi non videri scribant [There are, however, authors that oppose this continuation of the Great Sanhedrin – on the power of which indeed the establishment and authority of the lesser Sanhedrins depended – so that they write with confidence regarding the number or authority of this same institution that it does not appear to have endured in its own right]' (Book 2, 604). To exemplify this disbelief among the authorities, Selden quotes Bishop Spondanus: 'cum admodum obscura sit eorum (Synedrii illius collegarum) memoria in sacra Scriptura ac probatis historiis à Mose usque ad Christum, falsum quoque putamus, eos semper eodem numero vel suprema autoritate perseverasse, quamvis probabile crediderimus, extitisse semper imaginem quandam eiusmodi magistratûs quem & aliquando restituisse videtur Josaphat Rex Judae [With the remembrance of the Sanhedrin judges becoming utterly obscured over the course of those sacred scriptures spanning from the history approved with regard to Moses up through Christ, we deem it false that this same institution always persevered in number or in supreme authority, although we believe it probable that there always existed some image (semblance / mental picture / model) of this kind of magistrate, an image that at one time Josaphat, King of Judea, appears to have restored]' (Book 2, 604). It is unclear exactly what kind of image Selden's source has in mind here, or what kind of image Selden assumes he has in mind. Is it an image captured in writing or an oral tradition of the kind that Drayton idealizes in dreaming of British Bards? Is it a fantasy motivated by desire or loss, an ideal that might prompt action, or an accurate transmission of a faded fact? As an image, Selden's own version of the great Judaic court faces the same challenges from the conflicting criteria of scholarly critics and rhetorical moralists that Jonson's praise for a country estate or Drayton's romanticized Britannia must confront. Even if Selden cannot claim, as Jonson can with regard to the Sidney estate 'Penshurst,' that he has visited a meeting of the Sanhedrin, his imagined Sanhedrin might prove every bit as real in the Platonizing sense of the truth-telling lie or foreconceit in Sidney's *Apology*: an image of what ought to be rather than what is. In his final great work, Selden might be able to claim the moral war-

rant of a Sidneyean golden world, at best a higher truth, at worst a provocation to think about religious society otherwise than has previously
been the case.

The massive scholarship of the books tells another story. Selden is
without question attempting to reconstruct the Sanhedrin as it was in
fact, and he strongly resists the position that the Sanhedrin has persisted
only as an image. Philology, not poetic device, is the queen of his
method. According to his own thesis, it is true, this famous court and its
judicial decisions have always borne the status of a human invention
that, even if divinely commanded, needed to be fashioned and refashioned over the course of their roughshod history. Invention in this case
is rather social than fanciful, however, an intellectual, discursive, and
practical collaboration among a people across history rather than the
golden dreams of solitary poets and prophets. At times, Selden purveys
the ancient vehicle of this fashioning as if it were an unbroken oral
transmission; but he is aware of those critics who charge that such a tradition is fictive, not simply made but made up. In response, his scholarly
persona resists the seductions of normative poetics, the elevation of a
carefully idealized model over the intricacy of historical detail, or the
delight in a well-turned phrase over the critical analysis of often barbarous evidence. Selden maintains his distance from his invention, as well
as from the readers and the turbulent English context to which, if the
readers choose, the model of the Sanhedrin might be applied. If the
scholar insists that his subject was more than an image, then, he is also
prepared to leave his invention as something less than Sidney's foreconceit, the wonder, instruction, and delight of which is meant boldly and
powerfully to change men into heroes. The danger, then, of simply
approximating the Sanhedrin as it was is that no contemporary will be
moved to imitate its benefits in future times.

In one of the few passages reflective of an agenda on the author's
part, Selden voices his desire for change in the plaintive mode of longing for judicial ideals that might have been realized at a turning point in
history but simply were not. Had the Jews early on embraced their
reformed party, the Christians, he surmises, then the best of law and
spirit would have survived Roman persecution together. Jews and Christians failed to recognize that they were in pursuit of the same ideal, a
just society in which spiritual zeal and redemption are reconcilable with
law. Yet Selden offers little if any glimpse of the future of his invention.
Might the Sanhedrin be re-established as the Jews dreamed or fancied
(*somniant*) that it would be?

In Selden's final years, there was a prominent drive in England either to restore the Jews to Israel or to allow them back into England; and English readers could read in their own tongue the extraordinary book by Menasseh Ben Israel called *The Hope of Israel*. But to the incomplete end of his work on the Sanhedrin, Selden is elusive on the question that perhaps mattered most in the 1650s: Was the Sanhedrin a useful, viable model for advancing religious society into a prosperity worthy of the Messiah, or a beautiful, poetical dream from which Philo-Semites would sadly awaken? Was the great Judaic court a malleable yet reliable standard through which the best of spirituality in war-torn England might be preserved and the impostors rectified? Or was the image of the Sanhedrin an arbitrary and unreliable wisp in the historical currents of a turbulent time? Selden's volumes on the Sanhedrin sometimes lament the missed opportunities for prudent and earnest Jews to have embraced the new gospel of God's spirit as a means of eventually preserving their laws and institutions in the centuries beyond Constantine. Yet he himself never quite clarifies just how much hope the debacle of contemporary Christianity can afford in looking to Judaic images of hewed stone.

In lamenting the death of Selden in a preface to Book 3, the publisher of *De Synedriis* enumerates the projected sections that the author never completed. There has been no attempt to finish the work, he acknowledges; for who could do it? But he does attempt to justify Selden's tendency to digress into densely learned discussions of points such as the history of consecration and dedication. At first, the publisher claims that Selden's digressions were as useful as they were learned and diligent. Yet he also wishes that the author had completed the work; for 'Optandum est hanc pulcherrimam Diatribam ad umbilicum fuisse perductam [it is desirable that he had prolonged this most beautiful/grand discourse to its conclusion]' (Book 3, A3v).

This piece of praise is not simple or obvious in meaning. Perhaps it was desirable for Selden to reach the end of the umbilical cord in the sense that only then might he move his readers beyond a discourse understood largely as a holiday in a *locus amoenus* of great beauty. Readers of the treatise might well remember that the umbilicus figures in rabbinical allegories, based on the Canticles, of the Sanhedrin itself. Perhaps the publisher wishes that Selden simply had protracted the reader's pleasure in the beauty of learning. Is beauty or grandeur the

vehicle of instruction or a distraction from utility? Selden has left his
readers – people already living in a time of great uncertainty about the
future of England – with a further perplexity about whether his or any
scholarly pursuit of a measure in religion will prove a golden dream
from which, finally, the readers, like the fisherman in Theocritus, wake
up or remain forever impoverished in apparent bliss. Thus the critic
who aimed to rectify the British Bards becomes in his death a Bard who
himself must be rectified, whose indirection must be followed or abandoned in the abyss of archaic and obscure scholarship.

The publisher's praise of the beauty as well as the use of Selden's
digressive scholarship approximates Horace's famous advice that in
order maximally to succeed, a poem needs to delight and instruct. Like
his old friend Ben Jonson, however, Selden found the maximum efficacy of his discourse – the accomplishment of delight and utility – an
almost impossible bill to fill. Indeed, he was wary of the legitimacy of
both pleasure and relevance in his scholarship; for either one could subvert the critical rigour and complex evidentiary thrust of his historiography. In the preface to Book 3 of *De Synedriis*, beauty and grandeur
amount to the consolation left over from Selden's failure to follow his
own threads out of the abyss. The disjunction between pulchritude and
utility epitomizes Selden's own lifelong conflict over whether a religious
society is better served by being prodded in the direction of golden
worlds or by having its imminent positive standards textually rendered
and practically administered as justly as humanly possible. Selden
looked to and refashioned ancient Judaism not simply because it was
uncompromisingly devoted to both spiritual zeal and legal rigour, but
also because it prompted him to coordinate all the different warrants to
which Selden believed a religious society should and would have debts,
to poesy and to nature, to spiritual labours and to legal contracts, and
(above and encompassing them all) to a wilful divinity first made manifest in the Paradise of Genesis.

Occasionally, Selden acknowledges the direct relevance of his work
on the Sanhedrin for contemporary Christian societies. Whether it is his
insistence on the Jews as a model for the early Christians, or his careful
analysis of how bodies of elders have jurisdiction over kings, Selden at
least hints at some topical points of contact between the world of Oliver
Cromwell and the world of Moses and Jethro. But he also resists such
relevance, whether it is because a topical comparison might endanger
him or because he has a distaste for the reduced scope to which a harp-
ing on relevance might force a careful and critical scholarship. The

table of contents anticipating the unfinished part of the work gives readers no reason to believe that he simply never arrived at the application
of his researches. Selden leaves his publisher to address the problem of
whether scholarly diligence yields hope in a measured religion or distraction in the ornate details of the past, or both. At home at Whitefriars
or in the Inner Temple, Selden dwelt in scholarship like a monk in his
cell; but he also sought vindication from the critics who charged him
with kowtowing to autocrats. Selden embraced public office, yet he also
closed his door to it. His life and works wrote large for his contemporaries a great dilemma of his time – whether it is better to make grand and
beautiful ideals that might shine on and even benefit a people from
afar, or to open oneself to the vicissitudes, manipulation, and injustices
of history in striving through social, political, and legal practices that
might effect direct changes in the world. As the third Sanhedrin volume
spirals haplessly into the incoherent abyss of scholarly detail, Selden's
readers are left to ponder whether he has left them with a pastime or a
promise. More than this, they are faced with deciding whether the
answer to that dilemma bears implications for the very future and
nature of religious society. For if the great Selden has failed to make
spirituality and civility hang together, it is possible that they simply will
not and cannot cohere.

Conclusion: 'Ghostly Authority against the Civill'

For half a century, John Selden 'took part in the great movements that reformed the European spirit, reordered its polity, and restructured its culture in the early modern period.'[1] But like that of so many other great participants in these 'movements,' his part was inventive, complex, and *sui generis*. Selden experimented with what Rosenblatt has called 'a plurality of discursive communities' both in posing the possible ways in which a religious society might best be regulated or normalized, and eventually in rethinking the warrant according to which the biblical dispensations of law and of spirit might be reintegrated or better co-ordinated.[2] By the 1640s Selden was participating in England's unprecedented struggle over how to save the concept and the core of religious society, threatened as it was by the rival excesses of forced conformity and anarchic fancy. Unlike Hooker and Laud, Selden had done more than try to justify and enforce the canonical religious polity as is. Unlike his dear friend Archbishop Ussher, who despite his own frail old age preached Selden's funeral sermon, Selden had tried to think outside the limited terms of debate among his partisan contemporaries. If, in trying to moderate episcopacy with an element of Presbyterianism, Ussher had 'met with the common fate of Arbitrators, to please neither party,' he preached to the impressively large and important audience at Selden's funeral that he, Ussher, 'was scarce worthy to carry his [Selden's] Books after him.'[3] But Ussher understood as well as anyone what all those books comprised: knowledge about the Judaic ways, so old and yet so new, of conceiving and accomplishing the holy commonwealth.

Once the episcopal model of church polity had been supplanted by the Presbyterian model in the 1640s, it was time for the Presbyterians to fret that the breakdown of English religion into particles referred to by Thomas Browne as 'atoms in divinity' was threatening the very existence of a charitably disposed and comprehensively religious society. Doubtless the most frantic of the many Presbyterian alarmists was Thomas Edwards, author of the tripartite *Gangraena*, otherwise known as 'A Catalogue and Discovery of many of the Errours, Heresies, Blasphemies and pernicious Practices of the Sectaries of this time, vented and acted in *England* in these four last years,' that is, 1642 to 1646. Among the parties guilty of disintegrating religious society in England were the various sects of antinomians, Brownists, Anabaptists, Familiasts, and Seekers, but also Selden's own Erastianism, the position holding that 'there is no distinction concerning Government of Ecclesiasticall and civil, for all that Government which concerns the Church, ought to be civil, but the maintaining of that distinction is for maintaining the interests of Church-men.' Whether it was the Erastians set on erasing church polity, the Congregationalists crying rape whenever Parliament might 'use any civil coercive means to compell men of different judgement,' or the antinomians erasing all the carnal forms and strictures outside 'the experience of the spirit in a mans self,' Edwards was eager to support the Long Parliament in its efforts at reform by taking it upon himself to offer that body of governors a refresher course in the fundamental notion of a religious society. Such a notion, Edwards argued, can be threatened only from within; for outside enemies such as the papists will tend to confirm a religious community's sense of identity and purpose. A toleration of the 'whirlegigg spirits' throughout England will produce nothing short of the 'dissolution of all Religion and good manners.' Parliament had better realize, Edwards warns, that in 1646 the handwriting is on the wall, and that it was the responsibility of that 'supreme Judicatory' to guarantee the survival of the Calvinist and Presbyterian vision of a comprehensive, well-regulated, spiritually and morally reformed society.[4]

There was no shortage of disputants against Edwards's claim that England was facing a 'no presbyter, no religious society' crisis. Independents or Congregationalists were refuting the notion of their 'Incompatiblenesse with Magistracy' in *An Apologeticall Narration*,[5] then laying out a new understanding of how compatibility might work. Labourers in the spirit would have 'no new Common-wealths to rear ... no State-ends or Politicall interests to comply with; No Kingdoms in our eye to subdue unto our mould.' The fact that the Congregationalists 'had nothing else to doe but simply and singly to consider how to worship God acceptably' would mean that their religion would 'be coexistent with the peace of

any form of Civil Government on earth.'[6] 'Presbytery is the rival of Episcopacy,' John Goodwin argued in 1647, 'But Independency is of
another strain, and admitteth not of human prudence in church government. For the Church is a spiritual building, framed of such lively
stones as are not of the world, nor [is it] of the wisdom of the world, but
founded only upon the wisdom of God, revealed in the word by his
Spirit, [which] is sufficient to constitute and maintain a church without
assistance from the kingdoms of the world – whose power they leave
entire to itself.'[7] Such an extraordinary claim on pure apolitical spirituality was bound to run aground, especially given the Independents'
overlap with the Erastians in the project of delineating the separate
realms of coercive civil jurisdiction and suasive spiritual labour. Indeed,
Independency accumulated as much political currency as religious,
Congregationalists found themselves needing to justify their support of
coercive actions such as Pride's purge, and by the early 1650s it was
undeniably the case that their emphasis on autonomous gathered
churches was understood not to exclude a loosely organized national
church with its tithes.[8] Both in the aspirations to compatibility with the
magistrate and in their own designs on national politics and control, the
Independents were committed to fashioning and realizing a plan for
religious society even as they were perceived to be eroding the very possibility of such an entity.

In extending the autonomy of congregations both inward to the conscience and outward to the nation, Milton meanwhile was moving
beyond Independency towards a bolder, more sectarian vision of religious society that would authorize the militancy of the New Model Army
concurrently with each citizen's strenuous and unfettered exertion of
virtue, honest intellect, and godly devotion. Likening the newly tolerant
character of England to the great societies of democratic Athens, republican Rome, and the early Christian church, he filled his closet oration
known as *Areopagitica* with celebrations of the strong virtue, true liberty,
and championship of truth that an England beyond bishops and presbyters might just accomplish – by means of war to be sure, but more
emphatically by means of a spiritual, moral, and intellectual trial of the
individual conscience whose benefits Milton attributed to the scholarly
adventures of Selden himself. Off the battlefield but in the wars of
truth, Milton's brave new England would require a generous spirit of
charitable cooperation in reassembling the pieces of a metaphorical
temple that imaged for Milton the imperfect coherence of truth as it is
grasped by the penultimate religious commonwealth.

Even the most mystical of the adventurous thinkers and writers in the 1640s and 1650s had plans for refashioning a holy commonwealth. A few years after *Areopagitica*, in the final years of Selden's life, the Digger Gerrard Winstanley would be connecting the radical new claims on the experience of the Holy Spirit to a wholly new social order in which the earth would be converted back into a communal treasury and in which there would be no hierarchical propriety or mastery in families and society at large. Such was the vision of the 'true levelers,' he declared, who would proceed with a mattock rather than a sword or simply a miracle. Looking to swords and miracles rather than mattocks, Fifth Monarchists touted the return of King Jesus together with a vision of religious society opposite to Selden's Erastianism, a society in which the saints, not the magistrates, wielded the power. Welcoming the Nominated Parliament of 1653 as an approximation of the Sanhedrin, some of the Fifth Monarchists were prepared to fight in ending the long and corrupt monarchy of Rome and bringing about the final monarchy of their Saviour. We know that, at the same time, Selden himself was trying to finish his massive representation of the Sanhedrin and, in general, of the ancient Judaic institutions and arrangements by means of which the legalistic and spiritual extremes of a society might be corrected. These extremes, the excessive cold of conformity and the scalding heat of inspiration posited throughout the history of the English Reformation in John Denham's *Cooper's Hill* (1st ed., 1642; extensively revised in the early 1650s), had been encountered by the Jews themselves, and while Selden was to avoid direct applications of his work on the Sanhedrin to contemporary problems, his scholarship and activities in the 1640s had spoken quite directly to England's conflicts over magistracy's relationship to spirituality and over the tensions between devotional prescription and extemporization. In addition, the *Table Talk* took as its main theme Selden's sense that the closer England was edging towards the complete collapse of measure in its religious society, the more that it was up to lay scholars like him to imagine the possible ways of either saving its measure or providing it authentically for the first time.

In fact and in the popular imagination, the 'Ranters' embodied both the fear and the hope that England might move beyond the human devices, instruments, and circumstances of polity into the all-in-all apocalypse of pure spirit – without forms or scripture or any human mediation whatsoever. Dismissing the 'material sword' of the New Model, but also the 'Mattock' of the Diggers, Abiezer Coppe grasped simply 'the Sword of the Spirit' and, better, a formless God of universal love replacing all selves, filling all creation, and supplanting all forms.[9] Yet much as the so-called Ranters touted and were feverishly accused of bringing about the demise of those human, social, and ecclesiastical forms impeding the effusion of the spirit, Selden's late Erastianism was interpreted by some as signalling the endpoint of religious society and the inception of a purely civil society. Even among some of Selden's advocates, the great scholar's posthumous reception involved some concession to the conclusion that the great scholar had not entirely succeeded in his massive efforts to rescue a comprehensive religious society from collapse into secularity on the one hand and antinomian fantasy on the other. While some purveyors of his afterlife studied this shortcoming as symptomatic and symbolic of the overall contemporary failure to move beyond the spiritual fantasies of the Ranters and the drastically coercive and wholly civil will of the Hobbesian sovereign, others forgave Selden his limits by imagining the scene of his death as a showdown between two masters, Leviathan and God; but they disagreed on the master that Selden had chosen at long last.

In an eighteenth-century testimony to Selden's scholarship, it is true, one admirer would declare that the great English lawyer 'Lamented and Endeavour'd to correct the follies' of both sides in the Civil War; and that even his work on tithes had 'since beene found to be of real service to the Church.'[10] And there is no missing the influence of Selden's legal work on Matthew Hale, the authority of his work on natural law in the philosophy of the later century, and his presence in debates over the Exclusion Crisis and the Glorious Revolution.[11] Regarding Selden's most normatively ambitious enterprise, the search for the natural laws of religion shared by all peoples, however, Samuel Pufendorf criticized the English scholar for having squandered his opportunity to 'deduce natural law from any principle or hypothesis for which the evidence is acknowledged by all nations, or which they could be brought to acknowledge by arguments drawn from the light of reason.' The problem: Selden 'expounds what Hebrew scholars thought; he does not sufficiently examine whether their opinion accords with sound reason.'[12] In the decades after his death, Selden's Judaic scholarship and his case for ancient Presbyterianism in his Eutychius edition especially drew polemical responses, with very few readers concluding that Selden had found the key to the welfare and coherence of the holy commonwealth. Some conceded that his readers had been unable to understand his advice, blaming the reception of his learning rather than Selden himself for having sent such mixed and inaudible signals that readers finally could not say whether his chief obligation was to civility or to divinity. Others were far less kind. For if Baxter was prepared to be convinced by Hale that Selden was not on the devilish side of Hobbes, there were those mid- to late-seventeenth-century readers who argued that Selden had done everything in his power simply to remove holiness from the commonwealth altogether. Still others concluded that Selden's vision of the holy commonwealth, for instance, in the Eutychius, was sufficiently ecclesiastical but simply wrong and partisan. Selden's contemporaries agreed that the legacy of his scholarship was a powerful, unusual, and learned one; but they were at odds about what his scholarship meant for the future of the holy commonwealth in England. With the publication of the *Table Talk*, they could have seen just how concerned Selden was with relations between church and magistracy in contemporary times; laughed at the homespun simplicity with which he rephrased the knottiest problems in the holy commonwealth; and experienced a certain shock at the bald claims that he apparently made for the control of the church by the magistrate. But they also would have come across a remark according to which Selden himself had putatively despaired that 'Disputes in Religion will never bee ended because there wants a Measure by wch the business should bee decided ... One sayes one thing & another another, & there is, I say, no measure to end the controversie' (*Table Talk*, 119).

The fact that Selden's supporters and admirers struggled over the question of his legacy is in itself a testimony to their recognition that it was a legacy worthy of their close attention. On 28 November 1653 Gerard Langbaine wrote to Selden with his response to the second book of *De Synedriis*. Regarding the question of how the civil and spiritual orders should relate to one another, Langbaine worried: 'you have told us a great deale of serious truth, but I feare whether wee shall be so prudent as to conforme to it.'[13] Obviously, Langbaine regarded Selden's work on Judaic institutions as normative, as a full and legible standard for a contemporary society whose members will lack the shrewdness or the will to follow. In the 1640s Ralph Cudworth's letters to Selden were especially enthusiastic about the windfall that the scholar's work on calendars, Eutychius, and the Sanhedrin promises to yield the lovers of truth in beleaguered England.[14] Similarly, but with reference to *De Jure Naturali* and *Uxor Hebraica*, Milton found support in Selden's scholarship for his own defences of liberty against the evils of force and hire.[15]

After Selden's death in 1654 numerous panegyrists lamented the loss of his massive learning yet rarely went so far as to emphasize the ready and remedial utility of his scholarship. According to one obsequy, he was 'great Learnings *Atlas*,' the 'Grand Oracle of *Antiquity*! th' Immense / Master of *Language*, and profounder *Sense*! / Gulf of unfathom'd *Reading*, total *Summe* / Of all our *Laws*, both extant, or to come.' Selden has become the kind of mysterious, remote law for mankind that panegyrists often made of their ostensibly heroic subjects, from Donne on deceased teenager Elizabeth Drury to Jonson on the aristocratic friends Cary and Morison. One image in the obsequy suggests the possibility that the heroic ideal embodied in Selden might possess an instructive value, since the dead scholar is praised as 'great *Britains* chief Mirror.' Yet the poem never commits itself to what 'profounder *Sense*' might be glimpsed therein, to whether the mirror manages to clarify the oracular tendencies of the author, or whether British readers are likely to look that way for a vision of what ails their war-torn, topsy-turvy society.[16] Much like the apocalyptic scholarship of Joseph Mede, so too Selden's Judaic researches: each person's appreciation of the work's merit reflects that reader's own partisan affiliations far more than it cites the express contemporary aims of Selden himself. Selden sets a standard for carrying out the intensive religious, political, and cultural debates of the 1640s but leaves very little notice of exactly how or even whether the standard ought to be set up in England. His separation of excommunication from spiritual labour appears to embody a thesis of what 'ought' to be as well as what 'was'; but what about the specifics of the Sanhedrin itself? In his afterlife, Selden's work and ethos gain the monumental stature of a panegyric fiction, the ghostly vestige of some now-distant ideal, some hero of justice flown from the world, one whose presence in the world cannot be hoped for beyond the memory of a few feeble interpreters.

In lamenting the great scholar's death, panegyrists struggle for metaphors that might capture his now-lost value. With some images drawn from nature and others from art, Robert Fletcher lends Selden a mythic stature here, a mortal vulnerability there; the admirer states the obvious of Selden's immense capacity for learning, yet juxtaposes such praise with the panegyric convention according to which the great man has lost to death the majority of his normative presence, 'Since the grave Pole-star of the groaping sky / Has suffer'd ship-wrack in mortallity.' The same poem laments that Selden once helped to hold Britain together, but Britain itself – and Selden's place in it – is a fragile human invention as well as a subject of natural mortality: 'But when such brawny sinews of a state / As thee break loose; 'tis like a clock whose weight / Being slipp'd a side all motion's at a stand.'[17] If in the 1640s Selden sketched the horizon of a new polity for English society, in the 1650s the sun shining on that horizon has quickly risen and set.

The best that can be said is that Selden's potentially instructive mirror was so refined as to belong elsewhere: 'But since there's no perfection here, thy glass / To become gold indeed translated was.' Fletcher puts a great, if not entirely clear, distance between Selden and the world: 'Thy furnish'd soul being fill'd with all that could / Be here extracted from the grosser mould / Of earth's *Idea*, in a brave disdain, / Drew to its proper Center, that vast Main / Of truth and knowledg, great *Jehovah*, hee / That's all in all to all eternitie.'[18] God is the great alchemist, turning baser metals into gold through death, but not converting the brazen world into a golden one. Selden, too, is the great Neoplatonic magician, absorbing from the corrupt world some purer extraction, though Fletcher suggests that the great scholar has not so much turned the base world into an Idea as he has paid close attention to such a desirable transformation. In the final assessment, Selden's oceanic learning reduces appropriately to that mind in which the creatures of the world find no resemblance and in which there is only divinity, the greatest monism of God's all in all. Alternatively, the centre of Selden's circle is not the circle whose centre is everywhere and circumference nowhere, but the more contracted target of Jonson's retreating Stoic heroes, for instance, the Infant of Saguntum: 'How summed a circle didst thou leave mankind / Of deepest lore, could we the centre find!'; or, in the vein of Jonson's own image for Selden: 'And like a compass keeping one foot still / Upon your centre, do your circle fill / Of general knowledge.'[19] Before the great man's death, there is the outside chance that the profound centre or the compass's stable inner foot will effect some difference at the circumference of the abnormal world. Fletcher emphasizes, however, that with the return of the great man into nature's womb, there is no hope of regaining the presence of that Idea, not unless transmigration – that Pythagorean theory that for Selden had such fascination – comes true for 'Old souls to inform new bodyes.' Fletcher knows better: 'But this we hope not for.' Selden's 'season'd Judgment' must give way to the 'Sects' and 'parties' that either 'rave' in the pretence of zeal or repress free souls in the pretence of law. With Selden's body, English religious society comes apart until the Second Coming. Yet even in life, Selden's measure, his 'Plummet'[20] was sunk too deeply for him ever to have held it together, at least so long as that gauge is understood to be embodied in the scholar's writings.

For unlike the kind of praise that Jonson bestows on Shakespeare, according to which the works outlive the man, Selden's eulogizers seldom make this case. They largely agree on what is lost with Selden, in essence, the prospect of the rightly tempered measure in religious society. Most parties test a 'measure ... Not by their judgment, but their interest,' one poet complains. By contrast, Selden sought measure so judiciously as to render that search a Herculean labour: 'When 'twas thy excellence to pursue the chase, / Till there was left to scruple no more place. / So long *Alcides* thought his work unsped, / As he to Hydra left or tayle or head. / Thy Plummet sinks into the deepest sound, / Still plunging onward till it finde the ground.' 'Still' – always – 'plunging': the search for measure is at once 'stamp'd authentick' and left unfinished by Selden's scrupulous and 'teeming brain.'[21]

In emphasizing that Selden's influence might well conclude with his life, eulogizers testify to the more local, intimate, and conversational authority of the great scholar. Like the small communities of zealots in the law that he praises in *De Synedriis*, Selden himself is celebrated for his normative guidance among friends. In his recollection of their friendship, Whitelocke stresses Selden's gift of 'good counsell & incouragement in my studyes,' including advice which the receiver describes as a 'rule': 'That I should not neglect to study men as well as bookes, & as often as I could, to be in the Company of ingenious, & learned men, by whom I might gaine more by conversation, then I could by study.' Here was a lesson that Selden had gathered in the company of Jonson and his coterie, that society must be refashioned from the small group outward. Selden lived out that notion at his own table, much as he imagined that the ancient Bards had done with their lords, or the ancient critics with their Bards. In doing so, he also anticipated the eighteenth-century moral philosophy that 'mankind's intrinsic sociability, and with it the moral instinct, become obstructed in large societies because they have too much material to contend with ... "To cantonise is natural," writes Shaftesbury, "when the society grows vast and bulky."'[22] Yet, like Ben Jonson, Whitelocke's Selden puts greater stock still in a larger yet invisible and still selective community, the community of authors to which he instructed Whitelocke to return: 'yett though I should be in Company late att night, he advised me att my returne home to reade somwhat, that there should be *nulla Dies sine linea*.'[23] As valuable as social experience might be, each day of a man's life needs a boundary or level, the geometrical termination that only reading can bring, presumably the careful reading of appropriate material, but Whitelocke does not say.

Selden's advice testifies more surely to the inward largesse that society might yield the individual than it does to the social benefits that any one citizen might produce within society as a whole.

In the years after his death, Selden's influence was felt to be both moral and scholarly. In speaking of the arrogance of Selden's good friend John Vaughan, Clarendon lamented 'that all Mr. Selden's instructions, and authority, and example, could not file off that roughness of his nature, so as to make him grateful.'[24] In his preface to *The Divine History of the Genesis of the World Explicated and Illustrated* (1670), Samuel Gott credited Selden with teaching him the value of collaborative research.[25] In *Plato Redivivus* (1681), Henry Neville felt no need even to name the 'learned gentleman of our nation' whose *De Synedriis* his interlocutor has found to be excellent.[26]

When in the 1650s, Selden's contemporaries narrowed their focus ever more intensely on the state of religious society in the British Isles, they persevered in imagining Judaic scenarios in which coercive law and capacious spirit might be reconciled or at least coordinated. Accordingly, in 1656 the participants in a conference at Whitehall debated whether England ought to readmit the Jews in anticipation of the return of the Messiah. In carrying out these discussions, interlocutors considered two factors that Selden himself rarely entertained: the imminence of the apocalypse and the toleration of living Jewish people. But neither the Messiah nor the Sanhedrin was forthcoming, and, in fact, one sticking point in the discussions remained: whether the Jews would be allowed to retain their separate judicial system. As the 1650s proceeded, there were other signs that English intellectuals – even apocalyptic radicals such as Milton – might be tiring of their efforts to unite law and spirit in one holistic vision. Indeed, the indecision and disagreements over the question of whether to readmit the Jews had a way of accentuating the extremes of law and spirit rather than harmonizing the two warrants in anticipation of the divine all-in-all. Picking up where the Erastian Selden was erroneously perceived to have left off, in *Leviathan* (1651) Hobbes mounted a theory of religious society in which a religious society would find a stable measure only if the civil magistracy relieved spiritual warrant of its place in the world of men.

—— 2 ——

With the pronounced increase in their time of studies in rabbinical literature, and especially in Maimonides' *Mishneh Torah*, seventeenth-century

Hebraists such as Petrus Cunaeus came to believe that, as Aaron L. Katchen writes, 'the Israelite commonwealth was the most perfect, because of the harmony and, especially, the indivisible bond between Church and state that existed in it.' Theirs 'was an indissoluble link between institutions and faith,' if only they could be true to their covenant.[27] So, too, Tuck explains, the upshot of Selden's rabbinical studies came to be that 'It was God who had to be the sole superior capable of imposing general rules upon men and backing them up with punishments, and Selden nowhere considers the question of whether God might *not* be a legitimate superior.' In the *De Jure Naturali et Gentium*, Selden posited 'the divinely inspired character of the Hebrew tradition' as well as the conduit of some '*external* force, a god or angel, capable of giving illumination to the human mind.'[28] Then, in his last great work, Selden strove to represent the civil authority that would best suit his premises about the ancient Jews, only to run out of time in the final volume. Unlike Francis Bacon, as he was praised in the 1640s and 1650s, the Judaic Selden was not declared a Moses who had glimpsed the promised land and led the way to it, but simply did not arrive there himself. Selden's measures of religious polity were not propositions or recommendations so much as enquiries, histories, and inventions without express directions for how others might use them well. Selden had no Great Instauration and carved out no '*novum organum*.' He drew a detailed picture of an ancient and godly institution that, it is suggested, might well help the English to think otherwise about the rifts in their holy commonwealth. To dogmatize about the Sanhedrin doubtless would have served to reduce its possibilities to the level of mere polemics.

Just before and after Selden's death, however, there was good reason to believe that Selden's Judaic work might directly serve the needs of an apocalyptic commonwealth; for Menasseh Ben Israel came to England in search of a homeland for the Jewish people. His mission began in 1649; took flight with the publication and translation of *The Hope of Israel* in the early 1650s; culminated in the indecisive Whitehall Conference of 1655; and, at the very least, cleared the legal path for the Jews to re-enter England. The time for readmission was indeed ripe; for, as David S. Katz explains, the rabbi's mission 'took place at the juncture of a number of important intellectual movements ... The more speculative concerns with the Mosaic law, the supernatural qualities of Hebrew, millenarianism, and the lost ten tribes reached the peak of their persuasiveness and intensity about the time of the Conference,' that is, of the Whitehall Conference held in December 1655.[29] Yet, if there was great interest in the possibility of Jews living again in England, there was also great opposition in response and, even among supporters, a diversity of sometimes conflicting motivations. Some supporters hoped to relieve the Jews of oppression, some to profit from their putative economic savvy, some to convert them to true religion, and some to have English Christianity uplifted by an infusion of Judaism. Hebraic covenants with God had always figured centrally in English Puritan thought, but in the 1640s and 1650s the calling of the Jews announced with extraordinary vigour the Messianic desire for a perfected and unified society under the watch of a single God.

Of what would the Judaic infusion consist? The ancient Jews had shared a great intimacy with God, but what about their successors far into the future? When Selden ventured thoughts on the matter, he noted that the Jews tend to prosper, support the prince with loans, and cohere as a society. But he had a more elaborate explanation for why the Jews would thrive in any society: theirs was a comprehensively religious society in which a normative yet adaptable law existed in full harmony with a deeply experienced love, zeal, and inspiration directly owed to God. Embracing Maimonides' taxonomy of prophecy despite its occasional inconsistencies, Selden's argument for the benefits of Judaism was fundamental if also mostly indirect: that at its best ancient Judaism already comprised the coordination of law and spirit of which Christian societies in the 1650s stand in such dire need. Had the early Christians (or reformed Jews) and the traditional Jews embraced one another, he lamented, the search for a measured spirituality existing in harmony with civil society would have been long over. Yet Selden tended to keep his Judaism in the realm of invention, scholarship, and ideas: rarely did he have anything to say about the Jews alive in his own time, those who might come to be his neighbours – this, despite the fact that Sir Henry Finch, Selden's brother in the common law, had called the Jews to begin the restoration of the world as early as 1621.

Selden was not alone among his contemporaries in his belief that Jewish law might normalize a zealous, capacious spirituality without evacuating that spirituality of its light, truth, and richness. For the Cambridge Platonists, Harold Fisch explains, Maimonides helped to lay 'stress on the normality of the prophetic experience.'[30] Not simply any acceptance of the intricacies of Jewish law could provide such a rationalized normalcy for spiritual experience; Maimonides was instrumental in accommodating that body of law to a seventeenth-century Christian's sense of a properly rational religion. Yet virtually no other English writer of

Selden's time was so consistently blithe about the normative idea of ancient Judaism as was he. Far from it: by the 1650s Judaic religion had accrued extreme and largely negative associations with an irrational, base, and oppressive legalism on the one hand and – irony of ironies – with the uncontrollable zeal of antinomian fancy on the other hand. The latter had been developing since the first decades of the century when the 'Judaizers' or 'Traskites' came to be numbered among the zealots laying claim 'to that priuate spirit or holy ghost which our *Puritanes* glory in.'[31] This sentiment persisted through the millenarianism of the 1640s and 1650s, as did the fundamentally Pauline charge that Judaism was mired in a ceremonial law from which Christians were graced to be free. For Alexander Ross, the Jews were so 'blind, hard-hearted, [and] stiff-necked' that they 'always resisted the Holy Ghost.' Moreover, 'Their Religion consisteth most in needlesse and ridiculous ceremonies, in Rabbinical fables, Cabalistical whimsies, Thalmudical Traditions, large Fringes, and Phylacteries, and in a meer outside.'[32] Others reviewed the 'history' of the Jews in England to remind the people of that country of how, in the Middle Ages, Jews had committed atrocities against Christians – indeed, against children – old stories that Selden himself had prepared for inclusion in the work of Purchas.[33] Such rabid attacks on the Jews attempted to undercut any conviction that Jewish law could exert a calming and normative effect on English Christianity in the 1650s. In fact, the implication of such attacks tended to be that the contemporary craving for all things Judaic was a symptom rather than a cure of senseless fancy and disgusting antinomianism run amuck.

For those writers neither so committed to the study of ancient Judaic religious society as Selden nor so critical of contemporary Judaism as Ross, the decade of the 1650s was a time of considerable conflict over whether there was hope to be found for a traumatized yet heady English religious society in visions of Israel. Each in his or her own way, these writers were torn between an optimistically monist vision of Hebraic society and the Pauline demolition of the perpetual childhood and bondage of Jewish law. One and the same writer, say, the Cambridge Platonist John Smith, could invoke Maimonides in an effort to normalize and rationalize the spirit behind true prophecy and to differentiate that spirit from 'the Pseudo-Prophetical' enthusiasm fuelling the millenarian wildfire of the 1650s; then, in the same book unleash a full-scale assault on the 'legal righteousness' of the Jews. In the latter case, Maimonides embodies the arrogance behind the belief that 'in that Model of life contained in that Body of Laws, distinguished ordinarily into Moral,

Judicial & Ceremonial, was comprised the whole Method of raising Man to his perfection.' Lest this aim of perfecting mankind seem rather attractive, Smith drove home the charge that legal religion was, in fact, a '*Lean* and *Spiritless Religion* ... a Souleless and Liveless form of External performances, which did little or nothing at all reach the Inward man, being nothing but a mere Bodily kind of drudgery and servility.'[34] Thus, the law that might provide spirituality with normalcy so easily slid into the ritualism that had no soul; intimacy with God the Father ended up squandering the grace of God the Son and Holy Ghost.

The complexity and intensity of the Interregnum commentaries on Judaism arose in response to those contemporaries of Selden who shared with him in some measure a hope in Israel. English religious society had been vacillating between the extremes of legalistic force or conformity and the chaos of the spirit. The ancient Jews had followed the instructions of God in establishing a religious society that masterfully and vitally harmonized law and spirit, even in the face of enormous adversity and ongoing change. The sense of loss afflicting conceptual Judaizers – the sense that Jewish customs, institutions, and dispensations were long gone – might be reversed with the influx of living and breathing Jews whose ways and beliefs were on display for all English readers to see in the 1650 translation of a work by Leo Modena, *The History of the Rites, Customes, and Manner of Life, of the Present Jews, throughout the World.* Making a workable whole out of Jewish and English citizens living together for the first time in centuries would not be easy: the English would be asked to make concessions to Jewish religious, judicial, and economic practices; the Jews would have restrictions placed on their station in English society; and Jews and Christians would have to recast themselves in such a way as to minimize the long-standing and deeply seated offence mutually taken. On 14 October 1663 Pepys paid a visit to a London synagogue where he marvelled at 'the men and boys in their Vayles, and the women behind a lettice out of sight,' the Hebrew service and prayer for the king, and the transportation of the law. In the end, however, he found the service ridiculous: 'But Lord, to see the disorder, laughing, sporting, and no attention, but confusion in all their service, more like Brutes then people knowing the true God, would make a man forswear ever seeing them more; and endeed, I never did see so much, or could have imagined there had been any religion in the whole world so absurdly performed as this.' In a 'strangely disturbed' state Pepys left the synagogue; one year later gentiles were prohibited from visiting the synagogue.[35]

For writers like Selden with little to say about – perhaps little toler-
ance for – living and breathing Jews, ancient Judaism afforded both a
best-case and a last-ditch model for saving religious society. In *The
Commonwealth of Oceana*, for instance, James Harrington introduces his
largely agrarian and electoral prescriptions for remaking the commonwealth of England with a warning: it is all well and good to apportion a
separate if nearby isle for habitation by the Jews, but 'To receive the Jews
after any other manner into a commonwealth were to maim it; for they
of all nations never incorporate but, taking up the room of a limb, are of
no use or office unto the body, while they suck the nourishment which
would sustain a natural and useful member.'[36] Yet Harrington maintains
that though the Jews would never 'incorporate' into some other body
politic, the corollary of this warning is that their own commonwealth
has accomplished an exemplary balance between civil government and
spiritual liberty.

The Sanhedrin figures prominently in Harrington's vision of this
much needed but delicate balance; it is the senate that, he believes,
must always complement the people and the magistracy; lawful society
needs a 'senate debating and proposing,' a 'people resolving,' and a
'magistracy executing.' It might be true that the Sanhedrin lacked what
Harrington considers sufficient rotation among its members; but this
fault did not prevent that body from overseeing the greatest master-
piece of all, the accommodation of law as the 'national conscience' with
'the liberty of private conscience' as the latter was most powerfully
embodied by the prophets. 'In Israel,' Harrington argues, 'the law ecclesiastical and civil was the same; therefore the Sanhedrim, having the
power of one, had the power of both.' National conscience thrived
together with private conscience no less than the religious law prospered with the civil, for 'as the national religion appertained unto the
jurisdiction of the Sanhedrim, so the liberty of conscience appertained
from the same date and by the same right unto the prophets and their
disciples.' Far from destroying one another in conflict, the magistrate's
'losing the power of religion, loseth the liberty of conscience which in
that case hath nothing to protect it.'[37]

Harrington warns his readers that they will be taught otherwise, that
'there is a meanness and poorness in modern prudence, not only unto
the damage of civil government, but of religion itself.' Some of the enemies preventing a reciprocity between law and prophecy come from
within the religious domain itself: 'The parties that are spiritual are of
more kinds than I need mention: some for a national religion and

others for liberty of conscience, with such animosity on both sides as if these two did not consist; of which I have already sufficiently spoken to show that the one cannot well consist without the other.'[38] But Harrington's ongoing and imaginary debate with 'Leviathan' leaves no doubt about the party most immediately threatening to the future of that prudence inducing senators and prophets to benefit one another. The enemy is Hobbes, and the threat is his pessimistic brief against the possibility that civil parties can share sovereignty or that civil and spiritual agents can share authority. Lord Saye had feared during the sessions of the Westminster Assembly that a Judaic model of religious society would mix the civil and sacred realms too thoroughly. Hobbes represented to his critics the nightmare of a society in which peace and security depended on the evacuation of the sacred from the world.

—— 3 ——

In the 1650s a virtually unprecedented possibility arose in England, namely, that the notion of a comprehensively religious society might have to be abandoned. Interpretations and responses to Judaism were often gauges of this hypothesis. On the one hand, the debate over the readmission of the Jews, while apocalyptic and homogenizing in its ultimate aims, considered a policy of permitting a substantial and quasi-autonomous subset of English society to practise its separate religion – and to practise it separately. On the other hand, Judaic models were at times interpreted as edging English society towards legalism and civil coercion rather than towards the perplexing mix of civil and religious affairs that Lord Saye had resisted in the 1640s. Thus, when in 1653 Clement Barksdale brought out a translation of Cunaeus's *De Republica Hebraeorum*, the volume comprised only the first of three books, the one concerned with civil government. The motto of the volume was 'nec omnia, nec nihil,' a reminder that even in its incomplete state, the book might offer Interregnum England a model for government, not least in the renowned Sanhedrin.[39] If, as Katchen argues, the full Cunaeus volume had a tendency to loosen its own 'indissoluble link between institutions and faith,'[40] the Barksdale translation reversed the author's subversion of law on behalf of faith; in the 1653 volume, faith as it fills the heart or as it holds a community together was sacrificed on the altar of civil order and law.

Two years earlier, in *Leviathan*, Hobbes had set the standard for placing overwhelming emphasis on a coercive civil sovereign as the remedy for the violence and disorder wracking religious society in England. It is true that he made some effort to reserve a place in civil society for specifically divine dispensations and religious practices, and that he delineated the grounds of faith and the nature of the kingdom of God. However, not least in the eyes of those early critics disinclined to weigh Hobbes's every concession – indeed, eager to posit atheism behind the lines of his monumental argument – the political theorist's watchword was simply that religion ought to direct us without exception and almost exclusively to civil obedience: better to obey the instituted sovereign by means of worship than to labour over the truth value of his and one's own habits of worship. But Hobbes went even further: 'spirit' and 'inspiration' are insubstantial and, as such, are polemical words naming nothing real. 'If this superstitious fear of Spirits were taken away,' he argues, then the 'simple people' would be less vulnerable to the machinations of ambitious men and 'would be much more fitted than they are for civill Obedience.'[41] Claims on insubstantial spirits or on the infusion of spirit into human nature 'are as absurd and insignificant, as a *round quadrangle*' (108). Worse, they issue in 'the Seditious roaring of a troubled Nation' (141). Concerning the biblical passage that occupies Selden's attention for so long, the one in which God redistributes the spirit bestowed on Moses to the seventy elders, Hobbes concluded that 'The Scriptures by the Spirit of God in man, mean a mans spirit, enclined to Godlinesse' (143).

Far from neglecting religion, Hobbes devotes the second half of his book – and many sections of the first – to proving that its practices are best controlled and interpreted by the coercive civil sovereign. If at times Hobbes's distribution of authority resembles Selden's in *De Synedriis*, it is also the case that Hobbes's view of human nature has no room for the powerful love and conscience so carefully laid out in Selden's work, nor does he develop the bonds of religious community or the substantial realities of the spirit in the way that Selden does. Hobbes's point is that the concretion of the divine spirit in either individuals or communities creates a warrant or authority bound to conflict with that of civil authority and to lead human society back to its nasty brutal wars. But there is no such thing as an insubstantial spirit. What this means is that human beings must confess the incomprehensibility of all divine reality and fall back on the mediatory authority and coercive will of the civil sovereign. For 'whereas some men have pretended for their disobedience to their Soveraign, a new Covenant, made, not with men, but with God; this also is unjust: for there is no Covenant with

God, but by mediation of some body that representeth Gods Person; which none doth but Gods Lieutenant, who hath the Soveraignty under God.' Pretenders in a covenant with God are credited with a lying, 'vile, and unmanly disposition' (230).

It is not surprising that, when Hobbes cites the passage from the twenty-second chapter of Matthew, in which followers of Christ are instructed to 'pay Caesar what is due to Caesar, and pay God what is due to God,' he tends to omit the second half. Subjects are rather to worry about their offences against 'the publique Conscience' of the civil law than they are about any 'private Consciences, which are but private opinions' tending to disorder and disrupt the commonwealth. Allow any subject to lay claim to inspiration and it becomes impossible to 'see why any man should render a reason of his Faith; of why every Christian should take the Law of his Country, rather than his own Inspiration, for the rule of his action.' Selden had introduced his *De Synedriis* with a highly provisional metaphor according to which civil and spiritual realms might coexist in the world as two suns in a sky or two souls in a body. Hobbes mocks the very notion: 'As there have been Doctors, that hold there be three Soules in a man; so there be also that think there may be more Soules, (that is, more Soveraigns,) than one, in a Commonwealth; and set up a *Supremacy* against the *Soveraignty*; *Canons* against *Lawes*; and a *Ghostly Authority* against the *Civill*; working on mens minds, with words and distinctions, that of themselves signifie nothing, but bewray (by their obscurity) that there walketh (as some think invisibly) another Kingdome, as it were a Kingdome of Fayries, in the dark' (370). Such divisions set up two masters, one temporal and the other ghostly, and in an extraordinary reversal of the biblical injunction, Hobbes makes the case that human beings must serve the worldly god or perish.

Hobbes proceeds to explain that civil sovereigns do not replace God in the hearts and lives of their obedient subjects. Rather, the civil authority is responsible for bringing God to them – in the Scriptures that are authorized, in the readings of Scripture that are legitimized, in the insistence that prophets conform to law, and in the public imagination and worship of God. The 'church' never exceeds the bounds of the commonwealth. Similarly, 'spirit' signifies air, breath, understanding, affections, gifts, life, zeal, even (in the case of the seventy elders) 'a subordination to authority,' but Hobbes never tires of repeating that it must not be rendered literally as some ghost, 'which signifieth nothing, neither in heaven, nor earth, but the Imaginary inhabitants of mans brain' (428–33).

At one point, Hobbes edges closer to Selden's coordination of law and spirit when he acknowledges that subjects are entitled to believe privately a teaching against the grain of public law, for their 'internall Faith is in its own nature invisible, and consequently exempted from all humane jurisdiction' (550). Subjects must only keep those beliefs hidden, shorn of words and actions, couched in the form of hopes and wishes. But if for Hobbes religion is reducible to faith in Christ and obedience to laws, and if it might be imagined that a civil sovereign might require of subjects an action that would condemn them to hell, the burden of his argument is that faith virtually never carries civil subjects outside the strictures of obedience. 'All that is Necessary to Salvation,' he concludes, 'is contained in two Vertues, Faith in Christ, and Obedience to Laws. The latter of these, if it were perfect, were enough to us' (610). So it is that Hobbes arrives at a civil redaction of the Pauline convention that grace and faith help us to satisfy the justice of those laws that, left to their own devices, corrupt human beings cannot follow. Hobbes believes that with the careful invention of the civil sovereign, the master – and our own fears of violence and death – will coerce us into obedience, whether or not we have faith in God. In Hobbes's argument, 'the Supreme Pastor' is identical to 'the Civill Sovereigne,' and there is no need for the struggles involved in coordinating the warrants of law and spirit when the law, or the sovereign's will, is all in all.

In his own, very different, way, the Milton of the late 1650s expressed exasperation with the failures of a radicalized England to arrive at a just and true coordination between law and spirit in the newly constructed temple of religious society. In *A Treatise of Civil Power* (1659), his remedy is utterly to separate Christian spirituality from the domain of civil law and magistracy. According to Milton, religious liberty involves three – and only three – agents, the Holy Spirit interpreting the scriptures to the individual conscience; and it is the very essence of Protestant religion that these three be untouched by, and uninvolved in, the forms and forces of civil life and authority. Given this state of affairs, there is no point in invoking Moses or any other ancient Jewish authority for two reasons: Moses 'did all by immediate divine direction' and the Jews 'had a commonwealth by [God] delivered them, incorporated with a national church exercised more in bodily than in spiritual worship: so as that the church might be called a commonwealth, and the whole commonwealth a church.'[42] In short, Moses is far too holy for modern Protestants to imitate, and the subsequent Jewish polity is far too monistic at best, carnal at worst.

No such separation between civil power and spiritual dispensation is ever absolute in Milton: it remains the duty of his ideal magistrate to strengthen the moral integrity of the commonwealth and to defend 'things religious settled by the churches within themselves.'[43] Much the same notion can be seen in Milton's sonnets and in the prose of the early 1640s. What is more, in the *Ready and Easy Way* (1660) as well as in the concluding book of *Paradise Lost* (1667–74), Milton models his ideal senate on the Jewish Sanhedrin, always mindful of his monistic ideals of a godly world in which all difference, including the difference between law and spirit, is by degree not kind; in which human beings can contribute to their comprehensive welfare as spiritual, physical, and communal entities; and in which body and soul exist along a continuum, all of which is made holy and beautiful by the divine creator.

As Rosenblatt has argued, however, Milton is torn between Hebraic monism and Pauline dualism; between a continuum between law and spirit, and the repudiation of childish, enslaving, and carnal law for the sake of grace and spirit; between the acceptance of the body (and of poetry) as godly delights, and the metaphysical (and visceral) disgust at the fallen body's stench.[44] The optimistic Milton – the one who believes that human abilities and institutions adhere to natural law and divine wisdom as they succeed in regaining liberty in the fallen world – tends towards monism; the pessimistic Milton opts for dualism. In the prevalence of the former Milton in the heady 1640s, Rosenblatt shows that the Hebraic scholarship of John Selden is perhaps Milton's greatest English model. Selden stands virtually alone in his eyes as the man who understands God's holy fusion of law and spirit in Paradise and then again in the early covenants with the Noachian and Hebrew peoples. Such a monistic Milton emerges once again in the pre-fall books of *Paradise Lost*, though he largely gives way to the dualistic Milton in the Pauline, post-fall books in which Hebraic law converts into Old Testament law useful only as foreshadowing symbols of and severely limited provocations to the covenant of grace.

For Milton, that is, Selden's Hebraic project of working out the best coordination between law and spirit is the primary condition of Paradise. In this Paradise God watches his human creations cherish their bodies and their souls, their verses and his laws, the natural truths that they inherit and the community that they freely devise and sustain. In Milton's *Paradise Lost*, written after the collapse of the revolutionary attempts to refashion England's religious society, Selden's vision of the world is converted into the most attractive *locus amoenus*, a world in which it is requisite yet clearly possible to harmonize what God wants restricted and what he wants open in the practice of human liberty. For the unfallen Adam, then, the dream of Paradise and the reality were entirely the same. Yet fleetingly so: even before their fall, Adam and Eve are bombarded with the ever-new trials of negotiating the needs of the conscience with those of the community, of sifting between the egalitarian spirit of moral trial and the coercive institutions of marriage, of enjoying the fullness of experience in the garden and cosmos without transgressing the ostensibly simplest of laws. When they leave Paradise on their way through a fallen wilderness, it is altogether uncertain whether they will ever find another paradise outside the garden lodged in their innermost souls. Yet Milton has a way of making the unfallen world resemble the fallen insofar as the success of a religious society can never be taken for granted. In looking to Selden for superior guidance in reconstituting the nature and boundaries of England's religious society, he ignores the charges made against Selden by critics of Erastianism from the 1640s onward, namely, that Seldenesque thought was essentially dualistic in privileging civil authority over ecclesiastical polity and in inverting the traditional hierarchy according to which the beautiful soul was imprisoned in the filthy body. Other admirers of Selden could not ignore these charges that the great scholar had sought to free civil society from its incarceration in the human dispensations of the divine spirit. Mr Selden and Mr Hobbes, these charges held, were pushing for the end of religious society. In looking to the evidence both textual and biographical, some (like Richard Baxter) reaffirmed their belief that Selden might well point the way to the survival of a holy commonwealth. Others (such as Edward Stillingfleet and Thomas Barlow) expressed their admiration for the learning but made the case, with varying degrees of politeness, that Selden had participated willy-nilly in the secularization of the holy commonwealth.

—— 4 ——

It was to Matthew Hale that Richard Baxter turned for reassurance that Selden, far from having sold his soul to Hobbes, was truly what Baxter had hoped and imagined, a great hero and guardian of the holy commonwealth. In his correspondence as well as in his works, Baxter insists that obedience to magistracy was as badly neglected by contemporary Christians as spirituality was slighted by Hobbes; for 'far be it from any Christian to reproach King Jesus, King of Kings, and to deny his Royalty, or his Royall officers, by the name of *Erastian*, and so deny an essential part of Christianity.'[45] As William Lamont summarizes the point, 'respect for the magistracy ... is the ark of [Baxter's] faith,' and so long as Selden had not given way to Hobbesian secularism, Baxter was prepared to understand the lawyer's Erastianism as having respected 'the office properly ministerial,' with the clergy's 'doctoral, priestly power, and power over their own sacramental communion in the church which they guide.'[46] It was fitting, then, that the great lawyer and historian of the common law from whom Baxter received his assurances about Selden, Sir Matthew Hale, perpetuated not only the historical methodology and legal premises of his mentor, but also some of Selden's most cherished religious convictions as well. Not least, Cromartie explains, was that controversial notion of 'the agency of an "Intellectus Agens" ... which gave access to the truths that were normally said to be written in men's hearts,' and withal to 'the possibility of moral knowledge.' This agent 'was not a moral sense (as it were, a moral sight), but just a precondition of the sense's exercise' and, one should add, its guarantor; for Hale inherited from Selden the idea that the '*Intellectus Agens*' amounted to a virtually direct assistance from divine illumination. More pervasively, Hale understood Selden's legacy to comprise not the secularization of the sacred but the 'sacralisation of secular things,' its essence 'heightening the significance of everyday life' by means of consecrating the duties shared among human beings as much as the obligations owed by human beings to God.[47]

Selden's staunchest critics either ignored or refused to believe that the massive scholarship on behalf of the sanctity of the secular was anything other than Hobbesian secularization of religion. As a respondent to the case of conscience of whether the Jews ought to be readmitted into England, Thomas Barlow expressed his conviction that Selden's Erastian work on the Sanhedrin was essentially Hobbesian, evacuating the spiritual realm of any power and authority it might have possessed. In posing the question of whether the Jews should be tolerated, Thomas Barlow divides the issue into four subsections, in the first of which he addresses 'What Power is to give this Toleration.' For this first consideration, he explains, and 'notwithstanding what (a) *Erastus* with his (b) Followers, and (c) *Selden* of late have said, I believe it to be a manifest Truth, That in every Christian Nation there are (or should be) two divine distinct Powers.' Referring to Hobbes's *Leviathan* as item 'b' and to Selden's *Libris de Synedriis Judaeorum* as item 'c,' Barlow simply asserts that there should be a 'Sacred or Spiritual' power and a 'Civil or Temporal' power in every commonwealth. Even so, he makes no effort to incorporate the Jews into English religion or the English into Jewish religion, for 'the Jews neither desiring, nor intending to be Members of our Church, but only of our Common-weal; their Admission or Exclusion depends only on the Civil Power.' Toleration is a civil matter in this case, which (Barlow reminds us) itself is an essentially Judaic position if one is to credit Mr Selden's 'large Discourse,' *De Jure Naturali et Gentium.* In that work, Barlow summarizes, Selden shows how 'very scrupulous' the Jewish governors were 'in admitting those Proselytes which did voluntarily come unto them.'[48]

When next Barlow refers to Selden's *De Jure Naturali,* it is the law of nature, not of nations, that he isolates, with reference accordingly to those proselytes who live among the Jews but do not convert to Judaism. 'For though [the Jews] did not require of their Proselytes (those of the Gate I mean) to submit to the positive Law, and Precepts of *Moses*,' Barlow paraphrases Selden, 'yet they did universally require of them to abstain from Blasphemy, Idolatry, and all natural Injustice, as is manifest in *Josephus*, the Sacred Text it self and their Rabbinical and Talmutical Writers.' In this instance, the Jews tolerated any religious practices in keeping with what Tuck has called a 'pretty minimal' slate of precepts. The naturalized Jews were civilly tolerant of other religions to an extent that the nationalized Jews were not; for the latter required the proselyte to abandon his entire identity in order to obey a comprehensive and complicated set of positive laws dubbed by Barlow the height of 'senceless irrationality.'[49]

Two questions about the implications of Selden's scholarship arise from Barlow's reading of his work. First: Was Selden's vision of a religious society for the most part tolerant to sectarian groups so long as they understood and respected the civil authority of the magistrates, or was it premised in Erastian and Hobbesian fashion on the total uniformity of a state religion? That is, was Milton right about Selden when he claimed that the great scholar's *De Jure Naturali* promulgated a liberating thesis: 'that all opinions, yea, errors, known, read, and collated, are of main service and assistance toward the speedy attainment of what is truest'? Milton makes this claim in *Areopagitica*, a work in which he exhorts Parliament and the English people to tolerate each other's sectarian and wandering searches for truth. Yet in the same breath, Milton captures a dogmatic side to Selden, the 'exquisite reasons and theorems almost mathematically demonstrative.'[50] In keeping with Milton's own provision that certain fundamental religious truths and moral precepts

are obligatory if a religious society is not to undo itself, his Selden purveys a natural law whose spirit of toleration on matters of 'indifference'
might metamorphose into the spectre of forced conformity when it
comes to guaranteeing consensus on the supposed essentials of faith and
practice. Whether the focus is Selden's natural law or his Sanhedrin, is
Barlow right about Selden's normative religious society – that in the final
analysis it was tailor made for service as or under Hobbes's leviathan?

The second question lingering from Barlow's conflation of Hobbes
and Selden is whether Selden's religious society is finally religious at
all. Barlow does not acknowledge the considerable efforts made in *De
Synedriis* to find a freedom for spiritual labourers in coordination with
the dominion of magistracy and law. Nor does Barlow concede the
simple truth about Selden's Leviathan, the agent who coerces human
beings into obeying their contracts. For, as Selden makes clear in the
Table Talk and in his Judaic scholarship in general, his Leviathan is the
creator of leviathan, the God of the Hebrew Bible. As Tuck emphasizes,
there is no denying the theological basis of Selden's last solution for the
conflict between spirit and law: 'he argued that there are good historical
grounds for supposing that God gave his orders to mankind first at the
creation of Adam, and secondly at the renewal of the human race with
Noah – the latter set of commands being the *praecepta Noachidarum* of
Talmudic tradition.'[51] There is also no denying Selden's shift from an
emphasis on those precepts in *De Jure Naturali et Gentium* to an emphasis
on civil human inventions in *De Synedriis*. It was an emphasis that Simon
Lowth, the one hostile critic remembered in Wilkins's biography of
Selden, deemed the most repugnant and risible of all the enemies of
the holy commonwealth in the latter half of the seventeenth century.

In his treatise *Of the Subject of Church Power* (1685), Lowth returns time
and again to pummel Selden.[52] Seeking 'to vindicate our Church from
Erastianism' ('To the Reader'), Lowth maintains in his 1683 letter to the
reader that the Seldens of the world have been only too successful in
spreading the belief that there is only one kind of authority in the
world, the civil magistrate; 'that the Church is nothing at all' (2); and
'that the Prince is invested with whatever belongs to a Churchman' (3).
The world, Lowth believes, has been 'so much unhing'd and discom-
pos'd ... of late' because the church and its officers have been robbed
of their proper authority; the world is now under the mistaken impression that religious authority cannot safely coexist with civil power (4).
Selden, he complains, has unleashed a double attack on church jurisdiction, mocking the power of the church as a fraud in his 'common Dis-

course,' then more seriously subverting clerical authority in 'his First Book *De Synedriis*' (4). Lowth's thesis is that the clergy possess 'a Power and Offices peculiarly theirs, as to the execution, with its special force and Laws, reaching to all that come to Heaven by Christ Jesus, and as not derived from, so no ways thwarting or interfering with the Civil Government' (7). There is nothing new in this argument, he insists; innovation is all on the side of Hobbes and Selden. Yet the consequences of removing the boundary between the civil and the sacred offices in a Christian commonwealth are catastrophic: 'if once these Land-marks be displaced, become promiscuous and common, making inrodes on one another, not only he will be at a loss that engages in the Debates and Resolutions in these cases, but Mankind it self, the Christian Part of the World to be sure, can no more continue in Peace, but with Invasions and Usurpations, Disorders and Confusions here upon Earth, than the earthy Globe it self, can subsist, or keep its *Equilibrium*, should the Elements of which it is made lose their Native qualities, and become blended together' (72). Lowth offers no careful reading of Selden's work on the Sanhedrin; he makes no concession to Selden's own sophisticated attempts to protect the realm of all spiritual labour from encroachments. Lowth's perception of Selden operates on the level of the sound bite, the kind of nugget he might find in the *Table Talk*. In Lowth's hands, Selden's elaborate temple complex has been traded in for a scapegoat with two faces, one Erastus, the other Hobbes. Indeed, Lowth finds Judaism irrelevant for the concerns of a Christian commonwealth (75).

Lowth has no shortage of abuse for the Judaic scholar. At best, Selden finds himself at impasses about the Sanhedrin, especially regarding its relevance for seventeenth-century England. Selden is unsure, he mocks, of 'whether the *Sanedrim* might whip their Kings or not,' but, more important, about the extent to which 'the Kings of *Judah* are proposed as Patterns to our Kings for the exercise of Power in the Christian Church, in our Nine and thirty Articles, and may authorize them in it' (77). At worst, Selden has violated the most basic tenets of the Pauline Reformation: 'no man sets these two Powers of the Church and State more apart than does St. *Paul*' (94); beguiled his readers into believing 'that himself is the great Searcher of Records and Authors, and Laws, of the Books and Practice of all Ages; and if the mighty, the laborious, *Selden*, has said it, it must be so, there can be no doubt of, there needs no other search after it' (145–6); traded in his 'Integrity' for a scholar's 'Zeal and Industry' together with the fraudulent application of that

industry in his plot against the church (146); and replaced the truths of
church history with a utopia (a '*Eutopian* Plot'), but this a *locus amoenus*
whose contrived designs against the clergy were malicious and opportu-
nistic in a time of chaos and libertinism, another version of his 'Traiter-
ous Actings' together with the Long Parliament against the king (151).
Far from failing in his evil enterprises, Lowth concludes, Selden's Sanhedrin joins Hobbes's leviathan in dominating the thoughts and imaginations of contemporary English society at the disastrous expense of the
holy commonwealth. With the help of 'the horrid Anarchy, and dismal
Confusion' of the 1640s and 1650s, Lowth bitterly laments, Selden was
'imboldned' to direct his own 'incessant Industry' against the church of
Christ and the Apostles; for he took the argument against church
authority 'to a greater height of irreligion and audaciousness' (189–90).
What makes Selden's scholarship such an insidious 'Plot, for the over-
throwing the Power of Christ's Kingdom, in the Polity, Laws and Rights
of it,' is that he dressed up his designs in the Judaic Bible, using the
Hebraic conflation of church with state to deny that the Christian clergy
have 'any Sword or Head that is Spiritual' (192, 188).

Lowth does eventually attempt a summary of Selden's views on excommunication. In continuing to mock the scholar's evil plot against
the church, however, Lowth adds one refinement to his attack on
Selden's industry and method that raises a possibility introduced by the
sympathetic editor of the *De Synedriis* itself – that what Selden creates has
more to do with poetics than with serious argumentation. But Lowth
finds poison in the pretty matter of research. 'And indeed,' Lowth
scoffs, 'had he not intended more to amuse the World with a bulk of
Stuff and Reading, as is his usual way, and by a confusion of things first
to confound his Reader, the easier to impose upon him, the usual way of
Hereticks ... First, to involve and entangle; he would have omitted all the
Impertinencies, and gone directly to the Business, As whether such a
Kingdom was once erected? Such Power was left upon Earth or not?
[A]nd this indeed he attempts, but 'tis in the After-Game, the Bustle,
and Distraction' (215). Selden's way, that is, tends to distract or please
the reader with the games of philology, the sideshows of learning, with
very little if any straightforward argumentation about what all this detail
means for contemporary England. Then, when the reader has enjoyed
the game sufficiently and is trying to make his way out of the elaborate
theatre, Selden presents him with his onslaught against the very basis of
the holy commonwealth. The reader accepts out of politeness or perhaps simply out of impatience, overlooking Selden's false applications,

dubious interpretations, and conflation of Christian with Jew. Selden builds a utopia of scholarship in which the reader amusingly loses his way for a while, a scholar's version of the poetic pleasures to which a parasitic Bard's reader might be brought. But unlike the parasite, who simply wants pay or a meal, Selden (Lowth concludes) wants much more: the soul of the reader and the essence of the very real, if imperiled, religious society.

―――― 5 ――――

Towards the end of his attack on Selden, Lowth pauses to make a concession to his nemesis, 'yielding to him in some measure, what he contends for, That the Kingdom, Government and Jurisdiction of the Gospel is not, cannot be outwardly forcing and Coercive, by the either Instruments or Penalties of this World. To assert such a Power erected by our Lord and Saviour Jesus Christ, is immediately and with the same breath, to publish it a Cheat, an Imposture and Usurpation, 'tis in the very letter to Affront and Contradict, the very Plot, Frame, and Constitution of it, since Christ himself has declared that his Kingdom is not of this World ... only he came of a different Errand and Design, than some others had come of before him, he was of another Spirit, and to work his work quite in another manner, and by other Weapons; not such as were Carnal, but Spiritual, mighty indeed, to the beating down strong holds, but of Sin and Sathan' (235–7). This is no small concession, though Lowth would have the reader think so. In his work on the Sanhedrin and in his debts to Erastus, Selden has striven to carve out a domain for the purity of spiritual labour. Lowth's point is that Selden has cut away the true authority and power of the church in the process, but Lowth himself must insist that by power and authority in the church, he means something entirely different from the power and authority in the civil magistrate. Lowth is not prepared to admit what his concession betrays: that there is far more to Selden's scholarship than a devilish plot against the holy commonwealth. What is more, eventually Lowth himself must say precisely what role he believes the king and the civil officers ought to play in determining the religion of a people: making religion law, stamping out heresy, protecting true religion 'with Penalties to be inflicted on such as oppose and violate it' (445). When Lowth says, 'Nor can our Religion since the Reformation be any otherwaies called a *Parliament* Religion then it might have been called so before, where the same Secular Power is equally extended and executed, as in case of the *Lollards* certain supposed Hereticks' (445), it is hard to decide whether he is assigning Parliament less importance for religion than Selden would assign, making its role humdrum, as it were; or, more important, extending the influence of Parliament back before the Reformation. Polemics is much easier than exposition when one is considering exactly how to keep the holy commonwealth together. So Lowth returns to mocking Selden's scholarship, offering the satirical apology that poor country vicars lack the resources of a great city scholar: 'we that live remote in the Countrey, and but poor Vicars there, have not the advantage of Sir *Robert Cotton's* Library, cannot attend Auctions, or but common Booksellers Shops, and have not Money to imploy others, especially for the obtaining such Authors as these, most of which are out of Print, and some very rarely to be had by any' (477). Yet learning has not ensured Selden's Christian integrity, Lowth reminds his readers, nor for that matter 'his skill as Divine' (477). Lowth even does battle with the deceased Selden over who gets to be friends with Lancelot Andrewes, all as a distraction from the real burden of saying precisely how the civil and the clerical are 'two distinct things,' how 'they ought to be united, but not confused together' (492).

To the English intellectuals searching for remedies to contemporary ills during the years of the Civil War, Interregnum, and Restoration, Selden was such a complex figure, and his scholarship was so richly detailed and massive, that it is no wonder that a Lowth or a Barlow wanted to reduce him to partisanship. Selden, they believed, could not possibly have served both leviathan and God – this was Baxter's feeling as well, though Baxter understood better than most that Selden's defence of the holy commonwealth would find a way to reconcile the serious claims of the magistrate with the supreme authority of the divine.

One especially ironic instance of the reduction of Selden's scholarship to partisanship comes from the unlikely legacy of his friend and fellow scholar, Edward Pocock. In 1656 Pocock finished a work that Selden had started in the 1640s: Pocock published a complete edition of Eutychius, a passage of whose annals Selden had clipped and used to show the presence of Presbyterianism in antiquity. Pocock's edition advertises its debt to and reverence for Selden on the title page, in its frontispiece (a portrait of Selden, with rows of books visible behind the great scholar), and in the prefatory matter, which portrays the dying Selden as virtually begging Pocock to complete the work. Here, then, is Pocock's fulfilment of the urgent final wishes of his friend.

An early eighteenth-century life of Pocock attached to his works by the editor, Leonard Twells, however, offers a different reading on the Eutychius behest.[53] In 1641 Pocock and Selden had become friends when they corresponded over Selden's work on the patriarch. Such friendships were critical during that 'Deluge of Miseries,' Twells points out (30). In a letter dated 8 November 1653 Gerard Langbaine vividly made the same point about fellow scholars when he wrote to Selden that a particular 'Problem might suit very well for the Fire-side, in a Winter night; but I am sorry I have Occasion to say, that I fear we must be forc'd, e'er long, to bid good Night to our *Noctes Atticæ*' (42). It is a time, Langbaine feared, when visitors to the universities would, in essence, 'banish' learning altogether. This state of affairs lent an urgency, then, to Selden's requests (beginning in early 1652) that Langbaine and Pocock carry on his work on the Eutychius.

Selden does not say in his letter exactly why he is so keen on having the edition brought to completion – whether it will reinforce his earlier use of it on behalf of Presbyterianism (a strange goal for a man who has come to hate the Presbyterians), or correct that impression. He says nothing about whether the edition would complement his Judaic scholarship as a contribution to the holy commonwealth; but Selden 'seems overjoy'd' to learn that the friends will carry on with the edition and he wills to them the impression of his edition as well as 'all Letters or Notes concerning that Author' (43). By contrast, Twells emphasizes, Pocock had no inclination to work on Eutychius, no fondness for the Arabic author, and above all 'was unwilling to give any seeming Ground for being thought a Partner in it' (53). As Twells tells the story, Pocock believed that Selden's selection of a passage from Eutychius, as well as his commentary on the passage, was simply revenge against certain bishops with whom he had fallen out. 'And tho' afterwards' – that is, through the 1620s and 1630s – Selden 'met with a great deal of Respect from them, on account of his very great learning, yet the Resentment of that former Usage lay deep in his Mind, and was at length sufficiently discovered by him, as he found an opportunity for it' (53). As episcopacy sank in the early 1640s, Twells concludes, Selden parlayed his learning into vengeance, his contribution to the holy commonwealth nothing more than unadulterated anger.

The worst is yet to come however. Twells maintains that Pocock's real reason for accepting the behest was his desire to show how ineptly the angry Selden had translated and interpreted Eutychius. Not only was his translation poor, critics argued, but the passage that he had chosen for publication was patently fabulous: 'the whole Passage was a perfect

Fable' (53). The great scholar had botched the Arabic, the shrewd historian had been blind to blatant fictions, and the brilliant interpreter had
taken a passage out of a context that would have shown it 'in a truer
Light.' Selden should have known that the Patriarch's 'bare Authority
cannot be sufficient in any Matter to overthrow the general Consent of
the *Greek* and *Latin* Fathers, and Church Historians' (54). What Selden
refused to understand was that bishops, not presbyters, were the constant in the history of the church.

With Twells fashioning Pocock's response to Selden's Eutychius, Selden's extraordinary work on religious history became a pawn in the
polemics of those controversialists fighting over the holy commonwealth
in an England picking itself up after the Civil War and Interregnum.
Selden had been thus used far more positively, for instance, in John
Cleveland's mock of the Westminster Assembly: 'And Selden is a galliard
by himself, / And well may be; there's more divines in him, / Then in all
this their Jewish Sanhedrin.'[54] Some intellectuals, however, left behind
clear evidence of the earnest engagement with the future of the holy
commonwealth that Selden had provoked during their readings of his
large and diverse corpus of scholarship.

In *An Elegant and Learned Discourse of the Light of Nature*, for instance, a
text that was published in 1652 but originated in lectures at Cambridge
in 1646, Nathaniel Culverwell responds in a decidedly mixed fashion to
Selden's scholarship. Like the work of Grotius and Salmasius, he complains, Selden's *De Jure Naturali* actually leaves the most careful reader
with no sense of natural law whatever; each fails to recover that universal
law from the 'cloudy and obscured manner' in which philosophers have
handled it. It would not have surprised Culverwell to hear Selden's
remark that virtually no one understands what is meant by the law of
nature. Culverwell makes considerable use of 'the renowned' Selden's
elucidation – 'very full and satisfactory' – of Judaic rites and laws; yet
without blaming Selden per se, he also opposes the influential error
that natural law derives from the Jews as though it were one of their traditions and a fire to be kindled only at their candle. Culverwell is apt to
thank Selden for allowing him access to an authenticated ancient Judaism; but that early body of laws and rites does not impress Culverwell as
the panacea against scepticism, persecution, fragmentation, and secularization. Nor does he ever acknowledge that Selden himself is impressed by the Jews. Rather, Selden is represented as reporting the arrogance with which the Jews arrogate to themselves a monopoly on the
universality of nature. What is more, the author of *De Jure Naturali* is

credited with calling attention to the 'Intellectus Agens,' as that controversial force is clarified and heralded in the Stoic tradition. According
to 'that learned and eminent writer of our own,' the Stoics do not finally
make the mistake of identifying the human soul with divinity; rather,
they posit 'much similitude between the soul and a Deity; many bright
resemblances of God stampt upon it, which is not only sound Philosophy, but good Divinity too; that the soul was made according to the
image of its Creatour.'[55]

For Culverwell, then, Selden alternates between failing to help mid-
seventeenth-century Christendom gain access to the much-needed universal of natural law; exposing the hubris of the Jews in such a way that
gentiles might feel empowered once again to seek out nature; and helping his contemporaries to isolate and understand that complex yet crucial legacy of natural law in the ancient Stoics. By contrast, Edward
Stillingfleet, writing after the publication of Selden's work on the Sanhedrin, after Hobbes's *Leviathan*, and in the early years of the Restoration
rather than the midst of the Civil War, is intent on grappling with a wide
range of Selden's scholarship, but in particular with the work on ecclesiastical polity from the 1630s (on priestly succession among the ancient
Jews), through the edition of Eutychius in the 1640s, up to the books on
the Sanhedrin in the 1650s. He is also intent on refuting Selden's claims
that the church should have no jurisdiction in the matter of excommunication, that the business of the church is wholly suasive and doctrinal,
and that excommunication does not entail the transgressor's expulsion
from the services of worship.

Throughout *Irenicum: A Weapon Salve for the Churches Wounds*,[56] Stillingfleet makes extensive use of Selden's researches: on the warrant of
natural law as it resides in the will of God (15); on Hebraic terms for
and notions of religious society (74) and on the Hebraic construction of
the priesthood (90–1); on the early church (the Eutychius) but also on
the ancient Jewish institutions (*De Synedriis*). Stillingfleet is grateful for
the access that Selden has afforded him, as well as respectful towards the
theses that Selden has 'strongly pleaded' (148). But Stillingfleet's goal is
expressly remedial, his hero an updated Richard Hooker, and his bogey
the Erastian disenfranchising of the church for which Selden so earnestly advocates. According to Stillingfleet, the ancient Judaic unification of jurisdiction in the magistracy is untenable for early modern
Christendom. The church must retain its own polity, not least because
(as Selden would agree) its orientation should be heavenly and its goals
spiritual. Yet that difference does not spell for Stillingfleet the removal

of jurisdiction from churches; for religion is as much social as it is inwardly spiritual, and the welfare of the church depends upon its authority to expel the incorrigibly transgressive members from its midst. It is not surprising that Stillingfleet shifts the emphasis of his Judaic studies from Selden's civil Sanhedrin to the clearly ecclesiastical synagogue. Indeed, he argues, Christ would never have looked to the Sanhedrin to resolve disputes among his followers.

Stillingfleet is equally if not more concerned with helping the English church to grope towards a peaceful accommodation of conflicting parties, the Episcopalians, Presbyterians, and the moderate type of Congregationalists (that is, the type who can stomach or even encourage an organized national church). To arrive at this accommodation, he makes the case that no single ecclesiastical polity is divinely ordained. Setting aside the Old Testament, Stillingfleet maintains that the New Testament offers general guidelines for church polities but nothing more, at least nothing about which early modern readers can have any certainty regarding 'the hovering light of unconstant tradition' (320). In the vein of Hooker, Stillingfleet understands these guidelines to emphasize order, edification, governance, and decency, but then to allow each society to exercise its prudence in developing a specific polity that will translate these qualities into an acceptable form for contemporaries. Unlike Hooker, however, Stillingfleet is eager to show that at the end of so much bloodshed and conflict the best possible form is apt to accommodate Presbyterians and Episcopalians alike, 'both as asserting the due interest of the Presbyteries, and allowing the due honour of Episcopacy, and by the joynt harmony of both carrying on the affairs of the Church with the greatest Unity, Concord, and Peace' (282).

Stillingfleet's recommendations for peace have their own uncertain moments. Having argued that early modern Christians are not bound by ancient practice and cannot grasp that practice with any certainty, he makes an about-face and concludes with the reminder that contemporary church polities should approximate the practices of the primitive church. Having argued that the ancient Jews cannot help early modern Christians with their establishment of a church polity, he lingers on the synagogue and presses on to discover how much the primitive church imitated it. Citing Hooker as the great English voice behind his prudential argument, he imagines a hybrid church with which Hooker would strongly disagree, then (rather than make the case that circumstances have changed since the 1590s) he argues that English theologians prior to the Civil War essentially agreed that no one church polity was necessary. Arguing that the church must remain separate from the magistracy, Stillingfleet makes the case for the sensibility of the national church and never elaborates on what he means by positing 'a fair, amicable, and mutual aspect these two powers have one upon another, when rightly understood, being far from clashing one with the other; either by a subjection of the civil power to the Ecclesiastical, or the civil powers swallowing up, and devouring the peculiarity of the Ministerial function' (43). On such points one can readily understand Stillingfleet's attraction to Selden's massive efforts to explore the history and the theory of this 'mutual aspect,' but if Stillingfleet is thankful to Selden for so heroically assisting in this crucial enterprise, the former sidesteps the nagging problems with the application of his salve on the wounds of the church by setting Selden's Erastianism up as an easy target and a distraction. Ironically, Stillingfleet finds further distraction in the very manner of Selden, for he shares with the great scholar a tendency to get lost in the details of antiquity from which, for Stillingfleet though not for Selden, the pay-off is believed to be minimal.

Stillingfleet's choice of the weapon salve for his titular metaphor verges on archaism. For the debate over whether that magical salve might effect a cure over a large distance culminates in the 1630s, with clear evidence that the new atomic and mechanical philosophies are either replacing or appropriating the pneumatic and occult theories of Robert Fludd. In his own works, Selden proves to be stretched between natural philosophies, between the occultists and mechanicians of his world. In the 1650s and 1660s Selden's views of polity are possibly nostalgic for the primitive and ancient, one last voice for the holy commonwealth to which the secularists are bringing ruin. Yet Stillingfleet represents Selden as helping to bring that Erastian ruin almost without volition. Selden is rarely labelled an Erastian, though it is clear enough that Stillingfleet sees him as one, and Erastianism itself is said to derive from a misinterpretation of the very nature of religious societies and their powers to censure (136). Stillingfleet also senses the need to distance his argument for the mutability of church polity from the errors of 'the *Proselytes* of *Erastus*' (403). Indeed, Erastianism is credited with a 'just *zeal* against the *extravagancies* of those who scrued up *Church power* to so high a peg, that it was thought to make perpetuall *discord* with the *Common-wealth*' (appendix, 2). These zealots for the civil magistracy 'could never think themselves free from so great an inconvenience, till they had *melted down* all *Spiritual power* into the *Civil State*, and *dissolved* the *Church* into the *Common-wealth*' (appendix, 2). Thanks to these followers of the physician Erastus, the church was rendered unable to salve its own illnesses and was deprived 'of her *expulsive* faculty of *Noxious humours*' (appendix, 2). But the church, Stillingfleet insists, is a society with rights and powers, divinely instituted and thus independent of the civil state. Its unity with the civil state is only accidental, he argues, though (like Selden) he entertains natural metaphors for that junction, not least the pneumatic connections between the soul and the body in the human constitution. So it is that the fortunes of the church and the state tend to rise and fall together but remain ontologically distinct.

At best, Stillingfleet concludes, the Erastian conception of the relationship between the polities of magistrate and minister is 'crude' and distracted by the irrelevance of Judaic ritual. He never quite says, however, whether Selden considered the Sanhedrin a workable and final measure for the ills afflicting English religious society. Among his admirers, Selden's death brought with it not only the incomplete state of that normative solution but also conflicting perceptions of whether Selden believed that religious and civil warrants could be harmonized or coordinated in a single vision of human society. According to one account, found in Aubrey, a minister came to visit the dying scholar while Hobbes was in attendance. When Hobbes chastised Selden for having lived and written courageously only to die like a coward, 'the Minister was not let in.'[57] Whatever the historical veracity of the anecdote, Tuck concludes, its symbolic value for Selden's contemporaries was clear, for the story links Selden's famous anticlericalism to a much less certain affinity for Hobbes.

According to another account, the dying Selden confessed to two close friends, the illustrious cleric and theologian James Ussher and Dr Gerard Langbaine, 'that he had his study full of books and papers of most subjects in the world; yet at that time he could not recollect any passage wherein he could rest his soul, save out of the holy scriptures; wherein the most remarkable passage that lay most upon his spirit was Titus ii.11, 12, 13, 14.' In this passage, 'the grace of God has dawned upon the world with healing for all mankind; and by it we are disciplined to renounce godless ways and worldly desires, and to live a life of temperance, honesty, and godliness in the present age, looking forward to the happy fulfillment of our hope when the splendour of our great God and Savior Christ Jesus will appear' (NEB, 272). Given his inability to find a shred of comfort in his other, worldly books, according to this reckoning, Selden refuses entrance to the magistrate at the door. Unlike the testimony of Sir Matthew Hale to Richard Baxter 'that Selden was "a resolved serious christian, and a great adversary to Hobbes's errors,'"[58] this account of Selden's favourite biblical passage has little if anything to do with preserving Selden's support for a holy commonwealth in this world of human polities.

For all their differences, however, and whatever their unreliability, these two emblems agree in what they demonstrate about Selden's posthumous reception: both insist that at his death, Selden came to realize the fraudulence of any hope in a meaningful reconciliation between civil power and spiritual redemption. In these anecdotes, Selden is shown to glimpse the tragic irony of his own scholarship, to understand a future in which, as a character in *The Karamazov Brothers* proclaims, 'this mingling of elements, that is, of the essence of Church and state, taken separately, may very well go on for ever, in spite of the fact that it's impossible and cannot be brought into any normal, let alone reconcilable relationship.'[59] In taking sides on whether Selden was Hobbesian or anti-Hobbesian, the next generation's inventors of the great scholar's demise epitomized their sense of a monumental change taking place in the mid-seventeenth century, namely, the movement from a comprehensively religious society to a comprehensively civil society in which religious society is relegated to smaller units or cantons. Both anecdotes ignore the fact that even if he unavoidably left his Sanhedrin incomplete, until Selden went to his grave, he was hard at work on the lifelong project of 'mingling' civil and religious elements that had consumed him for so many years.

As Langbaine let on in his response to *De Synedriis*, this massive enterprise also made Selden something of a lone, misunderstood figure, a prophet whose supposed obscurity was really a symptom of an obtuse people. Apparently, Selden deemed it more suitable to work on his historical reconstruction of the Sanhedrin than to accept those commissions rumoured to have come his way from Cromwell, who, it is reported, wanted Selden to defend the regicide and to draft the constitution of the new government under way in England.[60] Selden died in search of a paradise in which the Bards and their judges, the judges and their seers, inspired prophets and coercive leviathans might dwell in peace. On his deathbed, his more polemically minded contemporaries believed, Selden had been forced to face and dispel his life's illusion.

In the eighteenth century, Selden's first major biographer and editor, Archdeacon David Wilkins, worried that the *Table Talk* would establish a diminished image of the great scholar for posterity. For Richard Milward's collection of putative sayings from Selden's mouth at dinner – an anthology that Wilkins considered of dubious credit – would doubtless detract from a full understanding of Selden's learning, and it neither captured his inclinations nor portrayed his mores and principles ('nec mores aut principia depingunt').[61] As an antidote to the caricatures of the 'Erastian' Selden that would surely continue to appear, Wilkins concluded his 'vita authoris' with an explanation of the scholar's religion. Selden always wanted to steer religion towards the middle course, Wilkins argues, and any conflict that he had with the clergy was designed to pursue this basic goal. He was, in essence, a latitudinarian before its time, which meant that his several enemies were in a good position to declare him heterodox.

In order to epitomize Selden's creed, Wilkins quotes a passage from the scholar's prolegomenon to the De Successionibus, in which Selden hails the sincere Protestant who renounced the Catholic church for its opposition to true divinity, but did not wish to establish a new church without knowledge of early church history, the fathers, councils, and canons. This kind of a genuine Protestant he differentiates from the peevish, morose kind who rejected such historical resources merely for the sake of their own audacious and ingenious explications of scripture. The latter Protestants wanted to disturb the peace of Christendom, while the former wanted to restore its truth. Wilkins makes no mention of the fact that Selden's words were addressed to Laud. The controversial archbishop has been pruned from the learned catholicity of Selden's Protestantism.

In what follows in Wilkins's account, there does emerge a roundabout emphasis on the Englishness of that Protestantism. Since these words speak to the reformation of the English church in particular, Wilkins explains, the editor has decided to complete his account of Selden's religion and, consequently, of his life with words taken from a manuscript copy of a French life of Selden written by Paulus Colomesius. According to Colomesius, Selden's words may well have suited the beginnings of the English Reformation, during which there was high regard for antiquity. The English reformers proceeded deliberately in sorting out the good from the bad in their enterprise. They respected the succession and dignity of the clergy and retained traditions from the past, all in a spirit without the affected humour of contradiction but with a willingness to incorporate elements of the Roman church that were not at odds with the law of God. In France, Colomesius laments, reform was entirely otherwise. Reformers pursued tumult and innovation, rejecting the whole of Christian history in an effort to assert their own wills and wits. In short, even the Roman Catholics admit that England, and only England, had managed truly to reform its church.[62]

Wilkins draws no conclusions from this French source as a commentary on Selden's distinction between two types of Protestant, but one conclusion appears to be that Selden either did look or should have looked homeward for the best norm of a holy commonwealth. The scholar had no need to have travelled so far in his pioneering efforts, Wilkins implies in his layered conclusion; for in the spirit of Anglicanism lay the hope of Israel. That latitudinarian spirit would have less room for the intricacies of the liturgy, for the pressurized conformity of a Laudian prelacy, or for complex problems of theology. No doubt like similar versions of the 'spirit of Anglicanism' in the twentieth century, it would be capaciously open to learning both ancient and modern, anchored in solid moral problem-solving rather than in the niceties of soteriology, and distil a peaceful Christian essence from the volatile history of Christian conflict.[63]

It is hard to say exactly why Selden's religion was handled last in Wilkins's life. No doubt it was the aspect of the scholar most difficult to explain, and the aspect that most needed explaining, especially for Wilkins, a clergyman himself with disregard for the *Table Talk*. In some measure, however, Selden's religion had become an irrelevant afterthought, for the eighteenth century and for Selden scholars thereafter, because Selden's most triumphant legacy was believed to lie elsewhere: at home in England, to be sure, but in the progress of the common law rather than in the bulwark of the holy commonwealth. Even a cursory reading of Sir Matthew Hale's *History of the Common Law* clarifies how fervently Selden's contribution to scholarship was venerated in the understanding of England's legal history, institutions, and practices. In the *Jani Anglorum*, we are told, Selden 'has given a full account of those laws' basic to property and criminality. Selden's commentary on the *Fleta* has helped the English law to gain a sense of autonomy from and superiority over Roman civil law, an attitude all the more important insofar as the civil law continued to be practised in certain jurisdictions in England. Selden's Eadmer is cited several times as a boon to understanding the history of English law. The common law is 'the great foundation (under God) of the peace, happiness, honour and justice of this kingdom'; for it 'declares and asserts the rights, and liberties, and the properties of the subject; and is the just, known, and common rule of justice and right, between man and man, within this kingdom.' Hale clearly cared about Selden's piety, and he comforted Baxter on this score. We learn from an early life of Hale that he enjoyed grasping 'the most curious points of rabbinical learning' from Selden, and was himself 'particularly attached to the study of divinity.'[64] But in *The History of the Common Law* he testifies to Selden's heroic efforts on behalf of the just measures of human society, and Hale's 'under God' actually means 'aside from God,' that is, taking it for granted that God is always to thank for any happiness in this life of ours.

The ways and means of unifying England's religion – or of religiously unifying English society – continued to vex and increasingly perplexed the cultural brokers of the Restoration. Dissenters resisted what Richard Baxter called 'pursuing union the wrong way, by persecuting the godly'; but persecution was intense, sweeping, and eventually (if perversely) more attributable to parliament than to Charles II, who would tolerate Dissenters if doing so allowed breathing room for English Catholics.[65] Writing from exile, Edmund Ludlow mourned the end of accommodation upon hearing that John Dury, a leading proponent of the unification of the Protestant churches, had departed England like a fleeing Astraea: 'And Mr. Dureus, who had for many yeares endeavoured reconcilliation betweene the Calvinist and Lutheran against their common enemy the papist, that he might have a full taste of the principles and resolution of the Bisshop of London, who was looked upon as the intellectus agens of their King *in matter of religion*, acquaints him with certeine propositions lately put forth by the popish party in Germany for the accomodating of the difference betweene the papist and Protestant; one whereof being that auricular confession should not be imposed, but left ad libitum. The Bisshopp blaming that moderation, as a duty *judgeing that confession* absolutely necessary to be used, Mr. Dureus *thereby becomeing satisfyed in their intentions, and being* thereby destitute of all hopes for the promoting of his interest for the present in England, betakes himselfe to the work of accomodation beyond the seaes.'[66]

If from the dissenting standpoint the persecutions of godly persons subverted accommodation, staunchly Anglican clergy, among them Samuel Parker, indicted all manner of non-conformity as destructive of the holy commonwealth, with complex political results. As Jon Parkin has said, 'Charles II's controversial decision to suspend the penal laws against dissenters in March 1672 decisively broke the linkage between Church and Crown which had been precariously sustained since the Restoration. For Anglican churchmen like Samuel Parker, who had rested their ecclesiology, and their intolerance of dissent, upon the right of the sovereign to order the Church, this *volte-face* left them in a potentially embarrassing situation.' Parkin adds, 'After the failure of attempts to find a suitable accommodation with the Established Church, discussion about tolerating a pluralist religious culture based on rights and interests replaced the wrangling over specific doctrine and Scripture.'[67] By 1669 Louis du Moulin was pointing out to Baxter the irony that 'men as ill-principled as Grotius and Selden, yea Hobbes as bad as can be, should come nearer the truth than many good men.'[68] By lumping Selden with Hobbes, du Moulin epitomized the perception that the holy commonwealth's worst enemy had proved the struggling civil commonwealth's best friend. As Baxter understood, du Moulin was mistaken about Selden's principles.

By the eighteenth century, neither Selden nor anyone else had managed to save the holy commonwealth in England. Opposition to the Catholicism of James II did provide an opportunity for the Protestants in England to join forces against the common enemy; but in the wake of the 1688 revolution, the Act of Toleration meant the end of the dream of religious unity; as J.P. Kenyon states the point, 'the division between Protestants created in 1662 was confirmed,' and the Comprehension Bill was 'predictably talked out.'[69] Another historian, Paul Seaward, agrees that by the end of the 1680s 'dissent itself had changed. Decades of frustration and moments of temptation to separatism had brought many to change their minds about the virtues of a single national church. The numbers of presbyterians who were still committed to securing comprehension within the Church of England had shrunk: presbyterians, wrote an anglican minister in 1689, "are but few now, most of them being run into Independency."'[70] In 1689 Selden's *Table Talk* was published for the first time, featuring shocking paradoxes such as the answer to the question of 'Whether ... the Church or Scripture [is] Judge of Religion.' The answer attributed to Selden: 'In truth neither, but the state' (117). Gone from this character of an Erastian was the complexity of precisely what Selden had meant by 'Judge.' Readers of the *Table Talk* might have had their breath taken away by such saucy language (in the passage he goes on to compare the matter to the medical treatment of a boil), but Milward's caricature of Selden's Erastian views signalled that England was on the verge of waking up from the dream of the holy commonwealth to find its society comprehensively civil.

Notes

A variety of texts will be cited for the works of Selden; unless otherwise noted, the reference is to the *Opera Omnia*, by volume and column number.

Introduction

1 Berkowitz, *John Selden's Formative Years;* Christianson, *Discourse on History, Law, and Governance;* Tuck, *Philosophy and Government,* 205–21; and Rosenblatt, *Torah and Law,* 94–103, 123–31. Article-length studies will be cited in the appropriate places.

2 Calvin, *Institutes of the Christian Religion,* Book IV, chap. xx, sect. 2, quoted by Goldsmith and Roots in *Gangraena,* 'Introduction,' 10.

3 'Preface to *Gondibert,*' in Spingarn, *Critical Essays of the Seventeenth Century,* vol. 2, 10.

4 *Works Moral and Religious,* vol. 1, 112.

5 Lamont, ed., *Richard Baxter's 'A Holy Commonwealth,'* xxviii, 14, 25, 49, 68, 129.

6 Ibid., 126–7.

7 See Wilkins, 'Vita authoris,' in *Opera Omnia,* lii. I discuss each of these responses in the conclusion.

8 Reinert, *Regulating Confusion,* 18.

9 Rosenblatt, *Torah and Law,* 123–9.

10 For a discussion of how this image of the Lesbian rule had an impact on English humanism, see Baker, *Divulging Utopia,* 53. Aristotle's discussion is in the *Ethics,* Book 5.

11 Milton's views are taken here from *Areopagitica* and *Of Civil Power,* in *Complete Poetry and Major Prose,* 717–49; 839–55; quotation on 743.

12 Tuck, 'The Institutional Setting,' in *Cambridge History of Seventeenth-Century Philosophy,* ed. Garber and Ayers, vol. 1, 24.

13 Ibid., 12.

14 Botero, *Reason of State*, 61–9, 222–3.

15 Marsilius of Padua, *Defensor Pacis*, lxv.

16 See Bodin, *Colloquium of the Seven about Secrets of the Sublime*, 182–94.

17 Wootton, *Divine Right and Democracy*, 59.

18 Ibid., 61–2; and quoted by Wootton, 63.

19 For the importance of religion in Restoration England, see Harris, *Politics of Religion*. For the metaphor of 'cement,' see Wootton, *Divine Right and Democracy*, 60.

20 Pocock, 'Thomas May,' 120.

21 Sharpe and Zwicker, *Politics of Discourse*, 6–7.

22 David Loewenstein, *Representing Revolution*, 8.

23 Wootton, *Divine Right and Democracy*, 63, 74; and *The Grounds of Sovereignty and Greatness* (1675), quoted by Wootton, 74.

24 Lamont, 'Pamphleteering,' 80.

1: A Scholar's Life

1 This paragraph is indebted in its entirety to Skinner, *Foundations*, vol. 2.

2 See Franklin, *Jean Bodin and the Rise of Absolutist Theory*.

3 See Donne, 'Satire 3,' ll. 17–26. For England's responses to Henry of Navarre, see Voss, *Elizabethan News Pamphlets*.

4 Skinner, *Foundations*, 2.304.

5 Hooker, *Of the Laws of Ecclesiastical Polity: Preface, Books I to IV*, 232–3.

6 Ibid., 29, 32, 43.

7 Quoted in Aiken, *Lives of John Selden*, 43.

8 Norbrook, *Writing the English Republic*, 10–11.

9 For links between canon and Canaan, see Gassendi, *Animadversiones*, 117–19.

10 *Michael Drayton*, vol. 4, 240.

11 See Wilkins, 'Vita authoris,' *Opera Omnia*, lii, and further discussion in my conclusion below.

12 Wedgwood, *Coffin for King Charles*, 9.

13 'The Dedication of a Sermon to Mr. Selden,' quoted by Berkowitz, *John Selden's Formative Years*, 30.

14 Barbour, *Literature and Religious Culture*, chaps 1–2.

15 Cockburn, 1.

2: Ancient Bards and Inmost Historians

1 Worden, *Sound of Virtue*, 253.

2 Worden, 'Ben Jonson among the Historians,' 68.

3 'An Apology for Poetry,' in Smith, *Elizabethan Critical Essays*, vol. 1, 185; Selden's praise for Sidney is found in Hebel, *Michael Drayton*, vol. 4, 65.

4 The text for Selden's letter, which appears in the *Opera Omnia* (vol. 3, cols 1690–6), is Rosenblatt and Schleiner, 'John Selden's Letter to Ben Jonson'; the text in the article is based on a transcription of the manuscript, Selden supra 108 fols 64-64 Bodl. L.

5 Spalding, *Diary of Bulstrode Whitelocke*, 74.

6 For a poetry quite contrary to court culture in the 1620s and 1630s, see Norbrook, *Writing the English Republic*.

7 *Complete Poems*, 148.

8 Clayton, *Sir John Suckling*, 71.

9 Patrick, *Poetry of Robert Herrick*, 194.

10 'To My Most Dearely-Loved Friend Henery Reynolds Esquire, of Poets and Poesie,' in *Michael Drayton*, vol. 3, 231.

11 Prescott, *Imagining Rabelais*, 184.

12 The text for Selden's poem to Browne is *Opera Omnia*, vol. 3, col. 1720.

13 *Opera Omnia*, vol. 3, col. 1720.

14 Selden invokes Plato in the margins to the verses on Drayton, ibid. See also Plato, *Phaedrus*, 476–81.

15 'Ad v. c. Th. Farnabium de Lucano perpetuis illius notis explicato & in lucem iam prodituro,' *Opera Omnia*, vol. 2, col. 1720. Farnaby's Lucan appeared in 1618 with Selden's poem.

16 Grafton, *Joseph Scaliger*, vol 1, 16.

17 Kelley, *Modern Historical Scholarship*, 69.

18 Bolton, 'Hypercritica,' in Spingarn, *Critical Essays*, vol. 1, 99, 93.

19 Johnson, *Rise of English Culture*, 521–2.

20 For Woolf, see *Idea of History*, 238.

21 For Whear on Selden, see Woolf, *Idea of History*, 190; for Peacham on Selden, see Berkowitz, *John Selden's Formative Years*, 49.

22 Jonson, *Complete Poems*, 461.

23 Sharpe, *Sir Robert Cotton*, 11.

24 *Complete Poems*, 214.

25 Sharpe, *Sir Robert Cotton*, 228.

26 *Britannia*, 32–3.

27 *Poly-Olbion*, in *Michael Drayton*, vol. 4, v.

28 *Church History of Britain*, vol. 1, 4.

29 *Poly-Olbion* in *Michael Drayton*, vol. 4, 2.

30 Prescott, *Imagining Rabelais*, 181–2.

31 *Poly-Olbion*, in *Michael Drayton*, vol. 4, 46.

32 Ovid, *Fasti*, 141.

33 Quintilian, *Institutio Oratoria*, vol. 1, 131.

34 *Poly-Olbion*, in *Michael Drayton*, vol. 4, xii.

35 Book 3, 156–7.

36 For Ammianus, see the Loeb edition, *Ammianus Marcellinus*, vol. 1, 179; for Lucan, Brown and Martindale, Lucan, *The Civil War*, 22. Selden quotes Ammianus and Lucan in the *Analecton*, in *Opera Omnia*, vol. 2, col. 890.

37 Selden quotes Diodorus Siculus in *ibid.*

38 See *Britannia*, 118. Selden cites Aelian in his preface, *Analecton*, col. 865.

39 Athenaeus, *The Deipnosophists*, vol. 3, 109.

40 Ibid., vol. 2, 195ff.

41 This paragraph is based in its entirety on Hornblower and Spawforth, *Oxford Classical Dictionary*, 1003–8, 1047.

42 Athenaeus, *Deipnosophists*, vol. 6, 373–5.

43 *Marmora*, 83: 'In Nomis hisce & qui fuere caeteris diis dicati, mira erat & ridicula theogoniarum, amorum, peregrinationum, fraudum, portentorum seges, & sexcenta tam puerilia quam fabulosa.' Selden cites Strabo, X.

44 Vol. 1, 95 (italics mine); see also *Marmora*, 83.

45 In addition to his swipes at unreliable rabbinical fictions in the commentary on Drayton, Selden disparaged the Jews in 'Of the Jews sometimes living in England' (1617), written for Samuel Purchas.

46 For *depravatio* and *norma*, see *De Dis Syris*, 2d rev. ed., the prolegomena, 30–4. For an account of the reception and edition of the work on the Continent, see Sellin, *Daniel Heinsius*, 104–6.

47 See Drayton, *Poly-Olbion*, in *Michael Drayton*, vol. 4, 15–16.

48 O Hehir, *Expans'd Hieroglyphicks*, 127, 153.

49 *Imagining Rabelais*, 181–2.

3: Legal Sages and Parliamentary Religion

1 Burgess, *Absolute Monarchy*, 166.

2 Brooks, *Lawyers, Litigation*, 7–8, 196–7, 206–7.

3 Caesar, *Conquest of Gaul*, 139–42; and Tacitus, *Annals*, 154–7.

4 Cromartie, *Sir Matthew Hale*, 30, 32.

5 Tubbs, *Common Law Mind*, 194–5.

6 Prest, *Inns of Court*, 157.

7 Helgerson, *Forms of Nationhood*, 103–4.

8 Plutarch, *Moralia*, 321, 325.

9 Vol. 1, 13–17; cf. Bracton's model, Mommsen and Watson, *Digest of Justinian*, vol. 1, 1.

10 Coke, *Reports*, preface to part II, viii; preface to part III, iv.

11 Little, *Religion, Order, and Law,* 175–7; Little cites G.P. Gooch on lawyers as priests.

12 Tubbs, *Common Law Mind,* 195.

13 *Reports,* preface to part IV, xvi; preface to part VI, xv, xvii.

14 Cited in Gough, *Fundamental Law,* 41.

15 Tubbs, *Common Law Mind,* 21.

16 Quoted in Eusden, *Puritans, Lawyers, and Politics,* 122.

17 Knafla, *Law and Politics,* 50.

18 Ibid., 105–6, 106–7.

19 *Law, or a Discourse,* 74. Bacon's text is *The Elements of the Common Laws of England.*

20 Lambarde, *Archeion,* 43, 66–7.

21 Prest, *Rise of the Barristers,* 189.

22 Ibid., 218, 217.

23 Ibid., 226, 226–7.

24 Dodderidge, *Lawyers Light,* 87, 64–5.

25 Fulbecke, *Direction or Preparatiue,* 1v, 2v.

26 Ibid., 7r, 10r, 21v.

27 Ibid., 34v, 52v–53r, 53r.

28 Ziskind, 'John Selden,' 22–39; Sommerville, 'History and Theory,' 249–61; Christianson, *Discourse on History*; and Tuck, '"Ancient Law of Freedom,"' 137–61, 238–41.

29 Tuck, '"Ancient Law of Freedom,"' 139.

30 Kelley, *History, Law and the Human Sciences*; the quotations appear on 48–50 of the eleventh essay, separately paginated and entitled 'History, English Law and the Renaissance.' Kelley derives his distinction between antiquity and authority from Maitland.

31 White, *Sir Edward Coke,* 22, 29.

32 Tite, *Impeachment and Parliamentary Judicature,* 32.

33 Christianson, *Discourse on History,* 87, 88.

34 Ibid., 108.

35 Jonson, 'Conversations with Drummond,' in *Complete Poems,* 478; the Selden passage is quoted by Berkowitz, *John Selden's Formative Years,* 83.

36 Berkowitz, *John Selden's Formative Years,* 83.

37 Johnson et al., *Commons Debates, 1628,* vol. 2, 2–3, 23, 302; vol. 3, 17, 18, 19, 129.

38 Ibid., vol. 2, 332–3, 333, 334, 250, 146.

39 For the consensus, see Burgess, *Politics of the Ancient Constitution.*

40 Johnson et al., *Commons Debates, 1628,* vol. 2, 85–6, 86–7; vol. 3, 514; vol. 4, 61.

41 Notestein and Relf, *Commons Debates for 1629,* 12–13, 14, 18–19.

42 Johnson et al., *Commons Debates, 1628*, vol. 4, 64–9, 102, 115, 143, 169.

43 Berkowitz, *John Selden's Formative Years*, 193.

44 Johnson et al., *Commons Debates*, 1628, vol. 2, 342; vol. 3, 25, 406, 432, 438, 442; vol. 4, 39.

45 Ibid., vol. 3, 97; vol. 2, 150, 342.

46 Ibid., vol. 3, 451, 455–6, 514, 519.

47 Notestein and Relf, *Commons Debates for 1629*, 28.

48 Ibid., 36, 49, 58–9, 78–80, 117.

49 *Commons Debates for 1629*, 119, 120.

50 For continental concern about Selden's imprisonment, see Grotius's letter to Pieresc, quoted in Aiken, *Lives of John Selden*, 79.

51 Brooks, *Lawyers, Litigation*, 1.

52 Stow, *Survey of London*, vol. 2, 49

53 Fuller, *History of the Holy War*, 92, 191, 243–7, 271.

54 See, for instance, Bracton, *De legibus*, vol. 1, 3.

55 Prest, *Inns of Court*, 95.

56 Squibb, *High Court of Chivalry*, xxvi, 37.

57 Prest, *Rise of the Barristers*, 87–8.

58 Christianson, *Discourse on History*, 38.

59 Prest, *Rise of the Barristers*, 315–16.

60 See Brooke, *Discourse*, 3–5, 33–5.

61 *Titles of Honor*, first published in 1614, with a dedication to Heyward; the second edition (1631) offered Heyward a new dedication; the edition cited is the third (1672), a corrected edition, a1r; it includes the dedication of the second edition.

62 Jonson, *Complete Poems*, 213.

63 Pocock, *Machiavellian Moment*, 14–15, 16.

64 *Classical Humanism*; for Eliot and Lipsius, 286; for Leighton, 287.

4. Natural Law and Common Notions

1 *Civil War*, 22.

2 Caesar, *Conquest of Gaul*, 141.

3 *Poly-Olbion*, in *Michael Drayton*, vol. 4, 122, 192, 193.

4 Ibid., 193.

5 Ibid., 214–16, 119.

6 Quoted in Feingold, 'John Selden,' 71.

7 Ibid., 61.

8 *Poly-Olbion*, in *Michael Drayton*, vol. 4, 108.

9 Feingold, 'John Selden,' 62.

10 For the distinctive, if overlapping, mentalities regarding nature in the seventeenth century, see Vickers, *Occult and Scientific Mentalities*.

11 *Poly-Olbion*, in *Michael Drayton*, vol. 4, xi, 20–1, 234–5, 300–1.

12 Feingold, 'John Selden,' 69.

13 'John Selden,' 73.

14 *Three Works of Francisco Suárez, S.J.*; for a translation of the Latin in volume 1, see vol. 2, 178–350.

15 Tuck, *Natural Rights Theories*, 93.

16 For the encomium to Hopton, see *Opera Omnia*, vol. 2, cols 1717–19.

17 Bacon, *Opus Majus*, vol. 1, 3.

18 Ibid., 49.

19 Holdsworth, *English Law*, 145.

20 On this point, see Tuck, *Philosophy and Government*, 215. For a recent review of Tuck, see Sommerville, 'Selden, Grotius,' 318–44.

21 *Areopagitica*, in *Complete Poems and Major Prose*, 727.

22 Christianson, *Discourse on History*, 251.

23 See Barbour, *English Epicures and Stoics*, chaps 4 and 5.

24 Sommerville, 'Selden, Grotius,' 334.

25 In his first major study of Selden, Richard Tuck depicts his subject as a forerunner of Hobbes, that is, as a theorist of natural law who attempts to answer the sceptics by accommodating a person's or a state's rights within a minimal slate of fundamental moral obligations. But motivated in part by J.P. Sommerville's critique, Tuck's second, revised reading of Selden emphasizes the proximity between the English lawyer and Grotius. In this reading, Selden retains some kinship with Hobbes, but Selden's formulation of a Hebraic natural law emerges into the spotlight. Tuck's first reading can be found in *Natural Rights Theories*, 82–100; the second can be found in *Philosophy and Government*, 205–21. Cf. Sommerville, 'John Selden,' 437–47.

26 Jonson, *Complete Poems*, 432.

27 Barbour, *English Epicures and Stoics*, chap. 4.

28 *De jure belli*, vol. 2, 12–13. Subsequent page references are given parenthetically in the text.

29 Tuck, *Natural Rights Theories*, 90.

30 Tuck, *Philosophy and Government*, 215–16.

31 On the *intellectus agens*, see Sommerville, 'John Selden'; and Tuck, *Philosophy and Government*, 216.

32 In *Areopagitica* Milton proclaims that Selden's appreciation for both mathematical method and trial-by-error is 'of main service and assistance toward the speedy attainment of what is truest' (*Complete Poetry and Major Prose*, 727).

33 Maimonides, *Guide for the Perplexed*, 2. Subsequent page references are given parenthetically in the text.
34 Novak, *Natural Law in Judaism*, 3.
35 Maimonides, *Mishneh Torah*, 4b.
36 'Atque haec sanè sive velut columnae cui innitantur caetera, robustissimae munus obeunt, sive qualem ferè habet ad vectis, librae, cunei, trochleae, aliorum in Staticis & Mechanicis motum Circulus ... rationem praestant JURIS NATURALIS nomen simul induere solita, atque in re Civili & Morali plane fiunt ... *universaliter prima*' (*De Jure Naturali*, 2).
37 Barbour, *English Epicures and Stoics*, chap. 5.
38 'Capita Juris Naturalis seu Universalis, juxta Ebraeos, designaturo subit in mentem illud S. Ambrosii; *Lex Naturalis Tres habet Partes*' (*De Jure Naturali*, 118).
39 A sizable portion of Selden's second book is given over to proselytes; see *De Jure Naturali*, 138–267. He returns to the matter often over the course of the work, for instance, in Book 5 on questions of marriage.
40 Barbour, *English Epicures and Stoics*, chap. 4.
41 *Marcus Aurelius*, 123.
42 *Vindiciae secundum integritatem existimationis suae*, in *Opera Omnia*, vol. 2, cols 1415–38.
43 See Barbour, *English Epicures and Stoics*, chaps 4 and 5.

5: The Canons of the Church

1 Christianson, *Discourse on History*, 5, 9–12, 202.
2 Hall, *Episcopacy by Divine Right*, vol. 10, 246–64.
3 Quoted in Carruthers, *Everyday Work*, 180.
4 See ibid., 175–6.
5 Ironically, the manuscript on which Selden based his edition, now BL, Cottonian MS. Titus Aix, is considered far less reliable than Corpus Christi College, Cambridge, MS. 452; for the Cotton manuscript 'leaves out many of the documents that help to give the History its importance.' See Eadmer, *History of Recent Events*, xiii.
6 Gransden, *Historical Writing*, 136.
7 See Stephen and Lee, *Dictionary of National Biography*, vol. 21, 414.
8 *Historical Writing*, 139.
9 Southern, *Saint Anselm*, 310.
10 Eadmer, *History of Recent Events*, 2.
11 See the *Opera Omnia*, vol. 3, cols 1393 (the letter to the Marquess of Buckingham), and 1399–458 (the three treatises).
12 See Wilkins, 'Vita authoris,' in *Opera Omnia*, li–ii and the conclusion, below.

13 Laud, *Works,* vol. 1, 70.

14 Ibid., 82, 112.

15 Ibid., vol. 6, 11, 17, 20.

16 Laud, *Works,* vol. 3, 399; vol. 6, 42; vol. 3, 408.

17 Helmholz, *Spirit of Classical Canon Law,* 4–5.

18 The phrase 'juridical community' is in Chodorow, *Christian Political Theory,* 65.

19 I owe this point to one of the anonymous readers for the University of Toronto Press.

20 'Quemadmodum verò id de quo in Jure Caesareo Proculeianis cum Sabinianis, in Theologia Pontificiis cum Reformatis, Calvinianis cum Lutheranis, in doctrina Judaica Scholae Hillelianae cum Sammaeana, aliisve id genus cum aliis convenit, id, inquam insigniori multò veritatis charactere apud homines eminere admitti solet, quam quod pars inter hos alterutra aut oppugnat aut sola affirmat, & pro indubitato quidem inde non rarò sumitur; ita de consensu heic Sectarum, quas diximus, binarum illustrium toties invicem aliàs discrepantium Scriptisque pugnantium, merito in re tum ad sacrorum suorum regimen tum ad mores civiles adeò spectante, est statuendum' (*De Anno,* preface, 4–5).

21 See Ziskind, *John Selden on Jewish Marriage Law: The 'Uxor Hebraica,'* 10. Subsequent references are to this edition.

22 Rosenblatt, *Torah and Law,* 88.

23 Ibid., 82, citing Helgerson, *Forms of Nationhood,* 300.

24 Bulstrode Whitelock, quoted in Aiken, *Lives of John Selden,* 128.

25 Heylyn, *Aërius Redivivus,* preface.

26 Ziskind, *John Selden on Jewish Marriage Law,* 14.

27 'Gravissima atque plurimùm vexata dudùm recruduit Quaestio, de Ordine Hieratico' (*Eutychii Aegyptii,* preface, 1).

28 Ziskind, *John Selden on Jewish Marriage Law,* 127n.

29 Ibid., 160n.

30 Warfield, *Westminster Assembly,* 14.

31 Milton, 145. 'On the New Forcers of Conscience under the Long Parliament,' in *Complete Poetry and Major Prose.*

32 Lightfoot, *Whole Works,* vol. 13, 6–7, 80, 82, 101, 113, 119, 121, 128, 153, 165–8, 172, 182, 185, 189, 191, 204.

33 Quoted in Carruthers, *Everyday Work,* 125–6.

34 Chidley, *Justification of Independent Churches* is quoted in Milton, *Complete Prose Works,* vol. 1, 140–1.

35 Milton, *Complete Poetry and Major Prose,* 676.

36 Milton, *Areopagitica,* in *Complete Poetry and Major Prose,* 732–3.

37 Ibid., 677.

38 Ibid., 676–7, 679.

39 Lightfoot, *Whole Works*, vol. 13, 205.

40 Milton, *Complete Poetry and Major Prose*, 122, 680; Rosenblatt's argument appears throughout *Torah and Law.*

41 *Complete Poetry and Major Prose*, 161.

42 Ibid., 727.

43 Milton praises the Sanhedrin in *The Ready and Easy Way* (889), and in *Paradise Lost* (459), both in *Complete Poetry and Major Prose.*

44 Lightfoot, *Whole Works*, vol. 13, 120, 189.

45 Figgis, *Divine Right of Kings*, and Paul, *Assembly of the Lord.*

46 Figgis, *Divine Right of Kings*, 321–2.

47 Ibid., 333.

48 Ibid., 335.

49 Paul, *Assembly of the Lord*, 2.

50 See Lightfoot, *Whole Works*, vol. 13, 83.

51 Ibid., 106.

52 Ibid., 126.

53 Ibid., 108, 119, 121, 128, 147, 179–80.

54 Ibid., 141, 78.

6: The Hope of Israel

1 See Fincham, *Prelate as Pastor.*

2 Cary, *Speech*, 5.

3 Ibid., 14–15.

4 The phrase is from Davis, *Fear, Myth and History*, 92.

5 *De Synedriis et Praefecturis Juridicis Veterum Ebraeorum* appeared in three books, in 1650, 1653, and 1655. Citations will refer parenthetically to book and page numbers. Thus, the metaphors under discussion appear in Book 1, preface, ix.

6 For Selden's discussion of the allegory, see Book 2, 253–6; and Epstein, *Babylonian Talmud*, 37a.

7 Ibid.

8 For Selden's keystone, see Book 1, preface, xi; and *Ausonius*, vol. 1, 174–9.

9 *Ausonius*, vol. 1, 176.

10 Norbrook, *Writing the English Republic*, 242.

11 Marvell, *Complete Poems*, 128, 129, 56.

12 Lightfoot, *Whole Works*, vol. 13, 83.

13 Herrup, 'Law and Morality,' 111. For ridings and rough music, see Ingram,

'Ridings, Rough Music'; and Ingram, 'Ridings, Rough Music and Mocking Rhymes.'

14 Selden quotes the Jerusalem Gemara on shame in Book 1, 113; for Milton, see *Complete Poetry and Major Prose*, 679–80.

15 Baker, *Divulging Utopia*, 149–51.

16 Tertullian, *Apologeticus*, 175.

17 Ibid., 183; also *De Synedriis*, Book 1, 299.

18 Quoted in Reinert, *Regulating Confusion*, 19.

19 Ibid., 18.

20 Neusner, *Mishnah*, 590.

21 Ibid., 265; also *De Synedriis*, Book 3, 133–5.

22 Theocritus, *Greek Bucolic Poets*, 246–53; also Book 1, 181.

23 Cf. Maimonides, *Guide*, 219–50.

24 Ibid., 241, 242.

25 Minucius Felix, *Octavius*, 413.

Conclusion

1 Copenhaver and Schmitt, 38; these words are applied to Bacon, Bruno, Charron, Lipsius, Montaigne, and others.

2 Rosenblatt, *Torah and Law*, 82.

3 Parr, *Life of James Ussher*, 68, 74–5.

4 Edwards, *Gangraena*, part 1, 32, 20, 24; Epistle Dedicatory, A4v, A2r.

5 The words of the licenser, Charles Herle, whose inclination to Presbyterianism did not prevent him from approving *An Apologeticall Narration* for publication in 1644. See Haller, *Tracts on Liberty*, vol. 2, 306.

6 Haller, *Tracts on Liberty*, vol. 2, 311, 312, 311.

7 Goodwin, *Independency God's Verity*, 186.

8 See, for instance, Goodwin, *Right and Might Well Met*, 212–20.

9 Smith, *Ranter Writings*, 87. For an emphasis on the ways in which 'Ranterism' was a feature of contemporary fears about the radical dispensation of the Spirit, see Davis, *Fear, Myth and History*.

10 Jean Le Clerc in BL Additional MS 4462, ff. 2–5b, *Vindication of His Character* (after 1729).

11 See Hale, *History of the Common Law*, Tuck, *Natural Rights*; and the translation and reprinting of the *Jani Anglorum*.

12 Quoted and translated by Sommerville in 'Selden, Grotius,' 336.

13 Langbaine to Selden, 28 November 1653, Selden supra 109, fol. 452r.

14 Selden supra 109, fols. 258–72.

15 Hughes, ed., *Complete Poems and Major Prose*, 572, 603, 727, 831, 868, 1003, 1040.

16 From a broadside whose title begins, 'Viro verè pietatis, integritatis, & prudentiae ...,' the author given as one G.D. (1654).
17 *Poems and Translations*, 216–19.
18 Ibid., 219.
19 Jonson, *Complete Poems*, 212, 148.
20 Fletcher, *Poems and Translations*, 220, 222.
21 Ibid., 222.
22 Reinert, *Regulating Confusion*, 18–19.
23 Spalding, *Contemporaries of Bulstrode Whitelocke*, 320.
24 Quoted in Craik, *Life of Edward Earl of Clarendon*, vol. 1, 26.
25 Gott, *Divine History*, A2r.
26 See Robbins, *Two English Republican Tracts*, 86.
27 Katchen, *Christian Hebraists*, 42, 54.
28 Tuck, *Philosophy and Government*, 215, 216.
29 Katz, *Philo-Semitism*, 5.
30 Fisch, *Jerusalem and Albion*, 191.
31 The words of King James in *Meditation Vpon The Lords Prayer* (1619); cited by Katz in *Philo-Semitism*, 25.
32 For Ross, see *View of all Religions*, 37–9.
33 Hughes, *Anglo-Judaeus*, 18.
34 Smith, *Certain Discourses (1660)*, 289, 303.
35 Latham and Matthews, *Diary of Samuel Pepys*, vol. 4, 335, and n. 1.
36 Harrington, *Commonwealth of Oceana*, 6.
37 Ibid., 38–40.
38 Ibid., 40, 63.
39 Cunaeus, *Republica Hebraeorum*, 1.
40 *Christian Hebraists*, 54.
41 Hobbes, *Leviathan*, 93. Subsequent page references are given parenthetically in the text.
42 Milton, *Complete Poetry and Major Prose*, 845.
43 Ibid., 848.
44 Rosenblatt, *Torah and Law*, passim.
45 Quoted in Lamont, *Richard Baxter and the Millennium*, 64, 92. Cf. 132–3 for Baxter's relationship to Erastianism in both its proper and popular senses.
46 Hale, *Works Moral and Religious*, vol. 1, 112.
47 Cromartie, *Sir Matthew Hale*, 40–1, 169, 161.
48 Barlow, 'Case of the Jews,' 35, 37, 20.
49 Ibid., 43; Tuck, *Philosophy and Government*, 216; Barlow, 'Case of the Jews,' 17.
50 Milton, *Complete Poetry and Major Prose*, 727.
51 Tuck, *Philosophy and Government*, 216.

52 Subsequent page references are given parenthetically in the text.

53 *Theological Works*, vol. 1. Subsequent page references are given parenthetically in the text.

54 'Vita authoris,' *Opera Omnia*, xxxv.

55 Culverwell, *Light of Nature*, 23, 43, 60–1, 75, 87.

56 Subsequent page references are given parenthetically in the text.

57 Tuck, *Philosophy and Government*, 220.

58 Cited in Aiken, *Lives of John Selden*, 151–2; see also 165.

59 Dostoevsky, *Karamazov Brothers*, 76.

60 See Tuck, *Philosophy and Government*, 220; Worden, *Rump Parliament*, 339.

61 'Vita authoris,' *Opera Omnia*, xiv.

62 Ibid., lii.

63 For the modern tendency to associate this spirit with the Caroline period, see Barbour, *Literature and Religious Culture*, introduction.

64 Hale, *History of the Common Law*, 7, 61, iii, iv.

65 For Baxter, see Lamont, 'Religion of Andrew Marvell,' 152.

66 Ludlow, *Voyce from the Watch Tower*, 283; italics in the original.

67 Parkin, 'Liberty Transpros'd,' 270.

68 Ibid., 276.

69 Kenyon, *Stuart England*, 265.

70 Seaward, *The Restoration*, 146.

Bibliography

Aiken, John. *The Lives of John Selden, Esq. and Archbishop Usher.* London: Mathews and Leigh, 1812.

Ammianus Marcellinus. Trans. John C. Rolfe. 3 vols. Cambridge, Mass.: Harvard University Press, 1982.

Aristotle. *Metaphysics.* Trans. Hugh Tedenick. 2 vols. Cambridge, Mass.: Harvard University Press, 1956.

Athenaeus. *The Deipnosophists.* Trans. Charles Burton Gulick. 7 vols. Cambridge, Mass.: Harvard University Press, 1967.

Ausonius. Trans. Hugh G. Evelyn White. 2 vols. Cambridge, Mass.: Harvard University Press, 1919.

Bacon, Francis. *The Advancement of Learning.* Ed. Michael Kiernan. Oxford: Clarendon Press, 2000.

Bacon, Roger. *Opus Majus.* Trans. Robert Belle Burke. 2 vols. Philadelphia: University of Pennsylvania Press, 1928.

Baker, David Weil. *Divulging Utopia: Radical Humanism in Sixteenth-Century England.* Amherst: University of Massachusetts Press, 1999.

Barbour, Reid. *English Epicures and Stoics: Ancient Legacies in Early Stuart Culture.* Amherst: University of Massachusetts Press, 1998.

– *Literature and Religious Culture in Seventeenth-Century England.* New York: Cambridge University Press, 2002.

Barlow, Thomas. 'The Case of the Jews.' In *Several Miscellaneous and Weighty Cases of Conscience.* 1692.

Berkowitz, David Sandler. *John Selden's Formative Years: Politics and Society in Early Seventeenth-Century England.* Washington, D.C.: Folger Library, 1988.

Bodin, Jean. *Colloquium of the Seven about Secrets of the Sublime.* Trans., ed., and intro. Marion Leathers Daniel Kuntz. Princeton, N.J.: Princeton University Press, 1975.

Botero, Giovanni. *The Reason of State*. Trans. P.J. and D.P. Waley. London: Routledge & Kegan Paul, 1956.

Bracton, Henrici de. *De legibus et consuetudinibus Angliae*. Ed. Sir Travers Twiss. London: 1878.

Brooke, Robert Greville, Lord. *A Discourse Opening the Nature of that Episcopacie, Which is Exercised in England*. London, 1642.

Brooks, Christopher. *Lawyers, Litigation and English Society Since 1450*. London: Hambledon Press, 1998.

Brown, Sarah Annes, and Charles Martindale, eds. Lucan, *The Civil War*. Trans. Nicholas Rowe. London: Everyman, 1998.

Burgess, Glenn. *Absolute Monarchy and the Stuart Constitution*. New Haven, Conn.: Yale University Press, 1996.

– *The Politics of the Ancient Constitution: An Introduction to English Political Thought, 1603–1642*. University Park: Penn State University Press, 1992.

Caesar, Julius. *The Conquest of Gaul*. Trans. S.A. Handford; rev. Jane F. Gardner. New York: Penguin, 1982.

Camden, William. *Britannia*. Trans. Philemon Holland. London: 1637.

Carruthers, S.W. *The Everyday Work of the Westminster Assembly*. Ed. J. Ligon Duncan III. Greenville, S.C.: Reformed Academic Press, 1994.

Cary, Lucius, Viscount Falkland. *A Speech Made to the House of Commons Concerning Episcopacy*. 1641.

Chodorow, Stanley. *Christian Political Theory and Church Politics in the Mid-Twelfth Century: The Ecclesiology of Gratian's Decretum*. Berkeley: University of California Press, 1972.

Christianson, Paul. *Discourse on History, Law, and Governance in the Public Career of John Selden, 1610–1635*. Toronto: University of Toronto Press, 1996.

Cicero. *De Oratore*. Trans. H. Rackham. Cambridge, Mass.: Harvard University Press, 1942.

Clayton, Thomas, ed. *The Works of Sir John Suckling: The Non-Dramatic Works*. Oxford: Clarendon Press, 1971.

Cockburn, J.S. *A History of English Assizes, 1558–1714*. Cambridge: Cambridge University Press, 1972.

Coke, Sir, Edward. *The Reports*. 13 parts. Ed. John Henry Thomas and John Farquhar Fraser. London: Joseph Butterworth and Son, 1826.

Copenhaver, Brian P., and Charles B. Schmitt. *Renaissance Philosophy*. New York: Oxford University Press, 1992.

Cromartie, Alan. *Sir Matthew Hale, 1609–1676: Law, Religion and Natural Philosophy*. New York: Cambridge University Press, 1995.

Culverwell, Nathaniel. *An Elegant and Learned Discourse of the Light of Nature*. Ed.

Robert A. Greene and Hugh MacCallum. Toronto: University of Toronto Press, 1971.

Cunaeus, Petrus. *De Republica Hebraeorum (The Commonwealth of the Hebrews)*. Intro. Lea Campos Boralevi. Florence: Centro Editoriale Toscano, 1996.

Davis, J.C. *Fear, Myth and History: The Ranters and Their Historians*. New York: Cambridge University Press, 1986.

Dodderidge, John. *The Lawyers Light*. 1631.

Dostoevsky, Fyodor. *The Karamazov Brothers* (1880). Trans. Ignat Avsey. New York: Oxford University Press, 1994.

Drayton, Michael. *The Works of Michael Drayton*. 5 vols. Ed. J. William Hebel. Oxford: Basil Blackwell, 1961.

Eadmer. *Eadmeri Monachi Cantuariensis Historia Novorum*. Ed. John Selden. London: 1623.

– *Eadmer's History of Recent Events in England. Historia Novorum in Anglia*. Trans. Geoffrey Bosanquet. Foreword R.W. Southern. London: Cresset, 1964.

Edwards, Thomas. *Gangraena*. Ed. M.M. Goldsmith and Ivan Roots. Ilkley, U.K.: The Rota, 1977.

Epstein, I., Rabbi Dr, ed. *The Babylonian Talmud: Sanhedrin*. Trans. Jacob Schachter and H. Freedman. London: Soncino Press, 1994.

Eusden, John Dykstra. *Puritans, Lawyers, and Politics in Early Seventeenth-Century England*. New Haven, Conn.: Yale University Press, 1948.

Feingold, Mordechai. 'John Selden and the Nature of Seventeenth-Century Science.' In *The Presence of the Past: Essays in Honor of Frank Manuel*. Ed. Richard T. Bienvenu and Mordechai Feingold. Boston: Kluwer Academic, 1991.

Figgis, John N. *The Divine Right of Kings*. Rpt. ed. Bristol, U.K.: Thoemmes Press, 1994.

Finch, Sir Henry. *Law, or a Discourse thereof, in Four Books*. Buffalo, N.Y.: William S. Hein, n.d.

Fincham, Kenneth. *Prelate as Pastor: The Episcopate of James I*. Oxford: Clarendon Press, 1990.

Fisch, Harold. *Jerusalem and Albion: The Hebraic Factor in Seventeenth-Century Literature*. New York: Schocken Books, 1964.

Fortescue, Sir John. *De laudibus legum Angliae*. Ed. John Selden. 1616.

Franklin, Julian H. *Jean Bodin and the Rise of Absolutist Theory*. Cambridge: Cambridge University Press, 1973.

Fulbecke, William. *A Direction or Preparatiue to the Study of the Law*. 1620.

Fuller, Thomas. *The Church History of Britain*. 6 vols. Ed. J.S. Brewer. Oxford: Oxford University Press, 1845.

- *The History of the Holy War.* London: William Pickering, 1804.

Garber, Daniel, and Michael Ayers, eds. *The Cambridge History of Seventeenth-Century Philosophy.* 2 vols. New York: Cambridge University Press, 1998.

Gassendi, Petrus. *Animadversiones in decimum librum Diogenis Laertii.* 1649.

G.D. *Viro ver pietatis.* London, 1654.

Goodwin, John. *Independency God's Verity* and *Right and Might Well Met.*1649. In *Puritanism and Liberty.* Ed. A.S.P. Woodhouse. London: Dent, 1938.

Gough, J.W. *Fundamental Law in English Constitutional History.* Oxford: Clarendon Press, 1955.

Grafton, Anthony. *Joseph Scaliger: A Study in the History of Classical Scholarship.* 2 vols. Oxford: Clarendon Press, 1993.

Gransden, Antonia. *Historical Writing in England, c.550–c.1307.* Ithaca, N.Y.: Cornell University Press, 1974.

Grotius, Hugo. *De jure belli ac pacis libri tres.* Trans. Francis W. Kelsey. Intro. James Brown Scott. New York: Oceana, 1964.

Hale, Sir Matthew. *The History of the Common Law.* 2 vols. Notes Charles Runnington. London: 1794; rpt. Holmes Beach, Fla.: William W. Gaunt & Sons, 1993.

- *The Works Moral and Religious of Sir Matthew Hale, Knt.* Ed. T. Thirlwall. 2 vols. London: H.D. Symonds, 1805.

Hall, Joseph. *Episcopacy by Divine Right.* Vol. 10 in *The Works of Joseph Hall.* 12 vols. Oxford: Talboys, 1837.

Haller, William, ed. *Tracts on Liberty in the Puritan Revolution, 1638–1647.* 3 vols. New York: Columbia University Press, 1934.

Harrington, James. *The Commonwealth of Oceana and a System of Politics.* Ed. J.G.A. Pocock. New York: Cambridge University Press, 1992.

Harris, Tim, et al., eds. *The Politics of Religion in Restoration England.* Oxford: Basil Blackwell, 1990.

Helgerson, Richard. *Forms of Nationhood: The Elizabethan Writing of England.* Chicago: University of Chicago Press, 1992.

Helmholz, R.H. *The Spirit of Classical Canon Law.* Athens: University of Georgia Press, 1996.

Herrup, Cynthia B. 'Law and Morality in Seventeenth-Century England.' *Past & Present* 106 (1985), 102–23.

Heylyn, Peter. *Aërius Redivivus: Or the History of the Presbyterians.* 2nd ed. London, 1672.

Hobbes, Thomas. *Leviathan.* Ed. C.B. MacPherson. New York: Penguin, 1968.

Holdsworth, W.S. *Sources and Literature of English Law.* Oxford: Clarendon Press, 1925.

Hooker, Richard. *Of the Laws of Ecclesiastical Polity: Preface, Books I to IV.* Ed. Georges Edelen. Cambridge, Mass.: Harvard University Press, 1977.

Hornblower, Simon, and Antony Spawforth. *The Oxford Classical Dictionary.* New York: Oxford University Press, 1996.

Hughes, William. *Anglo-Judaeus, or The History of the Jews Whilst Here in England.* 1656.

Ingram, Martin. 'Ridings, Rough Music and Mocking Rhymes in Early Modern England.' In *Popular Culture in Seventeenth-Century England.* Ed. Barry Reay. London: Croom Helm, 1985.

– 'Ridings, Rough Music and the "Reform of Popular Culture" in Early Modern England.' *Past & Present* 105 (1984), 79–113.

Johnson, Edwin. *The Rise of English Culture.* New York: G.P. Putnam's Sons, 1904.

Johnson, Robert C., et al., eds. *Commons Debates, 1628.* New Haven, Conn.: Yale University Press, 1977–78.

Jonson, Ben. *Ben Jonson: The Complete Poems.* Ed. George Parfitt. Baltimore: Penguin, 1975.

Kahn, Victoria, and Lorna Hutson, eds. *Rhetoric and Law in Early Modern Europe.* New Haven, Conn.: Yale University Press, 2001.

Katchen, Aaron L. *Christian Hebraists and Dutch Rabbis: Seventeenth Century Apologetics and the Study of Maimonides' Mishneh Torah.* Cambridge, Mass.: Harvard University Press, 1984.

Katz, David S. *Philo-Semitism and the Readmission of the Jews.* Oxford: Clarendon Press, 1982.

Kelley, Donald R. *Foundations of Modern Historical Scholarship: Language, Law, and History in the French Renaissance.* New York: Columbia University Press, 1970.

– *History, Law and the Human Sciences: Medieval and Renaissance Perspectives.* London: Variorum Reprints, 1984.

Kenyon, J.P. *Stuart England.* New York: Penguin Books, 1978.

Knafla, Louis A. *Law and Politics in Jacobean England: The Tracts of Lord Chancellor Ellesmere.* New York: Cambridge University Press, 1977.

Lambarde, William. *Archeion, or, A Discourse upon the High Courts of Justice in England.* Ed. Charles H. McIlwain and Paul L. Ward. Cambridge, Mass.: Harvard University Press, 1957.

Lamont, William. 'Pamphleteering, the Protestant Consensus and the English Revolution.' In *Freedom and the English Revolution: Essays in History and Literature.* Manchester: Manchester University Press, 1986.

– 'The Religion of Andrew Marvell: Locating the "Bloody Horse."' In *The Political Identity of Andrew Marvell.* Ed. Conal Condren and A.D. Cousins. Aldershot, U.K.: Scolar Press, 1990.

– *Richard Baxter and the Millennium: Protestant Imperialism and the English Revolution.* Totowa, N.J.: Rowman and Littlefield, 1979.

- ed. *Richard Baxter's 'A Holy Commonwealth.'* New York: Cambridge University Press, 1994.

Langbaine, Gerard. Letter to Selden. Selden supra 109, fol. 452r, 1653.

Latham, Robert, and William Matthews, eds. *The Diary of Samuel Pepys.* 9 vols. Berkeley: University of California Press, 2000.

Laud, William. *The Works.* 7 vols. Ed. William Scott and James Bliss. Oxford: John Henry Parker, 1847–60.

Le Clerc, Jean. *Vindication of His Character.* After 1729. BL Add. MS 4462, ff. 2–5b.

Lightfoot, John. *The Whole Works.* 13 vols. Ed. John Rogers Pitman. London: J.F. Dove, 1824.

Little, David. *Religion, Order, and Law: A Study in Pre-Revolutionary England.* New York: Harper & Row, 1969.

Loewenstein, David. *Representing Revolution in Milton and His Contemporaries: Religion, Politics, and Polemics in Radical Puritanism.* New York: Cambridge University Press, 2001.

Lowth, Simon. *Of the Subject of Church Power.* 1685.

Ludlow, Edmund. *A Voyce from the Watch Tower, Part Five: 1660–1662.* Ed. A.B. Worden. London: Royal Historical Society, 1978.

Maimonides. *The Guide for the Perplexed.* Trans. M. Friedländer. 2nd rev. ed. New York: Dover, 1956.

- *Mishneh Torah: The Book of Knowledge.* Ed. and trans. Moses Hyamson. New York: Feldheim, 1974.

Marcus Aurelius. Rev. ed. Trans. C.R. Haynes. Cambridge, Mass.: Harvard University Press, 1979.

Marsilius of Padua. *Defensor Pacis.* Trans. and intro. Alan Gewirth. New York: Columbia University Press, 1956.

Marvell, Andrew. *The Complete Poems.* Ed. Elizabeth Story Donno. New York: Penguin, 1972.

Milton, John. *Complete Prose Works of John Milton.* Ed. Don M. Wolfe. Vol. 1. New Haven, Conn.: Yale University Press, 1953.

- *John Milton: Complete Poetry and Major Prose.* Ed. Merritt Y. Hughes. New York: Odyssey Press, 1957.

Minucius Felix. *Octavius.* Trans. Gerald H. Rendall. Cambridge, Mass.: Harvard University Press, 1931.

Mommsen, Theodor and Alan Watson, eds. *The Digest of Justinian.* Philadelphia: University of Pennsylvania Press, 1985.

Neusner, Jacob, trans. *The Mishnah.* New Haven, Conn.: Yale University Press, 1988.

Norbrook, David. *Writing the English Republic: Poetry, Rhetoric and Politics, 1627–1660.* New York: Cambridge University Press, 1999.

Notestein, Wallace, and Frances Helen Relf, eds. *Commons Debates for 1629.* Minneapolis: University of Minnesota Press, 1921.

Novak, David. *Natural Law in Judaism.* New York: Cambridge University Press, 1998.

O Hehir, Brendan, ed. *Expans'd Hieroglyphicks: A Critical Edition of Sir John Denham's Coopers Hill.* Berkeley: University of California Press, 1969.

Ovid. *Fasti.* Trans. James George Frazer; rev. G.P. Goold. Cambridge, Mass.: Harvard University Press, 1996.

Parkin, Jon. 'Liberty Transpros'd: Andrew Marvell and Samuel Parker.' In *Marvell and Liberty.* Ed. Warren Chernaik and Martin Dzelzainis. New York: St Martin's Press, 1999.

Parr, Richard. *The Life of the Most Reverend Father in God, James Ussher, Late Lord Archbishop of Armagh, Primate and Metropolitan of all Ireland.* London, 1686.

Patrick, J. Max, ed. *The Complete Poetry of Robert Herrick.* Garden City, N.J.: Anchor, 1963.

Paul, Robert S. *The Assembly of the Lord: Politics and Religion in the Westminster Assembly and the 'Grand Debate.'* Edinburgh: T. & T. Clark, 1985.

Peltonen, Markku. *Classical Humanism and Republicanism in English Political Thought, 1570–1640.* New York: Cambridge University Press, 1995.

Plato. *Phaedrus.* Trans. Harold North Fowler. Cambridge, Mass.: Harvard University Press, 1914.

Plutarch. *Moralia.* Trans. Frank Cole Babbitt. Vol. 5. Cambridge, Mass.: Harvard University Press, 1936.

Pocock, Edward. *The Theological Works of the Learned Dr. Pocock.* 2 vols. Ed. Leonard Twells. London: 1740.

Pocock, J.G.A. *The Ancient Constitution and the Feudal Law.* New York: Cambridge University Press, 1957; rev. ed., 1987.

– *The Machiavellian Moment: Florentine Political Thought and the Atlantic Republican Tradition.* Princeton, N.J.: Princeton University Press, 1975.

– 'Thomas May and the Narrative of Civil War.' In *Writing and Political Engagement in Seventeenth-Century England.* Ed. Derek Hirst and Richard Strier. New York: Cambridge University Press, 1999.

Pollock, Sir Frederick, ed. *Table Talk of John Selden.* London: Quartich, 1927.

Prescott, Anne Lake. *Imagining Rabelais in Renaissance England.* New Haven, Conn.: Yale University Press, 1998.

Prest, Wilfrid R. *The Inns of Court under Elizabeth I and the Early Stuarts, 1590–1640.* London: Longman, 1972.

– *The Rise of the Barristers: A Social History of the English Bar, 1590–1640.* Oxford: Clarendon Press, 1986.

Quintilian. *Institutio Oratoria*. 4 vols. Trans. H.E. Butler. Cambridge, Mass.:
   Harvard University Press, 1920.

Reinert, Thomas. *Regulating Confusion: Samuel Johnson and the Crowd*. Durham,
   N.C.: Duke University Press, 1996.

Ross, Alexander. *A View of all Religions in the World*. 2nd ed., rev. and enl.
   1655.

Rosenblatt, Jason. *Torah and Law in 'Paradise Lost.'* Princeton, N.J.: Princeton
   University Press, 1994.

Rosenblatt, Jason, and Winfried Schleiner. 'John Selden's Letter to Ben Jonson
   on Cross-Dressing and Bisexual Gods.' *English Literary Renaissance* 29 (1999),
   44–75.

Saint German, Christopher. *Doctor and Student*. Ed. T.F.T. Plucknett and J.L.
   Baron. London: Selden Society, 1974.

Sandmel, Samuel, ed. *New English Bible* (NEB). New York: Oxford University
   Press, 1976.

Seaward, Paul. *The Restoration*. New York: St Martin's Press, 1991.

Selden, John. *De Anno Civili et Calendario Veteris Ecclesiae seu Reipublicae Judaicae
   Dissertatio*. 1644.

– *De Dis Syris*. 1st ed. 1617. 2nd rev. ed. Lyon: 1629.

– *De Jure Naturali et Gentium Juxta Disciplinam Ebraeorum*. London: 1640.

– *De Successionibus in Bona Defuncti ad Leges Ebraeorum; De Successione in Pontificatum Ebraeorum*. 1636.

– *De Synedriis et Praefecturis Juridicis Veterum Ebraeorum*. Book 1: 1650. Book 2:
   1653. Book 3: 1655.

– *England's Epinomis*. In *Tracts Written by John Selden*. London: 1683.

– *Historiae Anglicanae Scriptores Decum*. 1652.

– *The Historie of Tithes, That Is, the Practice of Payment of Them*. Facsimile of the
   1618 ed. New York: De Capo, 1969.

– *Jani Anglorum Facies Altera*. 1610. Trans. as *The Reverse or Back-face of the English
   Janus* by Redman Westcot (Dr Adam Littleton), 1682.

– *Joannis Seldeni Ad Fletam Dissertatio*. Rpt. from 1647 ed. Trans., intro., and
   notes, David Ogg. Cambridge: Cambridge University Press, 1915.

– *Marmora Arundelliana*. 1628.

– *Mare Clausum. Of the Dominion, Or, Ownership of the Sea*. Trans. Marchamont
   Nedham. New York: Arno Press, 1972.

– *Opera Omnia*. 6 vols in 3. Ed. David Wilkins. London: 1726.

– *Titles of Honor*. 1st ed. 1614.

– *Titles of Honor*. 2nd ed. 1631.

– *Titles of Honor*. 3rd ed. 1672.

– ed. and trans. *Eutychii Aegyptii, Patriarchae Orthodoxorum Alexandrini*. 1642.

Sellin, Paul R. *Daniel Heinsius and Stuart England.* Leiden: Leiden University Press, 1968.

Sharpe, Kevin. *Sir Robert Cotton, 1586–1631: History and Politics in Early Modern England.* New York: Oxford University Press, 1979.

Sharpe, Kevin, and Steven N. Zwicker. *Politics of Discourse: The Literature and History of Seventeenth-Century England.* Berkeley: University of California Press, 1987.

Skinner, Quentin. *The Foundations of Modern Political Thought.* Vol. 2, *The Age of Reformation.* New York: Cambridge University Press, 1978.

Smith, G. Gregory, ed. *Elizabethan Critical Essays.* 2 vols. Oxford: Clarendon Press, 1904.

Smith, John. *Certain Discourses (1660): A Facsimile Reproduction.* Delmar, N.Y.: Scholars' Facsimiles & Reprints, 1979.

Smith, Nigel, ed. *A Collection of Ranter Writings from the Seventeenth Century.* London: Junction Books, 1983.

Sommerville, J.P. 'History and Theory: The Norman Conquest in Early Stuart Political Thought.' *Political Studies* 34 (1986): 249–61.

– 'John Selden, The Law of Nature, and the Origins of Government.' *Historical Journal* 27 (1984), 437–47.

– 'Selden, Grotius, and the Seventeenth-Century Intellectual Revolution in Moral and Political Theory.' In *Rhetoric and Law in Early Modern Europe.* Ed. Victoria Kahn and Lorna Hutson. New Haven: Yale University Press, 2001.

Southern, R.W. *Saint Anselm and His Biographer: A Study of Monastic Life and Thought, 1059–c. 1130.* Cambridge: Cambridge University Press, 1963.

Spalding, Ruth. *Contemporaries of Bulstrode Whitelocke, 1605–1675.* Oxford: Oxford University Press, 1990.

– ed. *The Diary of Bulstrode Whitelocke, 1605–1675.* New York: Oxford University Press, 1990.

Spingarn, J.E., ed. *Critical Essays of the Seventeenth Century.* 3 vols. Oxford: Clarendon Press, 1908.

Squibb, G.D. *The High Court of Chivalry: A Study of the Civil Law in England.* Oxford: Clarendon Press, 1959.

Stephen, Sir Leslie, and Sir Sidney Lee, eds. *Dictionary of National Biography.* Vol. 21. Oxford: Oxford University Press, 1917–.

Stillingfleet, Edward. *Irenicum: A Weapon Salve for the Churches Wounds.* 2nd ed. London, 1662.

Stow, John. *A Survey of London.* 2 vols. Ed. Charles Lethbridge Kingsford. Oxford: Clarendon Press, 1908.

Suárez, Francisco. *Selections from Three Works of Francisco Suárez, S.J.* 2 vols. Ed. James Brown Scott. Oxford: Clarendon Press, 1944.

Tacitus, *Annals.* Trans. John Jackson. Cambridge, Mass.: Harvard University Press, 1937.

Tertullian. *Apologeticus.* Trans. T.R. Glover. Cambridge, Mass.: Harvard University Press, 1931.

Theocritus. *Greek Bucolic Poets.* Trans J.M. Edmonds. Cambridge, Mass.: Harvard University Press, 1977.

Tite, Colin G.C. *Impeachment and Parliamentary Judicature in Early Stuart England.* London: Athlone Press, 1974.

Tubbs, J.W. *The Common Law Mind: Medieval and Early Modern Conceptions.* Baltimore: Johns Hopkins University Press, 2000.

Tuck, Richard. '"The Ancient Law of Freedom": John Selden and the Civil War.' In *Reactions to the English Civil War 1642–1649.* Ed. John Morrill. London: Methuen, 1982.

– *Natural Rights Theories: Their Origin and Development.* New York: Cambridge University Press, 1979.

– *Philosophy and Government, 1572–1651.* New York: Cambridge University Press, 1993.

Vickers, Brian, ed. *Occult and Scientific Mentalities in the Renaissance.* New York: Cambridge University Press, 1984.

Voss, Paul J. *Elizabethan News Pamphlets: Shakespeare, Spenser, Marlowe and the Birth of Journalism.* Pittsburgh, Pa.: Duquesne University Press, 2001.

Warfield, Benjamin Breckinridge. *The Westminster Assembly and Its Work.* New York: Oxford University Press, 1931.

Wedgwood, C.V. *A Coffin for King Charles: The Trial and Execution of Charles I.* New York: Macmillan, 1964.

White, Stephen D. *Sir Edward Coke and 'The Grievances of the Commonwealth,' 1621–1628.* Chapel Hill: University of North Carolina Press, 1979.

Woodhouse, A.S.P. *Puritanism and Liberty.* London: Dent, 1938.

Woodward, D.J., ed. *The Poems and Translations of Robert Fletcher.* Gainesville: University of Florida Press, 1970.

Woolf, D.R. *The Idea of History in Early Stuart England: Erudition, Ideology and 'The Light of Truth' from the Accession of James I to the Civil War.* Toronto: University of Toronto Press, 1990.

Wootton, David, ed. and intro. *Divine Right and Democracy.* New York: Penguin, 1986.

Worden, Blair. 'Ben Jonson among the Historians.' In *Culture and Politics in Early Stuart England.* Ed. Kevin Sharpe and Peter Lake. Stanford, Calif.: Stanford University Press, 1993.

– *The Rump Parliament, 1648–1653.* Cambridge: Cambridge University Press, 1974.

– *The Sound of Virtue: Philip Sidney's* Arcadia *and Elizabethan Politics.* New Haven, Conn.: Yale University Press, 1996.

Ziskind, Jonathan R., trans. and ed. *John Selden on Jewish Marriage Law: The 'Uxor Hebraica.'* New York: E.J. Brill, 1991.

Ziskind, Martha A. 'John Selden: Criticism and Affirmation of the Common Law Tradition.' *American Journal of Legal History* 19 (1975): 22–39.

Index